AMERICAN HORTICULTURAL SOCIETY
Northeast
SMARTGARDEN™ REGIONAL GUIDE

AMERICAN
HORTICULTURAL
SOCIETY

AMERICAN HORTICULTURAL SOCIETY

Northeast

SMARTGARDEN™ REGIONAL GUIDE

RITA PELCZAR AND
TREVOR COLE

DK Publishing Inc

LONDON, NEW YORK, MUNICH,
MELBOURNE, AND DELHI

Senior Editor Jill Hamilton
Designers Megan Clayton, Susan St. Louis
Creative Director Tina Vaughan
Project Director Sharon Lucas
Production Manager Chris Avgherinos
DTP Designer Milos Orlovic
Picture Research Jo Walton
Image Coordinator Chrissy McIntyre
Publisher Chuck Lang

Horticultural editor Ray Rogers

Contributing writers Pat Cullina, Madeline Farbman,
Peter Punzi, S. Jane von Trapp
Design assistance Miesha Tate, Mark Johnson-Davies,
Jaye Tang, Stephanie Sumulong
Editorial assistance Christine Heilman, Jane Perlmutter, John Searcy
DK Photo Access Library: Mark Dennis, Emily Angus,
Neale Chamberlain, Kate Ledwith
Additional photo research: Louise Thomas

First American Edition, 2003
04 05 10 9 8 7 6 5 4

Published in the United States by
DK Publishing, Inc.
375 Hudson Street
New York, New York 10014

DK Publishing, Inc. offers special discounts for bulk purchases for sales
promotions or premiums. Specific, large-quantity needs can be met with
special editions, including personalized covers, excerpts of existing guides,
and corporate imprints. For more information, contact Special Markets
Department, DK Publishing, Inc., 375 Hudson Street, New York, NY 10014
Fax: 800-600-9098.

Library of Congress Cataloging-in-Publication Data

Cole, Trevor J. (Trevor Jack)
Northeast / by Trevor Cole -- 1st American ed.
p. cm. -- (SMARTGARDEN™ regional guide)
ISBN 0-7894-9495-7 (PBF)
1. Gardening--Northeastern States. I. Cullina, Patrick. II. Title.
III. Series.
SB453.2.N82C66 2003
635.9'0974--dc21
2003010172

Reproduced by Colourscan, Singapore
Printed and bound in the USA by RR Donnelly

See our complete product line at

www.dk.com

CONTENTS

Foreword 6

PART I

THE TEN
SmartGarden™ TENETS

FOREWORD

The Cornell campus in upstate New York was a challenging experience for a North Carolina native. The plants were different not only in growth rate but in the species commonly selected. I saw new dogwoods, magnolias, and crabapples while my favorite peonies, irises, and daylilies flourished as well in New York as in North Carolina. I learned the importance of the winter form of a plant rather than placing all of my hopes in the short season foliage or flowers.

Gardening is based on assembling and coordinating factors such as light, temperature, water, nutrients, and coping with wind, rain, critters, and the gardener's age. I am beginning, however, to become aware of the mistakes that people live with in their garden day after day that disrupt the pleasures of managing a garden. The SMARTGARDEN™ is the answer. This time, let us create a garden that utilizes all of the new ideas available for gardening.

Maps, zones, and ecoregions were considered in discussions of where plants would grow, but summer tolerances of plants to heat were never proposed. Only now in 2003 have we developed a series of concepts, created the technology to analyze the data collected over 14 years from thousands of weather stations. Our USDA Plant Hardiness zones have been updated, and the addition of the AHS Plant Heat Zone Map in 1997 completed the circle of information available to determine a plant's total range of temperature tolerance. The American Horticultural Society's SMARTGARDEN™ Guides are the outcome of my years as a research horticulturist.

Too many gardeners put up with plants that have outgrown their space or are barely surviving. The question that follows goes to the heart of gardening – how can I replace and replant with the most desired effects and create a SMARTGARDEN™? And how do I accomplish this while being a good steward of the Earth? This Northeast SMARTGARDEN™ Regional Guide is the best resource for those questions and more. I hope that you enjoy looking at your garden and your gardening practices with new eyes, a new vision!

H. MARC CATHEY, PHD
PRESIDENT EMERITUS,
AMERICAN HORTICULTURAL SOCIETY

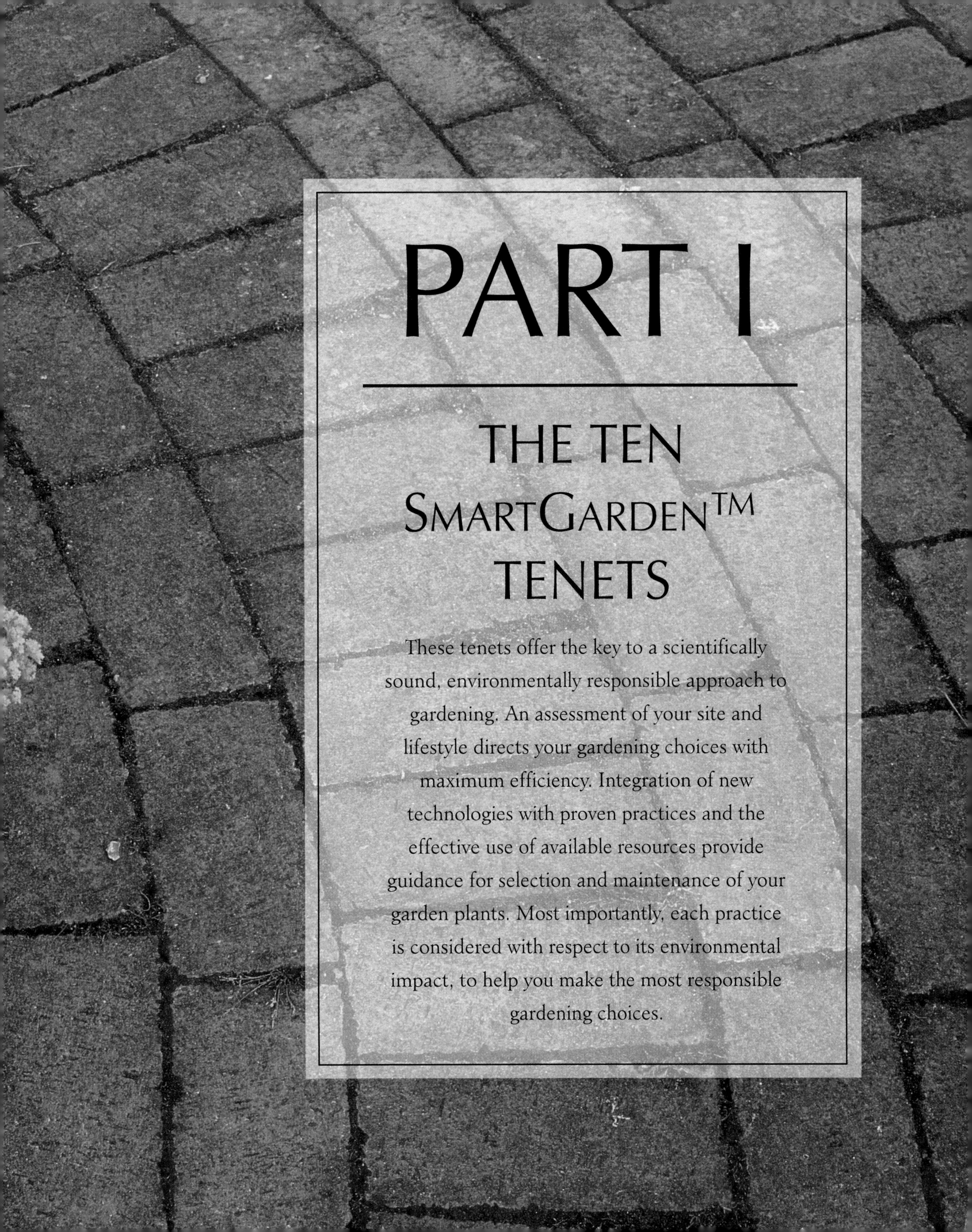

PART I

THE TEN SmartGarden™ TENETS

These tenets offer the key to a scientifically sound, environmentally responsible approach to gardening. An assessment of your site and lifestyle directs your gardening choices with maximum efficiency. Integration of new technologies with proven practices and the effective use of available resources provide guidance for selection and maintenance of your garden plants. Most importantly, each practice is considered with respect to its environmental impact, to help you make the most responsible gardening choices.

KNOW YOURSELF

A lot of thought should go into gardening before you even pick up a trowel. Since you are going to determine the garden's dimensions, style, and makeup – and you will be primarily responsible for its maintenance – the best place to begin is to take a reading of your personal likes and dislikes and your abilities and limitations. In subsequent tenets we will consider the characteristics of the site, appropriate criteria for selecting plants, and ways to ensure that your gardening efforts reap successful results by using an environmentally responsible approach. But before you can begin to put that important information to good use, it is critical to examine your preferences, priorities, and point of view.

Be realistic

As much as you would enjoy spending many hours in your garden, you have other commitments that limit your availability, and you may be sharing your outdoor space with others who prefer nongardening activities. Physical constraints might also inhibit your gardening pursuits, and your budget may not accommodate your elaborate gardening visions. However, with some thoughtful planning and a bit of compromise, your SMARTGARDEN™ can oblige your varied outdoor requirements, limitations in time and physical ability, and, yes, even a budget that lacks a certain desired heft.

In a nutshell: think about your time, your physical condition, and your budget, and take on a garden only of the size and complexity you can handle.

What you want
The owners of this property made careful decisions about how they wanted to use their space. Another owner might well have decided to plant the area entirely in grass and shrubs, and a third could have created a playground.

The space-time continuum

Once you know where a garden best fits within the overall landscape, the next step is to determine its size and shape. While the shape is largely a design consideration, the size depends a great deal on the plants you want and the time you have to tend them.

Some gardens will require little of your time once they are established. A bed of flowering shrubs underplanted with a groundcover needs only occasional attention. An extensive flower bed or large vegetable patch, on the other hand, needs regular tending throughout the growing season. Of course, the bigger the garden, the more time it requires to plant, weed, harvest, deadhead, edge, and prune. The best plan is to start small, then expand if you find you have the space, time, resources, and energy.

Planning the site

When you are deciding where you should place your garden and what size to make it, you need to consider not only the conditions that make it suitable for growing plants, but also how the garden will be integrated into the landscape as a whole. For example, if you have children who need space for a swingset or to play basketball or frisbee, siting your garden at the other end of the yard might be wise – at least until they outgrow these activities. Obviously, you need a plan.

Fully integrated
A carefully considered mixture of plants and hardscaping – the nonplant elements – results in a garden that beautifully blends with and complements the house. Container-grown plants generally require more care than those that are grown in the open ground.

Garden plans

Whether your garden aspirations are complex and ornate or you are planning on a somewhat more modest scale, you should map out your garden on paper before you pick up your trowel or buy your first plant. Although these garden plans may vary in complexity from a rough sketch to an exquisitely executed artwork, there are just a couple of basic types of sketches that you need to use at this stage. The first one is used to map out existing features and microclimates, information that you need to determine which plants will thrive and where. A more detailed garden sketch, which should be done on graph paper to scale, shows your entire property – both physical features and garden areas.

Unless you are starting with an empty lot, you will need to sketch the existing features of your landscape, such as the house, walkways, and driveway. The more accurate your sketch, the more useful it will be for planning. Don't forget to note sunny and shady areas, hedges and fences that block the wind, unusually wet or dry spots, neighboring buildings, attractive or unattractive views, and other positive and negative features.

You may find that you want to make adjustments: remove a tree, repair or improve a walkway, relocate the doghouse. Some of these changes will be easy; those that are more complex can be completed over time. Make corresponding notes on your plan to track the direction in which you are heading.

Next make a list of the activities that you enjoy doing in the yard. Of course, you also need to consider anyone who may spend a significant amount of time in the yard, whether it be your spouse or partner, children, or anyone else. The landscape use checklist (opposite) will help you identify the various uses and activities that fit your space and budget.

Once you have a prioritized list of gardening and nongardening activities for your yard, you can begin designating areas for each. Some areas will overlap, so make sure that the activities are compatible for use of the same space – playing football in the herb garden just won't work. On the other hand, patios and decks are perfect locations for container gardens and adjacent raised beds. Keep in mind that different kinds of plants (for example, perennials, vegetables, and shrubs) can often be combined in the same garden area as long as they have similar cultural requirements.

Making a Plan

This exercise is useful for those who have just acquired a new property as well as for those who are considering a major (or even minor) relandscaping project. Documenting existing conditions will point you in the right direction when the time comes to choose specific elements.

FEATURES TO CONSIDER FOR THE SKETCH

When drawing a sketch of your property, include all features that are permanent or at least long-term. Once your sketch is completed, you may want to make several copies. That way you can try out different designs for arranging beds and hardscaping features on paper before you actually get to work.

Don't forget to include any of the following features that are applicable. There may well be more features in your yard that you should include.

- Perimeter of the yard
- House
- Driveway
- Walkways and paths
- Garage, shed, or other service outbuildings
- Gazebo, patio, deck
- Hammock
- Swingset/sandbox
- Pool

- Doghouse, kennel, run
- Existing trees
- Existing beds or gardens
- Hedges, fences, walls
- Water faucets
- Areas of sun and shade
- Wet or dry areas
- Views to highlight
- Views to hide

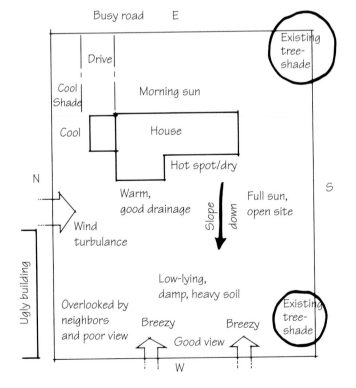

Putting it down on paper

All of the important cultural and design elements of the property have been included in this sketch. Note that there are no specific plant features indicated except for the trees, which are being considered more as producers of shade than as living plants. Consideration of individual plants comes later.

KEEP YOUR PLANS FLEXIBLE

Don't fret if there isn't room in your landscape to accommodate all of the activities you have in mind. Long-range planning can extend your choices, and spreading the implementation of your plan over the course of several years also reduces the shock to your bank account.

As you and the others who use your yard mature, priorities for landscape use will change. The area designated for a sandbox for youngsters might be transformed into a patio after a few years. Once the old swing set in the back yard has lost its appeal, it can be replaced with a mixed border or small vegetable garden.

Like children, plants grow up, and their increasing size alters the landscape. Perennials that once filled in between young evergreen shrubs may need to be moved as the shrubs reach their mature size. Aggressive perennials may be overrunning your borders. Choices must be made; something will need to go. As your trees expand in height and spread over the years, the area beneath them becomes shadier. If the grass growing in the trees' shadow becomes thin and weak, it may be time to replace it with a shade-loving groundcover or a simple mulch, or perhaps you will choose to thin or raise the crown of the tree (*see p. 29*) to allow more light to reach the grass.

Remember: plants don't live forever. The demise of a plant often opens up opportunities for including new and perhaps more interesting plants in its place.

Adapting to physical challenges

If you or members of your household have physical limitations, these need to be considered in your planning. Raised beds and containers can be built and placed with accessibility in mind. Paved walkways can put outlying beds within easy reach of those who might otherwise be able to enjoy them only from a distance, and stepping-stones or paths within planting areas afford easier and safer movement through the garden for maintenance.

Careful selection and placement of plants within the landscape is important for physically challenged gardeners. Once established, many trees, shrubs, and groundcovers will require a minimum of care. These can be placed at the periphery of the yard. More labor- intensive gardens should be placed where they are most easily accessed and where tools and water

LANDSCAPE USE CHECKLIST

Planning space to accommodate your outdoor pastimes will help you determine the best placement and size of your plantings, and prioritizing these areas will help you develop a working plan.

Nongarden areas/activities:
- Relaxing (including deck and/or patio)
- Outdoor cooking/eating
- Swimming
- Sports and active play
- Sandbox, tree house, playhouse, swing set
- Utility areas: trash cans, air conditioning/heating units, compost pile

- Work and storage spaces: garden shed, cold frame, firewood storage
- Pet areas
- Paths and walkways
- Driveway/parking
- Lawn
- Other, including walls and fences and overhead structures

Garden areas:
- Vegetable/fruit
- Herbs
- Flowerbeds
- Woodland garden
- Shade trees
- Wildflower meadow or naturalized area
- Foundation planting

- Pond
- Containers
- Raised beds
- Cut flowers
- Hedges
- Specimen trees and shrubs

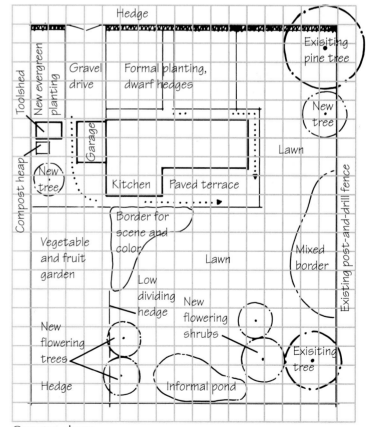

One step closer
The first sketch shown to the left is now fleshed out with desired planted areas (beds, borders, hedges, and the like) and hardscape features (driveway, terrace, and pond). The template is now ready to be made into a reality.

Easier access
If gardening is difficult for you, growing plants in a raised bed such as this one will bring them up to your level. Even if you are not an active gardener, the plants will be closer to your eyes and nose.

are located nearby. Also remember the potential danger posed by thorny trees and shrubs, low branches, and surface roots. Of course, these points apply to any sensibly designed garden, but they are of more obvious and immediate importance to the physically challenged.

A number of ergonomically designed gardening tools make gardening easier if physical ability is limited. Despite our best efforts to remain fit, chances are that eventually we will all lose some

mobility or strength. Your SMARTGARDEN™ should become easier to maintain as plants mature, but no garden is maintenance-free. Fortunately, physical limitations needn't eliminate gardening activities, especially if they are considered in your garden plan.

Lawns and turf alternatives

The majority of homeowners consider a lawn an essential part of the garden, although it is the most labor-intensive and the most demanding in terms of resources and money. A well-maintained lawn, fertilized in spring, mown regularly, and watered during periods of drought, forms a solid green sward that stands up to traffic. Given little maintenance and no supplemental water, however, lawns go brown and dormant during drought, and they quickly become infested with perennial weeds that smother the grass.

One repetitive chore that consumes a great deal of gardening time is mowing the lawn, and maintaining a healthy lawn can be a genuine challenge in many parts of the country. Irrigation systems may be necessary in areas that experience extended periods of dry weather during the growing season. Weeds, insect pests, and diseases may necessitate the use of pesticides or biological controls that can be costly and time-consuming to apply. This doesn't mean that

LAWNS AND ALTERNATIVES

A healthy lawn ties the garden together and creates space.

It is important to choose the correct grass species for your conditions: shade-tolerant grasses, for example, do not thrive in full sun. In most of the Northeast, Kentucky bluegrass is the species of choice for sunny and mostly sunny locations. This forms a dense lawn and spreads by underground runners, so it quickly refills any damaged areas but needs watering during summer to retain its color. It does not grow well on poor soils and needs fertilizing regularly to grow properly. Tall fescue is more drought and shade tolerant and very durable,

but it cannot be mown as closely as Kentucky bluegrass and has a slightly coarser texture. Perennial ryegrass is similar to Kentucky bluegrass but does not spread or mow as well and may die after severe drought or cold. It establishes quickly and is often included in seed mixtures to act as a nurse grass for other species. Bentgrasses make a very fine-textured lawn but need frequent mowing. They grow best in regions close to bodies of water, where humidity is high. In the southern parts of the Northeast zoysiagrass forms a thick, green lawn. This is started from small individual plants, known as plugs, rather than as seed or sod. It is slow to green up in spring and goes dormant in fall earlier than regular grasses. Clover is occasionally added to seed mixtures to help keep a lawn green during summer. It also provides a source of nectar for bees but is more likely to stain clothing than grass.
In areas where traffic is light, many other plants can be used to form a lawn. Bugleweed (*Ajuga reptans*) and goutweed (*Aegopodium podagraria*) are tough, will withstand some wear, and need mowing only occasionally if at all, but both are invasive and can

spread into other areas of the garden. Crown vetch (*Coronilla varia*) is excellent for slopes and spreads very rapidly. Chamomile (*Chamaemelum nobile*) makes a lush green mat (given enough water) but will not stand up to more than occasional foot traffic. The cultivar 'Treneague' is nonflowering and hardy to Zone 5.

Both a conventional lawn and a graveled area fill the roles of unifier and provider of spaciousness.

you should exclude all turf from your landscape, but be aware that it is an area that requires a significant investment in time and money. To reduce the expense, reduce the size of the lawn. A small area of grass is much easier to maintain than a large expanse.

If you decide to reduce the lawn area of your yard, you have a number of options. Consider a wildflower meadow or a large bed of groundcovers, which will require some seasonal care – perhaps two or three times a year – but not nearly the time and effort involved in trying to maintain a perfect lawn.

Another alternative to lawns are the various soil coverings, such as paving, gravel, or mulch. These can serve as walkways or seating areas. Individual planting beds and trees can be extended by removing the turf between them and connecting the areas with mulch. Use broad curves for the outline of the mulched area to facilitate mowing, because mowing around a large area that contains several trees takes much less time than mowing around individual trees. Although the initial cost and labor output of creating these areas may be greater, the reduction in maintenance time and expense over the long run may be significant.

Low-maintenance plantings

Every garden – even the simplest container garden – requires some maintenance, but there are definitely some plants that require less attention than others. Consult your nursery, extension service, and other local experts (*see* Appendices, *pp.384–389*) to identify such plants for your immediate area. Also, there are certain strategies that minimize the effort you must put into a planting for it to look good.

Many of these strategies are simply a matter of working with nature rather than against it: select plants that are adapted to the specific conditions present in your yard; water plants deeply rather than frequently so that roots grow downward and are capable of retrieving water over a greater area; remove weeds before they set seed and spread; and use mulch to conserve water and suppress weeds. Building raised beds and containers and filling them with soil may seem like a lot of work initially, but once constructed, they can provide a planting area that is within easy reach for maintenance.

A SMARTGARDEN™, when carefully analyzed, designed, implemented, and maintained, can reward any gardener for years.

Stay off the grass
Not a single blade of grass figures into this part of the property. Designed for low maintenance, it provides a pleasant sitting and socializing area while incorporating easy-care plants in both gravel and a raised bed. The solitary but exuberant container provides some color and serves as a focal point.

ASSESS YOUR SITE

The best place to begin your journey toward a SMARTGARDEN™, as with any project that involves major change, is first to determine where you stand. Take a look around your property. Observe the existing vegetation, the lay of the land, the soil, the degree of light and shade, and determine both your average temperature range and your first and last expected frost dates.

Evaluating strengths & limitations

If your yard is shady, plants that thrive in low light levels will be the most successful. If part of your yard is shaded and another area receives full sun, your options increase; however, siting a plant in the area that satisfies its particular light requirement is essential. If your region receives limited precipitation during the growing season, consider xeriphytic plants (those with low water requirements); if you have wet areas, a bog garden might be your best choice. Although these factors limit gardening options, each can be viewed as a strength if the appropriate plants and garden style are chosen.

Examine the existing plants carefully. Are there trees or shrubs that are struggling to survive or that require excessive maintenance? Plants that outgrow their space or suffer from chronic disease or pest problems may be the wrong ones for your site, and it may be best to remove them entirely.

Evaluating the existing nonplant features in your landscape is an important part of your site analysis. Are there problem areas – a steep slope or an awkward swale? Are your walkways functional? Have you set aside areas for relaxation? Does everyone have space to pursue outdoor interests?

Your observations will point you toward those improvements that need to be made to maximize your gardening success and satisfaction with the least amount of strain on you, your resources, and the environment. Your site analysis will also provide clues for selecting plants (or other nonplant features) that will fit in with your conditions.

It helps to know something about basic plant requirements with respect to the environment, including aspects of soil; how temperature, shade, and exposure define your selection of garden plants; and how microclimates present options for savvy gardeners. After you examine your existing growing conditions, you may decide to make some changes or improvements. In Tenet 3, methods for modifying your site will be outlined. But first let's take a look at what you have to work with.

Get to know your soil

Becoming familiar with the character of your soil is key to your gardening success. Important aspects include texture, structure, drainage and water-holding capacity, pH (acidity or alkalinity), and fertility.

One way to get to know your soil is to have it professionally analyzed. A soil test reveals details about your soil's chemistry that cannot be observed with the naked eye. Soil test kits for home use are available in a wide range of prices and sophistication. You can also send a soil sample to a local soil-testing lab. Public soil-testing labs are relatively inexpensive, but they may be slow during peak seasons. Private soil-testing labs may be a bit more costly, but they are often faster and some offer more extensive tests than those available through the extension labs.

Metamorphosis
Combining careful planning with smart horticultural practices will transform this neglected yard into a beautifully integrated area (opposite) that will easily accommodate a wide variety of gardening and leisure activities.

SOIL TEST REPORT

A soil test report provides basic information about the fertility of your soil. It is very useful when you are determining the amounts of fertilizer to add (or to hold off on adding) to your soil.

Potassium moves through soil slowly and is rarely present in low levels

Magnesium is essential for plant activites, most notably for photosynthesis, and its chemistry is closely linked to pH and calcium levels

High levels of calcium are usually linked to a high pH reading and interfere with the availabilty of other minerals

Phosphorus moves through soil fairly quickly but is easily replaced

NOTE Optimum levels are based on general garden conditions for a wide range of plants. Some vegetable crops and ornamentals require different levels.

Macronutrients (pounds/acre)

Phosphorus: 67 (Below Optimum)
Potassium: 360 (Above Optimum)
Magnesium: 202 (Optimum)
Calcium: 1917 (Above Optimum)

by Mehlich 3 extraction

	Below Optimum	Optimum	Above Opt.
P			
Mg			
Ca			

| Very Low | Low | Medium | High | Very High |

Soil texture

All soils are made up of solid material and spaces between the solids – in roughly equal proportions by volume. About 90 percent of the solid portion of most soil is weathered rocks and minerals. These particles are classified according to size, and are, from smallest to largest, clay, silt, and sand. Most soils are a combination of particle sizes, often with one or another predominating. The relative amounts of each type of particle determines the soil texture. Loam is a soil that contains roughly equal amounts of all three soil particle types and is usually well suited for growing a very wide range of garden plants.

A soil's texture has a major influence on such soil characteristics as water retention and nutrient movement. For example, a sandy soil drains faster than a clay soil, and a clay soil retains nutrients better than a sandy one; therefore, watering and fertilizing schedules should be adjusted accordingly.

Soil texture will also influence your selection of plants. Some plants – those that generally have low water requirements – thrive in a sharply drained, sandy soil. Others benefit from a more constant supply of moisture and nutrients; these usually grow better in a loam or clay loam, which hold on to water longer and release it more slowly than sandy soil. You can get an idea of the texture by rubbing some dry soil between your fingers. Sandy soil has a gritty feel to it; silt is much smoother; and clay, when dry, forms dense, hard clumps that are not easily broken apart. When wet, clay can be formed into balls or ropes.

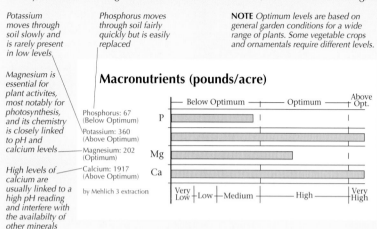

50% pore spaces (air and water)

45% weathered rock and mineral particles

About 5% organic matter

The space between Healthy, productive soil contains the same amount of space (taken up by air and water) as it does actual particles. Smart gardening practices strive to preserve this balance.

Soil structure

The structure of a soil is determined by how the various solid portions of the soil are arranged – particles can be separate, as in the case of pure sand, or bind together to form clusters, or aggregates (tiny clusters of particles). The arrangement has significant impact on the movement and retention of water, nutrients, and air in the soil.

The remaining solid part of the soil is organic matter, which makes soil more conducive to plant growth by enabling the formation of soil aggregates. Aggregates form when soil organisms break down organic matter into humus, an amorphous, gummy material that binds particles together (see The nature of humus, p. 31). Pore spaces between the aggregates are relatively large, and yet smaller spaces between soil particles occur within the aggregates. This combination provides a balance between the movement of water and air and the retention of moisture and nutrients, and makes it easier for plant roots to grow down through the soil.

To improve soil structure, spread organic matter on the soil surface and incorporate it into the upper six to eight inches (15–20cm) of soil every year in areas that are cultivated on an annual basis. For more permanent areas, work organic matter into the soil at planting time. After that, organic mulches can be applied around plants each year; the activities of soil organisms and other natural processes will incorporate much of the organic matter into the soil.

Drainage/water-holding capacity

Plant roots require both air and water for healthy growth. The pore spaces in soil accommodate both, but during rain or irrigation, water forces air out of the pores. Drainage refers to the movement of water through the soil; water-holding capacity is the ability of a soil to retain water after rainfall or irrigation. During dry periods, air-filled pores predominate. Coarse-textured (sandy) soils tend to drain quickly, retaining little water. They also warm up faster in the spring and are generally easy to work. Fine-textured (clay) soils retain both water and nutrients longer than a sandy soil and may become waterlogged. The same material – organic matter – that improves the drainage of a heavy clay soil can increase the capacity of a light sandy soil to retain water.

Different areas of your property may drain very differently. After a heavy rain, one area may stay wet much longer than others. If you plan to garden in a wet spot, you should choose plants that are well adapted to such conditions.

SOIL DRAINAGE TEST

To assess your soil's drainage, perform the following test. Wait at least a few days after the last rain until your soil has dried a bit, then dig a hole 4 inches (10cm) deep, large enough to accommodate a 46-ounce (1.4kg) can. Remove the top and bottom of the can and place it in the hole, firming the soil around the outside. Fill the can to the top with water, then observe how long it takes to drain. Ideally, the water level will drop about 2 inches (5cm) in an hour. This indicates that your soil drains well but also will retain the moisture necessary for the healthy growth of a wide variety of garden plants.

If the water level drops less than an inch (2.5cm) after an hour, your soil does not display sufficient drainage to accommodate many plants. Either limit your choice of plants to those that like constant moisture, or take measures to improve the drainage. If the water level drops 4 inches (10cm) in an hour, your soil drains too fast, and unless you plan to grow only plants that tolerate very dry soils, you will need to add organic matter to help retain soil moisture (and will also need to water as necessary).

Remember that different areas of your landscape may display marked differences in drainage and this test should be done in each one.

Soil pH

The acidity or alkalinity of your soil is critical to plant health. The measurement of the degree of acidity or alkalinity, the pH scale, rates solutions from most acidic (0) to most alkaline (14), with 7 being neutral.

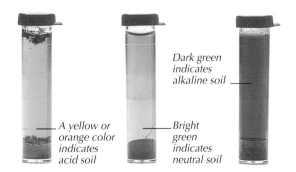

Dark green indicates alkaline soil

A yellow or orange color indicates acid soil

Bright green indicates neutral soil

Determining pH
Kits are available for testing the acidity, neutrality, or alkalinity of your soil at home. They give a good general indication of pH.

The pH of your soil is determined by many factors, such as the type of rock from which the soil originated, the amount of precipitation, and the type of vegetation growing in it.

The optimal soil pH for most plants is between 6.0 and 7.0. Deficiencies of essential nutrients often

occur outside of this range, damaging plants and sometimes making them more susceptible to diseases and pests. Furthermore, acidic soils inhibit the survival of certain beneficial organisms, including earthworms, mycorrhizal fungi, and many bacteria. These organisms are responsible for the decay of organic matter and thereby help plants obtain nutrients.

Soil pH can be modified (to change soil pH, *see* p.30), but to determine which materials and how much you will need to add to your soil, you will first need to perform a soil test (see the opposite page).

Soil fertility

There are 16 essential nutrients necessary for plant growth. Carbon, hydrogen, and oxygen are derived from air and water, and the remaining nutrients are supplied from the soil. The macronutrients – nitrogen (N), phosphorus (P), and potassium (K) – are needed by plants in large quantities; the secondary nutrients – calcium (Ca), magnesium (Mg), and sulfur (S) – are needed in moderate quantities; and the trace elements – boron (B), chlorine (Cl), copper (Cu), iron (Fe), manganese (Mn), molybdenum (Mo), and zinc (Zn) – are essential but needed only in very minute quantities. Determining the existing nutrient levels in your soil can help identify the kind and amount of fertilizers needed.

The acid test
Some plants, including azaleas (left) and rhododendrons and their relatives, thrive only in acidic soils. They will fail if not provided the conditions that maintain acidity.

Not all are alike
The availability of nutrients in the soil depends on the pH level. Note how many of them are less available in acidic soils.

pH

4	5	6	7	8	9
Acidic			Neutral		Basic

nitrogen

calcium and magnesium

phosphorus

potassium

sulfur

iron, magnesium, zinc, copper, cobalt

molybdenum

boron

Avoiding chlorosis
Yellow leaves with dark green veins on citrus, azaleas, and some other plants is a sign of chlorosis, a mineral deficiency often caused by soggy or alkaline soils. To control, improve drainage, add organic matter, and/or treat the soil with chelated iron.

Types of fertilizers

There are many different kinds of fertilizers available that can supply essential nutrients to your plants. Derived from a variety of sources, both natural and synthetic, they are available in a range of formulations that have been developed for different uses, from fast-acting foliar sprays to timed-release pellets. Some contain a single nutrient, and others multiple nutrients.

The three mineral nutrients used in the greatest quantity by plants are nitrogen (N), phosphorus (P), and potassium (K). A fertilizer that contains all three macronutrients is called a complete fertilizer. The three numbers on a bag of a complete fertilizer – the analysis – refer to the percentages by weight of nitrogen (N), phosphorus (phosphate, expressed as P_2O_5), and potassium (potash, expressed as K_2O), in that order.

Many complete fertilizers contain other nutrients that are also essential for healthy plants but are used in smaller quantities (secondary and micronutrients). These are usually listed on the label.

Organic fertilizer is derived from an organic – or once-living – source. Cow, horse, poultry, and sheep manures, fish emulsion, alfalfa and soybean meals, wood ashes, and compost are examples of organic fertilizers. Since most are somewhat lower and more

Apply it correctly
Spread the appropriate amount of fertilizer in a ring around a plant at and beyond its dripline – the outermost reach of its branches – then work it into the soil or cover it with mulch.

variable in nutrient content than chemical fertilizers, you will need to use more of the material to obtain the nutrition your plants require. Because organic fertilizers are typically slow to break down in the soil, they have several advantages over chemical fertilizers: they remain available to plants over a longer period of time, they don't leach out of the soil as quickly, and they don't usually "burn" (dehydrate) roots. One of the most significant qualities of organic fertilizers is that they improve the structure and ecological balance of soil, which promotes healthy plant growth.

FERTILIZER FORMULATIONS

Fertilizer comes in many forms. Many synthetic fertilizers are available in a dry, granulated form, which is easy to spread, and the nutrients are usually readily available. Some granulated fertilizers are coated with sulfur or plastic so that their nutrients are slowly released over time.

Some synthetic fertilizers are sold as concentrated liquids or powders that require diluting. These are applied as liquids to the soil around plants or as a foliar spray. Foliar fertilizing using a water soluble solution can provide quick relief for plants that are suffering from a nutrient deficiency.

Fertilizer spikes are compressed, dry fertilizer that has been formed into a stakelike solid. Commonly used for trees and shrubs, they are inserted into holes drilled into the soil around the root zone.

Manure can be fresh or dried, resulting in a considerable difference in weight and nutrient content, not to mention smell.

NUTRIENT CONTENT OF FERTILIZERS
(ALL VALUES ARE APPROXIMATE)

	% Nitrogen (N)	% Phosphorus (P_2O_5)	% Potassium (K_2O)
Organic			
Animal manure	0.6	0.1	0.5
Compost	0.5	0.3	0.8
Bone meal	2	14	-
Sewage	7	10	-
Seaweed meal	2.8	0.2	2.5
Blood meal	12	-	-
Mushroom compost	0.7	0.3	0.3
Rock phosphate	-	26	12
Wood ash	0.1	0.3	1
Cocoa shells	3	1	3.2
Inorganic			
Balanced fertilizers	available in various proportions		
Ammonium nitrate	35	-	-
Superphosphate	-	20	-
Muriate of potash	-	-	60
Potassium sulfate	-	-	49

Urban soils

Soils in urban environments often suffer from detrimental effects of construction and high-density populations. Compaction, contamination, poor drainage, nutrient imbalances, and excess temperatures are common. When the force of foot and vehicular traffic is exerted on the soil, it compresses and compacts the soil and breaks up soil aggregates. Compacted soil is a major cause of tree decline in urban environments.

Soil contamination often occurs when building materials are spilled or dumped. Some contaminants are toxic to plants, while others cause more indirect damage, such as altering the soil pH. On badly contaminated sites, gardening may be limited to raised beds and containers filled with imported soil.

In addition to suffering nutrient imbalances, many urban soils are infertile simply because topsoil and organic matter are often removed during construction, leaving an infertile subsoil that drains poorly and has very poor aeration. Taking the time to improve your soil is usually the best solution (*see* Building soil with organic matter, *p. 30*).

Heat absorbed by buildings, roads, sidewalks, and vehicles adds considerably to the air temperature of the urban environment, which in turn raises the soil temperature. This "heat-island effect" can significantly alter the chemical and biological characteristics of soil. One of the easiest and safest ways to counteract this effect is to apply an organic mulch to the soil surface (*see* The mulch advantage, *p. 47*).

Temperature ranges

All plants have an optimal temperature range for growth. They also have temperature limits (both high and low), beyond which injury or death is likely to occur. These temperatures vary from one plant to another – some plants have a wide temperature range, others are far more limited – a major reason that locations with widely different climates support distinct plant species. Gardeners deal with this preference for temperatures on a daily basis.

Bring on the cold
Bunchberry (*Cornus canadensis*) tolerates severe cold (to USDA Zone 2).

Sheltered beauties
Irises such as this *Iris innominata* thrive in a protected spot.

Keep me warm
Most gardeners in the Northeast need to provide a protected spot for a common fig tree (*Ficus carica*).

USDA Hardiness Zones

Winter hardiness is the ability of a plant to survive the winter conditions in a given location. Other factors in addition to cold influence hardiness, including soil moisture, humidity, and buffeting winds. While a dianthus may tolerate frigid temperatures in a garden, it often fails to survive winters where soils stay wet, and although a number of broad-leaf evergreens thrive in cold temperatures, these evergreens may suffer severe desiccation if exposed to winter winds.

To help American gardeners identify plants that survive winter temperatures in their region, the USDA created the Plant Hardiness Zone Map. The 1990 edition includes 11 hardiness zones based on average annual minimum temperature. An updated edition of the map, under development, will include 15 hardiness zones – the four new zones will help gardeners in subtropical regions select appropriate plants. Plants in this book have been assigned hardiness codes that match the 15 zones on this map.

Thousands of plants have been coded to the USDA Plant Hardiness Zone Map according to the lowest temperatures they will survive. Also considered in the rating is the plant's cold requirement: many plants require a certain amount of cold in order for their buds to break dormancy in the spring. Therefore, the hardiness rating is actually a range from the coldest zone in which the plant will survive to the warmest zone that satisfies its cold requirements.

The influence of cold temperatures on plant survival is more complicated than simply the lowest temperature experienced by the plant. Other factors such as the rate of temperature drop, the duration of the cold, the amount of temperature fluctuation, and the snow or mulch cover on the soil around the plant.

°F	Zones	°C
below -50°	1	below -46°
-50° to -40°	2	-46° to -40°
-40° to -30°	3	-40° to -34°
-30° to -20°	4	-34° to -29°
-20° to -10°	5	-29° to -23°
-10° to 0°	6	-23° to -18°
0° to 10°	7	-18° to -12°
10° to 20°	8	-12° to -7°
20° to 30°	9	-7° to -1°
30° to 40°	10	-1° to 4°
above 40°	11	above 4°

AHS Heat Zones

On the opposite end of the thermometer, the amount of heat that plants are exposed to in summer is equally critical. For this reason, the American Horticultural Society Plant Heat Zone Map was developed in 1997. AHS President Emeritus Dr. H. Marc Cathey supervised the development of the map, using data collected from the National Climatic Data Center and the National Weather Service. The map divides the US into 12 heat zones according to their average annual number of "heat days." A heat day is defined as a day in which temperatures reach or exceed 86° F (30° C). AHS Heat Zone 1 averages less than one heat day per year, while Zone 12 averages more than 210 heat days.

Like hardiness zones, the heat zones for a particular plant are given as a range. The first number indicates the hottest zone in which it will grow successfully; the second represents the zone with the minimum amount of summer heat necessary for it to complete its annual growth cycle.

As for cold hardiness, heat tolerance in plants involves more than just temperature. Summer rainfall – and the lack of it – limits the successful cultivation of many plants. High humidity rings the death knell for many plants that thrive in drier conditions with similar heat. Some plants are able to thrive in warmer zones if nights are cool. Qualities of the soil – its fertility, acidity or alkalinity, and drainage – also influence the summer survival equation. These factors should also be taken into account when selecting plants.

Although temperature is not the only determinant involved in a plant's ability to thrive in summer conditions, it is an important factor, and one that has been extensively assessed for the use of gardeners. For specific zones for many plants that grow in the Northeast, see the Plant Catalog.

Average Number of Days per Year Above 86°F (30°C)	Zone
<1	1
1 to 7	2
>7 to 14	3
>14 to 30	4
>30 to 45	5
>45 to 60	6
>60 to 90	7
>90 to 120	8
>120 to 150	9
>150 to 180	10
>180 to 210	11
>210	12

Identify light and shade levels

As you stroll around your yard, observe which areas receive full sun and which areas are shaded by trees or surrounding structures. Because light levels change with the time of day, the season, and from one year to the next, this is an ongoing project. As the sun travels across the sky, a shady morning garden may be basking in full sun by early afternoon. In summer, when deciduous trees are in full leaf, a bed that received spring sun may be densely shaded. The angle of the sun as seasons change also alters the level of light in a garden. Furthermore, as trees mature, they cast increasingly broader shadows – beds that were planted in full sun several years ago may become cloaked in the shade of trees that grow nearby.

As your garden matures, stay abreast of changing light levels and the impact on your plants.

To assess your garden's current level of light, examine the shade patterns several times during the course of a sunny day. Note areas that receive shade in the morning, midday, and early and late afternoon. By noting the position of surrounding trees (taking into consideration whether they are deciduous or evergreen) and estimating the changing angle of the sun, you should be able to approximate the light levels in your garden for the entire year with reasonable accuracy.

Identifying your garden areas according to the light categories on this page will help you select plants with corresponding light requirements.

Full sun
Areas that receive at least six hours of direct sun during the day are considered in full sun and are desirable for vegetables, fruit, roses, and a wide range of flowering plants. Some plants that thrive in full sun in cooler northern climates, however, may require some afternoon shade in warmer areas of the Northeast.

Full shade
Areas beneath trees with a dense canopy where no direct sunlight penetrates and reflected light is reduced, or that stand in the all-day shadow of tall buildings or evergreens, are considered to be in full shade. Careful selection of plants for such minimal light levels (and the reduced moisture levels that often occur in areas with low light) is necessary.

Partial shade
Some gardens receive dappled shade throughout the day. If you stand in dappled shade, you should be able to glimpse portions of the sky through the leaves above. Other gardens are more densely shaded for a part of the day but receive bright sunlight for two to six hours. Both are considered partially shaded. A wide variety of plants are suited to this level of light.

Identify your microclimates

Areas within the same yard can present quite a variety of growing conditions, and it is important to recognize the garden limitations and possibilities of each. A microclimate – a portion of your yard where growing conditions differ from surrounding areas – can be a dry, shady spot or one that is constantly wet. It may be a narrow strip that is protected by a hedge, or an area warmed by its proximity to a building or stone wall.

To identify microclimates in your yard, note areas that seem slightly out of sync with the rest of the yard or other yards in the neighborhood – spots where spring flowers open earlier or later than others of the same kind, locations where blooms last longer, or areas that require more or less frequent watering than surrounding areas. These observations will suggest the need for plants that accommodate the nuances of your microclimate. They may also offer the opportunity to grow plants beyond the prevailing cultural limitations (particularly the overall hardiness and heat zone ratings) of your landscape.

EXISTING VEGETATION

Trees provide shade, and shady areas are typically several degrees cooler than adjacent areas in the sun. Shady spots also tend to stay wetter longer. Some plants that thrive in the sun where summers are cool can be grown in warmer climates if they are provided some shade. Dense vegetation can also block or reduce winds that cause a rapid loss of moisture by plants and soil. Planting a windbreak to provide protection from prevailing winds is one way you can help create a microclimate in your yard.

Microclimates are not static, however, especially those influenced by vegetation. As plants grow or are pruned or removed, conditions can be dramatically altered: a sunny garden may become shaded as the tree canopy expands; a wet area may become drier as groundcover plants grow and absorb more water; and a shade garden may be exposed to full sun if an old tree becomes damaged and needs to be removed. The gardener, as always, must be adaptable.

STRUCTURES AND HARDSCAPING

A house, garage, fence, or wall can also serve as a windbreak. These structures cast shade as well – the north side of a wall running east to west tends to be cooler and damper; the sunny south side will be notably warmer and drier. Such a wall creates two distinct microclimates that are separated by mere inches. Each side will support a culturally distinct set of plants. Although the difference in climate on either side of a wall that runs north to south is more subtle, the west side will tend to be warmer than the east side.

In temperate zones, a south-facing wall, particularly if it receives full sun, is a great place to grow sun-loving tropical or subtropical vines – such as *Bougainvillea* and black-eyed Susan vine (*Thunbergia alata*) – as annuals. The soil warms earlier in the spring, boosting early growth, and because the wall collects and holds heat,

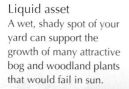

Liquid asset
A wet, shady spot of your yard can support the growth of many attractive bog and woodland plants that would fail in sun.

Dry oasis
A shady dry spot has been transformed into a refuge with the masterful use of gravel, water, and adaptable plants.

moderating cooler night temperatures, growth will continue later into the autumn.

Because the area is cooler, plants growing on the north side of a building emerge from dormancy later than those on the south side. Air temperatures are influenced by the material and color of nearby structures: white or light colors reflect daytime light and heat back onto the plants; dark colors absorb heat.

SOIL SURFACES
The color of paved surfaces and mulch has a similar effect on nearby plants. Dark mulches absorb heat and can be used to warm the soil. Light-colored paving reflects light and heat back to surrounding areas. Heat-tolerant plants that thrive in sunny locations are usually the best choices near unshaded driveways and sidewalks.

WATER
Large bodies of water have a moderating effect on temperature, but even a backyard pond or pool can contribute a similar influence. Plants located at the edge of a pond not only have more water available in the soil, but they also benefit from a more humid environment created by evaporation from the pond.

COASTAL GARDENS
Gardens located near the seashore have special requirements. Plants must be able to tolerate salt spray, strong winds, and sandy soil. However, the moderate temperatures and higher humidity allow

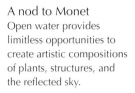

A nod to Monet
Open water provides limitless opportunities to create artistic compositions of plants, structures, and the reflected sky.

for growing a broader palette of plants, including marginally hardy ones. Soil can be improved by adding organic matter, and windbreaks can provide protection. Surprisingly, solid walls do not afford as much protection as salt-tolerant trees and shrubs, which act as filters to the salt spray as well as a buffer to the wind. Once a living barrier is established, less tolerant plants can be grown and benefit from the nurturing aspect of the ocean.

TOPOGRAPHY
Unless your yard is flat, its topography will influence your growing conditions. Marginally hardy plants and those that produce cold-sensitive, early spring flowers are more likely to be damaged by frosts if they are located in a frost pocket. Slopes also affect runoff: water can collect in a low area, making an ideal location for a bog garden. Steep slopes can be tamed and runoff reduced by using retaining walls to create level planting areas. Now let's explore ways to modify your existing garden conditions.

A little protection
Even a thinly constructed fence can provide enough wind protection to give shelter to delicate ferns and marginally hardy plants.

ADAPT WHEN NECESSARY

So you've assessed yourself and your lifestyle and have critically analyzed your site. Now it's time to make some decisions about your gardening conditions. Reconciling your personal interests, style, and budget with the physical limitations of your yard may require some compromises. But if any reasonable improvements to your site will enhance the long-term success of your garden, they should be considered. Drastic changes are not recommended for a SMARTGARDEN™, particularly those that will be difficult or time-consuming to maintain.

Fixed and variable factors

Certain aspects of a gardening site – temperature extremes, rainfall, elevation, proximity to city or the ocean – cannot be altered, and the plants you grow should be inherently compatible with those existing conditions. Radical attempts to change your microclimate are generally unfruitful and a frustrating waste of your time.

On the other hand, some modifications can alter the growing conditions significantly to the advantage of your gardens. Adding soil amendments such as organic matter (*see p. 30*) or limestone or iron sulfate to decrease or increase the acidity (*see* Adjusting soil pH, *p. 30*) is often necessary, particularly in areas

Staying dry
Make the best of a fast-draining area by creating a dry garden, using drought-tolerant plants set among stones, gravel, and sand.

where builders have removed topsoil. Regrading a backyard to improve drainage, or removing trees to allow more light into an area, may dramatically expand your gardening opportunities. The cost of such major modifications should be evaluated against the potential results. Sometimes compromises in garden size, placement, plant selection, and hardscaping options (nonplant features, such as patios) offer satisfying and less costly solutions.

Conditions vary, depending on the location of your garden within the landscape. Parts of your yard may be in full sun while others are shaded; some areas may be exposed to persistent winds from which other areas are protected; drainage patterns may result in a wet zone in one part of the yard and dry conditions in another. Identifying the distinct characteristics of each area provides the gardener with an opportunity to grow plants with varied requirements within a single landscape. Matching the requirements of the plants you want to grow as closely as possible to the conditions of a particular site will minimize adaptations that are necessary for healthy growth.

Smart redirection
Instead of trying to grow grass in a wet spot, the owners of this property converted part of their land into a lush planting of woodland plants shaded by small trees.

Raise it up
Raised beds and supplemental irrigation enable this gardener to grow larger, better-quality vegetables.

The benefits of time

Keep in mind that time is an important dimension in gardening. An instant SMARTGARDEN™ is an oxymoron. Good things take time. Building a healthy soil doesn't happen overnight; it is an ongoing process. Likewise plants, particularly trees and shrubs, increase in size over the years, and they should be spaced with an eye toward their mature size. Although you may be tempted to purchase large plants in order to give your garden an established feeling from the start, this strategy has its drawbacks: larger plants are more expensive, and they often have more difficulty becoming established than smaller stock. By the time a large plant has settled in and has begun to produce significant growth, a specimen that was smaller at planting time might even have caught up with the larger one.

Time can be viewed as a wonderful dynamic – you can witness your garden's change with the passage of the seasons and the years as the design you envisioned becomes a reality. As plants and beds mature, they often require less maintenance because after their roots become well established, appropriately selected trees and shrubs will not require much attention, and, as groundcovers fill in, the need for weeding is reduced.

Worth the wait
Starting from scratch may seem daunting at first, but the satisfaction of watching a landscape grow over time is one of the major pleasures of gardening. Heavy work gives way to installing the structural "bones" of a garden area, followed by planting and then enjoying the rewards of all of your planning and hard work.

Raised beds for variety

Sometimes the plants you want to grow are at odds with your soil. Plants that require excellent drainage are poor choices for heavy, clay soils. On the other hand, a light, sandy soil will not sustain plants that require abundant moisture without reliable, abundant irrigation. If you want to include plants in your landscape with requirements that vary significantly from your native soil, consider growing them in raised beds or containers. Given the finite quantity of soil involved, its characteristics can be easily manipulated to suit the needs of desired plants.

Although limited in space, these gardens can be constructed or placed in sun or shade, protected or exposed locations, and watered frequently or minimally. They can also be built to accommodate easy access for gardeners who have difficulty bending or working in ground beds. The flexibility of raised beds gives the gardener an enormous selection of plants that might otherwise be ill suited for the conditions of the site (*see also p. 13*).

Culling the existing landscape

Before you begin adding plants to your landscape, it is important to review those that are already there. Some may have suffered damage or neglect and are now simply eyesores. Others may require a bit (or more) of maintenance. Certain plants in your yard may require significant time and energy to keep them healthy and attractive. This is particularly common with plants that were sited in inappropriate conditions in the first place. Transplanting to a different spot in the landscape or removing them altogether may be necessary.

Small trees and shrubs are often planted too close together. Although the short-term effect may be pleasing, after a number of years plants eventually become too crowded for their space. If such plants exist in your yard, determine if their value is worth the effort of constant pruning. Is transplanting them to another location a possibility, or should you simply remove them?

Most suburban lots can accommodate very few large trees. If the trees that were planted decades ago have overtaken the lot, you may want to consider removing one or two, or at least thinning their branches to allow more light to penetrate. Limbing up the tree – that is, removing the lower branches – can increase light penetration as well, and it opens the area beneath the tree for use.

Severe damage from disease, insects, winds, lightning, or other environmental stresses may have affected some trees and shrubs in your yard. Ask yourself if they are worth saving – it may be time to consider a replacement. Pruning or removing large trees may require a professional arborist.

WHEN TO CALL THE ARBORIST

Trees are a common and essential element of the northeastern landscape, providing shade to your home, garden, and leisure areas while lending a graceful aesthetic presence to your surroundings with views of foliage, fruit, bark, and habit throughout the year. To protect these valuable horticultural commodities, there are times when a certified arborist must be brought in to evaluate or treat declining, sick, or damaged trees.

Arborists, popularly known as tree surgeons, are professionals trained in tree care. They can diagnose problems, recommend treatments, fertilize, prune, spray, and remove trees safely.

Contact an arborist if large or out-of-reach limbs have broken, often a result of storm damage, or when large-scale pruning must be done. A proper cut, made either from the ground or in the tree's canopy through the use of ropes and harnesses, will enable the tree to heal quickly and eliminate entry points for insects or disease. Birches, cherries, and magnolias can be especially vulnerable to wounds that are not properly treated.

When insects or diseases become a problem for your trees, arborists can recommend and provide a number of helpful remedies. In cases where a specific pest besieges a species of tree, such as with the wooly adelgid and the Eastern Hemlock (*Tsuga candadensis*), an arborist can prescribe a number of remedies to control the problem and, in some cases, encourage regenerative growth. Arborists can also recommend and perform removal of dead or declining trees. Consult your state association of arborists for a list of certified professionals.

A job for the professional
Removing large limbs and felling trees are both best left to trained professional arborists.

Thinning and limbing up

When large trees limit the opportunities for growing other plants in a yard, either because they take up a great deal of space, or they cast dense shade, removal is not your only option.

Thinning a tree involves removing a percentage of its branches so that more air and light can penetrate through the remaining canopy without stimulating a great deal of vigorous, new growth. This is accomplished by cutting specific branches back to where they connect to a larger limb. This type of pruning is often beneficial to the tree: weak, unhealthy, and crowded branches can be removed, and air circulates better through the canopy. Plants that are growing beneath the tree will receive more light. If you want grass to grow under a tree with a dense canopy, thinning is critical.

Limbing up involves removing low limbs back to the main trunk in order to allow access to the area beneath the canopy; it effectively raises the crown. Ideally this process should begin early in the tree's training, but it can be done to large trees as well. When you are removing lower limbs from a young tree, do it gradually – this will cause less shock and promote a stronger trunk. As the tree gains height and girth, continue to remove the lowest branches. Generally, the best time to prune trees is when they are dormant, during the fall and winter.

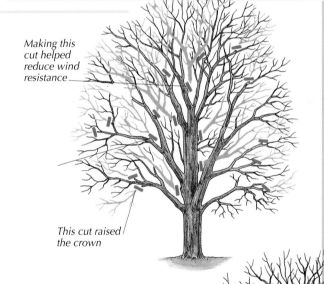

Making this cut helped reduce wind resistance

This cut raised the crown

Thinning a tree
This is often done to reduce the overall size of a tree, to allow more light and air to penetrate through the crown, and to reduce wind resistance and stress from wide-spreading, heavy branches. Thinning requires more skill than limbing up.

Limbing up (crown lifting)
Removing some of a tree's lower branches creates more room for people and vehicles to pass more freely or to expose a street light that has become hidden in the branches. This is generally the easier of the two options presented here.

Entire branch was removed

Part of this large branch was removed

Adapting soil conditions

Whether refining an existing garden or working an area that is new to cultivation, a number of conditions can be fairly easily modified, such as adjusting pH and modifying drainange and structure.

Many of these changes – particularly those involving the soil – are most easily addressed prior to planting. Once a garden has been planted, your ability to incorporate soil amendments is restricted. Whenever you dig soil, take the opportunity to incorporate amendments. It takes much longer for fertilizer and limestone to reach plant roots when placed on the surface of the soil than it does when those materials are mixed throughout the root zone.

ADJUSTING SOIL PH

As mentioned in Tenet 2, a soil test provides important information about your soil. If your existing soil pH restricts your selection of plants, you can adjust it by mixing certain minerals into the soil. Limestone – usually ground or dolomitic – is applied to raise the pH (decrease the acidity). Wood ashes also tend to raise the pH of soil. Elemental sulfur or iron sulfate are the most commonly recommended supplements for lowering pH. Aluminum sulfate can also be used to decrease acidity, but it may cause aluminum toxicity in some plants.

Many sources of organic matter, including pine needles, oak leaves, unlimed compost, and green manure (cover crops that are plowed into the soil), will increase the soil acidity as they are broken down by microorganisms. Peat moss is also an acidifier, but its use should be avoided because it takes so long – centuries, in fact – for it to regenerate in its native bogs. The amounts of various materials needed to produce the desired pH level will vary depending on your soil texture and the amount of change needed. Modifying the soil pH takes time; it may require repeated applications.

An extreme case
You may not have ducks taking up permanent residence in your yard, but many properties have spots that are poorly drained. Either take measures to drain the area, or consider creating a bog garden or even a pond.

DEALING WITH DRAINAGE

If your soil drains too slowly, you have several options. You can limit your selection to plants that like wet soils, add material to the soil to improve drainage, or build raised beds and fill them with good, loamy soil before planting. To improve drainage of a compacted soil, add organic matter. If the subsoil is compacted, you may need to break up the hardpan or add subsurface drainage tiles to carry excess water away from planting areas.

For vegetable gardens with poor drainage, a hill-and-furrow planting method can be used: broad rows can be built up above the soil surface, with furrows running between the rows to divert excess water. Conversely, if your soil drains too quickly, use the furrows for planting. Rain or irrigation water will be channeled into the furrows where plants are growing.

For gardens where the soil drains too quickly, the addition of organic matter will improve water holding capacity, and mulching will reduce evaporation loss. But supplemental irrigation may be necessary unless you choose plants that thrive in dry soils.

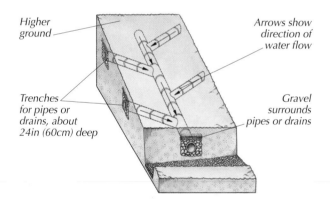

Higher ground

Arrows show direction of water flow

Trenches for pipes or drains, about 24in (60cm) deep

Gravel surrounds pipes or drains

Improving drainage
Connect pipes or tiles in a gravel-filled trench. On sloping ground, lay the pipes or tile drains to run parallel to the ground. On level ground, slope the pipes away from ground level.

Building soil with organic matter

Organic matter – compost, leaf mold, grass clippings, rotted manure, or any material that was once alive – has a nearly miraculous power to improve almost any soil. Added to a clay soil, it facilitates drainage by creating soil aggregates with pore spaces between them; in a sandy soil, it bolsters water retention. The best way to provide continuous, well-balanced nutrition for plants is to build up the soil with organic matter.

As both microscopic (for example, bacteria) and macroscopic (such as earthworms and fungi) soil organisms digest organic matter, they release

nutrients in a usable form for plants to absorb through their roots. Unlike quick-release chemical fertilizers that offer a glut of nutrients that may wash away with the next rain, decomposition of organic matter is a continuous process; nutrients are released slowly over a long period of time.

There are many good sources of organic matter, and many of them are free and readily available. Kitchen and yard wastes can be composted and within a few months yield a rich soil supplement (*see* Composting wastes, *p. 56*). Leaves raked during the fall become crumbly leaf mold, especially if they are chopped and mixed with a bit of soil to encourage their decomposition. Manure is often free for the hauling from a nearby farm or stable, or it can be

| Mushroom compost | Peat | Manure |

Brown gold
Here are just three of the many different kinds of organic matter that can be added to the soil in order to improve the structure and water retention.

purchased in bags from a home-supply or hardware store. Green manure is a cover crop that is sown, grown, and then turned back into the soil. A winter cover crop is an efficient method of adding nutrients and organic matter to a vegetable garden.

A distinction is often made between leguminous and nonleguminous cover crops. Both add organic matter to the soil, but legumes, such as clover and vetch, contribute additional nitrogen as a result of their symbiotic relationship with nitrogen-fixing *Rhizobium* bacteria in the roots. As the legume roots decompose, nitrogen is released back into the soil. Of course, the amount of specific nutrients any given organic matter contains depends on the source and condition of the organic matter. For example, most compost contains 1.5 to 3.5 percent nitrogen, 0.5 to 1 percent phosphorus, and 1 to 2 percent potassium. Wood ashes – which tend to raise pH – contain little nitrogen, 1 to 2 percent phosphorus, and 3 to 7 percent potassium.

A soil that is well furnished with organic matter will sustain a healthy population of organisms, resulting in both improved soil structure and a good source of the raw materials needed by your garden plants. This is recycling at its best.

USING SOIL AMENDMENTS

Given the diverse nature of soil conditions throughout the Northeast, there are a number of varying conditions that warrant the use of amendments. The region's large number of urban sites often feature conditions where soils have become compacted and depleted of nutrients. While tilling can ease compaction issues, organic amendments such as leaf mold or composted manure can enrich soils and create a more suitable nutritional environment for all of your plants.

There is also a wide array of regionally available organic amendments in the Northeast. Examples include blood meal, mushroom soil, fish meal, and fish emulsions. Such organic matter should also be used as amendments in areas where thin, lean, or sandy soils are common.

In areas where heavy soils predominate, such as those with a high component of clay where ample soil nutrition may be present, amendments such as organic matter can be introduced in order to improve drainage and air circulation. In troublesome areas where dense soils make amendment difficult, your best choice may be to create raised beds or berms with good quality topsoil that can support a variety of landscape plantings.

The nature of humus

After organic matter is thoroughly decomposed by soil microorganisms, it produces a material called humus, which exists as a very thin layer around soil particles. There is some misunderstanding about this term. The material commonly sold in bags that bear the label "humus" – usually compost or peat – would be more accurately labeled "humus-producing material," because microorganisms use it to make true humus, which is the end product of organic matter decomposition.

Humus contributes significantly to the soil environment by facilitating the aggregation of soil particles (which improves soil structure), holding nutrients against the force of leaching, increasing aeration, retaining water, and acting as a buffer to moderate a soil's acidity or alkalinity.

The carbon:nitrogen ratio

One of the most critical characteristics of organic matter in terms of plant nutrition is the carbon to nitrogen ratio (C:N ratio). Fresh organic matter has a high carbon content compared to its nitrogen content. As the organic matter breaks down, the ratio changes as the relative amount of nitrogen increases. In most fully matured compost, the C:N ratio is between 30:1 and 10:1. When organic matter with a high C:N ratio (above 30:1), such as sawdust or grass clippings, is added to soil, microorganisms use nitrogen from the soil, and a temporary nitrogen deficiency can occur in plants. To avoid this deficiency, use composted organic matter. If mulching with a noncomposted organic material, apply a top-dressing of a nitrogen fertilizer prior to spreading the material.

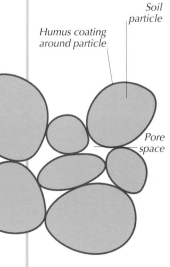

Humus coating around particle

Soil particle

Pore space

Up close
This diagram shows a much enlarged view of a few particles of soil. Each particle is coated with humus, the end product of microbial breakdown of organic matter. Humus aids in the retention of moisture and nutrients and promotes the formation of aggregates, which in turn leads to increased pore space: all very good things for soil.

PICK THE BEST PLANTS

One of the most important steps in establishing and maintaining a SMARTGARDEN™ is selecting the right plants. Matching the cultural requirements of plants with your specific garden environment significantly increases the likelihood of successful cultivation and minimizes the maintenance effort. Preferences for water, light, soil type and acidity, tolerance of wind, humidity, salt spray, and air pollution, and resistance to diseases and pests are important factors in plant selection. Some conditions, such as soil pH, can be adjusted to accommodate the needs of desired plants. Others, such as salt spray near coastal regions or air pollution near industrial areas, are essentially fixed and limiting factors in the selection process.

Practical considerations

Identifying the USDA Plant Hardiness and AHS Heat Zones of your site is a logical first step in choosing plants you would like to grow. If a plant does not have the hardiness or heat tolerance for the zone in which you garden, you should choose another plant, unless you are willing to take extra measures to protect it. For example, tropical and subtropical plants can be grown in a container outdoors in temperate zones and brought indoors for winter (*see* Growing tropical plants in the Northeast, p. 38). Consult the Zone maps on p. 22 to determine your USDA Hardiness Zone and your AHS Heat Zone. Use those numbers as a starting point to select plants that will thrive in your garden's temperatures.

There may be areas of your yard that are unsuitable or impractical for growing plants of any kind. Consider a nonplant alternative such as a fence (in place of a hedge), a walkway, patio, or deck (in place of a lawn, bed, or similar planting), or a gazebo (in place of a large shade tree). These spaces are important elements of a landscape because they provide you with a minimum-maintenance area for moving through your gardens comfortably, or room for relaxing and enjoying your planted areas.

So you have an area in your yard and you want it to do something, but you need to consider the options: Provide shade? Simply look nice? Attract birds? Smell good? Block a view? Separate one area from another? Cover the ground? Provide a space for active play?

What are the site's physical factors, including sun, water, soil, wind, and microclimate? Will it support plants? If no, use the site for some other purpose, or think hard about what you would need to do to modify it. If yes, consider the specific plant features you'd like and require: leaves, flowers, fruit, form, bark, fragrance, size, shape, longevity, adaptabilty, productivity, hardiness, specific needs such as pruning, support, or deadheading to look its best, and susceptibility to pests and diseases.

Choose plants that meet the desired criteria and will grow well in the available microclimate, and determine how many will be needed.

The next consideration is your budget. If you can wait for a small plant to grow to its mature size, or let groundcovers and other similar plants multiply, you will spend less. You should also determine when to buy the plant, and put it in the ground.

Two solutions
Using plants is not always the solution to a given landscape problem: the conditions and the planning process may logically lead you to choose a hardscaping option over a garden.

Compromise
Instead of draining this area, the gardener chose to create a pond feature with hardscaping leading right up to it. Plants adapted to the conditions thrive, and the entire area is a place of delight instead of one of constant maintenance.

Plant categories

Plants are grouped according to their lifespan. The major categories are annuals, biennials, perennials, and woody plants.

ANNUAL

An annual completes its life cycle in a single season. It grows from seed, develops vegetatively, bears flowers, and produces seed for the next generation and then dies, all in less than a year.

BIENNIAL

A biennial requires two growing seasons to complete its life cycle. Most biennials produce vegetative growth their first season; they flower, produce seed, and die their second season.

It takes two
In spite of its specific name, *Lunaria annua* (honesty) grows most commonly as a biennial, requiring two years to complete its life cycle.

Follow the sun
Sunflowers are annuals that must have full sun to thrive.

PERENNIAL

A perennial is a plant that lives for more than two years, and a herbaceous perennial is a nonwoody perennial that survives from one growing season to the next because its roots or underground storage organs (such as a bulb, corm, or tuber) persist.

Sun-lover
Achillea species (yarrows) are mostly tough, adaptable perennials that grow well in dry, sunny spots.

Shade seeker
Green-and-gold (*Chrysogonum virginianum*) grows best with some shade, especially in the hottest part of the afternoon.

WOODY PLANT

A woody plant is also a type of perennial, but it possesses a more permanent structure that persists above ground from season to season. Woody plants may be deciduous (shedding their leaves each year) or evergreen. Examples include shrubs, trees, and some climbers and groundcovers.

Always green
Daphne odora (near left) is a typical evergreen, always bearing leaves at any given time. However, evergreens normally shed some leaves periodically.

Leaf droppers
Hydrangea species and cultivars (far left) are all woody plants that are widely used in shrub borders and as specimens. Being deciduous, they shed their leaves for winter.

Perennials grown as annuals

Some plants are referred to as annuals, when they are actually perennial in their native habitat or in another Hardiness Zone. This has led to a bit of confusion among gardeners. True annuals – plants that grow, flower, produce seed, and die in a single growing season – have a Hardiness Zone of zero because they cannot tolerate cold winter temperatures, and so hardiness is not an issue.

Many plants that are grown as annuals in temperate climates, such as sweet basil, snapdragon, coleus, and moonflower, are perennial in warm climates; such plants are sometimes referred to as horticultural annuals, meaning that they can be grown as annuals in regions where they will not survive as perennials. They may also be referred to as tender perennials.

Four o'clocks (*Mirabilis jalapa*) produce rootstocks that will overwinter in milder areas if given protection, such as a deep loose mulch of straw or oak leaves.

Impatiens, perennials or shrubs where native, are widely grown as tender annuals in the Northeast.

Snapdragons (*Antirrhinum* species and cultivars) often overwinter and produce many flowers their second (and sometimes third) year.

Plant adaptations

Why do some plants flourish in full sun, while others languish or outright die unless they are provided with at least some shade during the hottest part of the day? Why do some plants thrive in bogs and open water, and others are perfectly at home in deserts or on cliffsides? Although most garden plants have roughly the same structure – roots, stems, leaves, flowers – nuances in their morphology equip them for a wide variety of conditions. This is fortunate, because this means there are plenty of plants, both naturally occcuring and selected, whose requirements and preferences match your conditions. Understanding the characteristics that make a plant suited to particular conditions will help you recognize those that are likely to do well in your garden environment.

SHADE

Plants that grow best in the shade tend to have large, flat leaves with a fairly thin outer layer of cells. This allows maximum area and minimum resistance for absorbing light needed for photosynthesis and growth. In general, plants that grow in shady conditions produce fewer flowers and seeds than those grown in sun – this limited reproductive activity conserves a great deal of energy that can be directed toward vegetative growth. Thus, the ornamental display of many shade gardens relies more heavily on foliage color and texture than on flowers.

Shady situation
Savvy gardeners prize shade for the opportunities it provides to create garden pictures using foliage color and texture as well as overall plant habit.

HEAT AND DROUGHT

Xeriphytic plants have developed several strategies for reducing water loss and dealing with high temperatures. Many have smaller leaves with a thick, waxy layer, called the cuticle, on the leaf surface that protects it from drying out as well as providing some protection against insects. The reduction in both

Desert grasses
A great many grasses are adapted to growing in very dry and often hot areas and thrive in well-drained soils and even gravel.

surface area and protective coating minimize moisture loss. Alpine plants that survive in areas where soil water is frozen for much of the year, and unavailable for absorption by plants, often exhibit similar traits.

Another adaptation that enables many plants to tolerate dry climates is pubescence – the presence of fine hairs – on leaves. These hairs help shade the leaf surface from the hot sun and trap moisture lost by the leaf through transpiration, thus maintaining a higher humidity level immediately around the leaf surface. The higher humidity reduces the transpiration pressure in the leaf, slowing the rate of moisture loss. Leaf arrangement and color also affect the absorption of heat. Leaves that point upward, arranged vertically toward the sun – such as *Yucca* and *Phormium* – absorb less heat than those with leaves oriented at right angles to the stem. Light-colored plants (typical of many heat-tolerant plants, including several species of *Euphorbia*, *Sedum*, and *Verbascum*) absorb less heat than dark plants.

Resistant roses
Rosa rugosa var *alba* and its many relatives thrive in hot, dry, cold, and windy sites.

COLD AND WIND

Some plants that grow well in cold, windy sites (such as along the coast, on open plains and priairies, or at the tops of mountains) have a prostrate growth habit, minimizing their exposure to drying winds. Trees and shrubs that survive in regions with cold winters are sensitive to environmental signals such as dropping temperatures and decreasing day length, initiating changes that induce dormancy to prepare them for winter, often indicated by leaf drop or a change in evergreen foliage color. As temperatures decrease, certain solutes – dissolved substances – accumulate in cells, reducing the likelihood of their freezing and rupturing. This is essentially making use of plant "antifreeze."

Site-specific challenges

Identifying the varied growing conditions of your site will help you select plants that will thrive with the least amount of assistance on your part. For example, an area of your yard that drains poorly and remains wet for long periods of the season is a likely site for a bog garden. The sunny strip alongside the street or driveway, subject to reflected heat and baking sun and far from the water faucet, lends itself to a xeriphytic planting of drought-tolerant plants. The shady north side of your house is a likely spot for shade-loving shrubs and groundcovers.

The conditions of some gardening sites are more challenging than others, and they may significantly restrict plant selection. If you live by the seashore,

Four combinations
You can create spectacular gardens in almost any given condition: sunny and dry (upper left), sunny and wet (upper right), shady and dry (lower left), and shady and wet (lower right). Only the most extreme conditions – such as the darkest, driest woodland or a sunny lake – will preclude you from achieving the garden you want.

you should select plants that tolerate salt spray and wind. If your soil is rich in limestone, plants that thrive in alkaline soil are a logical choice. Trees that have proven to adapt to the stresses of air pollution and compacted soil are the best options for planting alongside busy streets and in high-traffic urban areas. The lists in the Plant Catalog offer you a guide to regionally adapted plants to use in the variety of specific conditions that may be present in your garden.

Some areas may represent exceptions to the general conditions that are present in your yard and may offer possibilities for growing plants beyond those typically suited for your region or location (*see* Identify your microclimates, *p. 24*).

Plants for local conditions

For centuries, plant breeders have selected and developed varieties of plants with qualities that make them particularly well adapted to certain conditions, often extending the area in which that plant has traditionally been grown. Disease-resistant tomatoes are a notable example.

Many, if not most, of the cultivated plants that we grow have been selected because someone thought they were (for example) showier, bigger, smaller, healthier, or more fruitful than other plants like it. It may have been a planned cross that was part of a breeding program at a major seed company, or it may have been a serendipitous event – a gardener noticing a plant that was somehow different in some significant way than others. Sometimes seed of the selection observed and saved by a gardener is passed around to friends and handed down to children.

New varieties are continually being developed, grown, and compared at commercial seed companies and public institutions. Many regional plant breeding programs are associated with land grant colleges (*see* Appendix *p. 384*) or botanic gardens and arboreta (*see p. 385*).

Research has led to the breeding and selection of plants that better withstand environmental adversity. This means that certain varieties may extend the growing range or conditions where the plant can be successfully grown.

Discriminating variety selection can also reduce the impact of pests and diseases that frequently infest gardens in your locale. There may be varieties of the plants you want to grow that display an inherited resistance or tolerance to the problem. This preventive approach to pest and disease control is a simple way to reduce the need for applying pesticides. Local garden centers and Extension Services are often able to provide the names of disease- and pest-resistant varieties of fruits, vegetables, and ornamental plants for your area.

GROWING TROPICAL PLANTS IN THE NORTHEAST

Many plants commonly grown as annuals are in fact tender tropical perennials. These include such well-known plants as bedding geraniums, cannas, and fuchsias, and many species used in planters and hanging baskets, such as spike-dracaena, fan-flower, and bacopa. While these plants grow well during summer, they will not stand freezing and must be given protection over winter if you wish to save them. Many are easy to replace, while others become overly large if kept indoors for the winter. Some are easy to store dormant until spring, but most need to be kept in a cool but well-lit location. Avid gardeners who have suitable locations enjoy the challenge of bringing these plants through the winter and growing them on.

Dormant bulbs and corms, such as begonia, canna, dahlia, gladiolus, and four o'clock, should be lifted in fall after the first hard frost has blackened the stems. Turn them upside down to drain any water from hollow stems, and allow to air-dry in a frost-proof location for a day or so. Break off surplus soil but do not wash the roots clean, and store in barely moist peat moss or vermiculite in a cool but frost-free location. The ideal temperature is around 40°F (4°C). Inspect plants every few weeks, and water lightly if the storage material is very dry or if the roots shrivel.

Plants that don't become fully dormant should be dug and potted in fall before frost and kept in a sunny window, sun porch, or greenhouse where the temperature remains above 50°F (10°C). Bring plants indoors before night temperatures get close to freezing, or severe leaf-drop may occur. In spring, acclimatize overwintered plants to outdoor conditions gradually, since they may sunscald and desiccate badly if this process is hurried.

In addition to the commonly grown annual plants, many of the plants enjoyed as house plants, such as flowering maples, plumbago, lantana, and lemon trees, can benefit from a period outdoors during the summer. Be certain that they are hardened off properly in early summer and that they are brought back indoors well before first frost.

All plants that are being brought inside should be inspected closely for pests and diseases that can

Cannas (*Canna* species and cultivars) produce lush, bold foliage and brilliantly colored flowers.

spread rapidly in the close conditions of a sunny window ledge. It is far easier to treat a problem outside than to try to spray once it is indoors.

Mature size and growth habit

Trying to achieve a mature appearance in your new garden is tempting, but it can lead to problems. If you space your plants too closely together, the result is almost always unsatisfactory. Plants soon become crowded, they may become more susceptible to disease, and they compete for water and light. Flower and fruit production may be reduced. Often, their growth habit is altered – instead of full, wide-spreading branches, plants may appear sparse and gangly as they stretch in search of light.

When deciding which plants to include in your yard and where you want to place them, be sure you have room to accommodate the mature size of each selection, no matter what its eventual size will be. Repeated pruning of a shrub during the growing season will be made unnecessary if your initial selection is based on the desired mature size. Many nurseries supply the mature dimensions on the plant tag or label. Consult the Plant Catalog to avoid making a major mistake.

If the growth habit of a plant is something worth featuring, be sure to provide adequate room. For example, a Harry Lauder's walking stick (*Corylus avellana* 'Contorta') is best placed in an open area where its unusual form can be appreciated. A low, spreading plant such as creeping juniper needs plenty of lateral room to develop; otherwise, it may overtake nearby plants or walkways.

Training plants from an early age to enhance their natural habit or to direct growth in a certain manner can be an effective way to manage plant size.

Carefully pruned specimen plants can serve as focal points and accents, esepecially in a small garden. Some plants can be trained to grow against a wall, a technique known as espalier; this requires a minimum of garden space and is an effective use of a blank wall.

Another choice you will be confronted with when selecting your plants is which size to purchase. Although a larger plant may give you a fuller look than a smaller version of the same plant, you will need to weigh the additional expense against the immediate effect. In a few seasons, small plants often catch up to plants that were larger at the time of purchase (*see* The benefits of time, *p. 28*).

If you do start with young plants, it is still possible to achieve a mature look while waiting for them to grow. Maintain temporary herbaceous plantings in the space between young woody plants. Annuals survive for only a single season, and as your trees and shrubs spread in the coming years, perennials can be dug and transplanted to other areas.

Variations on a theme
Plants are very adaptable and respond to pruning and training to produce an amazing variety of shapes, including the espalier and standard shown here.

Tree forms

Trees may be the biggest of all the voices in your garden choir, but they do show a remarkable range of differences. Use these differences to create a varied backdrop for the rest of your garden plants and structures. Remember, it may take several to many years for the tree to develop its fully mature form.

Half-standard   *Fastigiate*   *Multistemmed*   *Weeping standard*

Growth habits

There are many shapes a plant can take, whether naturally or by manipulation though horticultural practices. It is often best to consider a plant's shape before thinking about its flowers – the shape will remain long after the flowers are gone. The Plant Catalog presents some options for selecting plants based on their habit.

Cushion- or mound-forming   *Clump-forming*   *Climbing and Scandet*

TAKE GOOD CARE OF THE EARTH

Every garden activity we undertake has a ripple effect on our plants, soil, water, and wildlife. We apply fertilizer to our lawns and, depending on the type and quantity, it can either bolster a healthy soil environment or leach through the soil and pollute local streams. By encouraging certain plants to grow and removing others, we influence whether and what wildlife inhabits our gardens. The material that we select to surface our paths and driveways also has an impact – positive or negative – on water runoff and soil erosion.

Choices and compromises

In our efforts to develop and maintain satisfying landscapes, we must try to achieve our goals without putting a strain on our environment. Simply by adjusting watering schedules, selecting the most effective mulch material, or timing the application of a pest control measure with precision, we can increase the efficiency of our gardening efforts and minimize the effect on the environment.

Some of the modifications we make in our gardens may require a balanced counteraction. For example, removing debris from a bed to keep it neat deprives soil of organic matter. Replacing the leaves with an organic mulch such as compost or shredded bark, however, supplies the organic matter while achieving the desired tidy appearance. Recognizing the impact of our activities, using resources efficiently and avoiding waste, must become second nature in the SMARTGARDEN™.

Whether planning a new bed, maintaining a lawn, or pruning a tree, gardening activities require choices. Consideration of environmental consequences should be an important part of the criteria you use for selecting one technique over another.

Basic decisions such as whether an area should be maintained as lawn or developed into a bed, whether to encourage wildlife (and if so, which kind), and whether a tree that casts dense shade should be removed all need to be weighed against their impact on the overall landscape. Sometimes a compromise in expectations, technique, or timing can be effective in achieving the desired change without causing significant environmental consequences.

Another example of compromise is reducing the amount of nitrogen fertilizer applied to plants that are subject to water stress – vegetative growth may be reduced, but so will the water needs of the plant.

Using every corner
Growing a wide range of plants makes efficient use of limited space and also attracts a diverse mix of wild creatures (many beneficial) into your garden.

Beneficial for all
Gardening in an age of shrinking habitats and resources should make every enlightened gardener consider both the plants and the wildlife that depend on them when making gardening decisions.

Serious disease or pest problems can be reduced by adjusting your planting schedule for several vegetable crops. Thinning a tree canopy that casts dense shade, rather than removing the tree, can accomplish the desired outcome of increasing light penetration without destroying a habitat and food source that supports a variety of wildlife.

Conserving water

Given the droughts and high average temperatures many parts of the country have been experiencing in recent years, not to mention the increase in population density, water consumption for

Someone's dinner table
Don't forget that lawns are still very popular with robins and other creatures that depend on them for food.

gardening is a growing concern. There are a variety of conservation strategies you can use in your garden to reduce water consumption

While all plants need water to thrive, some need less than others, and some plants are better equipped than others to obtain and retain water. For instance, succulent plants store water in their fleshy leaves or their stems and underground structures for use when needed. Leaves of lamb's-ears (*Stachys* spp.) and wormwood (*Artemisia* spp.) are covered with fine white hairs that shade the leaf surface and prevent moisture loss. Many ornamental grasses and prairie natives have deep roots that range far to seek water. Some leaves are oriented so that the minimum amount of sunlight falls on their surfaces, reducing leaf temperature. These and other characteristics of drought-tolerant plants minimize the need for supplemental watering (*see* Plant adaptations, p. 36).

You do not need to limit your plant selection to drought-tolerant species. Plants that require more frequent watering, however, should be grouped together, ideally close to a water source. By designing your garden according to the plants' water requirements, it is easier to develop efficient watering systems tailored to the needs of different sections of the garden.

REDUCING RUNOFF

A great deal of potentially beneficial garden moisture is lost to runoff. Grading your beds can help direct the flow of water to where it will be most useful. Studies suggest that significantly more water penetrates into the soil through a diverse planting of groundcovers than through turf, and reducing lawn area will increase water absorption.

A rain barrel that collects water from the roof saves water that would otherwise be lost as runoff. Several manufacturers produce plastic rain barrels with hardware to connect the downspout with the barrel, and a faucet so you can access the water. Rain barrels can be attached to drip irrigation systems or simply used to fill your watering can. An added benefit of collecting rainwater in areas with wells that supply hard water – water that contains a high level of soluble salts – is that since rainwater is soft, it will not cause mineral deposits that can clog up drip irrigation nozzles, and you can use the water on plants that need acidic soil conditions. Don't forget to cover barrels and other containers to control mosquitoes.

Solid-surface walkways and driveways prevent water from penetrating into the soil, and the water

Not thirsty
Drought-tolerant plants, such as junipers, lavender cotton, and sedums, grow well even with a limited water supply.

REDUCING RUNOFF AND RECYCLING NATURE

The Northeast region is filled with lakes, rivers, and wetlands that, along with underground aquifers, provide the water we take for granted when we turn on the tap. Many of these water sources are now in danger of contamination from chemicals and from over-consumption. Contamination comes from excess fertilizers and chemicals that leach into the soil from farming and gardening, from erosion of soil following snow melt in spring or after a summer storm, as well as from the runoff from roads, parking lots, and driveways. Contamination occurs when chemicals are carried into water sources, upsetting the balance of nature. The nitrogen in chemical fertilizers, for example, may leach through the soil and be carried into the groundwater following a heavy rainstorm. Using slow-release formulations of lawn fertilizers lessens the chance of this occurring, since the nitrogen is released over a period of time. Before manufacturers changed their formulas, phosphates in laundry detergents were responsible for the algae that clogged many lakes and rivers.

As gardeners, we can make a positive impact on our watersheds by following conservation practices in our garden. Apply fertilizers sparingly and at the proper time so they are absorbed by actively growing plants. Use compost whenever possible in preference to chemical fertilizers, because the nutrients need to be broken down by soil organisms and are not immediately soluble. Use garden chemicals only when needed, not "just in case," at the rate recommended by the manufacturer, and apply only enough to wet the foliage, not to the point where it is dripping on the soil. Watch the weather: applying garden chemicals just before rain is a waste of time and effort, and it adds to water contamination. Most garden chemicals degrade into nontoxic substances fairly quickly in contact with the soil, but this process is delayed if rain carries them through into the ground water.

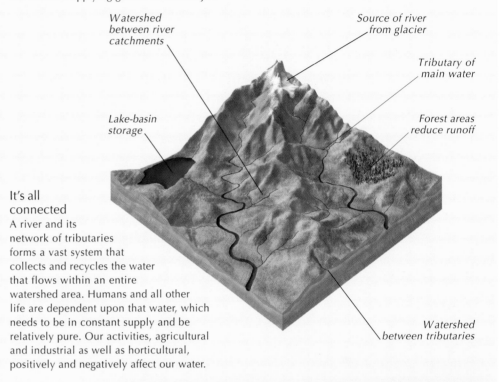

Watershed between river catchments

Source of river from glacier

Tributary of main water

Lake-basin storage

Forest areas reduce runoff

Watershed between tributaries

It's all connected
A river and its network of tributaries forms a vast system that collects and recycles the water that flows within an entire watershed area. Humans and all other life are dependent upon that water, which needs to be in constant supply and be relatively pure. Our activities, agricultural and industrial as well as horticultural, positively and negatively affect our water.

that runs off of these surfaces often leads to erosion or drainage problems. When installing a driveway or walkway, consider using a permeable surface through which rainwater can be absorbed. Driveways can be constructed of gravel, and beautiful walks and patios can be fashioned from unmortared stone set in sand.

Supplementing nature

Water requirements are affected not only by the type of plant and the density of the planting, but also by a number of environmental variables, such as temperature, wind, sunlight, and season. Soils also vary in their capacity to retain water. Thus there is no fixed rule for how often you will need to water: observing your plants and checking your soil offer the best clues.

Dry quarters
Even some tiny plants can get by without much water: saxifrages and *Aubrieta* are at home in a spot that provides little water; in fact, many grow best in such a setting.

Plants provide several clues when they are suffering from a lack of water. The observant gardener looks for these signs and waters thoroughly before the plant suffers long term or irreversable damage. The following are common symptoms or clues to water stress. The symptoms you first notice will vary somewhat from one kind of plant to another:
• dullness or a subtle change in foliage color
• reduced growth
• reduction in flowers or fruit
• wilting or curling of leaves
• footprints remain when grass is walked upon
• lawn turns dull, then bluish, and eventually straw-colored or brown

All plants should be watered when they are first set out, and regular watering should continue until their roots are well established. It is important to water thoroughly (and at the base of the plants; you don't need to give plants a shower when you water them) to encourage deep root development. Plants with an extensive and deep root system can obtain more water from the soil and are less subject to injury from temperature fluctuations.

Early morning or evening (in other words, before or after the heat of the day), are the best times to water – less will be lost to evaporation. Avoid wetting plant foliage, because wet leaves are more prone to disease.

HAND WATERING

Using a watering can or hose with a water breaker to deliver a drink to your gardens allows you to get "up close and personal" with your plants on a regular basis. You are likely to detect disease and insect problems soon after they appear. However, this system requires a great deal of time and may be impractical for large gardens. It is, however, perfectly suited for special, individual plants, small beds, and for those plants growing in containers.

WHEN TO WATER

Hard and fast guidelines about how often to water simply don't exist. You need to take into account the individual microclimate of your garden, the nature of your soil, and the quantity and size of the plants you are growing. Then you need to factor in the weather. Temperature, humidity, and wind velocity all contribute to the loss of moisture from the soil, especially when coupled with plants that have a relatively large leaf surface to transpire water. This loss of water from the soil is known as the evapotranspiration rate and, coupled with the water-holding capacity of your soil, determines how frequently supplemental water will be required. As you can see from the map below, the evapotranspiration rate is moderate to high throughout the Northeast, and you will need to keep a close watch on your plants for signs of stress (see symptoms above), and on weather forecasts for

predicted rain, to judge whether or not to water. Remember, too, that new plants do not have an extensive root system and are more likely to suffer from dryness than well-established plants. Also plants with large, soft leaves are more prone to dryness than those with stiff leaves. It is often possible to conserve water by watering individual plants showing signs of stress to save them, rather than by applying water to an entire bed.
Your soil type also governs the frequency of watering. On light, sandy soils, shallow soils, or those with a high proportion of rock and gravel, water will be required more often, and your soil will benefit greatly from the addition of large amounts of organic matter (see p. 31). Where soils are poor and water is at a premium, consider planting xerophytic plants (those requiring little water) in preference to more commonly grown woody plants and perennials.

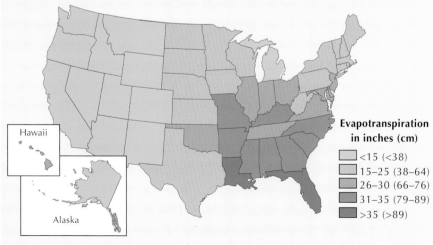

Evapotranspiration in inches (cm)
- <15 (<38)
- 15–25 (38–64)
- 26–30 (66–76)
- 31–35 (79–89)
- >35 (>89)

Hawaii

Alaska

Where to water
Knowing where to water is as important as knowing when. Direct it to the base of the plant and to the soil, so that the water goes directly to the root zone.

TRICKLE IRRIGATION

One of the most efficient watering systems is drip or trickle irrigation. Although it takes some effort to set up initially, in the long run it saves time. Trickle systems can be designed to accommodate any garden size or style. Water is delivered directly to the root zone of desired plants or areas through emitters at the end of water tubes. Little water is lost to evaporation or wasted on areas between plants. The spacing of emitters and rate of flow can be adjusted as necessary. This system can also be used for container plants.

If your water is hard, however, you may find that the narrow tubes of a trickle irrigation system become clogged with minerals. If a tube is clogged or becomes displaced, plants can suffer before the problem is noticed and rectified.

SOAKER HOSE

Also called a seep hose, a soaker hose allows water to drip out slowly into the soil along the length of the hose. Soakers are similar to drip systems but are easier to move from place to place. They are particularly useful in vegetable gardens, where they can be stretched along the rows, and in densely planted flower beds where they can wind through the entire planting area.

SPRINKLERS

For permanent plantings, an underground, automated sprinkler system can be installed, preferably before the garden is planted. The hardware of these systems must be checked and maintained for efficiency, and plants near nozzles must be monitored; if they grow over the nozzles, they may block or divert the spray. These systems can be programmed to run on a timer.

Portable sprinkler systems are relatively inexpensive and versatile, but they rarely deliver a uniform spray. Hoses connect the water source with a variety of sprinkler attachments – fans, oscillators, or pulsating heads. A significant amount of water from sprinklers is lost to

Wasting water
Sprinkler systems are a valuable method of applying water to lawns and gardens, but be sure to maintain the piping and hardware for maximum efficiency, and do your best to avoid waste by making sure the system is on only when water is needed.

Soaking a raised bed
Because soil dries out faster in a raised bed than in the open ground, growing vegetables or other plants this way often requires supplemental irrigation. A soaker hose provides water directly to the soil with very little loss by evaporation.

Mulchberries
They're called strawberries for a good reason: gardeners long ago realized the value of mulching these plants, so much so that straw became part of their standard culture and of *Fragaria*'s common name.

evaporation, and use of overhead sprinklers can sometimes lead to an increase in foliar disease problems in your plants.

Mulching for moisture

Mulching around plants conserves moisture in a number of ways. By physically covering the soil, less moisture is lost to surface evaporation, and the daytime temperature in the root zone in mulched soil is less than for bare soil, especially in hot sun. Mulches inhibit the growth of weeds that compete with your plants for water, and mulches help prevent soil crusting, the dry surface layer that impedes water penetration into the soil, leading to runoff and erosion.

Summer mulches are particularly important for soil moisture retention as well as weed control. But wait until the soil has had a chance to warm up in the spring before applying it, or new growth may be delayed. The best time to mulch depends on the plants that you are growing. In the vegetable garden, cool-season vegetables such as peas and spinach can be mulched much earlier than heat-loving tomatoes and melons. Give perennials enough time to emerge from the soil before mulching your flower beds. In a climate with cold winters and warm summers, mulching to provide

winter protection is most effective when applied after the ground has become cold and plants have entered dormancy.

Mulching too early can delay normal hardening of growth for winter. Many perennials will benefit from a winter mulch after their tops have died back. This helps moderate winter moisture and temperature levels in the soil, which are especially critical with new plantings.

There are some disadvantages to mulching that should be recognized; however, when and how much mulch you apply can minimize these. For example, some animals such as mice and rabbits may find an organic mulch to be a suitable spot to build their nests. These garden inhabitants can cause damage to shrubs and young trees in winter if they gnaw at the base of trunks or stems. Do not allow mulch to build up around the base of plants. This problem can be further minimized by waiting until after you have experienced several hard frosts before you apply the winter mulch. Mice and rabbits will likely have already found another location for their winter home by then. In spring, mulch needs to be pulled back from perennials to allow new growth to emerge and to prevent a buildup of excessive moisture around stems, which can lead to disease.

The mulch advantage

Mulching with the right material, applied at a proper depth and at the appropriate time, provides numerous advantages to garden plants in addition to retaining moisture and suppressing weeds. Mulch protects plant roots from extremes of heat and cold and creates a physical barrier between foliage and soil-splashing rain, which helps prevent the spread of disease. In vegetable gardens, mulch keeps fruit —such as tomatoes, cucumbers, and melons—clean, preventing direct contact with the soil, where fruit-rotting organisms likely lurk. Also, mulching may reduce the need for fungicides.

Mulching does not warm or cool a soil; rather, it moderates the temperature changes. This influence is accomplished by shading the soil from the hot sun during the day and by the retention of moisture. Water changes temperature more slowly than air. So the more moisture contained in soil, the slower the rate of temperature change around a plant's roots. Often winter damage occurs to the roots of plants, not because of the low temperature to which they are subjected, but because of rapid changes in temperature of a dry soil. These rapid

changes can cause perennials to heave out of the soil, exposing their roots to cold, dry air, killing the plant. Mulching helps minimize such losses.

HOW MUCH MULCH

How much mulch should you apply? Too much can impair plant growth by suffocating roots and preventing moisture from reaching the soil, but too thin a layer will not sufficiently suppress weed growth or retain moisture. In general, a 2–3 in (5–8cm) layer of organic mulch is appropriate. Replace the mulch as it breaks down instead of mulching too thickly at the beginning of the season. Always keep mulch away from the crown or stems of plants to avoid the buildup of excessive moisture and increase the likelihood of disease. In vegetable gardens and annual beds, organic mulch can be incorporated into the soil at the end of the season; it will improve soil structure and fertility. Around permanent plantings, mulch breaks down gradually, releasing nutrients that are carried to the roots by rain. In both cases, an organic mulch promotes a healthy soil environment.

MULCHING MATERIALS

The material you end up selecting for a mulch depends on its availability, your own personal taste, and the type of garden for which you intend to use

Mulching defense
For woody plants, apply a mulch to cover the entire root zone. Leave a 4-6in (10-15cm) gap around the stem base; mounding mulch onto woody stems may cause rot.

Recycling into mulch
All of the mulching materials above (from the top, they are bark, compost, and leaves) could come from the garden to which they are returned. Recycling all heathy plant debris makes good sense.

it. Both organic and inorganic mulches are available, and each is suited to several different types of garden applications.

Straw works well in the vegetable garden, but can look messy and contribute unwanted weed seeds to a perennial border. More attractive organic mulches, such as shredded bark, pine straw, or cocoa hulls, are better choices for flowerbeds, trees, and shrubs.

Weed barrier fabrics (landscape fabric or geotextiles) – material made out of polypropylene fibers – allow water and air to penetrate but prevent weed growth. They can enhance the efficiency of an organic mulch. They are usually placed directly on the soil surface and slits are cut through it for planting. An organic mulch, such as shredded bark or cocoa shells, is usually applied on top to hold it in place and provide a more attractive appearance.

Inorganic mulches include plastic, pebbles, and marble and stone chips. Black plastic is often used to mulch melons and cucumbers, since they benefit from the heat captured by the plastic in addition to a virtually total suppression of weeds. Rock gardens and beds of cacti and other succulents generally require drier conditions, and they may resent the moisture retained under a layer of shredded bark. Mulching with gravel or stone is probably the best solution for such gardens.

The color of the mulching material will affect its absorption or reflection of solar heat. Dark-colored mulches absorb more heat, warm the soil earlier in the spring, and maintain the heat later into autumn. Light-colored mulches absorb less heat, and they reflect heat and light upward toward the plants.

Plants themselves can serve as a useful mulch as they spread to cover the soil surface, crowding out weeds and shading the soil from the heat of the sun. Clematis benefit from such a mulch; many of them require a cool, shaded location for their roots, along with plenty of sun for the above-ground portions of the plant. These requirements can be met when the clematis is planted at the base of a coniferous shrub – the shrub provides a living mulch for the roots, as well as support for the clematis vine to grow upon.

Of course, plants require water, so although a mulch of living plants is an effective method of weed control and soil temperature moderation, it may actually increase the water requirement for the area.

In a woodland garden, trees and shrubs annually provide their own mulch of leaves and needles. Be sure that leaves and needles are raked off of desired groundcovers and herbaceous perennials growing beneath trees.

Managing without chemicals

Keeping your garden neat and preventing weeds from taking over doesn't require chemical warfare. Weeds can be pulled, cut, burned (where legal), smothered, and suppressed – the most effective method of control depends upon the types of weeds and the specific garden situation.

In a new garden, weeding can require a good bit of effort. But as garden plants become established and spread to cover the open ground, your

Don't wait
Don't let weeds progress this far before tackling them. Many methods can be used to keep them under control, including hand-weeding, if done on a regular basis.

weeding efforts will lessen, particularly if you practice some routine weed-management tasks. Eliminate your weeds before they become established and reseed themselves. It is more productive to spend a little time weeding on a routine basis than to let the weeds get an upper hand, eventually requiring a major cleanup effort. Mulching after you weed will prevent many weeds from returning (*see* The mulch advantage, p. 47).

Solarization provides excellent initial weed control for a new planting. The area to be solarized should be mowed very low and watered well. Cover it with black plastic, secured at the edges, and leave it for at least six weeks – longer if possible. The temperature in the top several inches of soil rises significantly, baking the surface vegetation as well as most weed seeds, roots, and soil pathogens.

To suppress the germination of weed seeds, corn gluten can be applied to a soil surface. This material, which is a natural byproduct of milling corn, is a good source of nitrogen, and it inhibits seed germination. Applied to established lawns, it prevents the germination of crabgrass and other annual weeds. It can be applied in a vegetable garden after vegetable plants have emerged. It is also useful in establishing a groundcover bed: groundcover plants are set, corn gluten is applied and watered in, the bed is mulched, and weeds are suppressed.

Edging a bed with a solid barrier, such as brick, stone, or wood, helps prevent creeping weeds from gaining entry.

A flame thrower is an effective tool for weeding nonflammable surfaces such as gravel paths, paved patios, and driveways as well as for spot treating persistent weeds. Never use a flame thrower close to desirable plants that may be scorched, or near a flammable mulch or other flammable surface.

Both useful and beautiful
A simple edging of wood or stone or similar material keeps creeping weeds such as Canada thistle and quackgrass at bay and will provide a very attractive addition to an otherwise very utilitarian part of your garden.

Boiling water, while somewhat cumbersome, has a similar effect on weeds as direct flame. It is particularly useful for hard-to-weed spaces between pavers or bricks.

Encouraging desirable wildlife

Useful "Plain Jane"
Even something as common and familiar as Queen Anne's lace (*Daucus carota*, from which carrots were bred) will attract butterflies and other beautiful and beneficial organisms.

Every year, more and more land is being cleared for homes and businesses, and wildlife habitats are being reduced or destroyed. Your SMARTGARDEN™ can be a haven for wildlife with a little planning. The three basic needs of wildlife – food, water, and shelter – can easily be met in a garden if you consider the type of wildlife you want to encourage and provide for them by including plants that produce nectar, flowers, seeds, and fruit, a source of water, and suitable habitats for nesting.

Adding feeders to your garden to supplement the plants will carry the banquet through the garden's lean times. Birdbaths or a small pond can provide sufficient water for your visitors, but remember to change the water frequently so it stays clean. If possible, leave some areas of the yard undisturbed for shelter. Dead trees and hollow logs provide homes for many wild creatures, as do unraked leaves (also see the Plant Catalog for plants to attract wildlife).

Maintaining a wildlife-friendly garden contributes to a well-balanced environment. Birds and bats feed on insects; butterflies, bees, and many other insects (and some bats) pollinate flowers; moles feed on grubs of root-eating beetles. Avoid using pesticides that will harm pollinating insects or birds, and be sure to read all pesticide labels carefully for warnings about potential dangers to wildlife.

Of course, not all forms of wildlife contribute to the health of your plants. Some wildlife may not be as welcome to your garden as others. There are some animals you would rather discourage from grazing in your azaleas, nibbling away at your bulbs, or feasting on your sweet corn. Like insect pests, take the approach of determining how much damage the critter is likely to inflict on your plantings, and if the level is unsatisfactory, take precautions to prevent the destruction.

Various techniques can be used to discourage deer, raccoons, voles, squirrels, and other potentially destructive forms of wildlife from damaging your plantings. Selecting plants that are unappetizing to the specific animal is a start – almost nothing eats daffodils! Other methods for discouraging foragers include fences or barriers, repellents, strategic placement of a scarecrow or an owl or snake lookalike, and a big dog.

Water magnet
Water attracts birds and others animals to your garden just as much as flowers and bird seed. They need to drink and bathe just like gardeners do, and some creatures, such as frogs, toads, and dragonfly larvae, will take up residence in a suitable water feature.

NORTHEASTERN WILDLIFE

Dark-eyed junco
These ground-foragers are a common winter visitor, feeding primarily on weed and grass seeds. If you dedicate part of your yard to wild plants, you will provide a food source far more extensive than any bird feeder.

As more and more land is taken over for housing and business, the areas left for wildlife shrink. Some wild species are becoming accustomed to existing close to man and, by creating a wildlife-friendly garden, you can do much to encourage and protect them. Many birds, butterflies, and small mammals can survive alongside man, and by adding a pool you can attract frogs and dragonflies. Depending on the size of your property and the diversity of planting, you can provide suitable habitats for a wide range of birds, animals, and insects. Many of these will be beneficial and will aid you in keeping pests under control. Snakes, spiders, and toads may not be your favorite garden guests, but they play an important role in reducing plant problems. The following lists contains some of the more common wildlife you may find in your garden, or want to encourage to come.

Ladybird beetle
This ladybug is looking for aphids and other pests to eat, as will its offspring.

Overwintering birds can help you by feeding on weed seeds and the egg masses of garden pests if you encourage them to stay around by putting out feeders. Those commonly found include:
• black-capped chickadee • purple finch • house finch • American goldfinch • common redpoll • house sparrow • European starling • blue jay • hairy woodpecker • downy woodpecker • pileated woodpecker • white-breasted nuthatch • brown creeper • cedar waxwing • evening grosbeak • pine grosbeak • northern cardinal • gray partridge • American kestrel • American crow

Spring brings an influx of birds either passing through or that will stay all summer. They all help by feeding on seeds and emerging insects. Some that you are likely to see are:
• American robin (some may overwinter) • common grackle • brown-headed cowbird • red-winged blackbird • tree swallow • barn swallow • purple martin • scarlet tanager • Baltimore oriole • song sparrow • chipping sparrow • gray catbird • brown thrasher • northern mockingbird • common flicker • yellow-bellied sapsucker • eastern bluebird • killdeer • whip-poor-will • house wren • Carolina wren • wild turkey • Acadian flycatcher • eastern kingbird • ruby-throated hummingbird • warblers (many species)

Eastern tiger swallowtail
The larvae of butterflies can eat garden plants, but few cause major damage.

Many small mammals will make their home in your garden and feed on seeds and insects, sometimes causing damage in the process. Some larger ones, such as skunks and raccoons, will also find their way in, but others, such as groundhogs and deer are best excluded if possible. You may catch glimpses of some of these: • hairy-tailed mole • eastern mole • smoky shrew • short-tailed shrew • bats (several species) • long-tailed weasel • eastern chipmunk • red squirrel • gray squirrel • flying squirrel • deer mouse • meadow mouse • house mouse • meadow vole • prairie vole • cottontail • striped skunk • groundhog (woodchuck) • raccoon • red fox • white-tailed deer.

Although they frighten many people, reptiles

and amphibians are gardener's friends, eating many of the pests that attack plants. Among those that should be encouraged are: • eastern garter snake • American toad • tree frog • leopard frog,

Butterflies and moths add movement to a summer garden. They will be attracted by

Eastern chipmunks
These rodents forage for seeds and nuts in mixed woods or brush.

plants rich in nectar and by a patch of wet mud or very shallow pool area. Some of the more common and striking are: • mourning cloak • monarch • black swallowtail • orange sulphur • great spangled fritillary • painted lady • luna moth • hawk moth • hummingbird moth.

Other garden invertebrates include: • earwigs • dragonflies • honeybees • solitary bees • bumblebees • wasps • spiders • millipedes • centipedes • sowbugs (pillbugs) • slugs and snails.

Red fox
Mammals also benefit from the conditions provided by gardens.

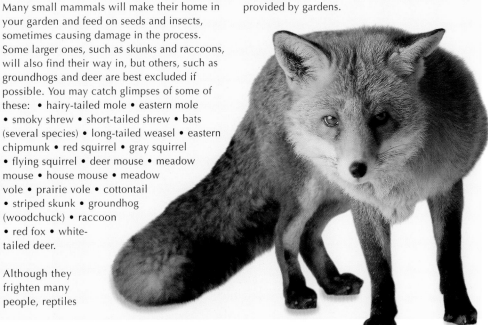

WORK WITH NATURE

Every aspect of gardening, from selecting your site and your plants to accommodating their spread and cleaning up debris, will be easier and more successful if you work with nature to achieve your goals. Although a garden alters a landscape to some extent, it should exist in harmony with its environment. The key is to follow nature's leads and to harness its forces to work on your behalf.

Learning from natural habitats

Plants with similar growth requirements should be grouped together in your garden, growing as they would in their natural habitat. Shrubs and perennials that thrive in low light can be planted beneath trees that furnish the necessary shade; those that require constant moisture can be grouped in a bog garden or at the edge of a pond; and those that thrive in full sun and dry soil can be combined in a sunny rock garden or xeriphytic planting.

In addition to grouping plants that share similar natural habitats, keep in mind any additional cultural requirements or special care that the plants might need when you are planning your garden. For example, vegetables and annual flowers generally require more fertilization and water than established perennials and woody plants. If the vegetable or annual flower beds are positioned within easy reach of a water faucet or rain barrel, their addition needs can be easily accommodated. Natural cycles of growth, reproduction, and decomposition can be put to work to your garden's advantage, and many problems can be avoided if you mimic natural patterns and solutions for reducing plant stress.

Just as the environment affects the growth of plants in your garden, everything you do in your garden has an impact on the environment. As environmentally responsible gardeners and stewards of the Earth, working in cooperation with nature rather than attempting to control it just makes good sense.

Natives and non-natives

One way to increase the odds that your plants are well adapted to your conditions is to select plants native to your region. By incorporating indigenous species, your garden not only reflects its geography, but it will also help sustain native wildlife.

Be sure that the natural habitats of your plant choices are reflected in the conditions within your yard. If your yard is open and sunny, it may be ideal for meadow wildflowers or rock garden plants. If it is heavily shaded, woodland natives are more appropriate. Regional wildflower and native plant societies can assist you with identifying native species and finding responsible retail sources.

Never collect plants from the wild without permission. Rare plants – those that may be difficult to obtain, but are not necessarily endangered – are put at risk when collectors dig them and remove them from their natural habitat. Many plants can be obtained without exploiting natural populations. Many nurseries, native plant societies, and private growers propagate their own rare plants and offer plants or seed for sale or exchange. Also, permission is sometimes given to individual plant collectors or native plant societies to dig and remove native plants from construction sites before the area is graded or built upon. In this way, many stands of both rare and common natives have been saved from the bulldozer.

Seize the shade
Although it may be considered a drawback by some, a shady spot – or entire property – presents a vast number of exciting opportunities for creating beautiful garden compositions and restful havens.

Worth copying
Many natural habitats are worth recreating in your garden, and some of the most popular are the wetlands: lakes, ponds, streams, bogs, wet prairies, and marshes. As with all habitats, it is important to know what constitutes a wetland and how it can be best and most easily maintained.

REGIONAL HABITATS WORTH EMULATING

Tallgrass Prairie, Pembina Trail Preserve, MN
Many common and uncommon plant and animal inhabitants can be found in this spectacular prairie in northwestern Minnesota.

There are several habitats in the Northeast. The transition is usually quite gradual, but the range of plants growing in each one is distinctive. As population pressure consumes remaining natural areas, plant diversity is decreasing. With a little effort, gardeners can recreate elements of a particular region and help conserve the rarities.

Deciduous woodland
Once the major habitat of much of the Northeast, most areas have now been logged and many cleared as well. The remaining areas have a surprising range of plants, and any well-treed lot can easily be adapted to recreate this habitat. Garden-friendly plants:
- Arrowwood Viburnum (*Viburnum dentatum*)
- Downy Serviceberry (*Amelanchier arborea*)
- Mountain Laurel (*Kalmia latifolia*)
- Silverbell (*Halesia carolina*)
- Summersweet (*Clethra alnifolia*)

- Bloodroot (*Sanguinaria canadensis*)
- Blue Cohosh (*Caulophyllum thalictroides*)
- Canada Columbine (*Aquilegia canadensis*)
- False Solomon's Seal (*Smilacina racemosa*)
- Lowrie's Aster (*Aster lowrieanus*)
- Round-lobed Hepatica (*Hepatica americana*)
- Spring Beauty (*Claytonia virginica*)
- White Baneberry (*Actaea pachypoda*)
- White Trillium (*Trillium grandiflorum*)
- Wood Anemone (*Anemone quinquefolia*)

Examples of deciduous woodlands found in:
Massachusetts – Garden in the Woods
Pennsylvania – Bowman's Hill Wildflower Preserve

Prairie
Where rain shadow from mountains causes little rainfall, or shallow soil precludes the growth of large trees, prairie grassland is the dominant habitat. Composed of grasses and perennial wildflowers, this is a popular garden subject, although not as labor-free as many imagine.
Garden-friendly plants:
- Little Bluestem Grass (*Schizachyrium scoparium*)
- Prairie Dropseed Grass (*Sporobolus heterolepis*)
- Switchgrass (*Panicum virgatum*)
- Black-eyed Susan (*Rudbeckia hirta*)
- Milkweed (*Asclepias syriaca*)
- New England Aster (*Aster novae-angliae*)
- New England Blazing Star (*Liatris borealis*)
- Purple Coneflower (*Echinacea purpurea*)
- Showy Goldenrod (*Solidago speciosa*)
- Wild Bergamot (*Monarda fistulosa*)

Examples of prairies found in:
Illinois - Chicago Botanic Garden
Wisconsin - University of Wisconsin Arboretum

Mount Desert Island, ME
Both this island and the adjacent Acadia National Park offer a variety of aquatic habitats to inspire gardeners to re-create a small bit of this natural splendor in their own home gardens.

Riparine and maritime
The many lakes and rivers and the long Northeast coastline provide ample opportunity to discover this type of habitat. Given a wet soil, it is easier to grow moisture-loving plants than to install drainage.
Garden-friendly plants:
- Bald Cypress (*Taxodium distichum*)
- Black Gum (*Nyssa sylvatica*)
- Beach Plum (*Prunus maritima*)
- Buttonbush (*Cephalanthus occidentalis*)
- Red Osier Dogwood (*Cornus stolonifera*)
- Smooth Alder (*Alnus serrulata*)
- Sweetgale (*Myrica gale*)
- Virginia Sweetspire (*Itea virginica*)
- Winterberry (*Ilex verticillata*)
- Bottle Gentian (*Gentiana andrewsii*)
- Cardinal Flower (*Lobelia cardinalis*)
- Joe Pye Weed (*Eupatorium maculatum*)
- Swamp Milkweed (*Asclepias incarnata*)

Examples of riparine or maritime habitats can be found at:
Maine - Acadia National Park
Wisconsin – Apostle Islands National Lakeshore

Shenandoah National Park, VA
More than 40 percent of this park has been designated as wilderness, an unusual occurrence in the eastern US. A vast array of native woody and herbaceous woodland plants thrive here.

Endangered and threatened plant species are those that the federal government has recognized as being in danger of extinction and are protected by law. The most common cause for this status is reduction or loss of the natural habitat of the species, but commercial collection of rare plants has also threatened their survival. Responsible propagation by native plant growers of species that are rare or at risk has increased considerably in recent years; this helps increase the population and the availability of these vanishing plants to consumers. You should always investigate commercial sources of rare plants to be sure they were nursery propagated and were not collected from the wild.

The term "native plant" is the source of some confusion. Plants have been introduced from one area to another throughout the history of mankind, and some plants have adapted so well to their new environments over such a long period of time that it is often hard to distinguish the natives from the introduced species. Some plant traffic between geographic areas predates human history, seeds having been conveyed by glacial movements, floods, prehistoric animals, or other means. The field of botanical archaeology has made interesting discoveries about prehistoric plant movement that continues to shed more light on natural plant history.

For the purpose of this book, a native species is one that, as far as can be determined historically, is indigenous – native – to the *state* or *region*. (More broadly, the issue is defining what is meant by the "region": is it a given continent, country, or state, or is it the area within 25 miles (40km) of your property?) An exotic species is one that has been introduced from outside the region. An invasive exotic is a species that has adapted so well to its new environment that it has escaped cultivation and is capable of overtaking the habitats of native plants, upsetting the balance of nature.

The nativity of species within a genus is often widespread. For example, the genus *Quercus* – the oaks – include species that are indigenous to various regions within North America, as well as Europe, the Middle East, Asia, and Northern Africa. Species of *Iris* hail from countries as widespread as China, Japan, Ukraine, Afghanistan, Turkey, Algeria, and the United States – from Alaska to the Mississippi Delta. Obviously, even though they are closely related, plants with such diverse native habitats have an equally wide range of cultural requirements. So although you can probably grow more than one species of oak or iris in your garden, there will be other members of those genera that require quite a different habitat.

Non-native plants from regions with similar climates and soils can add diversity to your landscape. To get ideas for plants that will grow well in your garden, observe plants that thrive in other nearby gardens, and ask your neighbors and staff at local public gardens as well. But take care to avoid those that are too well adapted. When these plants encroach upon your garden, diligent efforts are often necessary to limit their spread or eliminate them from your yard altogether.

Plants that are recognized as serious pests have been put on federal and state lists of noxious weeds. Legislation and regulation efforts to eradicate stands and control the spread of these pests is ongoing at federal, state, and local levels.

North American native
Commonly called New York aster, *Aster novi-belgii* is native to much of eastern North America. Many attractive cultivars have been selected.

Truly superb
Lilium superbum, the American turkscap lily, graces wild and cultivated spots where there is moist, acidic soil in sun to part shade.

A large clan
Phlox divaricata is a favorite for inclusion in woodland gardens. All but one of the genus' 70 species hail from North America.

INVASIVE PLANTS

While the majority of the plants we grow are well behaved, a few can be thought of as garden thugs, willing and eager to choke out their neighbors and colonize large areas. Others have escaped from cultivation and are invading natural habitats and replacing the native flora, *Lythrum* (purple loosestrife) being a prime example of this. These are termed "invasive exotics," and their cultivation should be approached with caution. For example, the seeds of Norway maple (*Acer platanoides*) carry for a long distance. If you live in town, this tree is unlikely to spread into natural areas, but if your home is close to a woodland, consider growing something else that poses less of a threat to the natural balance of things.

Invasive exotic trees and shrubs include: *Albizia julibrissin* (silk tree), *Berberis thunbergii* (Japanese barberry), *Euonymus alata* (winged euonymus), *Lonicera tatarica* (Tatarian honeysuckle), *Paulownia tomentosa* (empress tree), *Rhamnus cathartica* (common buckthorn), and *Rosa multiflora* (multiflora rose).
Climbers of concern include: *Hedera helix* (English ivy), *Lonicera japonica* (Japanese honeysuckle), and *Wisteria sinensis* (Chinese wisteria).
Perennials of note include: *Aegopodium podagria* (goutweed), *Coronilla varia* (crown vetch), *Lysimachia clethroides* (gooseneck loosestrife), and *Phragmites australis* (common reed).

Multiplication and division

Many garden plants reseed themselves. This natural process can work to your benefit – providing new plants for next year's garden and for giving to or exhanging with other gardeners – or it can create unnecessary weeding. Before selecting a plant and placing it in a bed, determine whether and how prolifically it self-sows.

Some biennials – plants that complete their life cycle over the course of two growing seasons – can become permanent features in your garden through the process of self-sowing. The flowers of woodland forget-me-not (*Myosotis sylvatica*), honesty (*Lunaria annua*), and several foxgloves (*Digitalis* spp.) produce seed that germinates and grows vegetatively the first season and develops flowers the next. With such plants, it is important to recognize the nonflowering plant so that it can be left to grow – and not inadvertently weeded – to bloom the following year.

A number of annuals and perennials also self-sow. Some are such prolific seed producers that weeding the seedlings becomes a chore. If this is the case, deadheading the spent blooms before they have a chance to form and disperse their seed will reduce or eliminate the problem. If there is already a problem, diligent weeding should remedy this.

Quite a few of the garden flowers that are sold in nurseries or by seed companies are hybrids – varieties produced by controlled crosses of specific parent lines – so their seedlings often do not resemble the parent plant in some important aspects. Be aware that your seedlings may be shorter, taller, less disease resistant, or a different flower or leaf color

(sometimes amazingly unattractively so) than their parent. Open-pollinated varieties, on the other hand, generally produce seed that is "true to type." Seed of such flowers or vegetables can be collected from these plants for growing the following year with some confidence about their inherited characteristics.

Herbaceous perennials that thrive in your garden may require dividing every few years. Take advantage of this natural increase to acquire more plants. For most perennials that bloom in spring, summer or fall division is recommended. Summer or fall bloomers are usually divided in spring.

Although the procedure varies somewhat with specific plants, division generally involves digging the entire clump, cutting it into smaller sections, discarding old, worn-out portions, replanting the vigorous divisions, and watering them thoroughly.

Composting wastes

One way you can work with nature to improve your soil is to build a compost pile or bin. Here, kitchen and garden wastes of many kinds can be converted into a nutrient-rich soil amendment. It takes several weeks to months for raw organic matter to become thoroughly decomposed and garden-ready in an active compost pile. There are a variety of factors that influence the rate of decomposition; the most important being the initial size of the organic matter, moisture in the pile or bin, temperature of both the surrounding air and the compost itself, air circulation

Composting bin
A simple cage constructed from lumber and chicken wire can hold garden refuse and other materials as it breaks down into compost.

within the pile, and the progressive status of the carbon:nitrogen ratio as the materials break down. Organic matter that has been shredded decomposes faster than if it has been left whole, because there is more surface area exposed. Decomposition rates are higher when conditions are warm and damp than when they are cold and dry. Air circulation increases the rate of composting, because the organisms responsible for decomposition need sufficient air to do their job. (For more on the carbon:nitrogen ratio, *see* p. 31.)

However, other than occasional turning, and a bit of added moisture when it's very dry, nature – in the form of industrious micro- and macroorganisms – does most of the work for you.

COMPOST BINS AND TOOLS

A number of useful products are available to help you produce your own compost. Compost bins can be constructed out of wood, heavy-gage wire fencing, cinder blocks, or other common materials. They can also be purchased ready-made. Designs range from simple bins to more elaborate constructions that feature cone-shaped tubs, interlocking layered shelves, and twist-top ventilation systems. Some designs feature tumblers or drums that rotate to facilitate mixing. Mixing or stirring an open compost pile can be done with a garden fork or a compost aerator, a tool specifically designed for the purpose, composed of a shaft with handles or a bar at one end

for holding, and short paddles on the other end that are inserted into the pile, then turned and lifted. Vermicomposting is a system using redworms, night crawlers, or earthworms in an enclosed container to break down organic matter such as grass clippings and kitchen wastes. The worm castings that are shed are a rich source of nutrients.

In an undisturbed woodland environment, the seasonal accumulation of leaves on the forest floor is part of a natural recycling process. As the leaves are decomposed by soil organisms, a steady supply of nutrients is released. In an effort to keep a garden neat, this cycle is often interrupted; leaves are raked and removed. The nutrients can be restored, however, and the neatness maintained, if the raked leaves are composted and the finished compost returned to the garden. Once the compost is ready, it can be incorporated into the soil or applied as a topdressing or mulch (*see* pp.47–49). It is also a useful addition to a soil mix for raised beds and containers. In an active compost pile, most weed seeds are killed by the heat generated during the decomposition process, but a few may survive and are usually easily removed.

By composting your kitchen and garden wastes, you are working in tandem with nature to improve the growing conditions for your plants while simultaneously reducing your contribution of solid waste to local landfills.

Prettier and stronger
A more sturdily constructed compost bin (which is easy to build) is more attractive and holds up longer than a simple cage (opposite). It should last for several years.

The view inside
Removing the front panel reveals the correct method of layering different materials, alternating "soft" (grass clippings and weeds) with "hard" (twigs and dead leaves) to speed decomposition.

General household waste
Plant remains are OK, but avoid including meat scraps and bones, which attract vermin.

Old straw
Make sure your compost pile heats up to destroy seeds contained in straw.

Weeds
As with straw above, a properly constructed and managed hot pile kills most weed seeds.

Hedge clippings
The smaller, thinner, and softer the clippings, the faster they will break down.

Bring it on
Good compost is best made from a wide variety of materials. Included on this page are just a few possibilities, including the spent bedding plants at left.

Aiding natural selection

Cleaning up a garden at the end of a growing season will improve its appearance through winter and, more importantly, contribute to its health the next season. This often involves a bit of "editing" – removing plants, plant parts, or pests.

- Branches of trees and shrubs that are damaged beyond repair should be removed with clean cuts. Stems displaying disease symptoms such as cankers or sunken lesions are usually best removed in order to prevent the further spread of disease.
- Minimize next year's insect pests by removing and disposing obvious signs of infestation such as the "bags" of bagworms and the nests of fall webworms.
- Remove weeds before they go to seed.
- Rake leaves to avoid matting that may suffocate lawn or groundcovers; compost both weeds and leaves (but remember: no pest- or disease-infested material onto the pile; this material is best discarded along with your household trash)
- After they have died naturally or succumbed to frost, cut annuals at ground level, leaving the roots to break down in the soil; this is a particularly good practice where erosion is a problem. Or remove the plants, roots and all, then compost everything.
- Clean structures and stakes you plan to reuse. Those that cannot withstand winter weather should be removed, cleaned, and stored until conditions are suitable again in spring.
- Perennial plants that die back in fall can be cut to the ground unless they contribute to your winter landscape or provide food or cover for desirable wildlife.

Eliminating flowered stalks
Removing flowered stalks of herbaceous plants improves their appearance and may also stimulate further flowering.

Reducing stress

Just like humans, garden plants look and perform better if their level of stress is reduced.

Transplanting can be traumatic for plants and may lead to a condition known as "transplant shock." To avoid this, allow seedlings grown indoors to acclimate to their new environment gradually (called "hardening off"). Place them in a protected spot outdoors for a few days before transplanting them. Transplant on a still, overcast day, and drench soil balls with a high-phosphorus liquid fertilizer to stimulate root growth.

During dry weather, wind can cause serious damage by increasing a plant's transpiration (moisture loss) rate. When moisture lost through leaves exceeds the rate at which it is replaced by roots, leaves appear scorched or may drop off. This can happen during cold weather as well, when soil water is frozen and little is available to plants. Siting a garden where plants are sheltered from prevailing winds can prevent such damage, or wind-tolerant plants can be grown as wind breaks to protect nearby plants.

Rapid fluctuations in soil temperature in winter can damage roots. This problem can be avoided by watering and mulching thoroughly in fall. The temperature fluctuates less rapidly in moist soil than in dry soil. In warm climates, mulching and watering provide similar protection, particularly during hot, dry periods when soil absorbs radiant heat during the day. Watering during dry periods and shading the soil with mulch reduce heat and moisture stress that lead to injury.

Safe haven
Hardening off under some sort of cover enables plants to make a safe transition from their early life indoors to growing in the open ground and in the face of the elements.

MANAGE PESTS FOR A HEALTHY GARDEN

Integrated pest management (IPM) is a sustainable and environmentally sensitive approach to garden disease and pest problems. IPM was initially developed for commercial growers as a means of merging all available information regarding a crop and its documented or potentially troublesome pests and diseases into a comprehensive plan of action to maximize production and quality and to minimize environmental risks. IPM has been adapted as a useful tool for home gardeners and is a perfect fit with the SMARTGARDEN™ philosophy: to follow nature's leads and to harness her forces to work on your behalf.

Keeping the proper perspective

IPM is a multistep process. It includes taking steps to prevent problems or to reduce their severity, identifying and monitoring problems that do arise (using physical and natural control measures first), and, if necessary, applying the least toxic pesticide at the proper rate and at the proper time. When dealing with garden diseases and pests, it is important to keep in mind that a certain amount of damage is tolerable. Trying to maintain every leaf and flower in perfect condition is impossible. Accepting a level of tolerable imperfection does not mean ignoring damage when it occurs. The SMARTGARDEN™ approach is to assess the damage, identify the cause, estimate the potential for further damage, and, depending on that assessment, continue to monitor the problem and adjust cultural practices to reduce its spread, or proceed with a specific control measure. The key is to strive for balance rather than perfection.

An ounce of prevention

One of the best methods for dealing with plant problems is to prevent them from occurring. Healthy, well-adapted plants are less likely to be seriously damaged by the diseases or pests that invade the garden. They can withstand an infection (from diseases) or infestation (from insects or other animals) better than a plant that is struggling from the stress of neglect or placement in an inappropriate site.

How much is too much? Gardeners who practice IPM know when the level of damage from a pest's activities has reached an unacceptable level.

Allies
Ladybird beetles (also widely called ladybugs) and a host of other insects and creatures can be recruited in the battle against plant pests.

How many should be tolerated?
This colorful caterpillar is the larva of the beautiful black swallowtail butterfly. A few will not cause much damage, but large numbers would pose a threat. It's up to you whether to reduce or eliminate them or leave them alone.

will do no damage to your trees or shrubs. An insect that bores into pine trees will probably leave your other trees and shrubs, as well as your herbaceous plants, alone.

Susceptibility to diseases and pests varies from one variety of plant to another. Plant breeders have used this phenomenon to impart disease- and pest-tolerance and resistance to an ever-increasing number of new varieties of the plants we grow in our gardens.

Selecting varieties that are resistant to pests and diseases that are common in your area is an easy way to give your garden plants an advantage. For example, some tomato varieties are resistant to several fungal wilts, viral diseases, and certain nematodes that can devastate a susceptible variety. By selecting varieties of hosta with thicker, more substantial leaves, damage by slugs is often avoided or at least lessened.

SANITATION

Removal and disposal of disease-infected or pest-infested plants and plant remains from the garden is an important cultural tool that should be incorporated into your gardening efforts throughout the growing season. It should also be a designated part of your annual cleanup activities. Remember: although the heat generated by a well-managed compost pile is sufficient to kill pests and most disease-causing organisms, seriously diseased plants are best kept out of the compost pile, just as a precaution.

Many pests and disease-causing organisms overwinter in or on the remains of their former host, and if left in the garden will be ready and waiting to cause problems come spring. When practical, remove the source before the pest or disease has a chance to spread. Also, before you introduce any new plant into your garden, inspect it for pests and the symptoms of disease.

OTHER PREVENTION TECHNIQUES

Other cultural methods for preventing pest and disease problems include mulching to create a physical barrier between soil-borne spores and potential hosts, using physical barriers such as netting or row covers to exclude egg-laying female insects, planting to ensure adequate air circulation between plants, planting early or late to avoid a pest or disease at a predictable time each year, and removal of garden plants or weeds that may serve as alternative hosts to disease organisms or pests.

Resistance or something else?

The hosta shown above is free of slug damage, while the one to the right has obviously been severely attacked. The difference between the two could be the result of thicker, tougher leaves than are common to many hostas, or it could be due to the the gardener's efforts.

RESISTANT VARIETIES

Most plant diseases and many pests are quite specific for the host plants that they will infect or infest. A disease that infects your lawn most likely

PEST-RESISTANT PLANTS

Some plants show a natural resistance to pests or diseases. Remember that resistance does not mean that the plants will not be attacked, just that they are not as susceptible to damage as others.

Bee balm: 'Aquarius' and 'Squaw'.
Birch: 'Heritage' river birch.
Crabapples: 'Adams', 'Beauty', 'Centennial', 'Centurion', 'Harvest Gold', 'Molten Lava', 'Prairiefire', 'Professor Springer', 'Red Snow', 'Sea Foam', and 'Sugar Tyme'.
Dogwoods: Hybrids between the flowering and kousa dogwoods, such as 'Appalachian Spring'.
Elms: New hybrids such as 'Homestead', 'Jacan', and 'Pioneer'.
Honeysuckle: 'Freedom'.
London plane tree: 'Bloodgood', 'Columbia', and 'Liberty'.
Phlox: Cultivars of *Phlox maculata* are more mildew resistant than those of *P. paniculata* and look very similar.
Roses: Many of the modern shrub roses of the Explorer (e. g. 'William Baffin') and Parkland (e. g. 'Morden Centennial') series.
Viburnums: Modern hybrids such as 'Mohawk' and 'Cayuga'.

CROP ROTATION

Rearranging (rotating) the placement of plants from one season to the next is a valuable means of outwitting pests and diseases in vegetable gardens and annual beds. Most diseases and many insects are rather specific in their selection of host plants, and many survive the winter as eggs or spores in the soil around the plant that was the pest's host during the previous growing season. Replanting the same crop in the same space increases the probability of reinfection. Make it more difficult for the pest or disease: move your beans to the other side of the garden, and plant marigolds where you had China asters last year. This simple avoidance technique can significantly reduce recurring problems.

Year 1

LEGUMES AND POD CROPS

Okra
Hyacinth beans
Scarlet runner beans
Lima beans
Snap beans
Peas
Broad beans

Year 2

ALLIUMS

Bulb onions
Pickling onions
Scallions
Shallots
Welsh onions
Oriental bunching
Onions
Leeks
Garlic

Year 4

BRASSICAS

Kales
Cauliflowers
Cabbages
Brussel sprouts
Sprouting broccoli
Broccoli
Oriental mustards
Chinese broccoli
Bok choi
Mizuna greens
Chinese cabbages
Komatsuna
Kohlrabi
Rutabagas
Turnips
Radishes

Year 3

SOLANACEOUS, ROOT AND TUBEROUS CROPS

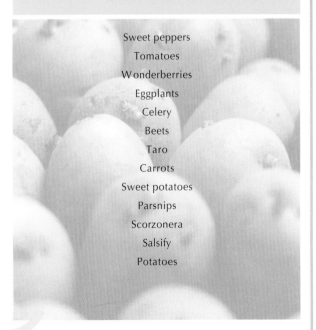

Sweet peppers
Tomatoes
Wonderberries
Eggplants
Celery
Beets
Taro
Carrots
Sweet potatoes
Parsnips
Scorzonera
Salsify
Potatoes

Rotation of vegetable crops
Vegetables are divided into four groups: legumes and pod crops; alliums; brassicas; and solanaceous, root, and tuberous crops. Sweet corn and summer and winter squash do not fit into the major groups, but they still should be rotated. If you are growing only a small amount of these, it may be possible to include them in one of the groups (such as alliums). Otherwise, treat them as a separate group and rotate everything on a five-year basis.

Diagnosing and assessing damage

If you are unfamiliar with the plant problem confronting you, take a Sherlock Holmes approach: use all available clues and resources to pin down the culprit. Numerous books and publications are available to assist your diagnosis. Furthermore, local Cooperative Extension offices, botanical gardens, nurseries, and plant societies maintain diagnostic clinics and horticultural hotlines. Many of these can be conveniently contacted on the Internet (*see* Appendix, *p. 384* for regional resources).

You may have an expert horticulturist to whom you can turn with any plant problems. But no matter whom you ask, the prognosis will be based on the information that you provide. The more detailed observations you make, the more accurate the advice you will receive. Whenever possible, you should provide one or more specimens of the plant that demonstrate progressive symptoms for the expert to examine. Each specimen should be more than just a single leaf; it is helpful and sometimes necessary to see more than one leaf attached to a bit of stem to identify the plant as well as the problem.

Once you identify the specific cause of your problem, the next step is to learn more about the disease or pest and determine how much damage is likely to occur and whether and what type of control measures are warranted.

NOTING DAMAGE

- When did you first notice the damage?
- What are the symptoms? Examine all parts of the plant and be as precise as possible.
- Are the symptoms on more than one plant or kind of plant?
- How rapidly do the symptoms progress?
- How long has the plant been growing in its current location?
- Which kinds of treatment (for example, fertilizer, insecticide, herbicide, mulching) have been applied to the plant or to surrounding areas recently?
- Have you ever noticed this problem before? If so, is it different this time?
- Has there been any change in soil grade in the area surrounding the plants?
- Has there been any other change in the area surrounding the plant?

Know your enemy

Familiarizing yourself with the most common pests and diseases of the plants you grow is a major step to outwitting them. By knowing their appearance, life cycle, feeding and overwintering habits, potential hosts, and natural predators, you can work with nature to tilt the balance in favor of your garden plants.

For example, fireblight is a bacterial disease that infests apples, pears, pyracantha, hawthorn, quince, and several other ornamental plants, typically causing sudden twig dieback. Serious damage can often be avoided by limiting the use of nitrogen fertilizer on susceptible plants, since succulent new growth, which is stimulated by nitrogen, is most prone to infection. If the disease does cause dieback, pruning out and destroying infected stems will generally stop (or at least slow down) the spread of the disease before it causes serious damage. Left untreated, the infection may move into older wood, where it forms cankers in which the bacteria overwinter. More extensive removal of branches displaying such cankers may be required at this point.

Knowledge of the life cycle of a pest or disease-causing organism enables the gardener to apply countermeasures at the time when they will be most effective. For instance, parasitic nematodes effectively control several

A ROGUE'S GALLERY

INSECTS

Aphids: Small and generally on the growing tips or underside of leaves. Attack a wide range of plants, sucking sap and covering foliage with a sticky deposit.

Bugs and beetles: A varied group of hard-bodied insects that feed mostly by chewing holes in leaves and stems.

Caterpillars: The young stage of butterflies and moths (such as gypsy moths) feed on leaves and shoots.

Grubs: The larvae of several beetles (and other insects) that live in soil and eat roots or suck sap.

Miners: Small larvae that tunnel inside a leaf leaving opaque areas or mines.

Mites: Tiny, red or yellowish, and live mostly on the underside of leaves and spin fine webs between stems. They cause tiny pale spots.

Slugs and snails: Feed on foliage and small plants, mostly at night. Slime trails make their presence easy to detect.

DISEASES

Anthracnose: Fungi that attack a wide range of plants, targeting foliage and fruit.

Blights: Shoots or branches wilt, growth stops, and the affected part dies. In fruit, development ceases and the fruit gradually withers.

Leaf spots: Caused by many different fungi, they occur on a wide range of plants. They start as small pale areas and spread, often coalescing to cover almost the entire leaf.

Mildews: Occur on many plants and are especially destructive during hot, humid weather and on dry soil.

Catch it in time
Diseases such as rusts (above), if caught early in their development, may be controlled by nonchemical means. Severe cases, however, may need chemicals for total control.

lawn pests, including Japanese beetle grubs. But they must be applied when the target pest is active; the nematodes persist for only about two weeks. By knowing that the grubs become active as the soil warms in spring, the nematodes can be applied when the grubs begin to feed.

PHYSICAL CONTROLS

Many pests and diseases can be controlled by physical means. For example, handpicking the pest or pruning diseased stems or branches is sufficient in many cases to prevent further spread. Brute force is sometimes effective: a hard spray of water can knock down a population of aphids or mites to a tolerable level. Colorado potato beetles and tomato hornworms can often be eliminated by hand – the pests are simply picked off the host plant and destroyed. This method is effective, however, only when the gardener is vigilant (and prepared for gore!).

Barriers can also prevent pest damage: a cardboard collar around young vegetable seedlings checks their destruction by cutworms. Tree wraps – sticky bands of material that are placed around the trunk of a tree – prevent the larvae of gypsy moths and similar leaf-eating caterpillars from reaching the tree's susceptible foliage. Tubular plastic cages and wraps placed around young trees protect their bark from the gnawing of mice or rabbits. Floating row covers made of a thin, light, and water-permeable fabric can block many flying pests from infesting vegetable plants. Birds can be thwarted from eating your cherries or blueberries by covering the trees or shrubs with a protective net before the fruit ripens.

When pesticides are necessary

The goal when using a pesticide is to achieve control with the minimum impact on the rest of the environment. Applying the right material at the wrong time, to the wrong plant, or at the wrong dilution can negate its effect or, even worse, cause more damage than the pest itself. Whenever you decide to use a pesticide, it is critical to follow all label instructions for safety.

DIRECTIONS FOR HANDLING

• Eliminate or minimize human, pet, and nontarget plant exposure to the pesticide. This is particularly important when dealing with concentrated formulations.
• Wear protective clothing, and wash it after use, separately from other laundry.
• Wash equipment used for measuring, mixing, and applying the pesticide, and store in a secure, designated location.
• Wash down or flush any hardscaped or soil areas that were exposed to pesticides or where pesticides may have been inadvertently spilled.
• Store pesticides in a safe, secure (preferably locked) location – out of the reach of children and pets – in their original containers and according to the label instructions.
• Thoroughly wash your hands and face – or better, shower – after applying pesticides.
• Dispose of unused pesticides and empty pesticide containers according to the label instructions.
• Keep a record of the application; include date, material applied, and plants treated.

Population explosion
Whiteflies are a widespread insect pest of both indoor and outdoor plants. Their populations can build up to large numbers quickly, and their sugary secretions support the growth of black sooty molds. As with most plant problems, early detection and diligent inspection will help keep them at bay.

Many synthetic chemical pesticides formerly available have been banned for environmental and safety reasons. A variety of environmentally friendly, nonchemical pest control alternatives have been developed, many derived from plants or minerals. These pesticides generally break down quickly into safe byproducts and thus are good choices for the pests they control. Like any pesticide, they may be toxic to humans or other nontarget animals and should be applied with care according to the manufacturer's instructions.

Types of pesticides

Pesticides work by direct contact, ingestion, or making the plant distasteful to pests. Some pests and diseases are susceptible just during one phase of their life cycle. Therefore, timing may be critical to achieving an acceptable level of control.

Contact pesticides require direct contact with an external part of the pest for effective control. They must be applied where the pest is or will be present. If a pest feeds on the underside of leaves, the pesticide should be applied to the leaf undersides. If only the upper surface of the leaf is sprayed, the pesticide may have little or no effect.

Other pesticides work only after ingestion – they must be consumed by the pest. Leaf-eating caterpillars and beetles are often controlled by an ingested pesticide that is applied to the foliage of the host plant. Many biological controls such as Bt (bacteria that control specific leaf and root eating pests) must also be ingested by the pest to be effective (*see* Beneficial microbes, *p. 69*).

Systemic pesticides are absorbed and carried within a plant. Sprayed on the foliage or applied to the soil, they are taken in by the plant and kill the pest when it feeds on plant tissues.

Repellents do not kill the pest but instead prevent it from harming the host plant by making it less appealing. Hot pepper sprays and predator urine are examples of repellents designed to keep animals from devouring garden plants. These generally require frequent application.

Chemical pesticide formulations

Some pesticides can be applied directly, while others require diluting prior to application. Be sure always to dilute concentrated pesticides to the correct strength for the pest you are trying to control, and the host to which it is applied. Most pesticides are available in one or more of the formulations detailed below:

- Aerosols are ready-to-use sprays – usually contact poisons – that are under pressure. The pesticide is emitted as a fine mist.
- Dusts are finely ground pesticides combined with a fine inert powder that acts as a carrier. These are generally ready to apply from the bag.
- Granular formulations are similar to dusts, but the carrier is a larger particle, usually an inert clay. This formulation is most commonly used for pesticides that are applied to the soil.
- Liquid concentrates are similar to wettable powders except that the concentrated pesticide is in liquid form.
- Wettable powders are water-soluble pesticides that are usually combined with a wetting agent to make mixing easier. They are mixed with water prior to application. They are usually applied as a spray but may be watered into soil when appropriate.

The way chemicals work
Different problems require chemicals to be applied in different ways. A combination of application methods may be needed to achieve a satisfactory level of control.

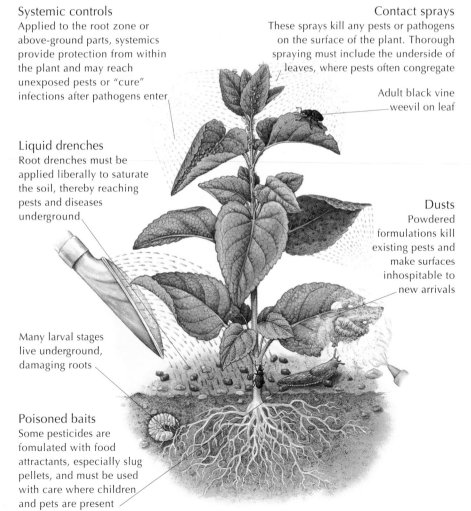

Systemic controls
Applied to the root zone or above-ground parts, systemics provide protection from within the plant and may reach unexposed pests or "cure" infections after pathogens enter

Liquid drenches
Root drenches must be applied liberally to saturate the soil, thereby reaching pests and diseases underground

Many larval stages
live underground, damaging roots

Poisoned baits
Some pesticides are fomulated with food attractants, especially slug pellets, and must be used with care where children and pets are present

Contact sprays
These sprays kill any pests or pathogens on the surface of the plant. Thorough spraying must include the underside of leaves, where pests often congregate

Adult black vine weevil on leaf

Dusts
Powdered formulations kill existing pests and make surfaces inhospitable to new arrivals

Chemical pesticide alternatives

There are many alternatives to chemical pesticides that are available for combating garden pests and diseases, and many are just as effective as stronger chemical pesticides if they are used correctly.

BOTANICAL INSECTICIDES

Certain compounds extracted from plants are effective in controlling a variety of pests. Some of the more commonly available are:

• neem: repels some pests and interrupts the life cycle of many plant-eating caterpillars and beetles after ingestion
• pyrethrum: an effective, broad-spectrum contact poison
• rotenone: commonly applied as a dust for short-term control of many leaf-eating caterpillars and beetles
• sabadilla: both a contact and stomach poison, effective against many true bugs, leaf-eating caterpillars, and thrips.
Keep in mind that just because a pesticide is classed as a botanical, it may still be very toxic; rotenone in particular is very toxic to fish. Like any other pesticide, these must be used with extreme care, and always read the label.

INSECTICIDAL SOAPS

Derived from fatty acids and potassium salts, insecticidal soaps are applied as a dilute spray. They damage cell membranes of soft-bodied pests such as aphids, leafhoppers, whiteflies, and spider mites, and make them slip off the plant. In order to be effective, insecticidal soaps must come into direct contact with the pest. Some particularly sensitive plants can be damaged by insecticidal soaps; check the manufacturer's instructions and, if you are unsure, test the product on a small part of the plant first.

HORTICULTURAL OILS

These are refined petroleum products that are commonly used on dormant plants to smother overwintering insects and mites. Formulations called summer-weight oils can be applied to many plants during the growing season for controlling scales, whiteflies, and certain diseases. However, some plants are susceptible to damage by oils so, as with all pesticides, you should read all of the instructions carefully.

Vegetable oils, derived from agricultural crops, may also be used to control pests such as aphids, spider mites, whiteflies, thrips, and scales. They should not be used on begonias, fuchsias, or seedlings because they can damage the leaves.

Double protection Rotenone (also called derris) has been applied to this plant to protect the leaves, and the square collar at the base protects the stem.

MINED MATERIALS

Another component of the arsenal of pest control weapons is material that is mined from the earth. Sprinkling diatomaceous earth – fossilized single-celled aquatic organisms – around plants provides a physical barrier against soft-bodied slugs and snails. Copper strips can be used as barriers to prevent damage by slugs and snails. Copper- and sulfur-based sprays and dusts can control fungal diseases such as powdery mildew and botrytis. These products can be detrimental to predatory mites, however, and should not be sprayed on young apples. Furthermore, the buildup of copper in the soil may be harmful to worms and, as it runs off into neighboring waterways, will affect fish.

Nature's pest control

Another method of thwarting garden pests is to enlist their natural enemies to work for you. Insects, nematodes, mites, microbes, and other organisms that feed upon or infect a plant pest are known as biological controls, and they are among the most effective ways of dealing with troublemakers in your garden. Beneficial organisms are fairly specific with respect to creatures they infect or consume, and they pose minimal danger to humans and other nontarget animals.

Some of the organisms that gardeners often lump together under the term "insects" are more correctly known simply as arthropods. Technically, true insects – such as ants, grasshoppers, butterflies, and beetles – are distinguished from other groups of common garden arthropods such as arachnids (spiders and mites) and crustaceans (pillbugs and sowbugs). Most of these creatures are neutral when it comes to their effect on garden plants; that is, they neither harm nor benefit them. They may, however, be a food source for birds, bats, or other wildlife, or they may help decompose organic matter. So in a sense, even though they do not directly help or harm plants,

arthropods help maintain a well-balanced environment. Many arthropods benefit garden plants by hunting and eating other insects and mites that feed on plants. Others parasitize pests, often by laying their eggs inside the body of the pest, where they eventually hatch and consume their host; then the emerging female adults complete the cycle by laying eggs in new hosts. Predatory mites often consume plant-feeding spider mites. Many spiders build webs and feed on whatever prey wanders in and gets stuck. Others, such as wolf, jumping, and crab spiders, actively seek their prey on plants or on the ground. Among the pests they help control are aphids, leafhoppers, and numerous beetles and caterpillars. Avoid spraying pesticides when these garden-friendly creatures are present.

Sowbugs may occasionally be a problem, however, because they are sometimes attracted in large numbers to seedlings, feeding on them at ground level. If necessary, a colony of sowbugs can be destroyed by pouring boiling water on them.

Attracting beneficial organisms

You can encourage predators and parasites of plant pests to inhabit your garden. Beneficial organisms can be purchased from distributors of natural pest controls. Make sure that when you release beneficial insects, there are pests for them to feed on; otherwise, they will seek another garden with a more tempting menu. Another potential problem is that some predaceous insects, such as the praying mantis, will feed on beneficial insects as well as your pests.

Either attracting or releasing beneficial insects into your garden will not give you instant results – your pests may be around for several days – but once the predators or parasites arrive, they will

work to control the pest until the pest population is depleted. Do not apply any insecticides to your garden while your beneficials are doing their job or you may eliminate them.

On target
Place containers of beneficial organisms on or near the plants you want to protect.

COMMON PARASITES AND PREDATORS

Centipedes: Not an insect but a good scavenger that feeds on soil-living pests, like millipedes and wireworms.

Ground beetles: These black beetles are often seen running away from an overturned piece of wood. They feed on many pests that live in or near the soil surface, such as cutworms, root maggots, and slugs and snails. Some species climb and help control Colorado beetles and tent caterpillars.

On patrol
A ground beetle actively searches for many kinds of garden pests to eat.

Hover flies: These look like tiny wasps and dart about, feeding on aphids.
Lacewings: Seen mostly in early evening, these feed on aphids, small larvae, mites, thrips, and scale insects.
Ladybird beetles (ladybugs): Both the well-known adult and the larvae devour aphids and other plant feeders. They are fairly specific on food choice, so buying them and releasing them in your garden may not work. A recently introduced species from Asia should be viewed with mixed feelings: while it eats aphids, it also gives people a painful sting.

Parasitic wasps: Varying in size from very small to rather large, these wasps lay their eggs in the bodies of host insects. The larvae then feed on the host and kill it. They may look frightening, but they do not sting people.
Spined soldier bug: One of the stink bugs, with a wide, flat shape, this has pronounced horns on either side of the shell. It feeds on many harmful caterpillars, sawfly larvae, and Colorado beetle larvae.
Tachinid flies: Similar in looks to house flies, these lay their eggs on many pests, including cutworms, army worms, gypsy moth larvae, and tent caterpillars. The resulting larvae feed on the host and pupate on the corpse.

Lone hunter
A solitary wasp has captured an insect to take back to its nest for its young.

Beneficial nematodes

Some nematodes – microscopic, eel-like roundworms – are plant pests, but others are beneficial, residing in soils and infecting and reproducing in garden pests that spend part of their life cycle in the soil. Beneficial nematodes are effective for managing black vine weevil larvae, white grubs, and Japanese beetle grubs, among others. The nematodes penetrate a host insect through natural body openings, multiply within the host's body, and release bacteria that multiply and kill the pest.

Native populations of beneficial nematodes are generally too low to provide effective pest control. However, beneficial nematodes can be purchased and applied to your lawns and gardens. Timing of the application is critical, and as with all pest-control products, it is important that you follow all of the label directions carefully. When correctly applied, beneficial nematodes not only provide excellent control of the target pest but are extremely safe to humans and other nontarget animals because they can only inhabit particular hosts, for example, the vine weevil.

Beneficial microbes

Some microbial organisms can be recruited to control pests. *Bacillus thuringiensis* (Bt) is a bacterium available in several different varieties, each of which is effective against specific pests. The bacterium produces a protein that is toxic to a variety of insects, causing paralysis of their mouthparts or gut. Bt var. *kurstaki* (Btk) controls several destructive caterpillars, such as cabbage caterpillars, cabbage loopers, gypsy moth, tomato hornworm, and codling moths, as well as corn borers. Other strains, Btt and Bt var. san diego, provide control of leaf-eating beetles such as the Colorado potato beetle. It is important to select the appropriate variety of the bacterium for the pest at hand. Bt degrades in sunlight and, consequently, it must be reapplied in order to remain effective.

A related species, *B. popilliae*, controls Japanese beetles by infecting the grubs – the soil-borne larval stage – with a disease known as milky spore. The bacteria reproduce in the host and remain in the soil when the host dies, providing a long-term source for infection of other grubs.

Attracting predators
Even a small bit of wildflower meadow will attract large numbers of beneficial predatory and parasitic organisms into your garden.

KEEP A GARDEN JOURNAL

The more you know about your site, your plants, and potential problems you may encounter, the more success you will experience in gardening. Although numerous resources are available to guide your gardening endeavors, the most important is your own experience. Keeping records is among the most valuable gardening activities you can perform. Both your successes and failures provide lessons that will make you a better gardener.

A garden diary

Interrupting your planting or weeding efforts to jot down notes in a diary might seem like a nuisance at the time, but it will help you plan your garden efforts this season and for years to come. Record the names of those plants that have performed famously as well as those you'd rather forget – and be sure to indicate which is which! The moments you take to note your observations will save you time in the long run. When you repeat a mistake because you forgot a previous failure, not only is it a waste of time and effort, but it may result in the loss of an entire growing season or even longer.

A gardening diary is a simple way to keep track of what is happening in your yard. Some allow for multiple years' entries on the same page. Typically, one page is allotted to every week of the year, and it is divided to accommodate four or five years' worth of

Making notes
Recording garden observations as you make them will produce a valuable record for the future. It can be as simple or as literary as you wish.

records. This allows you to look back to see what was going on in the garden at the same time in previous seasons. However, less elaborate systems can work just as well. A simple notebook or a calendar with enough room for your entries can accommodate any important details. The critical aspect of a garden diary is not what it looks like, but that you write in it. Regularly.

While garden notes needn't be lengthy, a few items are very important to include. Be sure to record the full name, including cultivar or variety, of any plant you acquire. Note the planting date and the plant's location in the yard. Then, when it's time to replant your strawberries and you want the same (or a different) variety than you planted half a dozen years ago (was it 'Surecrop' or 'Tristar'?), it is just a matter of checking your records. When you order vegetable and annual flower seeds, you can sit down with your notes, ordering those varieties you considered tops in the past and avoiding those that were disappointing. Having a record of where you purchased a given plant is sometimes helpful, especially for those hard-to-find varieties.

Diagrams of planting plans are also helpful. A sketch of your vegetable garden will assist planning future crop rotation schedules. A bed layout will remind you of the location of bulbs, ephemeral perennials (plants that complete their annual growth cycle in a very short time), or perennials that emerge late in the season, avoiding accidental damage when you are working in your garden before or after these plants are visible.

The four seasons
Many experienced gardeners strive to have something of interest in their gardens throughout the year. Noting when plants bloom or show other interesting features will be useful as you plan color combinations or theme gardens for a particular season. Clockwise from top left: Glory of the Snow (*Chionodoxa forbesii*), *Crocosmia* 'Lucifer', Christmas Rose (*Helleborus niger*), and Common Witchhazel (Hamamelis virginiana). Growing these four plants would provide all-season interest.

The march of time
Photographs, especially if taken at regular intervals, document the progression of a garden (or even a single plant) from the time of its establishment to mature beauty.

Information to include

Your records should include as much of the following information as possible about your plants and their basic and specialized care:

• Source: where you obtained the plant (nursery, friend, local plant sale)
• Provenance: the plant's place of origin (where it was previously grown)
• Date acquired
• Size and condition
• Special characteristics that set the plant apart
• Exact planting location
• Dates of application of fertilizer and pesticides
• Notes on propagation where applicable
• Pruning schedule
• Additional care required

• Flowering and fruiting times. Observations about plant growth are helpful as you plan additions. Perhaps you want a shrub that blooms at the same time as those in an existing planting, or a raspberry that ripens after your blackberries. Keeping track of planting and harvesting dates in the vegetable garden helps you plan for an extended harvest.
• Diseases, pests, cultural problems. Many pests can be avoided by planting earlier or later than the pest's arrival to the garden (doing this is especially useful in vegetable gardening). This necessitates, however, knowing when to expect the unwanted visitor. Because these dates vary even within a region, the best source of this information is your own garden records. The onset of a disease or pest infestation is equally important to note on ornamental plants so that you can be prepared to minimize damage.

On screen
Suitable computer software can be an invaluable aid in keeping track of the comings and goings (and successes and failures) of your garden plants over the years.

Planting Record.XLS

	PLANT NAME	SOURCE	DATE PLANTED	PLANTING LOCATION(S)	NOTES	
1						
2	Acer griseum x 3	Atlock	10/23/96	far corner	first things planted	
3	Viburnum plicatum tomentosum 'Shasta'	Veronica Nursery	5/17/97	lamp post	growing slowly as of '99 - too dry?	
4	Thuja occidentalis 'Smaragd' x7	B&B Nursery	5/30/97	far corner	3 dead spring '98 - take down the red maple!	
5	Liquidambar syraciflua	Bowman's Nursery	5/31/97	near rear spruce	excellent fall color	
6	Emmenopterys henryi	DCH Auction	6/5/97	near rear spruce	dead summer '97 - too hot and dry	
7	Buxus sempervirens upright selection x 10	Atlock	7/2/97	along front fence	hedge to block view	
8	Betula nigra 'Little King'	Scott Hort lecture '95	7/2/97	near front spruce	4" tall when received	
9	Heptacodium mikanoides	Atlock ex Haskell's	7/3/97	near Betula 'LK'	prune to reveal bark	

Sheet1 / Sheet2 / Sheet3

Many gardeners have developed a personal computerized plant record system. Data can be added to files quickly, and multiple years of records can be conveniently stored. You can develop a long-range plan and keep track of your progress. Be sure to keep a backup of all your gardening files just in case something happens to the computer!

Some of the most fascinating garden records are photographs. A spectacular garden is all the more dramatic when you can compare the "before" and "after" shots. Growth of trees, combinations of perennials, and successful container plantings can be documented for future referral. Also, a photograph can be very helpful to someone trying to diagnose a plant problem or identify a plant.

Other items for the record

Always record major modifications you make to your soil, such as double digging and adding replacement soil. Keep your soil tests from year to year, and make note of the kind and quantity of organic and mineral amendments you incorporate. Records of your soil fertility and pH are most useful when changes can be observed over time. Be sure to identify areas that receive different treatments.

Routine maintenance such as mulching, watering, fertilizing, and pruning should be recorded. Knowing the quantities of mulch and fertilizer you use in a season helps estimate future purchases.

By studying the phenology of the plants in your landscape – their cycles of growth and development over the course of the year – you can time gardening activities to your specific conditions. The optimum time to plant particular seeds, to apply insecticides, to release beneficial insects, and other gardening activities can be determined by observing the growth cycle of your plants and relating their various stages to the environment as a whole. Because plants respond to environmental stimuli, such as day length and temperature, their growth cycles can be used to indicate other similarly stimulated events such as the arrival of an insect pest or the emergence of a weed. Applying preemergent crabgrass control to the lawn as the forsythia flowers fade is an example of a phenologically based practice. Similarly, when an insect infestation is first observed in your yard, look around and take note of what is blooming. If the insect reappears in following years when the same plant is in bloom, you can reasonably schedule your pest control methods to coincide with that particular plant's blooming time.

Timing is everything
One way to control crabgrass is to apply a preemergent weedkiller to the soil as local forsythia flowers begin to fade. This is well before you would notice even seedling crabgrass, so make a note in your diary.

CONSULT THE PROS

In today's media-rich environment, the challenge is not so much to find information about whatever topic you seek as it is to filter the available resources to make sure you locate those that are most reliable and valuable to you and your gardening efforts. The books, periodicals, websites, television and radio shows, and gardens that are most useful to you are largely determined by two factors: your gardening interests and your location.

Gathering information

If you are investigating the possibility of developing a rock garden, heirloom vegetable plot, or water feature, for example, you can find books, magazines, and websites devoted to the subject. To apply the information you gather to your backyard, you can look to more regional resources, such as a nearby botanical garden, a local chapter of a rock garden society, your state's cooperative extension service, and periodicals with a regional focus. Obtain the best resources available to you, then integrate the information into your garden plan.

The printed word

Certain resources become like trusted friends – you return to them time after time for advice. A stroll down the gardening aisle of a well-stocked bookstore reveals that there are titles for nearly every conceivable aspect of gardening. But all gardening references are not equal. Although some books, like this one, have a regional perspective, many are written from a more general point of view, and some will reflect conditions quite unlike those you confront. Take this into consideration when looking for advice from a nonregional reference.

Magazines and journals can inspire you with examples of what other gardeners are doing as well as keep you up to date on advances in the field. There are many periodicals to choose from, for every level of gardening and for just about any specialty. Some of these are national with a broad scope. Every region and many gardening subjects – from prairie gardens to tomato culture to water gardening – are represented on the periodical shelf at the bookstore. Many plant societies, botanical gardens, and nurseries publish a newsletter, and many of these are packed with useful information. If you are considering subscribing to a gardening magazine or newsletter, ask a gardener who shares your interests for a recommendation.

Local and regional newspapers are another source of timely gardening information. Many run gardening columns each week or biweekly that offer growing tips on a local level. Newspapers may cover gardens worth visiting in your area, as well as local gardening programs and events.

The printed word
Many reference books are available to buy from bookstores or to research at libraries. It's a good idea to consult more than one volume to get multiple (and often different!) insights on a given plant's characteristics and garden potential.

Landscape painters
Employing a professional landscape designer or architect and contractor will not be inexpensive, but the results should be very rewarding.

The electronic approach

Websites on virtually every gardening specialty have cropped up over the last few years. A quick search on the Internet can reveal hundreds of articles about any gardening topic. You can spend many hours surfing the Net for specific information, or just enjoy exploring the breadth of subjects covered. Nearly every major garden club, plant society, and botanical garden, as well as many state cooperative extension services and university horticulture departments, have websites that you are welcome to peruse. In many cases, expert advice on almost any gardening subject is often only an e-mail away.

Many organizations may have regional chapters with individual websites. These can be a helpful source of local expert advice and can inform you of meetings, classes, and other events in your area. If you are looking for information on a specific plant, for example daffodils or roses, or a particular gardening topic such as rock gardens or bonsai, start with the appropriate national organization and go from there. Many organizations are listed on more general gardening websites, and the national organizations usually provide links to regional sites. *(For gardening websites see the appendix).*

A gardening list serve – an electronic conversation among a group of gardeners – provides opportunities to ask, receive, and offer advice, and to share gardening experiences. Many organizations sponsor

list serves. The accuracy of such advice, of course, depends upon the participants, but conversations are often lively and stimulating. If you are a member of the American Horticultural Society (AHS), you can learn about various list serves by visiting the Society's website (www.ahs.org), then join one of many ongoing conversations on just about any gardening subject that interests you.

Many local radio and cable television stations are getting into the gardening act with shows that highlight local gardens, gardeners, and timely and regionally appropriate gardening information. Tune in and see what's new.

Being there

Although written and electronic references are invaluable aids to gardening, nothing is quite the same as a visit to a real garden for learning what you need to know and for inspiring you with ideas. Regional botanical gardens and arboreta afford visitors a chance to see plants they have read or heard about in a real growing situation, and experts are often available to answer your questions.

Some public gardens offer classes and workshops on a variety of subjects, and some provide training for Master Gardeners (see Master Gardeners, page xx). Most offer volunteer opportunities – a great way to work with trained gardening staff, learning garden techniques first hand.

Chicago treasure
The 385-acre Chicago Botanic Garden, one of North America's premier gardens, has plants to see and events to enjoy all year.

Northern beauty
The Green Bay Botanical Garden's 47 acres of planted features and natural areas is open year-round and celebrates the glories of Wisconsin's four seasons and extensive gardening heritage. It offers classes and a full calendar of events

MASTER GARDENERS

The Master Gardeners program began in the early 1970s in Washington State as a way to train volunteers to help gardeners find reliable solutions to their gardening problems. Today there are master gardener programs in every state, coordinated by each state's Cooperative Extension Service.

Programs vary somewhat from one state to another, but in general, volunteers are selected and trained in basic horticultural practices. Training often includes plant identification, diagnosis of plant problems with appropriate recommendations for treatment, soil and fertilizer recommendations, lawn care, pesticide use and safety, organic gardening, ornamental gardening, and a variety of other topics.

In return for their training, Master Gardeners must volunteer a certain number of hours in public service. They may participate in plant clinics, assist with processing soil test reports, answer horticultural hotlines, conduct garden tours, or other activities that are aimed at disseminating reliable gardening information to the public.

Two hundred universities, public gardens, and nurseries throughout the United States and Canada are home to All America Selection (AAS) display gardens. These gardens provide visitors the opportunity to see how recent award-winning introductions (vegetables, flowers, and herbs) perform in a garden setting (See appendix for a list of AAS display gardens).

Close to home

Don't overlook a garden simply because it doesn't have a name: within your neighborhood there may be landscapes that deserve a closer look. Most gardeners love to show off the fruits of their labor, and some of the best advice available to you may be from the man or woman next door who shares both your growing conditions and your enthusiasm for gardening.

Observing the plants your neighbors grow, how they grow them, and how they tackle problems that arise can provide insight and ideas for your own yard. A gardening acquaintance may alert you to the arrival of a pest or show you a new plant that is just the ticket for your perennial border. Putting your heads together to find a solution for a problem multiplies your available resources.

As your garden comes of age, and neighbors can't help but observe your success, you are likely to be asked for advice from other interested gardeners. Be generous. Share your enthusiasm for gardening and your respect for the environment. You too are a valuable gardening resource.

Cutting edge
Faculty members at local and regional agricultural colleges often spend part of their time researching new techniques and breeding new plants. Their printed and electronic publications are a valuable resource.

EXTENSION SERVICE

While the Morrill Act served to establish and fund the land grant university system that began in earnest in the Northeast and Midwest in the 1860s and 1870s, it was 1887's Hatch Act and 1914's Smith Lever Act that created the foundation for the diverse network of resources that serve local gardeners in each northeastern state. The former established the Experiment Station program, originally dedicated to agricultural and mechanical research, while the latter created the Cooperative Extension Service, a vehicle for delivering the products of experiment station research and other valuable information to state residents.

Horticulturally speaking, land grant universities are very active in the Northeast, working in landscape plant selection, hybridization, evaluation, and production, as well as studying the organisms and conditions that dictate horticultural performance. More importantly, they target regional issues and offer results with genuine significance to state residents.

The Cooperative Extension Service delivers education and outreach to residents on a county level and tends to form specialties that reflect the characteristics of a given county's maekup. Urban counties will have a focus that differs a bit from those offices located in a rural, agrarian area. Northeastern Cooperative Extension Services distribute pertinent results of Experiment Station research and other valuable information to residents in the forms of lectures, bulletins, websites, telephone hotlines, and direct consultation. Topics include planting and maintenance techniques, farming information, plant pathology, and plant selection information. The Cooperative Extension Service also manages the Master Gardener program (see above).

HAVE FUN

Lots of people have yards; some have gardens. A yard is the area that surrounds your house. A garden, on the other hand, is a creation that enhances that space with sights, fragrances, and sounds that inspire and fulfill. The yard around your house is what you begin with; a garden is what it can become. Whether your garden is a woodland teeming with towering trees and flowering shrubs, a deep border of colorful perennials, a vegetable patch that stocks your table, or a simple windowbox overflowing with annuals, it should be fun for you and for those who visit.

The vision

Visualizing your dream garden can occupy many delightful hours looking through books and magazines for ideas, visiting botanical gardens, and imagining a bed here, a pond there, and over there, perhaps a trellis . . . it's a pleasant thing to daydream about your green activities. Planning for it to become a reality, and taking the measured steps necessary to assure success, is even more exciting. Witnessing the transformation of your yard into a SMARTGARDEN™ through choosing great plants, maximizing efficient practices, and nurturing a friendly, healthy environment, is a thrill that grows over time.

The challenge

Achieving a SMARTGARDEN™ is a challenge beyond simply planting a few perennials and trees around a patch of grass. It requires you to consider the question: how do you develop a garden, making the most of your landscape, while at the same time merging seamlessly into the rhythms and flow of nature? Your answer is both the task and the reward of its creation. Compromises will be necessary, and you may not see instant dividends on your investment, but over time you will enjoy the compounded benefits of a lovely garden and a healthy, balanced environment. Because you planned for it, your investment will continue to grow over time.

The gardening practices described in this book are designed to make the most of your gardening activities, using all available resources to streamline efforts so that you can concentrate on the gardening activities that you find particularly rewarding and have plenty of time to enjoy the fruits of your labor. Of course there will be some surprises. You will make changes as you go along, learning from and adapting to what works best for you. It is dynamic, challenging, and exciting, and, as every gardener comes to know, there is no such thing as a "finished" garden. The ongoing processes of planning, planting, maintaining, experiencing, refining, and sharing is part of the thrill.

The reward

Although many gardens are pleasant to look at, a SMARTGARDEN™ is a delight to experience on many different levels. It harmonizes with its surroundings, and enhances its environment without dominating it. The soil is alive and teeming with beneficial organisms. The plants fit their site and space – and they flourish! Birds and butterflies are welcomed, encouraged by the diversity of vegetation and friendly habitat. It's exciting to know your plants intimately while taking pride in their performances and anticipating their changes through the seasons as well as the years.

People garden for many reasons: to enjoy nature, get some fresh air and spend time outdoors, cultivate particular plants, grow their own food, attract wildlife, and create a pleasing, comfortable environment. For most gardeners, it is a combination of such goals. Some people garden because they enjoy the solitude, while others consider it an opportunity to spend time productively in the company of friends or family. It is a perfect activity for intergenerational bonding: senior gardeners have a wealth of experience they can share with young garden enthusiasts. Whether alone or with company, most of us garden because it's fun.

Some gardeners find satisfaction in neat rows of plump tomatoes, while others take more pleasure in a casual meadow of wildflowers or an elaborate pond for night-blooming waterlilies. No matter which type of garden you choose, it can be grown following these ten tenets. This kind of garden affords you the opportunity to express your taste and style and then to watch it grow, knowing that it is a healthy and safe environment for all who visit. That knowledge will amplify the joy you derive from your garden.

Whether you are beginning from scratch or you are improving an existing garden, smart gardening will help you embrace the vision, meet the challenge, and enjoy the rewards of bringing plants, animals, and structures together into a green and living whole.

Savoring the results
A well-planned and maintained garden that follows SmartGarden principles will bring endless pleasure to its owners, no matter the style or level of horticultural interest. The choices are up to you!

PART II

PLANT CATALOG

including Woody Plants *and*
Herbaceous Plants

One of the three most critical factors for the
success of any SMARTGARDEN™ is choosing the
right plant for the right spot. In this section, more
than 4,000 plants that grow well in the Northeast
region are grouped by physical characteristics or
horticultural requirements, with information on
light and moisture needs, cold and heat
tolerance, and maximum height and width. Below
is a key of the symbols:

☼	Sun	○	Moist	Zx–x	USDA hardiness zones
☼	Part shade	●	Wet	Hx–x	AHS heat zones
☀	Shade	pH	Acidic soil	↕ in/ft (cm/m)	Height of plant
○	Dry	Ⓝ	Native	↔ in/ft (cm/m)	Spread of plant

Plant catalog contents

HERBACEOUS

WOODY PLANTS

Often called "the bones of the garden," trees and shrubs should be the first plants to go in once the hard landscaping is done. They are slower-growing than perennials or annuals, taking longer to reach a good size, but they eventually make more impact on the landscape. Think before you shop, and consider eventual size, hardiness and heat tolerance, foliage color and density, and flowering time. Because of their importance in the landscape, it pays to do your homework and find just the right plant for every specific location. Trees in particular play a dominant role and can influence the other plants you can grow because of the shade they cast or their root systems. Shallow-rooted trees can take so much moisture from the soil that it is difficult to grow even grass beneath them.

Erica carnea 'Vivelli'
Spring heaths are low, spreading, evergreen shrubs with buds that form in fall and open in late winter or early spring.

Ilex x meservae 'Blue Princess'
These bushy, evergreen shrubs have berries that brighten a winter garden. Male and female flowers are on separate plants; a male is needed to ensure fruit.

Also take into account the winter effect; many trees have brightly colored bark or persistent fruit, which may be the only decorative feature in the garden at that time of year.

There is a shrub for every location, soil type, and exposure. Low groundcover species can take the place of grass, tall upright forms make ideal hedges or screens, and spiny ones can make an intruderproof barrier.

Acer saccharinum
Silver maples are tall, deciduous trees with silvery undersides to the leaves that turn a dull yellow in fall. They are best suited for use in parks and golf courses.

Different shrubs can provide flowers from late winter through to fall, with fruits and berries to bridge the gap. In summer, leaves may be yellow, purple, variegated, or green, and colored stems can add winter interest.

The diversity of evergreens is equally broad. Most conifers have needle- or fanlike foliage that may be green, blue, or yellow, while broadleaved evergreens have flowers and fruit. They range from small, columnar plants to large, towering trees. Many make excellent hedges that filter the wind, rather than blocking it, while others are better as specimen plants. In general, they act as a quiet backdrop to more flamboyant, brightly colored perennials and annuals.

Malus 'Snowdrift'
Aptly named for the blizzard of white blossoms in spring, this dense and rounded crabapple also bears glossy, dark green foliage. Its orange-red fruits attract a variety of wildlife in fall.

Trees with yellow or gold foliage

Yellow or golden foliage can brighten a garden and bring a touch of sunshine on a cloudy day. It stands out well against a dark background, such as a coniferous hedge or dark red brickwork. Planted at the end of a long, narrow garden, a yellow-leaved tree can make it appear shorter. Most yellow-leaved trees require full sunlight to retain their color.

Ptelea trifoliata 'Aurea'
GOLDEN HOP TREE

Ⓝ ☼ ☼ ◊ Z5–9 H9–5 ↕25ft (8m) ↔12ft (4m)

A low, spreading tree with very fragrant yellow flowers in early summer. Fruit are in small clusters of individual, winged seeds with the overall look of hops.

Alnus incana 'Aurea'
GOLDEN GRAY ALDER

☼ ◊ Z2–6 H6–1 ↕↔30ft (10m)

A conical tree with leaves that have gray hairs beneath. Clusters of red-tinged catkins are borne in late winter before the leaves. Will also grow in dry soils.

Acer shirasawanum 'Aureum'
GOLDEN FULLMOON MAPLE

☼ ◊ Z5–7 H7–5 ↕↔30ft (10m)

A small tree or large shrub closely related to the Japanese maple. New shoots are covered with downy hairs. Leaves turn orange in fall. Foliage burns in too much sun.

Catalpa bignonioides 'Aurea'
GOLDEN SOUTHERN CATALPA

Ⓝ ☼ ◊ Z5–9 H9–3 ↕↔30ft (10m)

Bright yellow when it unfurls in late spring, the foliage gradually turns green during summer. Fragrant white flowers produce long, persistent, beanlike fruit.

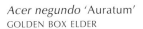

Acer negundo 'Auratum'
GOLDEN BOX ELDER
Ⓝ ☼ ☀ ◊ Z5–8 H8–3 ‡↔25ft (8m)
A slow-growing form of this vigorous tree. Bright
yellow young leaves become paler with age.
Withstands polluted urban locations.

Gleditsia triacanthos var. *inermis* 'Sunburst'
SUNBURST HONEYLOCUST
Ⓝ ☼ ◊ Z3–7 H7–1 ‡40ft (12m) ↔30ft (10m)
Bright yellow in spring, the leaves gradually darken to
green but new foliage opens all summer, giving a two-
toned effect. A broadly pyramidal, fast-growing tree.

Fagus sylvatica 'Dawyck Gold'
DAWYCK GOLD EUROPEAN BEECH
☼ ☀ ◊ ◊ Z5–7 H7–5 ‡60ft (18m) ↔22ft (7m)
Very tolerant of most soils, this makes an imposing
specimen tree. Yellow spring foliage turns green later
in summer, then pale brown, and hangs on all winter.

Quercus rubra 'Aurea'
GOLDEN RED OAK
Ⓝ ☼ ☀ ◊ ᵉᴴ Z5–9 H9–5 ‡70ft (20m) ↔50ft (15m)
An unusual form with yellow spring foliage that turns
green later, and has the characteristic red to pale brown
fall color. Grows best on sandy soils.

MORE CHOICES

• *Acer platanoides* 'Princeton Gold' Z3–7 H7–1
• *Cercidiphylum japonicum* 'Aureum' Z3–7 H7–1
• *Cornus mas* 'Aurea' Z5–8 H8–5
• *Liriodendron tulipifera* 'Aureomarginatum'
  Z5–9 H9–1
• *Metasequoia glyptostroboides* 'Ogon'
  Z4–11 H12–1

Robinia pseudoacacia 'Frisia'
GOLDEN BLACK LOCUST
Ⓝ ☼ ◊ Z4–9 H9–4 ‡50ft (15m) ↔25ft (8m)
The leaves retain their color all summer. Long, pendent
tassels of fragrant white flowers open in late spring.
A fast-growing, good tree for poor soils.

WOODY PLANTS

Shrubs with yellow or gold foliage

The unique tones of yellow- or golden-leaved shrubs make them invaluable for adding contrast in the garden. Some of these retain their bright color all summer and deserve to be in a prominent location; others gradually fade in intensity and should be sited where their spring brilliance can be seen but where other shrubs will assume center stage later in the year.

Cornus alba 'Aurea'
GOLDEN TATARIAN DOGWOOD
☼ ◊ ◐ Z2–8 H8–1 ↕↔10ft (3m)
Solid yellow at first, the leaves develop thin green margins as they age, but the overall effect is still golden. Winter twig color is not as bright as on other cultivars.

Spiraea japonica 'Goldflame'
GOLDFLAME SPIREA
☼ ◊ Z4–9 H9–1 ↕↔3ft (1m)
A very popular mounded shrub with foliage that opens an orange-red and turns yellow with age. Colors stay bright all summer. Remove shoots that revert to green.

Spiraea japonica 'Magic Carpet'
MAGIC CARPET SPIREA
☼ ◊ Z4–9 H9–1 ↕3ft (1m) ↔6ft (2m)
An upright plant with bright pink to red flowers in flat clusters all summer long. Tolerant of most soils, this is a new variety that is brighter-flowered than most.

MORE CHOICES

- *Berberis thunbergii* 'Bonanza Gold' Z4–8 H8–3
- *Cotinus coggygria* 'Golden Spirit' Z5–8 H8–1
- *Forsythia giraldiana* 'Golden Times' Z5–8 H8–5
- *Philadelphus coronarius* 'Aureus' Z4–7 H7–1
- *Physocarpus opulifolius* 'Dart's Gold' Z3–7 H7–1
- *Physocarpus opulifolius* 'Nugget' Z3–7 H7–1
- *Ptelea trifoliata* 'Aurea' Z5–9 H9–5
- *Rubus cockburnianus* 'Aureus' Z6–8 H8–6
- *Sambucus canadensis* 'Aurea' Z4–9 H9–1
- *Sambucus racemosa* 'Sutherland Gold' Z3–8 H8–1
- *Spiraea japonica* 'Gold Mound' Z4–9 H9–1
- *Spiraea thunbergii* 'Ogon' Z4–9 H9–1
- *Viburnum opulus* 'Aureum' Z3–8 H8–1
- *Weigela florida* 'Rubidor' ('Rubigold') Z5–8 H8–1

Viburnum opulus 'Aureum'
GOLDEN-LEAVED GUELDER ROSE
☼ ☼ ◊ ◐ Z3–8 H8–1 ↕↔5–10ft (1.5–3m)
White flowerheads of clustered, tubular fertile flowers, surrounded by flat sterile flowers, are of secondary interest. Foliage may scorch in strong sun and dry soil.

Ribes alpinum 'Aureum'
GOLDEN ALPINE CURRANT
☼ ◊ Z2–6 H6–1 ↕24in (60cm) ↔36in (90cm)
An erect shrub that makes a good hedging plant. Leaves turn green as they mature. Small greenish yellow flowers in summer produce red berries in early fall.

Cornus alba 'Spaethii'
SPAETHS TATARIAN DOGWOOD
☼ ◊ ◐ Z2–8 H8–1 ↕↔10ft (3m)
A very useful shrub, because it will keep its yellow variegation if grown in shade, where many variegated shrubs often revert to green. Red winter twigs.

Caryopteris x clandonensis 'Worcester Gold'
WORCESTER GOLD BLUE MIST SHRUB
Ⓝ ☼ ◑ ◊ Z6–9 H9–1 ↕3ft (1m) ↔5ft (1.5m)
Blue or purple-blue flowers produced in late summer
and early fall. Plant in a perennial border or shrub bed.
Cut back hard in spring. Dense and bushy.

Berberis thunbergii 'Aurea'
YELLOW-LEAVED JAPANESE BARBERRY
☼ ◊ Z4–8 H8–1 ↕↔5ft (1.5m)
This bushy, spiny shrub produces red-tinged, pale
yellow flowers ½in (1.5cm) long in midspring and red
berries in fall. May scorch in full sun in hot weather.

Sambucus racemosa 'Plumosa Aurea'
CUTLEAF GOLDEN ELDER
☼ ◑ ◊ Z3–7 H7–1 ↕↔10ft (3m)
Young spring foliage is tinged with orange,
turning to yellow as it unfolds and to
green by midsummer. The similar
cultivar 'Sutherland Gold' keeps its
yellow color all summer. Cut back
hard each spring for the
brightest foliage.

Lonicera nitida 'Baggesen's Gold'
BOXLEAF HONEYSUCKLE
☼ ◑ ◊ Z6–9 H9–6 ↕↔5ft (1.5m)
This evergreen honeysuckle produces flowers up to
1/2in (1.5cm) long, followed by glossy purple berries.
Makes a good hedge resembling boxwood.

Ligustrum 'Vicaryi'
VICARY GOLDEN PRIVET
☼ ◑ ◊ Z4–8 H8–1 ↕↔10ft (3m)
A semi-evergreen, upright shrub with leaves that turn a
bronzy purple in winter. The summer flowers produce
black fruit. Makes a good hedging plant.

WOODY PLANTS

Trees and shrubs with winter interest

Brightly colored twigs or fruit that persist into winter can add much to the pleasure of the garden once the leaves have fallen. Colorful stems glow in the winter sunshine, while bright berries or fruit in interesting shapes give visual interest and may also attract birds. Plants with twisted or contorted branches can also be a prominent feature of a garden during the winter.

Salix alba 'Britzensis'
CORALBARK WILLOW
☼ ◊ Z4–9 H9–1 ‡100ft (30m) ↔75ft (22.5m)
Color is more intense on new growth, so cut shoots back almost to the base every second spring. Will grow in most soils except very alkaline.

Salix alba subsp. *vitellina*
GOLDEN WILLOW
☼ ◊ Z4–9 H9–1 ‡100ft (30m) ↔75ft (22.5m)
This needs to be cut back hard in late winter or early spring to get the brightly colored new growth. May be grown as a small tree or a large shrub.

Betula platyphylla var. *japonica* 'Whitespire'
WHITESPIRE ASIAN WHITE BIRCH
☼ ◐ ◊ Z5–7 H7–5 ‡70ft (20m) ↔40ft (12m)
Has good heat tolerance, dark green summer foliage, and bark that doesn't peel. Shows good resistance to both bronze birch borer and leaf miners.

Acer griseum
PAPERBARK MAPLE
☼ ◊ Z4–8 H8–1 ‡↔30ft (10m)
Bark character develops at a young age. Dark bluish green leaves turn bronzy red and are held well into late fall. Native to central China. Pest-free.

Betula papyrifera
PAPER BIRCH
Ⓝ ☼ ◐ ◊ Z2–7 H7–1 ‡70ft (20m) ↔30ft (9m)
Bark turns white in its third or fourth year and stays white longer than many other white-barked birches. Yellow leaves in fall. Grows quickly.

Betula nigra
RIVER BIRCH
Ⓝ ☼ ◊◐ Z4–9 H9–1 ‡60ft (18m) ↔40ft (12m)
Often a multistemmed tree, this prefers acidic soil. Needs moist soil in spring but will grow where soil is dryer in summer. 'Heritage' is resistant to miners and borers.

Pinus densiflora 'Umbraculifera'
TANYOSHO PINE
☼ ◐ z4–7 H7–1 ↕2ft (4m) ↔20ft (6m)
A good specimen tree with horizontal branches and
attractive red bark. Develops a flat-topped appearance
with age. Best in a slightly acidic soil.

Rubus cockburnianus
GHOST BRAMBLE
☼ ◐ z6–8 H8–6 ↕↔8ft (2.5m)
A spreading shrub that forms dense thickets. The prickly branches are
purple with a white bloom (coating), and leaves are also white underneath.
The purple flowers are not very showy but produce black, inedible fruits.

Pseudocydonia sinensis
CHINESE QUINCE
☼ ◐ z6–8 H8–4 ↕↔20ft (6m)
Dense, upright tree with dark
green foliage that turns yellow to
red in fall. Light pink, early spring
flowers precede egg-shaped,
aromatic yellow fruit in autumn.

MORE CHOICES

- *Acer capillipes* z5–7 H7–5
- *Acer negundo* 'Violaceum' z5–8 H8–3
- *Acer palmatum* 'Sangokaku' z5–8 H8–2
- *Acer pensylvanicum* z3–7 H7–1
- *Acer tegmentosum* z4–7 H7–1
- *Acer triflorum* z5–7 H7–5
- *Betula populifolia* z3–6
- *Carya ovata* z4–8 H8–1
- *Clethra barbinervis* z5–8 H8–6
- *Cornus alba* z2–8 H8–1
- *Cornus florida* 'Autumn Gold' z5–8 H8–3
- *Cornus kousa* z5–8 H8–5
- *Cornus sanguinea* 'Midwinter Fire'
  z4–7 H7–1
- *Cornus sericea* cvs. z4–7 H7–1
- *Heptacodium miconioides* z5–9 H9–4
- *Kerria japonica* z4–9 H9–1
- *Maackia amurensis* z5–7 H7–5
- *Parrotia persica* z4–7 H7–1
- *Platanus occidentalis* z5–8 H8–5
- *Prunus maackii* z3–7 H7–1
- *Prunus mume* 'Peggy Clarke' z6–8 H8–6
- *Rosa sericea* f. *pteracantha* z6–9 H9–5
- *Stewartia koreana* z5–8 H8–4
- *Stewartia monadelpha* z6–9 H9–6
- *Stewartia pseudocamellia* z5–8 H8–4
- *Syringa pekinensis* z3–7 H7–1
- *Ulmus parvifolia* z5–9 H9–5

Pinus bungeana
LACEBARK PINE
☼ ◐ z4–7 H7–1 ↕↔30ft (9m)
Bark is smooth when young, becoming colorfully flaky
with age. Often has multiple trunks. Young shoots are
olive green. Growth rate is slow.

Trees with red or purple foliage

Dark-leaved trees are displayed to perfection against a pale background, and when featured against a green lawn, they make a bold statement. They are best used as individual specimens and lose their impact if overplanted. Some species are green in early spring and change color during the summer, adding a sense of mystery to the garden.

Acer platanoides 'Crimson Sentry'
CRIMSON SENTRY MAPLE

☼ ☼ ◔◔ ᵖᴴ Z3–7 H7–1 ↕15in ↔10in

This is a columnar form of 'Crimson King' with foliage that is almost as dark and that retains its color well through the summer. There is very little change in fall.

Acer platanoides 'Crimson King'
CRIMSON KING MAPLE

☼ ◔ Z4–7 H7–1 ↕100ft (30m) ↔75ft (22.5m)

Unlike some purple-leaved maples that change color during summer, the leaves open almost black and retain their dark color until fall.

Prunus cerasifera 'Thundercloud'
THUNDERCLOUD PLUM

☼ ◔ Z5–9 H9–4 ↕↔30ft (10m)

An adaptable tree that will thrive in most soils. Flowers in early spring, with the new leaves. Fertilize regularly to enable it to withstand many possible diseases.

MORE CHOICES

- *Acer palmatum* 'Burgundy Lace' Z5–8 H8–2
- *Acer palmatum* 'Crimson Prince' PP7217 Z5–8 H8–5
- *Fagus sylvatica* 'Riversii' Z5–7 H7–5
- *Malus* 'Cardinal' PP7147 Z5–8 H8–4
- *Malus* 'Red Splendor' Z4–8 H8–1
- *Prunus cerasifera* 'Newport' Z4–9 H9–1
- *Prunus serrulata* 'Royal Burgundy' PP6520 Z5–8 H8–5
- *Robinia pseudoacacia* 'Purple Robe' Z3–9 H9–1

Fagus sylvatica 'Dawyck Purple'
DAWYCK PURPLE EUROPEAN BEECH

☼ ☼ ◔◔ Z5–7 H7–5 ↕70ft (20m) ↔15ft (5m)

Makes a wonderful focal point in the garden and is relatively pest-free, except for bark diseases. Plant with green-leaved plants for foliage contrast.

Fagus sylvatica 'Purpurea Pendula'
PURPLE-LEAVED WEEPING BEECH

☼ ☼ ◔◔ Z5–7 H7–5 ↕↔10ft (3m)

Excellent mushroom-shaped weeper perfect for a large container or as a focal point. Grows slowly, and the leaves change to purplish green in summer.

Malus 'Liset'
LISET CRABAPPLE

☀ ☀ ◊ Z4–8 H8–1 ↕↔20ft (6m)

A rounded selection with good resistance to mildew and fireblight. Spring flowers produce small, dark red fruit that last well into winter.

Malus 'Royalty'
ROYALTY CRABAPPLE

☀ ☀ ◊ Z4–8 H8–1 ↕↔25ft (8m)

Bears sparse, dark red-purple fruits after the spring flowers. Upright grower, with brilliant purple foliage in fall. Severely prone to scab and fireblight.

Acer palmatum 'Bloodgood'
JAPANESE MAPLE

☀ ☀ ◊ Z5–8 H8–2 ↕↔15ft (5m)

Reddish purple flowers blossom in midspring, followed by winged red fruit. Foliage often turns bright red in fall. Grow as a shrub or small tree.

Acer palmatum f. atropurpureum
PURPLE JAPANESE MAPLE

☀ ☀ ◊ Z5–8 H8–2 ↕15–25ft (5–8m) ↔20ft (6m)

Needs a protected site to prevent the new foliage from damage by late frosts or cold winds. There are many named forms with leaves dissected in various ways.

Gleditsia triacanthos var. inermis 'Rubylace'
RUBYLACE HONEYLOCUST

Ⓝ ☀ ◊ Z3–7 H7–1 ↕30–80ft (10–25m) ↔25–35ft (8–11m)

Straggly tree with leaves opening dark red and changing to green. Grows in most soils; subject to webworm.

Shrubs with red or purple foliage

Whether used as foundation plants or in a mixed border, these shrubs add contrast and diversity. They vary from pale red to deep bronzy purple, so by careful selection, one can find the perfect shade to complement or tone with neighboring plants or structures. Some can be used for hedging, making an eye-catching change from the usual green.

Berberis thunbergii var. *atropurpurea* 'Rose Glow'
ROSE GLOW JAPANESE BARBERRY
☼ ☀ ◊ Z5–8 H8–5 ↕3ft (1m) ↔8ft (2.5m)
A spreading form that makes a rounded bush. The first flush of leaves in spring does not show the characteristic pale mottling; it develops later.

Physocarpus opulifolius 'Diablo'
DIABLO NINEBARK
☼ ☀ ◑ ◊ pH Z3–7 H7–1 ↕6ft (2m) ↔8ft (2.5m)
A new introduction. Pinkish-white flowers in summer are followed by bright red, eye-catching fruit. Leaf color lightens to a burgundy in fall.

Cotinus coggygria 'Royal Purple'
ROYAL PURPLE SMOKETREE
☼ ☀ ◊◑ Z5–8 H8–3 ↕↔15ft (5m)
A small deciduous tree or bushy shrub. Foliage turns scarlet in fall. Plumelike flower stalks turn a smoky grayish pink as they age.

Acer palmatum red-leaved selections
JAPANESE MAPLE
☼ ◊ Z5–8 H8–2 ↕↔20ft (6m)
Slow-growing, usually multistemmed trees. New foliage is often bright red, and fall color is scarlet, orange, or yellow. Tend to grow in horizontal planes.

Berberis thunbergii var. *atropurpurea* 'Helmond Pillar'
HELMOND PILLAR JAPANESE BARBERRY
☼ ☀ ◊ Z4–8 H8–1 ↕5ft (1.5m) ↔24in (60cm)
A narrow, upright shrub that makes a good specimen plant or narrow deciduous hedge. Like all barberries, it is very prickly and needs handling with care.

MORE CHOICES

- *Berberis thunbergii* 'Concorde' Z4–8 H8–1
- *Berberis thunbergii* 'Royal Cloak' Z4–8 H8–3
- *Corylopsis sinensis* 'Spring Purple' Z5–9 H9–2
- *Photinia x fraseri* 'Red Robin' Z8–9 H9–8
- *Pieris japonica* 'Mountain Fire' Z5–9 H9–1
- *Prunus x cistena* 'Schmidtcis' Z4–8 H8–1
- *Rosa glauca* Z2–8 H8–1
- *Weigela florida* 'Alexandra' Z5–8 H8–1

Sambucus nigra 'Guincho Purple'
GUINCHO PURPLE EUROPEAN ELDER

☀ ☀ ◐ Z6–8 H8–6 ‡ ↔20ft (6m)

The leaves open green and change color as they age, turning red in fall. Flowers are bright pink in bud and are borne on purple stalks. It grows well in most soils.

Corylus maxima 'Purpurea'
PURPLE-LEAVED FILBERT

☀ ☀ ◐ Z4–9 H9–1 ‡20ft (6m) ↔15ft (5m)

An upright, deciduous shrub or small tree. Purple-tinged yellow catkins hang in clusters before the leaves open, follwed by purple-husked, edible nuts.

Hypericum androsaemum 'Albury Purple'
ALBURY PURPLE TUTSAN

☀ ◐ Z6–8 H8–4 ‡30in (75cm) ↔36in (90cm)

A bushy, semi-evergreen plant with erect branches. Foliage remains colored all summer. Yellow flowers freely produced in summer produce juicy black fruit.

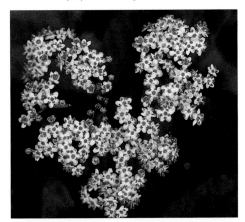

Prunus x cistena
PURPLELEAF SANDCHERRY

☀ ◐ Z3–8 H8–1 ‡↔5ft (1.5m)

A widely grown, upright, relatively slow-growing, deciduous shrub. The spring flowers are followed by dark red edible fruit that are hard to see against the foliage, but birds usually find them.

Sambucus nigra 'Gerda' ('Black Beauty')
BLACK BEAUTY EUROPEAN ELDER

☀ ☀ ◐ Z6–8 H8–6 ‡↔20ft (6m)

Nearly black foliage keeps its color all summer. The midsummer flowers have a light lemon fragrance and produce edible black berries in fall that birds also enjoy.

WOODY PLANTS

Trees and shrubs that twist or weep

Weeping trees have long been favorites of gardeners and landscapers because they add a different element to a design. They vary greatly in size, but remember they cover more ground space than conventional tree shapes, and it may be difficult to mow beneath them. Contorted and flattened stems are much prized by flower arrangers.

Cercidiphyllum japonicum 'Pendulum'
WEEPING KATSURA TREE
☼ ☀ ◐ ◊ Z3–7 H7–1 ↕20ft (6m) ↔25ft (8m)
Fast-growing tree that matures smaller than other weeping forms of Katsura tree. Bark becomes shaggy with age. Good focal point in a large rock garden.

MORE CHOICES

- *Acer palmatum* v. *dissectum* 'Viridis' Z5–8 H8–5
- *Cercidiphyllum magnificum* 'Pendula' Z5–8 H8–3
- *Cercis canadensis* 'Covey' Z5–9 H9–5
- *Chaenomeles speciosa* 'Contorta' Z6–9 H9–1
- *Cornus kousa* 'Elizabeth Lustgarten' Z5–8 H8–3
- *Cornus kousa* 'Weaver's Weeping' Z5–8 H8–3

Corylus avellana 'Contorta'
CORKSCREW HAZEL
☼ ☀ ◊ Z3–9 H9–1 ↕↔25ft (5m)
An upright, large shrub, this does best in a neutral to alkaline soil. The twisted branches are prized by flower arrangers. The catkins open in late winter.

Acer palmatum 'Waterfall'
WATERFALL JAPANESE MAPLE
☼ ☀ ◊ Z5–8 H8–2 ↕6ft (2m) ↔10ft (3m)
Regarded as the best green cutleaf form because of the deeply cut leaves and their larger size. Tolerates heat well. Good as an accent plant near a patio.

Laburnum x waterei 'Vossii'
VOSS'S GOLDENCHAIN
TREE

☼ ◊ Z5–8 H8–3
↕↔30ft (10m)

Has a denser habit and longer flower clusters than its hybrid parent, plus olive green, fissured bark. Plant in protected spots near buildings.

Larix decidua 'Pendula'
WEEPING EUROPEAN LARCH

☼ ◊ Z3–6 H6–1 ↕100ft (30m) or more ↔20ft (6m)

Branches are more pendulous than the species. Scaly gray bark becomes ridged with age. Deciduous.

MORE CHOICES

- Fagus sylvatica 'Tortuosa' Z5–7 H7–5
- Laburnum x watereri Z6–8 H8–3
- Prunus x 'Snofozam' Z5–8 H8–5

Prunus x subhirtella 'Pendula'
WINTER-FLOWERING CHERRY

☼ ◊ Z6–8 H8–6 ↕ ↔30ft (10m)

A graceful, artistic weeper that grows quickly. The bark is particularly distinct, with gray-brown lenticels (corky pores) in stripes on the younger branches.

Prunus x subhirtella 'Pendula Plena Rosea'
DOUBLE WEEPING CHERRY

☼ ◊ ◊ Z6–8 H8–6 ↕↔25 ft (8m)

Double flowers last a long time and are followed by red fruits that mature to glossy black. As with other cherries, many diseases and insects can attack.

Salix babylonica var. pekinensis 'Tortuosa'
CORKSCREW WILLOW

☼ ◊ Z5–9 H9–5 ↕50ft (15m) ↔25ft (8m)

Fast growing, small to medium tree with twisted shoots with bright green bark. It is greatly prized by flower arrangers and adds winter interest to the garden.

Fagus sylvatica 'Pendula'
WEEPING EUROPEAN BEECH

☼☼ ◊◊ Z5–7 H7–5 ↕80ft (24m) ↔50 ft (15m)

As branches touch the ground they root in place, often creating a cavernous shelter. Bronze fall color. Withstands heavy pruning but dislikes extreme heat.

Exotic and tropical-looking trees and shrubs

You can add a touch of the exotic to your garden with these unusual woody plants. Many are surprisingly hardy and relatively easy to find in the larger garden centers and nurseries or by mail order. Treat them as you would any regular tree or shrub: they may look tropical but they don't need any special pampering.

Albizia julibrissin
SILK-TREE, MIMOSA

☀ ◊ Z6–9 H9–6 ↕↔30ft (10m)

Light gray-brown seedpods persist through the winter. Grows quickly and normally is not long-lived. Very susceptible to wilt and webworm. Self-sows strongly.

Asimina triloba
PAWPAW

Ⓝ ☀ ◊ Z6–8 H8–6 ↕↔12ft (4m)

Both female and male plants are required to produce fruit. When fully ripe, the banana-flavored interior is yellow and custardlike. Has few pest problems.

Cotinus 'Grace'
GRACE SMOKEBUSH

☀ ◊ Z5–8 H8–5 ↕↔15ft (5m)

Wine-red new foliage, turning plum-red and then orange in fall. The individual flowers are inconspicuous but are carried in large clusters, giving a smokelike appearance.

MORE CHOICES

- *Aralia elata* Z4–9 H9–1
- *Aucuba japonica* 'Variegata' Z6–15 H12–6
- *Magnolia grandiflora* 'Bracken's Brown Beauty' Z5–9 H9–3
- *Magnolia grandiflora* 'D.D. Blanchard' Z7–9 H9–1
- *Magnolia grandiflora* 'Edith Bogue' Z7–9 H9–3
- *Magnolia grandiflora* 'Little Gem' Z7–9 H9–3
- *Magnolia tripetala* Z5–9 H9–5
- *Stachyurus praecox* 'Rubriflora' Z6–7 H7–6
- *Tsuga canadensis* 'Sargentii' Z3–7 H8–1
- *Ziziphus jujuba* Z5–10 H10–8

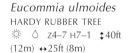

Catalpa x erubescens 'Purpurea'
PURPLE CATALPA, INDIAN BEAN TREE

☀ ◊ Z5–9 H9–5 ↕↔50ft (15m)

Leaves turn green during summer ,but leaf stalks remain purple. Flowers have gold centers and are smaller but more numerous than those of the northern catalpa.

Eucommia ulmoides
HARDY RUBBER TREE

☀ ◊ Z4–7 H7–1 ↕40ft (12m) ↔25ft (8m)

A spreading tree with glossy leaves. Flowers are inconspicuous. Interesting for the latexlike sap that pulls in strings if a leaf is torn.

Aucuba japonica
JAPANESE LAUREL

☀ ☽ ◊ Z6–15 H12–6 ↕10ft (3m) ↔10ft (3m)

Glossy-leaved evergreen shrub produces small red-purple flowers in midspring. In fall, female plants produce red berries. Disliked by rabbits.

Magnolia fraseri
EAR-LEAVED UMBRELLA TREE

Ⓝ ☼ ◐ ◊ Z6–9 H9–6 ‡30ft (10m) ↔25ft (8m)

Fast growing, often with multiple stems, and decorative bark in winter. One of the first tree magnolias to flower, blossoms measure about 8in (20cm) across. Red seed cones are also attractive.

Magnolia ashei
ASHE MAGNOLIA

Ⓝ ☼ ◐ ◊ Z7–9 H9–7 ‡30–70ft (10–20m) ↔25–50ft (8–15m)

Fragrant flowers open with the wavy-edged leaves. Free-flowering, even when young. Native to Florida.

Magnolia macrophylla
BIGLEAF MAGNOLIA

☼ ◐ ◊ Z6–9 H12–10 ‡↔30ft (9m)

Here is a leaf detail of the species more fully described below left. Note the silvery undersides, which create an attractive contrast when blowing in the wind.

Magnolia macrophylla
BIGLEAF MAGNOLIA

☼ ◐ ◊ Z6–9 H12–10 ‡↔30ft (9m)

A rounded tree with huge, fragrant flowers and large, oval, reddish, conelike fruit. Immense leaves are sometimes over two feet long. Needs a large setting.

Magnolia grandiflora 'Little Gem'
LITTLE GEM SOUTHERN MAGNOLIA

Ⓝ ☼ ◐ ◊ Z7–9 H9–3 ‡20ft (6m) ↔10ft (3m)

A slow-growing, compact, columnar tree. Leaves are dark green above, with a reddish down on the reverse. Flowers remain cup-shaped, rather than opening flat.

Magnolia grandiflora
SOUTHERN MAGNOLIA

Ⓝ ☼ ◐ ◊ Z7–9 H9–1 ‡↔30ft (9m)

Slow-growing, pyramidal evergreen that branches close to the ground. Fragrant, large white flowers bloom from late spring to early summer. Pest-free.

Ginkgo biloba
MAIDENHAIR TREE
☼ ◊ Z5–9 H9–3 ‡100ft (30m) ↔25ft (8m)
Narrow to spreading young tree becomes umbrella-shaped. Slow-growing, tolerant of pollution and heat, and free of pests. Outstanding yellow fall foliage.

Stachyurus praecox 'Magpie'
MAGPIE SPIKETAIL
☼ ◊ ۹ Z7–9 H9–7 ‡5ft (1.5m) ↔6ft (2m)
An early-flowering, upright, deciduous shrub with arching branches. The pointed leaves have a wide, creamy white edging. Needs shelter from cold winds, which could damage flower buds.

Kalopanax septemlobus
CASTOR ARALIA
☼ ◊ Z5–9 H9–4 ‡↔50ft (15m)
Upright when young, this deciduous tree becomes spreading at maturity and has very prickly stems. Clusters of small white flowers on the tips in summer.

Maclura pomifera
OSAGE-ORANGE
Ⓝ ☼ ◊ Z5–9 H9–5 ‡50 ft (15m) ↔40ft (12m)
Fast-growing tree with low, rounded, irregular head and stiff, thorny branches. Deep orange-brown bark with wavy, deep ridges. Very tough and durable.

Toona sinensis
CHINESE TOON
☼ ◊ Z5–8 H12–10 ‡↔50ft (15m)
A fast-growing, deciduous tree that may sucker and form a thicket. It will thrive in most soils. The summer flowers are small, white, and have a strange odor.

Aralia spinosa
DEVIL'S WALKING STICK

(N) ☼ ☼ ◊ Z4–9 H9–1 ‡30ft (10m) ↔15ft (5m)

Makes an impenetrable thicket in time, with spiny stems and leaves. Has white flowers in July and black fruit that attract birds. Grows well in poor soils.

Pistacia chinensis
CHINESE PISTACHE

☼ ◊ Z6–9 H9–6 ‡80ft (25m) ↔30ft (10m)

Shiny, dark green leaves hold on late into fall before coloring up. Flowers (before the leaves) are followed by fruit that ripens from light blue to red. Pest-free.

Catalpa bignonioides
INDIAN BEAN TREE, SOUTHERN CATALPA

(N) ☼ ◊ Z5–9 H9–5 ‡↔50ft (15m)

One of the last trees to leaf out in spring, this has a spreading growth habit. The early summer flowers become long, slender pods that persist all winter.

Aralia elata 'Variegata'
VARIEGATED JAPANESE ANGELICA TREE

☼ ☼ ◊ Z4–9 H9–1 ‡↔30ft (10m)

A vigorous, upright tree with spiny stems. Grows in most soils, including poor and stony. Large, spreading heads of small white flowers open in late summer/early fall.

Pterostyrax hispida
EPAULETTE TREE

☼ ☼ ◊ Z5–8 H8–5 ‡50ft (15m) ↔40ft (12m)

A round-headed tree that grows best in slightly acidic soil. The fragrant flowers open in early summer; even young trees flower well. The ribbed fruit are covered in bristles.

Catalpa bignonioides 'Aurea'
GOLDEN SOUTHERN CATALPA

(N) ☼ ◊ Z5–9 H9–3 ‡↔30ft (10m)

Similar in growth to the species (below left), this has leaves that remain yellow all summer in cooler climates. They turn greenish where summers are hot..

WOODY PLANTS

Trees with variegated foliage

In general, trees with variegated foliage grow more slowly than those with all-green leaves, which makes them desirable for smaller gardens, where they will not outgrow their allotted space as quickly. Be vigilant in pruning out branches that have reverted to green while still young. If left, they will grow faster than the variegated branches and spoil the shape of the tree.

Acer platanoides 'Drummondii'
NORWAY MAPLE
☼ ☀ ◊ Z3–7 H7–1 ‡80ft (25m) ↔50 ft
Situate carefully: the variegated leaves are prone to burning in full sun. Use as a focal point or with red-leaved trees and shrubs to set off the showy foliage.

Aralia elata 'Variegata'
VARIEGATED JAPANESE ANGELICA TREE
☼ ☀ ◊ Z4–9 H9–1 ‡↔30ft (10m)
A spiny-stemmed, upright tree that will grow in most soils and may sucker badly. In late summer, large heads of small flowers give the plant in a mistlike look.

Ilex aquifolium 'Argentea Marginata'
WHITE-EDGED ENGLISH HOLLY
☼ ◊ Z7–9 H9–7 ‡50ft (15m) ↔12ft (4m)
New foliage is pink-tinged. A female clone, this will produce berries if a male form is nearby. Several other cultivars of English holly have white or gold variegation.

MORE CHOICES

- *Cercis canadensis* 'Silver Cloud' Z4–9 H9–2
- *Cornus florida* 'First Lady' Z5–8 H8–3
- *Fraxinus pennsylvanica* 'Variegata' Z4–9 H9–1
- *Ilex opaca* 'Stewards Silver Crown' Z5–9 H9–5

Acer palmatum 'Butterfly'
BUTTERFLY JAPANESE MAPLE
☀ ◊ Z5–8 H8–2 ‡↔10ft (3m)
A small tree or large shrub with an upright habit. The deeply cut foliage is tinged pink when young, becoming creamier with maturity. In fall, the margins turn red.

Acer negundo 'Flamingo'
FLAMINGO BOXELDER
Ⓝ ☼ ☀ ◊ Z5–8 H8–3 ‡50ft (15m) ↔30ft (10m)
Pink young leaves age to green with white edges. To encourage production of more pink leaves, prune plants in late winter. Grows very quickly.

Shrubs with variegated foliage

Most shrubs are grown chiefly for their flowers or fruit; by choosing those with variegated foliage, you gain a plant that has garden interest throughout the growing season. However, they stand out best when grown with – and particularly in front of – shrubs and trees that have single-colored leaves, because too much variegation can be visually overpowering.

Weigela florida 'Variegata'
VARIEGATED WEIGELA
☼ ◊ z5–8 H8–1 ↕↔6–8ft (2–2.5m)
Dense, bushy shrub. Prune old, straggly plants hard. Can grow near roads and in urban environments, due to tolerance of air pollution. Easy to grow.

Buddleja davidii 'Harlequin'
HARLEQUIN VARIEGATED BUTTERFLY BUSH
☼ ◊ z6–9 H10–4 ↕↔20ft (6m)
Expanding leaves are yellow, old leaves almost white. Less vigorous and smaller than many butterfly bushes. Flowers can be cut, but they do not last long.

Daphne x *burkwoodii* 'Carol Mackie'
CAROL MACKIE DAPHNE
☼ ◐ ◊ z5–8 H8–4 ↕↔3–5ft (1–1.5m)
Fragrant, light pink flowers in early summer. May be semi-evergreen in the southern NE. There are other variegated forms of this hybrid; this is the most common.

MORE CHOICES

- *Abelia* x *grandiflora* 'Sunrise' z6–9 H9–1
- *Elaeagnus* x *ebbingei* 'Gilt Edge' z7–11 H12–1
- *Euonymus fortunei* 'Emerald Gaiety' PP1960 z5–9 H9–2
- *Forsythia viridissima* v. *koreana* 'Ilgwang' z5–8 H8–5
- *Kerria japonica* 'Picta' z4–9 H9–1
- *Sambucus nigra* 'Pulverulenta' z6–8 H8–6
- *Symphoricarpos orbiculatus* 'Foliis Variegatis' z2–6 H6–1
- *Weigela florida* 'Brigela' PPAF z5–9 H9–5

Cornus alba 'Elegantissima'
VARIEGATED RED TWIG DOGWOOD
☼ ◊ z2–8 H8–1 ↕↔10ft (3m)
Gray-green leaves have irregular white margins. White flowers appear in late spring and early summer, followed by white fruit. Shoots are bright red in winter.

Leucothoe fontanesiana 'Girard's Rainbow'
RAINBOW FETTERBUSH
Ⓝ ☼ ☼ ◊ ↺ z5–8 H8–3 ↕5ft (1.5) ↔6ft (2m)
Grows best in organic soil. It will not stand drying out and needs protection from drying winds. Plant container-grown specimens in spring.

Small trees for fall color

When deciding on which tree to plant, fall color is one of the factors that should be considered along with flowers, foliage, fruit, and winter interest. The trees suggested here are suitable for modern townhouse lots and other properties where space is limited. Remember: fall color is best when these trees are grown in full sunlight.

Cornus kousa var. *chinensis*
CHINESE DOGWOOD
☼ ☼ ◊ Z5–8 H8–5 ‡22ft (7m) ↔15ft (5m)
Tiny flowers are surrounded by showy white bracts that turn pink as they age and are held above the leaves. Red summer fruit and red fall color add appeal.

Photinia villosa
ORIENTAL PHOTINIA
☼ ☼ ◊ Z4–9 H9–1 ‡↔15ft (5m)
A spreading, deciduous tree or large shrub with flat heads of white flowers in spring that resemble hawthorn blossoms, followed by egg-shaped red fruits.

Amelanchier x grandiflora 'Autumn Brilliance'
AUTUMN BRILLIANCE APPLE SERVICEBERRY
☼ ☼ ◊ pH Z3–7 H7–1 ‡25ft (8m) ↔30ft (10m)
A spreading small tree or large shrub with white spring flowers. The blue-black fruit are edible and loved by birds. Emerging new foliage is bronze-tinted.

Rhus typhina 'Laciniata'
CUTLEAF STAGHORN SUMAC
Ⓝ ☼ ◊ Z3–8 H8–1 ‡15ft (5m) ↔20ft (6m)
Erect conical clusters of yellow-green flowers to 8in (20cm) long appear in summer. In fall, female plants produce dense clusters of bright crimson fruit.

Sorbus commixta
JAPANESE MOUNTAIN ASH
☼ ☼ ◊ Z6–8 H8–6 ‡30ft (10m) ↔22ft (7m)
A conical tree with erect branches. Young leaves are a copper shade becoming green, then turning yellow to red in fall. Heads of white flowers open in spring.

Acer buergerianum
TRIDENT MAPLE
☼ ☼ ◊ Z5–9 H9–5 ‡30ft (10m) ↔25ft (8m)
A spreading tree with leaves that are blue-green beneath in summer and change to red or orange in fall. Drought resistant.

Acer triflorum
THREE-FLOWERED MAPLE
☼ ☼ ◊ Z5–7 H7–5 ‡30ft (10m) ↔25ft (8m)
Like most maples, this tree is noted for its stunning fall foliage. Once the leaves have dropped, the peeling gray-brown bark is revealed.

Crataegus crus-galli
COCKSPUR HAWTHORN

☼ ☼ ◊ ◊ z4–7 H7–1 ↕25ft (8m) ↔30ft (10m)

A spreading tree with almost horizontal branches and long, sharp thorns. Rounded clusters of white flowers in spring produce red fruits in late summer.

Malus sieboldii
TORINGO CRABAPPLE

☼ ◊ z5–9 H9–5 ↕8ft (2.5m) ↔10ft (3m)

Small tree with dense, spreading branches. Masses of white flowers in late spring after other crabapples. Leaves have silvery undersides in summer.

MORE CHOICES

- *Acer palmatum v. dissectum* 'Waterfall' z5–8 H8–2
- *Acer pseudosieboldianum* z5–7 H7–5
- *Amelanchier laevis* z5–9 H9–3
- *Franklinia alatamaha* z6–9 H9–6
- *Prunus sargentii* z5–9 H9–5
- *Pyrus calleryana* 'Aristocrat' z5–8 H8–1
- *Sorbus commixta* z6–8 H8–6
- *Stewartia pseudocamellia* z5–8 H8–4

Acer japonicum 'Aconitifolium'
FULLMOON MAPLE

☼ ◊ z5–7 H7–5 ↕↔30ft (10m)

Leaf lobes are divided twice and sharply toothed; they change from light green to golden yellow and red in fall. Protect from wind and late spring frost.

WOODY PLANTS

Medium to large trees for fall color

Good fall color is a desirable trait in a tree, since it extends the ornamental value of the plant. In some cases the fall color is so striking it is the main reason for selecting that particular plant. Some of the trees shown here are suitable for average city lots, while others are better suited to larger properties, where they will have space to develop to their full potential.

Quercus coccinea
SCARLET OAK
Ⓝ ☼ ☀ ◊ pH Z5–9 H9–4 ‡70ft (20m) ↔50 ft (15m)
Round and open at maturity, with glossy dark green foliage in summer and brilliant red fall color. Intolerant of adverse conditions, but fine to garden beneath.

Fagus grandifolia
AMERICAN BEECH
Ⓝ ☼ ☀ ◊ Z3–9 H9–1 ‡↔80ft (25m)
An imposing tree with smooth, gray bark, even on older trees. Plant in slightly acidic soil that is neither compacted nor wet. Slow-growing, but worth it.

Fraxinus pennsylvanica 'Summit'
SUMMIT GREEN ASH
Ⓝ ☼ ◊ Z4–9 H9–1 ‡45ft (14m) ↔25ft (8m)
A fast-growing selection with large, glossy, light green leaves in summer. Very adaptable to soil type. Other named forms have wider crowns or purple fall color.

MORE CHOICES

- *Acer saccharum* 'Green Mountain' Z3–8 H8–1
- *Acer truncatum* Z4–8 H8–1
- *Acer x freemanii* cultivars Z4–7 H7–1
- *Betula lenta* Z3–7 H7–2
- *Carya glabra* Z5–8 H8–1
- *Cercidiphyllum japonicum* Z4–8 H8–1
- *Ginkgo biloba* Z5–9 H9–3
- *Populus tremuloides* Z1–8 H8–1

Zelkova serrata
JAPANESE ZELKOVA

☼ ☼ ◑ Z5–9 H9–5 ‡100ft (30m) ↔60ft (18m)

As it matures, smooth gray bark flakes off to reveal orange patches. Rough-textured, elmlike leaves have toothed edges. Native to Japan, Taiwan, and South Korea.

Pistacia chinensis
CHINESE PISTACHE

☼ ◊ Z6–9 H9–1 ‡80ft (25m) ↔30ft (10m)

Shiny, dark green leaves hold on late into fall before coloring up. Flowers before the leaves are followed by fruit that ripens from light blue to red. Pest-free.

Liquidambar styraciflua
AMERICAN SWEET GUM

Ⓝ ☼ ◑ Z6–9 H9–6 ‡100ft (30m) ↔75ft (23m)

Narrow and upright when young, but lower limbs spread with age. Furrowed bark and corky wings on twigs add to its winter interest. Native to eastern US.

Acer rubrum 'October Glory'
OCTOBER GLORY MAPLE

Ⓝ ☼ ☼ ◑ Z3–9 H9–1 ‡70ft (20m) ↔40ft (12m)

Forms a rounder profile and has glossier deeper green leaves than the species. One of the hardiest of the red maples, it is very fast-growing and nearly pest-free.

Taxodium distichum
BALD CYPRESS

Ⓝ ☼ ☼ ◑◑ Z5–11 H12–5 ‡80ft (24m) ↔25ft (8m)

The needles turn rust-brown in fall before dropping. Pale brown, shallowly fissured bark. Distinctive aerial roots around the base in wet sites. Moderate growth rate.

Nyssa sylvatica
SOUR GUM

Ⓝ ☼ ☼ ◑ Z4–9 H9–2 ‡70ft (20m) ↔30ft (9m)

Has a cone-shaped head with straight trunk and horizontal branches. Useful as a street tree or specimen. Tolerates coastal conditions, but not shade.

Trees with white flowers

White flowers are luminous, they stand out against the foliage and are far more visible on a cloudy day or at dusk than those of other shades. Many of the trees shown here also produce colorful berries that attract birds into the garden, or have attractive fruit that add interest in fall and winter. A few of these have attractive bark as well (*see* p.90).

Styrax japonicus
JAPANESE SNOWBELL
☼ ◐ ♌ Z6–8 H8–6 ↕↔50ft (15m)
This forms a broad crown with spreading branches. Slightly fragrant flowers in late spring, attractive fruit in summer. Plant in early spring in a humus-rich soil.

Crataegus x lavallei
LAVALLE HAWTHORN
☼ ◐ ♦ Z5–7 H7–4 ↕22ft (7m) ↔30ft (9m)
Bright red to orange-red fruit with brown speckles complement the bronze to coppery red leaves in fall. The fruit last well into winter if not eaten by birds, squirrels, and other wildlife.

MORE CHOICES

- *Amelanchier laevis* Z5–9 H9–3
- *Cladrastis kentukea* Z4–9 H9–1
- *Cornus alternifolia* Z4–8 H8–1
- *Cornus florida* 'Cloud Nine' Z5–8x H8–3
- *Cornus x rutgersensis* Z5–8 H8–3
- *Crataegus x mordenensis* 'Snowbird' Z3–8 H8–1
- *Davidia involucrate* Z6–8 H8–6
- *Lagerstroemia* x 'Natchez' Z6–9 H9–6
- *Malus* 'Snowdrift' Z5–8 H8–5
- *Sorbus decora* Z3–8 H8–1

Cercis canadensis var. *alba*
EASTERN REDBUD
Ⓝ ☼ ◐ ♦ Z5–9 H9–5 ↕↔30ft (10m)
Early spring flowers often last 2 to 3 weeks. This appealing small tree looks well used in a woodland border and other naturalized situations.

Magnolia virginiana
SWEET BAY MAGNOLIA
Ⓝ ☼ ◐ ♦ Z6–9 H9–6 ↕28ft (9m) ↔20ft (6m)
Smallish lemon-scented flowers are produced throughout summer. Grows well in soils ranging from dry to swampy, providing they are moderately acidic. Native from Massachusetts to Texas.

Magnolia x loebneri 'Merrill'
MERRILL MAGNOLIA
☼ ◐ ♦ Z5–9 H9–1 ↕25ft (8m) ↔20ft (6m)
The 15-petaled flowers, up to 6in (15cm) across, open in midspring, and even young plants flower freely. Grows best in a deep, preferably slightly acidic soil with plenty of organic matter.

Magnolia kobus 'Wada's Memory'
WADA'S MEMORY MAGNOLIA
☼ ◐ ♦ Z6–9 H9–6 ↕30ft (10m) ↔15ft (5m)
One of the earliest magnolias to flower, this has quite fragrant flowers. It is very adaptable to most soils, including alkaline. New foliage opens mahogany red.

Halesia monticola
MOUNTAIN SILVERBELL

Ⓝ ☼ ◐ ◊ Z6–9 H9–6 ↕↔50ft (15m)

A low-branched, conical tree that grows best in a slightly acidic, organic soil in sun or shade. Flowers open with the leaves, which turn yellow in fall.

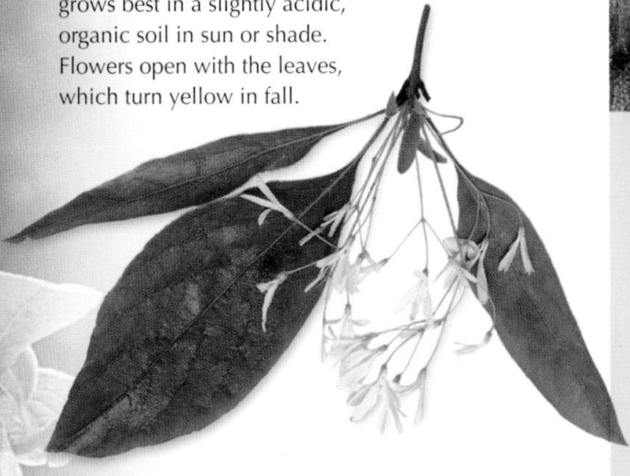

Chionanthus retusus
CHINESE FRINGE TREE

☼ ◊ Z5–9 H9–3 ↕↔10ft (3m)

Male and female flowers are on separate trees in spring; males are larger, but females produce attractive fruit. Tolerates most soils, providing they are deep and fertile.

Halesia diptera var. magniflora
TWO-WINGED SILVERBELL

Ⓝ ☼ ◐ ◊ Z4–8 H8–1 ↕20ft (6m) ↔30ft (10m)

Larger flowers than the species. Winged green fruit appear after the flowers. Foliage on this rounded tree turns yellow in autumn. Protect from wind.

Prunus x yedoensis
YOSHINO CHERRY, POTOMAC CHERRY

☼ ◊ Z5–8 H8–5 ↕↔30ft (10m)

Arching tree with almond-scented flowers in early spring before the leaves. Adaptable to most soils. Upright, weeping, and pink-flowered cultivars are available.

WOODY PLANTS

Trees with ornamental fruit

On some trees, the fruit are so striking that this is the main reason for planting them. In some cases, the fruit attract birds into the garden and their beauty is somewhat fleeting, in others, the fruit persist for the winter, adding color to the garden at the drabbest time of year. Occasionally, the fruit is edible and may be used for preserves or jellies.

Crataegus viridis 'Winter King'
WINTER KING GREEN HAWTHORN
Ⓝ ☼ ◐ ◊ ◊ Z5–7 H7–5 ‡20ft (6m) ↔15ft (5m)
Rounded and very thorny, with gray-green, waxy stems. Fruits persist into winter and are larger than the species. Less rust-susceptible than other hawthorns.

Crataegus crus-galli
COCKSPUR HAWTHORN
Ⓝ ☼ ◐ ◊ ◊ Z4–7 H7–1 ‡25ft (8m) ↔30ft (10m)
Makes a low-branched tree with dense foliage. White flowers in spring have a sharp odor. Long, sharp thorns make this an impenetrable hedge and bird haven.

Poncirus trifoliata
HARDY ORANGE
☼ ◊ Z5–9 H9–5 ‡↔15ft 95m)
A vigorous, spiny plant that does best on acidic soils. Fragrant white flowers in spring. Fruits prolifically in warmer areas. Can be grown as a prickly hedge.

Malus hupehensis
TEA CRABAPPLE

☼ ◊ z5–8 H8–5 ↕↔50ft (15m)

Deep pink buds open to fragrant white flowers in mid- to late spring. Fast growing and vase-shaped when young, then spreads. Fireblight prone. Native to China.

MORE CHOICES

- *Cornus kousa* z5–8 H8–5
- *Cornus mas* z5–8 H8–5
- *Euscaphis japonica* z7–8 H8–7
- *Ilex opaca* 'Jersey Princess' z5–9 H9–5
- *Ilex opaca* 'Dan Fenton' z5–9 H9–5
- *Ilex opaca* 'Jersey Knight' z5–9 H9–5
- *Ilex opaca* 'Old Heavyberry' z5–9 H9–5
- *Juniperus virginiana* 'Emerald Sentinel' z3–9 H9–1
- *Prunus* spp. z4–10 H9–1
- *Sorbus aucuparia* 'Black Hawk' z3–7 H7–1
- *Sorbus aucuparia* 'Michred' z2–7 H7–1
- *Zizyphus jujuba* z5–10 H1–8

Malus cultivars
APPLE, CRABAPPLE

☼ ◊ z3–8 H8–1 ↕↔3–20ft (1–6m)

Most apples and crabapples require an extensive pest-control program to produce the sort of perfect fruit seen in markets. Organic methods are available.

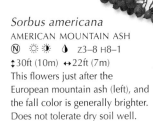

Maclura pomifera
OSAGE-ORANGE

Ⓝ ☼ ◊ z5–9 H9–5

↕50 ft (15m) ↔40ft (12m)

Fast-growing tree with low, rounded, irregular head and stiff, thorny branches. Deep orange-brown bark with wavy, deep ridges. Very tough and durable.

Asimina triloba
PAWPAW

Ⓝ ☼ ◊ z6–8 H8–6 ↕↔12ft (4m)

Both females and males are required to produce fruit. When fully ripe, the banana-flavored interior is yellow and custardlike. Has few pest problems.

Sorbus aucuparia
EUROPEAN MOUNTAIN ASH

☼ ◊ z2–7 H7–1 ↕↔50ft (15m)

Flat clusters of white flowers in spring. Fall foliage is reddish purple. Best grown on deep, acidic soils; may become chlorotic on alkaline ones. Many cultivars.

Sorbus americana
AMERICAN MOUNTAIN ASH

Ⓝ ☼ ☼ ◊ z3–8 H8–1

↕30ft (10m) ↔22ft (7m)

This flowers just after the European mountain ash (left), and the fall color is generally brighter. Does not tolerate dry soil well.

WOODY PLANTS

Shrubs with white or yellow fruit

Many of these shrubs have fruit that persist into winter and are very visible on a gray winter day. Plant them where the fruit can be enjoyed from the house, preferably against a dark background, such as an evergreen hedge. If snow usually falls early and lasts all winter, plant the yellow-fruited selections, since white fruit don't show up well against snow.

Viburnum opulus 'Xanthocarpum'
YELLOW-FRUITED CRANBERRY BUSH
☼ ☼ ◊ Z4–8 H8–1 ‡↔12ft (4m)
An arching shrub with dark green leaves that turn red in fall. Flowers in flat platelike heads, showy sterile flowers around the outside. Fruit last well into winter.

Symphoricarpos albus
SNOWBERRY
Ⓝ ☼ ☼ ◊ Z3–7 H7–1 ‡↔6ft (2m)
This shrub is tolerant of poor soils and pollution. Early summer flowers are white to pink and rich in nectar, making them attractive to butterflies.

Pyracantha 'Teton'
TETON FIRETHORN
☼ ☼ ◊ Z6–9 H9–5 ‡15ft (5m) ↔10ft (3m)
An upright, evergreen shrub with glossy, bright green foliage. Yellow-orange berries are freely produced in late summer. Makes a good barrier hedge or espalier.

MORE CHOICES

- *Cornus alba* Z2–8 H8–1
- *Daphne mezereum* f. *alba* Z5–8 H8–5
- *Ilex verticillata* f. *chrysocarpa* Z5–8 H8–5
- *Ilex glabra* 'Ivory Queen' Z5–9 H9–5

Chaenomeles speciosa 'Moerloosei'
MOERLOOSE FLOWERING QUINCE
☼ ☼ ◊ Z5–8 H8–5 ‡8ft (2.5m) ↔15ft (5m)
A rounded shrub with spiny branches that can also be used for a hedge or espalier. The fruit are yellow-green with black dots and can be used for jellies.

Symphoricarpos albus var. *laevigatus*
LARGE-FRUITED SNOWBERRY
Ⓝ ☼ ☼ ◊ Z3–7 H7–1 ‡↔6ft (2m)
Similar to the species but has larger leaves and slightly bigger fruit produced more prolifically. Coralberry (*S. orbiculatus*) has red fruits, better for snowy winters.

Shrubs with blue, black, or purple fruit

These fruit show up well against a pale background. Consider planting some of these near your foundations if your home has white, cream, or pale yellow paint or siding. On some species the fruit are the main attraction, and the shrubs can be planted as a specimen plant in a lawn or close to a path, where they can be admired as you walk by.

Viburnum farreri
FRAGRANT VIBURNUM
☼ ◊ Z6–8 H8–6 ↕↔10ft (3m)
Erect, deciduous shrub with leaves that turn red in fall. Highly fragrant flowers that open before the leaves can be damaged by a late frost; plant in a sheltered location.

MORE CHOICES

- *Aronia melanocarpa* 'Autumn Magic' Z3–8 H8–1
- *Aronia melanocarpa* 'Viking' Z4–9 H9–4
- *Callicarpa americana* Z5–9 H9–1
- *Callicarpa japonica* Z5–8 H12–3
- *Callicarpa dichotoma* 'Issai' Z5–8 H8–3
- *Callicarpa dichotoma* 'Early Amethyst' Z6–8 H8–3
- *Cornus alba* Z2–8 H8–1
- *Gaylussacia brachycera* Z3–7 H7–1
- *Ilex crenata* Z5–7 H7–5
- *Mahonia aquifolium* Z6–9 H9–6
- *Ribes aureum* Z5–8 H8–3
- *Vaccinium x* 'Northsky' Z3–7 H7–1
- *Vaccinium x* 'Top Hat' Z3–7 H7–1

Callicarpa bodinieri 'Profusion'
BODINIER BEAUTYBERRY
☼ ◑ ◊ Z4–7 H7–1 ↕10ft (3m) ↔8ft (2.5m)
An upright, deciduous shrub that needs a fertile soil to flower well. Small pink flowers open in midsummer. Grown mostly for the clusters of small, bright fruit.

Clerodendrum trichotomum
HARLEQUIN GLORYBOWER
☼ ◊ Z7–9 H9–7 ↕↔20ft (6m)
A small shrub best grown as a perennial at the northern end of its range. Flowering starts in summer and continues into fall; fruit and flowers often occur together.

Callicarpa dichotoma
PURPLE BEAUTYBERRY
☼ ◑ ◊ Z5–8 H8–7 ↕↔4ft (1.2m)
Slender, arching branches curve to the ground, and leaves grow in a single plane. Flowers and fruit are carried above the foliage in summer and fall.

Vaccinium corymbosum 'Herbert'
HIGHBUSH BLUEBERRY
Ⓝ ☼ ◑ ◊ ◔ Z4–8 H8–1 ↕↔5ft (1.5m)
Grow in sandy, organic soil. One of many named forms of blueberry selected for their fruit, 'Herbert' bears large berries of high quality. Red fall color.

Shrubs with red, pink, or orange fruit

Some of these shrubs have the most brilliantly colored fruit of all; on many of them, the fruit last through the winter, thereby giving added interest to the landscape. These fruit show up well against the snow and are a good choice where winters are long and snowy. The hard fruit of roses and some viburnums are softened by winter and attract birds in spring.

Viburnum setigerum
TEA VIBURNUM
☀ ◐ ◊ Z5–7 H7–5 ‡↔8ft (2.5m)
Upright growth with white flowers in flat-topped clusters in early summer. Foliage changes to reddish purple in fall. Can become leggy with time.

Viburnum dilatatum
LINDEN VIBURNUM
☀ ◐ ◊ Z5–8 H8–5 ‡10ft (3m) ↔6ft (2m)
Small, star-shaped white flowers are produced in late spring and early summer, preceding bright red berries. Dark green leaves turn bronze and red in fall.

Pyracantha 'Mohave'
MOHAVE FIRETHORN
☀ ◊ Z6–9 H9–6 ‡12ft (4m) ↔15ft (5m)
Upright grower with white flowers in spring giving way to the fruit, which ripen in early fall and hang on through winter. Resistant to scab and fireblight.

Hippophae rhamnoides
SEA BUCKTHORN
☀ ◊ Z3–8 H8–1 ‡↔20ft (6m)
A large deciduous shrub with small yellow flowers in spring, followed by fruit, but only on female plants. It is very salt-tolerant.

Arctostaphylos uva-ursi
BEARBERRY, KINNIKINICK
Ⓝ ☼ ◑ ◊ Z2–6 H6–1 ‡4in (10cm) ↔20in (50cm)
This mat-forming shrub can be grown as a groundcover or in a rock garden. White flowers are followed by round, bright scarlet fruit.

Cotoneaster horizontalis
ROCKSPRAY COTONEASTER
☼ ◊ Z4–7 H7–3 ‡↔5ft (1.5m)
A prostrate plant with congested branches that will follow the contours of a rock and flow down its face. Small white flowers in summer produce persistent fruit.

Cotoneaster adpressus
CREEPING COTONEASTER
☼ ◊ Z5–7 H7–1 ‡1ft (30cm) ↔6ft (2m)
A low, deciduous shrub that makes a goodground cover, because the branches root where they touch the soil. Fruits color early and persist into winter.

Ilex x meserveae 'Blue Princess'
BLUE PRINCESS HOLLY
☼ ◊ Z5–9 H9–5 ‡10ft (3m) ↔4ft (1.2m)
A hybrid holly with slightly prickly leaves. The spring flowers are small and white. A male pollinator is needed nearby for fruit set. Grows in most soils.

MORE CHOICES

- *Aronia arbutifolia* Z5–9 H9–4
- *Berberis thunbergii* cvs. Z4–8 H8–3
- *Cotoneaster apiculatus* Z4–8 H8–1
- *Daphne mezereum* Z5–8 H8–5
- *Euonymus americanus* Z6–9 H9–3
- *Lindera benzoin* Z4–9 H8–1
- *Lonicera* spp. Z4–10 H10–3
- *Nandina domestica* Z6–11 H12–4
- *Pyracantha* 'Rutgers' Z0–0
- *Rosa* spp. Z4–9 H9–3
- *Symphoricarpos x doorenbosii* 'Magic Berry' Z4–7 H7–1
- *Vaccinium macrocarpon* Z2–7 H7–1
- *Vaccinium vitis idaea* var. *minus* Z2–6 H6–1
- *Vaccinium vitis-idaea* Z2–6 H6–1
- *Viburnum opulus* Z3–8 H8–1
- *Viburnum plicatum* f. *tomentosum* Z4–8 H8–1
- *Viburnum sargentii* Z4–7 H7–4
- *Viburnum trilobum* Z2–7 H7–1

Ilex verticillata 'Red Sprite'
RED SPRITE WINTERBERRY
Ⓝ ☼ ◑ ◊ Z4–9 H9–1 ‡4ft (120cm) ↔3ft (1.5m)
A deciduous holly with nonprickly leaves, plus fruit that remain for a long time. Can grow in swamps but will also thrive in much drier locations.

Ilex verticillata
BLACK ALDER
Ⓝ ☼ ◊ Z5–8 H8–5 ‡↔15ft (5m)
Deciduous shrub bears bright green, saw-toothed leaves. White flowers are followed by fruit that may be dark red to scarlet, or sometimes orange or yellow.

WOODY PLANTS

Trees and shrubs with narrow or fringed foliage

Trees with broad leaves reduce the amount of light falling on the soil below and their leaves direct the rain outwards. Where the leaves are narrow or dissected, both light and rain can penetrate and the lawn or plants below thrive better. Narrow-leaved shrubs give a contrast of texture when interplanted with regular forms.

Rhamnus frangula 'Asplenifolia'
FERNLEAF BUCKTHORN

☼ ☼ ◐ ◖ Z3–8 H8–1 ↕↔15ft (5m)

A slow-growing, bushy, deciduous shrub that turns yellowish in fall. White flowers in summer give black berries. May become weedy from bird-spread seed.

Betula pendula 'Dalecarlica'
WEEPING BIRCH

☼ ☼ ◐ Z2–7 H7–1 ↕80ft (24m) ↔30ft (9m)

Both branches and leaves weep, making a very graceful statement. Yellow-green to yellow fall color. Transplant in spring, and prune in summer or fall.

Quercus phellos
WILLOW OAK

Ⓝ ☼ ☼ ◐ Z6–9 H9–3 ↕70ft (20m) ↔50ft (15m)

Fast-growing, with a cone-shaped growth habit. Smooth gray bark ages with shallow ridges. In warmer areas, dead leaves hang on through winter.

Sambucus racemosa 'Plumosa Aurea'
CUTLEAF GOLDEN ELDER

☼ ◐ Z3–7 H7–1 ↕↔10ft (3m)

Bushy shrub with arching shoots. Bears clusters of star-shaped flowers in mid-spring, followed by round red berries in summer.

Acer japonicum 'Aconitifolium'
FULLMOON MAPLE

☼ ◐ Z5–7 H7–5 ↕↔30ft (10m)

Small red flowers appear in early spring before the leaves. Leaves are very divided and sharply toothed on the edges. One of the best trees for red fall color.

Hippophae rhamnoides
SEA BUCKTHORN
☼ ◊ Z3–8 H8–1 ↕↔20ft (6m)
This grows best in a poor, very well drained soil. The yellow flowers open in early spring, before the leaves. Berries are produced on female plants only.

Fagus sylvatica 'Asplenifolia'
ASPLENIFOLIA EUROPEAN BEECH
☼ ☀ ◊ ◊ Z5–7 H7–5 ↕80ft (24m) ↔50 ft (15m)
Deeply cut, almost feathery foliage turns golden brown in fall. A fine specimen tree that withstands heavy pruning if needed to correct growth faults.

Stephanandra incisa 'Crispa'
LACE SHRUB
☼ ☀ ◊ ◊ Z3–8 H8–4 ↕2ft (60cm) ↔10ft (3m)
A low, spreading deciduous shrub that makes a good ground cover. Best in neutral to acidic soils. Leaves turn orange to purple in fall. Flowers in early summer.

Rhus glabra 'Laciniata'
CUTLEAF SMOOTH SUMAC
Ⓝ ☼ ◊ Z2–8 H9–3 ↕↔8ft (2.5m)
A suckering, deciduous shrub, that forms a dense colony of shoots and spreads slowly. The green flowers give red conelike fruit. Brilliant red in fall.

MORE CHOICES

- *Acer palmatum* 'Seiryu' Z5–8 H8–2
- *Acer palmatum* 'Tamukeyama' Z5–8 H8–2
- *Rhus* x 'Red Autumn Lace' Z4–9 H9–5
- *Salix babylonica* 'Crispa' Z6–8 H9–6
- *Sambucus canadensis* 'Acutiloba' Z4–9 H9–1
- *Sambucus nigra* 'Laciniata' Z5–6 H8–6
- *Spiraea* x *bumalda* 'Dolchica' Z3–9 H9–1
- *Stephanandra incisa* 'Crispa' Z3–8 H9–4
- *Syringa lacianata* Z4–8 H8–1
- *Vitex negundo* 'Incisa' Z6–9 H9–5

Acer palmatum dissectum 'Inabe Shidare'
INABE SHIDARE JAPANESE MAPLE
☼ ☀ ◊ Z6–8 H8–6 ↕6ft (2m) ↔10ft (3m)
Mound-forming shrub with arching shoots bears finely cut red-purple leaves that turn gold in fall. Produces tiny purple-red flowers in late summer.

Trees and shrubs with silver or blue foliage

Silver or bluish foliage looks cool, especially during the hot days of mid-summer. It also makes a good contrast for plants with dark red or purple foliage, showing both off to advantage, and forms a good backdrop for brightly colored flowers. Use this foliage color with moderation, because it has a greater visual impact than when overused.

Salix exigua
COYOTE WILLOW

☼ ◑ Z4–6 Hx–x ‡12ft (4m) ↔15ft (5m)

Grayish yellow catkins open in spring with the leaves, which are narrow, with toothed margins, and keep their gray color all summer. Grows well in sandy soils.

Elaeagnus angustifolia
OLEASTER

☼ ◑ Z2–8 H8–1 ‡↔20ft (6m)

Fragrant, creamy yellow flowers appear in summer, followed by edible yellow fruit. Branches are red-tinted with silvery scales. Deciduous.

Fothergilla gardenii 'Blue Mist'
BLUE MIST DWARF FOTHERGILLA

Ⓝ ☼ ◐ ● pH Z4–8 H8–1 ‡↔3ft (1m)

A bushy, deciduous shrub with blue-green foliage that turns red, orange, and yellow in fall. The fragrant flowers open in spring, before the leaves.

Hippophae rhamnoides
SEA BUCKTHORN

☼ ◑ Z3–8 H8–1 ‡↔20ft (6m)

A deciduous shrub with leaves that have silvery scales on both surfaces. Tiny yellow flowers produce fruit on female plants. A male plant is needed to produce them.

Caryopteris x clandonensis 'Arthur Simmonds'
BLUE MIST SHRUB

☼ ◐ ◊ Z7–9 H9–1 ↕3ft (1m) ↔5ft (1.5m)

Aromatic, gray-green foliage is silvery beneath. Rounded and deciduous shrub. Flowers late summer/ early fall.

MORE CHOICES

- *Calluna vulgaris* 'Silver Knight' Z5–7 H7–5
- *Elaeagnus commutata* Z2–6 H6–1
- *Hamamelis vernalis* Z4–8 H8–1
- *Salix elaeagnos* Z4–7 H7–1
- *Symphoricarpos albus* Z3–7 H7–1

Buddleja davidii 'Lochinch'
LOCHINCH BUTTERFLY BUSH

☼ ◊ Z6–9 H9–6 ↕8ft (2.5m) ↔10ft (3m)

A hybrid, with the common *B. davidii* as one parent. The fragrant summer flower spikes are up to 12in. (30cm) long. Flowers on new growth, so cut back hard in spring.

Zenobia pulverulenta
DUSTY BLUE HONEYCUPS

Ⓝ ☼ ◊ Z5–8 H8–5 ↕6ft (2m) ↔5ft (1.5m)

Pendent, bell-shaped, fragrant white flowers bloom in early to midsummer. Blue-green to dark green leaves have a bluish white underside when young.

Ilex x meserveae 'Blue Princess'
BLUE PRINCESS HOLLY

☼ ◊ Z5–9 H9–5 ↕10ft (3m) ↔4ft (1.2m)

Evergreen, shiny, blue-green foliage on a rounded shrub, with prickly leaves like those of English holly. Small white flowers in spring. Fruit persist into winter.

Ilex x meserveae 'Blue Prince'
BLUE PRINCE HOLLY

☼ ◊ Z5–9 H9–5 ↕15ft (5m) ↔12ft (4m)

Like all hollies, these hybrids have male and female flowers on separate plants. One male plant is needed for every 6–8 females to facilitate fruit set.

WOODY PLANTS

Shrubs with fragrant flowers

While fragrance in the garden is most enjoyable, not everyone reacts to floral scents in the same way. A shrub that is strongly scented for one may seem nearly without perfume for another. Before making a final decision on which to plant, try to find these shrubs in flower in a local nursery, garden center, or park to be sure their scent is one you can easily detect.

Viburnum carlesii
KOREAN SPICE VIBURNUM

☼ ◊ Z5–8 H8–5 ↕↔5ft (1.5m)

Rounded, upright shrub blooms in midspring. Foliage turns dark red in fall. Best on slightly acidic soil. 'Compactum' grows to only half the size indicated. 'Aurora' has red buds, pink flowers, and stronger fragrance.

Lonicera fragrantissima
WINTER HONEYSUCKLE

☼ ☼ ◊ Z4–8 H8–3 ↕6ft (2m) ↔12ft (4m)

Very fragrant, short-tubed flowers are produced during winter and early spring and are welcomed by bees. Berries are dull red and usually snatched by birds.

Viburnum x bodnantense 'Dawn'
DAWN VIBURNUM

☼ ◊ Z7–8 H8–7 ↕↔10ft (3m)

Often flowering during mild winter spells, branches can be cut and forced indoors. Flower buds may be damaged by late frosts, so plant in a protected site at the northern limits of its hardiness.

Buddleja davidii 'Black Knight'
BLACK KNIGHT BUTTERFLY BUSH

☼ ◊ Z6–9 H9–1 ↕10ft (3m) ↔15ft (5m)

Bears conical clusters of fragrant, dark purple flowers in summer. Attracts butterflies. Useful as an accent plant. Fast grower.

Viburnum farreri
FRAGRANT VIBURNUM

☼ ◊ Z6–8 H8–6 ↕↔10ft (3m)

An upright shrub that spreads slowly by suckers, this flowers in early spring and can also be forced indoors. Foliage has a bronzy sheen and turns maroon in fall. Adaptable to most soils, but best in a protected location.

Chimonanthus praecox
WINTERSWEET
☼ ◊ Z7–9 H9–7
↕8ft (2.5m) ↔10ft (3m)
In winter, this shrub produces fragrant, pendent, cup-shaped flowers. Leaves are lance shaped and glossy, arranged in opposite pairs.

Clethra alnifolia
SUMMERSWEET
Ⓝ ☼ ● ᵖᴴ Z3–9 H9–1 ↕↔8ft (2.5m)
Fragrant, bell-shaped white flowers form elegant spires. An upright shrub, it readily increases by suckering. Leaves turn yellow in fall.

Daphne mezereum
FEBRUARY DAPHNE
☼ ◊ Z5–8 H8–5 ↕↔5ft (1.5m)
Deciduous in the north, but semi-evergreen in the south, this erect shrub flowers in early spring. The bright red, poisonous berries, appear in late summer.

Daphne x burkwoodii 'Carol Mackie'
CAROL MACKIE DAPHNE
☼ ☼ ◊ Z5–8 H8–4 ↕↔3–5ft (1–1.5m)
Semi-evergreen, retaining its leaves until the end of winter. New foliage is yellow-edged at first, becoming white later. The flowers open in early summer.

MORE CHOICES

- *Abelia chinensis* Z5–9 H12–6
- *Calycanthus floridus* Z5–9 H9–1
- *Clerodendrum trichotomum* v. *fargesii* Z7–9 H9–7
- *Daphne caucasica* Z6–8 H8–6
- *Elaeagnus commutata* Z2–6 H6–1
- *Fothergilla major* Z4–8 H9–2
- *Hamamelis mollis* 'Pallida' Z5–9 H9–5
- *Hamamelis vernalis* Z4–8 H8–1
- *Hamamelis* x *intermedia* 'Arnold Promise' Z5–9 H9–1
- *Heptacodium miconioides* Z5–9 H9–4
- *Hippophae rhamnoides* Z3–8 H8–1
- *Magnolia grandiflora* 'Bracken's Brown Beauty' Z5–9 H9–3
- *Magnolia grandiflora* 'Little Gem' Z7–9 H9–3
- *Philadelphus coronarius* Z4–9 H9–4
- *Viburnum* x *juddii* Z5–9 H9–5
- *Viburnum* x 'Mohawk' Z4–8 H8–1

Daphne odora 'Aureomargnata'
WINTER DAPHNE
☼ ◊ Z7–9 H9–7 ↕↔5ft (1.5m)
Very fragrant flowers blossom from midwinter to early spring and followed by fleshy red fruit. Grow in a sheltered site where marginally hardy.

WOODY PLANTS

WOODY PLANTS

Rhododendron schlippenbachii
ROYAL AZALEA

☀ ◐ ◌ Z5–8 H8–5 ↕↔8ft (2.5m)

Deciduous, spring flowering shrub with buds that may be damaged by late frosts. New leaves are tinted purple and turn orange to crimson in fall if grown in sun. Grows well in neutral soils.

Pterostyrax hispida
EPAULETTE TREE

☀ ◐ ◌ Z5–8 H8–5 ↕50ft (15m) ↔40ft (12m)

The midsummer flowers produce attractive, ribbed fruits, and the bark is peeling and scented. Plant in deep, slightly acidic soil. Can also be grown as a tree.

Corylopsis pauciflora
BUTTERCUP WINTER HAZEL

☀ ◌◌◌ ᵖᴴ Z3–9 H9–1 ↕ 5ft (1.5m) ↔8ft (2.5m)

Fragrant flowers are produced in pendent clusters in midspring. This dense, bushy shrub has bright green leaves with bristlelike teeth.

Philadelphus x *lemoinei* 'Belle Etoile'
BELLE ETOILE MOCK ORANGE

☀ ◐ ◌ Z5–8 H8–5 ↕4ft (1.2m) ↔8ft (2.5m)

Small, extremely fragrant flowers are produced in clusters of 3–5 in early or midsummer. Upright or slightly arching; it makes a good specimen or addition to a shrub border.

Fothergilla major
LARGE WITCH ALDER

Ⓝ ☀ ◐ ◌ ᵖᴴ Z4–8 H9–2 ↕↔10ft (3m)

A multistemmed, erect shrub with dark green leaves that turn yellow, orange, and bright red in fall, with all three colors present at the same time. It may become chlorotic if grown on even slightly alkaline soils. Flowers open in spring.

Abeliophyllum distichum
WHITE FORSYTHIA, KOREAN ABELIA LEAF

☀ ◌ Z5–9 H9–1

↕↔4ft (1.2m)

Flowers bloom in late winter or early spring but may be damaged by hard frosts. Grows well when provided the shelter and warmth of a wall. Native to Korea.

Syringa vulgaris 'Madame Lemoine'
MADAME LEMOINE LILAC

☼ ◊ Z4–8 H8–1 ↕↔22ft (7m)

A very popular double-flowered lilac with creamy yellow buds. Plant where there is good air circulation to reduce the chance of mildew.

Syringa vulgaris 'Andenken an Ludwig Späth'
LUDWIG SPÄTH LILAC

☼ ◊ Z4–8 H8–1 ↕↔15ft (5m)

This cultivar has been used in breeding many modern hybrids. Often incorrectly labeled as Ludwig Spaeth. Introduced by Späth Nurseries in Germany in 1883.

Syringa vulgaris 'Charles Joly'
CHARLES JOLY LILAC

☼ ◊ ◑ Z4–8 H8–1 ↕↔22ft (7m)

Produces conical clusters of sweetly scented, dark purple-red, double flowers. Requires little pruning, although it may grow to be treelike.

Rhododendron mucronulatum
SNOW AZALEA

☼ ◑ ❀ Z5–8 H8–5 ↕↔4–5ft (1.2–1.5m)

A spreading, semi-evergreen shrub with fragrant flowers in late spring. Foliage is grayish green. Flower color varies from white to pink, so try to see this in flower before purchase.

WOODY PLANTS

Shrubs with blue or purple flowers

Shrubs with blue or purple flowers are in the minority, and many are not readily available, so this makes them all the more desirable. If you are growing the hydrangeas presented here, you will need to treat the soil with aluminum sulfate or similar acidifier each spring to make it acidic, or the flowers may be pink or even a muddy gray.

Daphne genkwa
LILAC DAPHNE

☼ ◊ Z6–9 H9–6 ↕5ft (1.5m)

The flowers open in spring, before the leaves, but have no fragrance. It needs a soil rich in organic matter and with perfect drainage. It must not dry out in summer.

Buddleja davidii 'Empire Blue'
EMPIRE BLUE BUTTERFLY BUSH

☼ ◊ Z6–9 H9–1 ↕10ft (3m) ↔15ft (5m)

Butterfly bush blooms in summer on the new growth produced that year. Cut back hard in early spring to encourage new shoots and to rejuvenate plants.

Buddleja davidii var. nanhoensis 'Nanho Blue'
NANHO BLUE BUTTERFLY BUSH

☼ ◊ Z5–8 H10–4 ↕↔4–5ft (1.2–1.5m)

Grows to half the size of the species but should be treated in the same way. This cultivar tends to revert to the mauve of the variety. Remove reverted shoots.

MORE CHOICES

- *Amorpha fruticosa* Z2–8 H8–1
- *Buddleja davidii* 'Dartmoor' Z5–9 H9–2
- *Caryopteris* x *clandonensis* 'Dark Knight' Z6–9 H9–1
- *Enkianthus perulatus* 'J.L. Pennock' Z5–7
- *Hibiscus syriacus* 'Blue Bird' Z5–9 H9–5
- *Hydrangea macrophylla* 'Blaumeise' Z0 H9–6

Vitex agnus-castus
CHASTE TREE

☼ ◊ Z6–9 H9–6 ↕↔8ft (2.5m)

Fragrant flowers appear through much of summer. Deadhead to encourage repeat bloom. Prefers hot weather. Native to southern Europe and western Asia.

Buddleja davidii 'Black Knight'
BLACK KNIGHT BUTTERFLY BUSH

☼ ◊ Z6–9 H10–4 ↕10ft (3m) ↔15ft (5m)

Bears conical clusters of fragrant, dark purple flowers in summer. Attracts butterflies. Useful as an accent plant. Fast grower. Same culture as other *B. davidii*.

Buddleja davidii 'Harlequin'
HARLEQUIN VARIEGATED BUTTERFLY BUSH

☼ ◊ Z6–9 H10–4 ↕↔20ft (6m)

Expanding leaves are yellow, old leaves almost white. Less vigorous and smaller than many butterfly bushes. Flowers can be cut, but they do not last long.

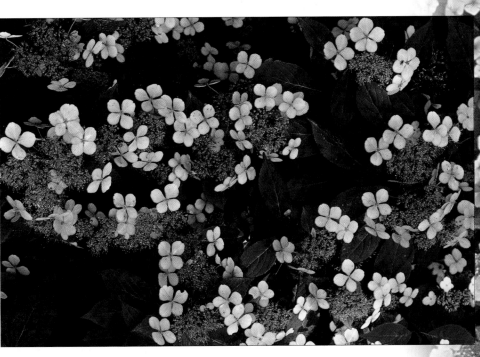

MORE CHOICES

- *Hydrangea macrophylla* 'Blue Wave'
  z6–9 H9–6
- *Hydrangea macrophylla* 'Nikko Blue'
  z6–9 H9–6
- *Hydrangea serrata* 'Blue Billow' z5–8 H8–3
- *Hydrangea serrata* 'Bluebird' z6–9 H9–6
- *Hydrangea serrata* 'Blue Deckle' z5–8 H8–3
- *Syringa vulgaris* 'President Lincoln'
  z4–8 H8–1

Hydrangea serrata 'Blue Bird'
BLUE BIRD LACECAP HYDRANGEA
☼ ☀ ◊ z6–9 H10–8 ‡↔4ft (1.2m)
Flowers, which are most colorful in acidic soils,
appear from summer to fall. Dark green leaves take on
red shades in fall.

Caryopteris x *clandonensis* 'Dark Night'
DARK NIGHT BLUE MIST SHRUB
☼ ☀ ◊ z6–9 H9–2 ‡3ft (1m) ↔5ft (1.5m)
Bears fragrant, small, dark purple-blue flowers
Compact, mounding shrub. Also grown for its silvery
gray foliage. Perfect for a mixed or shrub border.

Hydrangea macrophylla 'Blue Wave'
BLUE WAVE LACECAP HYDRANGEA
☼ ☀ ◊◊ z6–9 H9–2 ‡6ft (1m) ↔8ft (2.5m)
Sterile flowers in the center of the flowerhead are
surrounded by the showier fertile flowers. Color varies
in intensity, depending on soil pH.

Lespedeza thunbergii
BUSHCLOVER
☼ ◊ z6–8 H8–6 ‡6ft (2m) ↔10ft (3m)
A fast-growing shrub that quickly recovers from winter
injury at the northern limits of hardiness. Flowers
appear on arching stems in late summer.

Shrubs with red or pink flowers

Red and bright pink are hot colors that seem to leap out at you, so shrubs with these flower colors need careful placement if they are not to overpower other nearby plants. As the pink shade decreases in intensity, the impact lessens until, with the very pale pinks, they will blend with and enhance many other shades.

Hydrangea 'Preziosa'
PREZIOSA PINK HYDRANGEA
☼ ☽ ◊ Z5–8 H8–3 ↕↔5ft (1.5m)
A handsome, rounded shrub with purple-tinged stems and new foliage also tinted purple. The late summer flowers are purple to blue on acidic soils.

MORE CHOICES

- *Abelia* x *grandiflora* 'Edward Goucher' Z8–11 H12–8
- *Abeliophyllum distichum* 'Rosea' Z5–9 H9–1
- *Buddleja davidii* 'Dubonnet' Z5–9 H10–4
- *Camellia japonica* 'Betty Sette' Z6–9 H8–7
- *Chaenomeles speciosa* 'Cameo' Z5–9 H9–1
- *Cotoneaster horizontalis* Z4–7 H7–3
- *Daphne* x *burkwoodii* Z4–8 H9–2

Clethra alnifolia 'Ruby Spice'
RUBY SPICE SUMMERSWEET
Ⓝ ☼ ☽ ● Z3–9 H9–1 ↕↔6–8ft (2–2.5m)
This cultivar has pink flowers; the species' often have a pink tinge. Fragrant flowers appear from late summer to early fall. Tolerant of seaside conditions.

Hydrangea paniculata 'Pink Diamond'
PINK DIAMOND PANICLE HYDRANGEA
☼ ☽ ◊ Z4–8 H8–1 ↕10–22ft (3–7m) ↔8ft (2.5m)
A tough plant that is pollution-tolerant, thrives in cities, and will grow in most soils. The flowers open a creamy white, turn pink, and eventually go almost red.

Viburnum farreri
FRAGRANT VIBURNUM
☼ ◊ Z6–8 H8–6 ↕↔10ft (3m)
Flowering at the end of winter, this needs a sheltered location to prevent the new flowers from being damaged by frost. Can be forced into bloom indoors.

Enkianthus cernuus var. *rubens*
RED ENKIANTHUS
☼ ◊ pH Z6–8 H8–6 ↕↔10ft (3m)
Blossoms in late spring on a dense shrub with leaves that are tinged purple in summer and turn dark red-purple in fall. Dislikes dry soils. Native to Japan.

Buddleja 'Pink Delight'
PINK DELIGHT BUTTERFLY BUSH
☼ ☽ ◊ Z6–9 H9–1 ↕8ft (2.5m) ↔6ft (2m)
Produces larger flower spikes and deeper green leaves than the species. Orange-eyed flowers bloom from summer to fall. Prefers fertile soil.

Calluna vulgaris cultivars
SCOTCH HEATHER
☀ ◊ ᵖᴴ Z5–7
H7–5 ‡3–32in (8cm-80cm) ↔18in (45cm)
Heather cultivars flower from midsummer to late fall. Some have yellow or bronze foliage.

Rhododendron 'Olga Mezitt'
OLGA MEZITT RHODODENDRON
☀ ◊ ᵖᴴ Z4–8 H8–1 ‡4ft (1.2m) ↔5–6ft (1.5–2m)
Evergreen leaves turn a bronzy red in fall; the color persists throughout winter. The small, dense flowerheads are freely produced in late spring.

Calluna vulgaris 'Firefly'
FIREFLY SCOTCH HEATHER
☀ ◊ ᵖᴴ Z5–7 H7–5 ‡to 24 in (60cm) ↔20in (50cm)
Grow this in a poor, acidic soil with good drainage; heathers do not thrive in wet soils. One of many named varieties of heather, with flowers from white to dark red.

Rhododendron 'Solidarity'
SOLIDARITY RHODODENDRON
☀ ◊ ᵖᴴ Z5–9 H9–5 ‡3ft (1m) ↔3–4ft (1–1.2m)
A dense, rounded shrub with leaves that are white on the undersides. Like most rhododendrons, this is shallow-rooted and needs to be kept well watered in summer.

MORE CHOICES

- *Daphne cneorum* Z5–7 H7–5
- *Hydrangea macrophylla* 'Forever Pink' Z6–9 H9–3
- *Kalmia latifolia* 'Ostbo Red' Z5–9 H9–5
- *Lonicera tatarica* 'Arnold Red' Z3–9 H9–1
- *Spiraea japoica* 'Anthony Waterer' Z3–9 H9–1
- *Syringa microphylla* 'Superba' Z5–8 H8–5
- *Tamarix ramosissima* 'Pink Cascade' Z3–8 H8–1
- *Weigela florida* 'Bristol Ruby' Z4–9 H9–1

Rhododendron yakushimanum
YAKU RHODODENDRON
☀ ◊◊ ᵖᴴ Z5–9 H9–5 ‡↔3ft (1m)
A compact, rounded evergreen plant with leaves that are covered with a felty white down on the undersides. Native to Japan, this is one parent of many hybrids.

Rhododendron yedoense var. poukhanense
KOREAN AZALEA
☀ ◊◊ ᵖᴴ Z5–9 H9–5 ‡3–6ft (1–2m) ↔6ft (2m)
A deciduous, spreading shrub that can form a low mound. The dark green leaves turn orange to red in fall. Flowers occur in small clusters in late spring.

WOODY PLANTS

Shrubs with white flowers

There are more shrubs with white flowers than any other color. White gardens or borders are very popular, and the wide range of growth habits, flower form, and bloom time available in these shrubs makes the design process relatively simple. Using these as a background for white-flowered perennials, bulbs, and annuals will create a unified theme garden.

Hydrangea quercifolia 'Snow flake'
SNOW FLAKE OAKLEAF HYDRANGEA
Ⓝ ☼ ◐ ◊ Z5–9 H9–1 ‡6ft (2m) ↔8ft (2.5m)
A mounded, deciduous shrub with foliage that turns bronze in fall and attractive, peeling bark in winter. The late-summer flowers turn pink as they age.

Clerodendrum trichotomum
HARLEQUIN GLORYBOWER
☼ ◊ Z7–9 H9–7 ‡↔10ft (3m)
Fragrant flowers are produced from midsummer onward, and fruit and flowers are often present together. Cut back to live wood each spring.

Exochorda x macrantha 'The Bride'
THE BRIDE PEARLBUSH
☼ ☼ ◊ Z5–9 H9–5 ‡6ft (2m) ↔10ft (3m)
In late spring and early summer, arching branches form a mound of abundant white flowers and dense, dark green leaves.

Deutzia crenata var. nakaiana 'Nikko'
NIKKO DEUTZIA
☼ ◊ Z4–8 H8–1 ‡24in (60cm) ↔4ft (1.2m)
A dwarf selection that does well on a large rock garden or as a groundcover. The leaves turn burgundy red in fall.

Deutzia gracilis
SLENDER DEUTZIA
☼ ◊ Z5–8 H8–1 ‡↔5ft (1.5m)
A bushy, deciduous shrub that grows in most soils. Makes a good informal hedge. Abundant, fragrant flowers are borne from spring into summer.

Pieris japonica 'White Cascade'
WHITE CASCADE LILY-OF-THE-VALLEY BUSH

☼ ◐ ◊ pH Z6–8 H8–5 ↕↔20ft (6m)

A compact, evergreen shrub with bronze new foliage. Needs soil high in organic matter. The slightly fragrant flowers open in spring and last for several weeks.

Fothergilla major
LARGE WITCH ALDER

Ⓝ ☼ ◐ ◊ pH Z4–8 H9–2 ↕↔10ft (3m)

The fragrant flowers open in spring, and summer foliage is a dark, glossy green, turning yellow to scarlet in fall. An underused shrub.

Potentilla fruticosa 'Abbotswood'
ABBOTSWOOD SHRUBBY CINQUEFOIL

Ⓝ ☼ ◊ Z3–7 H7–1 ↕30in (75cm) ↔4ft (1.2m)

Dark blue-green leaves consist of five leaflets. Relatively large, saucer-shaped flowers are borne throughout summer and fall.

MORE CHOICES

- *Aesculus parviflora* v. *serotina* Z5–9 H9–4
- *Camellia* 'Snow Flurry' Z6–10 H8–7
- *Ceanothus americanus* Z4–8 H8–1
- *Clerodendrum trichotomum* Z7–9 H9–7
- *Daphne caucasica* Z6–8 H8–6
- *Daphne mezereum* Z5–8 H8–5
- *Exochorda racemosa* Z5–9 H9–5
- *Hydrangea arborescens* 'Annabelle' Z4–9 H9–1
- *Hydrangea paniculata* 'Tardiva' Z4–8 H8–1
- *Hydrangea quercifolia* 'Snowflake' Z5–9 H9–1
- *Osmanthus heterophyllus* Z7–9 H9–4
- *Philadelphus coronarius* Z4–9 H9–4
- *Philadelphus* x *lemoinei* 'Sybille' Z5–8 H8–5
- *Philadelphus* x *virginalis* 'Minnesota Snowflake' Z4–7 H7–1

Philadelphus x lemoinei 'Belle Etoile'
BELLE ETOILE MOCK ORANGE

☼ ◐ ◊ Z5–8 H8–1 ↕4ft (1.2m) ↔8ft (2.5m)

Small, extremely fragrant flowers are produced in clusters of 3–5 in early or midsummer. Upright or slightly arching; makes a good shrub border addition.

Fothergilla 'Mt. Airy'
MT. AIRY FOTHERGILLA

Ⓝ ☼ ◊ pH Z5–8 H8–1 ↕5ft (1.5m) ↔4ft (1.2m)

A free-flowering variety with excellent orange fall color. It increases by suckers. A hybrid introduced by the Mount Airy Arboretum, Cincinnati, OH.

Spiraea nipponica 'Snowmound'
SNOWMOUND SPIREA

☼ ◊ Z4–8 H8–1 ↕↔4ft (1.2m)

Flowers appear in midsummer. Fast-growing and spreading, this deciduous shrub prefers fertile soil. Also known as *S. nipponica* var. *tosaensis*.

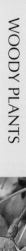

Buddleia davidii 'White Ball'
WHITE BALL BUTTERFLY BUSH
Z5–9 H9–3 ↕↔3ft (1m)
A new miniature variety from Holland that flowers on the current growth and should be cut back in spring. The flowers appear in late summer and fall.

Hibiscus syriacus 'Diana'
DIANA ROSE OF SHARON
Z5–9 H9–5 ↕10ft (3m) ↔6ft (2m)
This grows best in soils rich in organic matter. Cut back by half in spring for summer blooms, or almost to the ground for larger, later flowers.

Buddleja davidii 'White Profusion'
WHITE PROFUSION BUTTERFLY BUSH
Z6–9 H10–4 ↕10ft (3m) ↔15ft (5m)
Long spikes of fragrant flowers attract butterflies and bees. Best planted in groups in a border. Has no serious pests. Transplants easily and can self-sow profusely.

Stachyurus praecox
EARLY SPIKETAIL
pH Z6–8 H8–6 ↕3–12ft (1–4m) ↔10ft (3m)
An upright, arching, deciduous shrub that needs shelter from cold winds. The 4in. (10cm.) clusters of flowers open in late winter and early spring.

Clethra alnifolia
SUMMERSWEET
(N) pH Z3–9 H9–1 ↕24–36in (60–90cm) ↔8ft (2.5m)
Fragrant summer flowers last for several weeks and appear on new growth. An upright, deciduous shrub.

Cotoneaster dammeri
BEARBERRY COTONEASTER

☼ ◊ Z5–8 H8–3 ↕8in
(20cm) ↔6ft (2m)

A low groundcover plant that makes a dense carpet of evergreen foliage turning dull purple in winter. The early summer flowers produce persistent red berries.

MORE CHOICES

- *Physocarpus opulifolius* Z3–7 H7–1
- *Pieris japonica* 'White Cascade' Z6–8 H8–5
- *Potentilla fruticosa* 'Abbotswood'
  Z3–7 H7–1
- *Spiraea nipponica* 'Snowmound'
  Z4–8 H11–1
- *Stachyurus praecox* Z7–9 H9–7
- *Staphylea trifolia* Z3–8 H8–1
- *Viburnum plicatum* f. *tomentosum*
  Z4–8 H8–1

Syringa vulgaris 'Madame Lemoine'
MADAME LEMOINE LILAC

☼ ◊ Z6–9 H10–7 Z4–8 H8–1 ↕↔22ft (7m)

An old variety introduced in France in 1890, but still very popular and readily available. An exceptionally fragrant variety, not as prone to suckering as many.

Abeliophyllum distichum
WHITE FORSYTHIA, KOREAN ABELIA LEAF

☼ ◊ Z5–9 H9–1 ↕↔4ft (1.2m)

Flowers bloom in late winter or early spring but may be damaged by hard frosts. Grows well when provided the shelter and warmth of a wall. Native to Korea.

Itea virginica
VIRGINIA SWEETSPIRE

Ⓝ ☼ ◗ Z6–9 H10–7 ↕5–10ft
(1.5–3m) ↔5ft (1.5m)

Fragrant white flowers bloom in dense, elongated clusters. Open shrub grows upright, then arching. Dark green leaves turn red to purple in fall.

Magnolia stellata
STAR MAGNOLIA

☼ ◑ ◊ Z5–9 H9–5 ↕10ft (3m) ↔12ft (4m)

A bushy, deciduous shrub that needs protection from winter winds and late frosts. The furry flower buds open before the leaves. Many cultivars and hybrids are available.

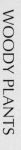

WOODY PLANTS

Shrubs with yellow flowers

Yellow is truly a happy color; it lifts our spirits and makes us feel good.
Planting groups of yellow-flowered shrubs helps make the garden a place
of relaxation and a place to unwind at the end of the day. Yellow is one
of the basic (primary) colors, and yellow flowers blend well with, and
complement, blooms of other shades.

Hypericum frondosum
GOLDEN ST. JOHN'S WORT
Ⓝ ☼ ☼ ◐ ◊ Z4–8 H8–1 ↕↔to 4ft (1.2m)
An upright shrub with peeling reddish bark on stiff
branches. The bright flowers open from mid- to late
summer. 'Sunburst' is a lower-growing form.

Hypericum 'Hidcote'
HIDCOTE ST. JOHN'S WORT
☼ ◐ ◊ Z6–9 H9–6 ↕↔5ft (1.5m)
Flowers from midsummer to early autumn This dense
and bushy hybrid bears evergreen to semi-evergreen
foliage and prefers moderately fertile soil.

Berberis verruculosa
WARTY BARBERRY
☼ ☼ ◐ ◊ Z6–9 H9–4 ↕↔5ft (1.5m)
A compact, slow-growing, evergreen shrub with rough,
warty stems and leaves that are white beneath. Late
spring flowers produce dark purple fruits.

Buddleja x weyeriana 'Honeycomb'
HONEYCOMB WEYER BUTTERFLY BUSH
☼ ◊ Z5–9 H9–2 ↕↔12 (4m)
Spreading, deciduous plant with long, arching shoots.
Fragrant flowers bloom from summer into fall on the
ends of the branchlets. 'Golden Glow' has lilac tints.

Corylopsis pauciflora
BUTTERCUP WINTER HAZEL
☼ ◊ ◐ ◑ ⬗ Z3–9 H9–1 ↕5ft (1.5m) ↔8ft (2.5m)
Dense and bushy. Young bronze leaves turn bright
green as they mature. Bears fragrant flowers in
profusion from early to midspring.

Cytisus x *praecox* 'Allgold'
ALLGOLD WARMINSTER BROOM
☼ ◊ Z6–9 H9–1 ↕4ft (1.2m) ↔5ft (1.5m)
Late spring flowers, deeper yellow than the species,
have an unpleasant odor. Effective in large groups to
light up the landscape.

MORE CHOICES

- *Berberis* x *gladwynensis* 'William Penn'
  Z6–9 H9–4
- *Calycanthus floridus* 'Athens' Z4–9 H8–4
- *Corylopsis spicata* Z5–8 H8–5
- *Diervilla sessilifolia* Z4–8 H8–1
- *Forsythia* 'Sunrise' Z4–9 H9–1
- *Hypericum calycinum* Z5–9 H9–4
- *Hypericum prolificum* Z5–8 H8–5
- *Mahonia bealei* Z5–8 H8–3
- *Mahonia* x *media* Z8–9 H9–8
- *Syringa vulgaris* 'Primrose' Z3–8 H8–3

Mahonia aquifolium
OREGON GRAPE HOLLY
Ⓝ ☼ ◊ Z6–9 H9–6 ↕↔5ft (1.5m)
This slow-growing, upright, evergreen shrub turns
purplish bronze in fall. Blue-black, wax-coated berries
ripen in early fall and hang on through winter.

Forsythia 'Northern Gold'
NORTHERN GOLD FORSYTHIA
☼ ☀ ◊ Z3–9 H9–1 ↕8ft (2.5m) ↔7ft (2.2m)
This is a good choice for the northern parts of the
Northeast, where forsythia blooms only below the
snowline. Flower buds are hardy to at least –25°F (-29°C).

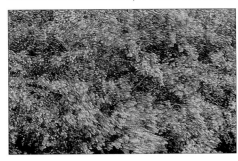

Caragana arborescens
SIBERIAN PEA SHRUB
☼ ◊ Z2–8 H8–1 ↕20ft (6m) ↔12ft (4m)
A tough shrub or small tree that grows in poor soil and
dry sites. It is a fast grower, but can be cut almost to
the ground if it gets too large.

Genista pilosa 'Vancouver Gold'
VANCOUVER GOLD BROOM
☼ ◊ Z5–9 H9–3 ↕18in (45cm) ↔3ft (1m)
A spreading, mounded plant that makes a good
groundcover. Free-flowering and
stays in bloom for a long time.
Leaves are lance-shaped
and silky beneath.

Kerria japonica 'Golden Guinea'
GOLDEN GUINEA JAPANESE KERRIA
☼ ◊ Z5–9 H9–1 ↕6ft (2m) ↔8ft (2.5m)
An arching shrub that is easy to grow and will survive
in most soils. This cultivar has larger flowers. There is
also a double-flowered cultivar that is not quite as hardy.

WOODY PLANTS

Evergreens for seashore environments

The long coastline of the Northeast means that for many of us, salt-laden winds are a fact of life. Evergreens are especially vulnerable to desiccation from salt because they retain their foliage in winter, when strong salt-laden winds are more likely to occur. The plants shown here are adapted to withstand high levels of salt.

Pinus banksiana
JACK PINE

Ⓝ ☼ ◊ Z3–8 H8–1 ‡70ft (20m) ↔15ft (3m)

This pine is able to survive in very poor and sandy soils, providing they are acidic; it does not grow well on alkaline ones. Useful for windbreaks and shelterbelts in exposed locations.

Juniperus virginiana 'Blue Cloud'
BLUE CLOUD JUNIPER

Ⓝ ☼ ◊ Z3–9 H9–1 ‡18in (45cm) ↔5ft (1.5m)

A low, spreading plant that originated in Holland and may be a hybrid. The branches are arching, with threadlike branchlets that have an unpleasant odor.

MORE CHOICES

- *Picea glauca* 'Conica' Z2–6 H6–1
- *Pieris floribunda* Z5–8 H8–5
- *Pinus mugo* Z2–7 H7–1
- *Taxus cuspidata* Z4–7 H7–1

Chamaecyparis pisifera 'Filifera Aurea'
GOLDEN THREADLEAVED SAWARA CYPRESS

☼ ◊ Z4–8 H8–1 ‡40ft (12m) ↔15ft (5m)

A slow-growing tree or large shrub that prefers a slightly acidic, moist soil. It forms a dense mound in time and can add winter interest to the garden.

Picea pungens
COLORADO SPRUCE

Ⓝ ☼ ◊ Z3–8 H8–1 ‡50ft (15m) ↔15ft (5m)

The gray-green needles are less prominent in the landscape than those of bluer cultivars. All selections are very tough and adaptable.

Pinus nigra
AUSTRIAN PINE, BLACK PINE

☼ ◊ Z5–8 H8–4 ‡100ft (30m) ↔25ft (8m)

A good choice for city planting; it is tolerant of most soils, pollution, and heat. Nice specimen plant, but also valued as a screen. Mature bark is grayish brown.

WOODY PLANTS

Ilex crenata
JAPANESE HOLLY

☼ ☼ ◐ ◊ Z5–7 H7–5 ↕15ft (5m) ↔12ft (4m)

An easy-to-grow holly that transplants readily into light, slightly acidic soil. Usually grown as one of the many named cultivars in different shapes and sizes.

Ilex opaca
AMERICAN HOLLY

Ⓝ ☼ ☼ ☼ ◊ Z5–9 H9–5 ↕45ft (14m) ↔4ft (1.2m)

In old age, the habit becomes more open and irregular. Fragrant white flowers in early summer are followed by small, persistent red fruit. Not for dry, windy areas.

Ilex x meserveae 'Blue Princess'
BLUE PRINCESS HOLLY

☼ ◊ Z5–9 H9–5 ↕10ft (3m) ↔4ft (1.2m)

Like many hollies, male and female flowers occur on separate plants. Plant a male cultivar (for example, 'Blue Prince' or 'Blue Boy') to ensure berries.

Ilex pedunculosa
LONGSTALK HOLLY

☼ ☼ ◊ Z6–9 H9–6 ↕30ft (10m) ↔22ft (7m)

This grows best in a loose, slightly acidic soil but will survive in heavier soils, providing they aren't too dry. Pollution-tolerant and thrives in fairly exposed sites.

Ilex glabra 'Compacta'
DWARF INKBERRY

Ⓝ ☼ ☼ ◊ Z5–9 H9–5 ↕10ft (3m) ↔6ft (2m)

An upright, suckering female shrub that forms colonies and makes a good hedge. It may eventually become bare at the base but can be cut back to rejuvenate it.

Chamaecyparis thyoides
WHITE FALSE CYPRESS, ATLANTIC WHITE CEDAR

Ⓝ ☼ ◊ Z3–8 H8–1 ↕50ft (15m) ↔12ft (4m)

An excellent species for low-lying sites that tend to remain wet. Loses its lower branches over time. Native to swamps and bogs from Maine to Florida.

Trees for seashore environments

Even for those of us who don't live near the ocean, salt may be a problem where it is used to clear snow off of roads in winter. High-speed traffic on major roads can create a fine spray that travels long distances on the wind and contaminates the soil where it falls. While this may not kill a tree outright, it does put it under stress. The trees here are quite salt-tolerant.

Crataegus x *lavallei*
LAVALLE HAWTHORN
☼ ◊ ◗ Z5–7 H7–4 ‡22ft (7m) ↔30ft (9m)
Red to orange-red, brown-speckled fruit follow the flowers in late fall, hanging on into winter. Oval-crowned and dense. Resists diseases better than many other hawthorns.

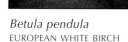

MORE CHOICES

- *Ailanthus altissima* Z4–8 H8–1
- *Amelanchier canadensis* Z3–7 H7–1
- *Fraxinus americana* Z6–9 H9–6
- *Platanus* x *acerifolia* Z5–8 H8–3

Acer platanoides 'Crimson King'
CRIMSON KING MAPLE
☼ ◊ Z3–7 H7–1 ‡100ft (30m) ↔75ft (22.5m)
A moderately large tree with leaves that hold their color all summer long. Bright yellow spring flowers in pendulous clusters contrast well with the dark foliage.

Acer rubrum
RED MAPLE
Ⓝ ☼ ☼ ◊ Z3–9 H9–1 ‡70ft (20m) ↔30ft (9m)
Tiny red flowers emerging before the leaves herald the arrival of spring in eastern North America. For the best display of vivid red fall color, grow in acidic soil.

Aesculus hippocastanum
COMMON HORSE CHESTNUT
☼ ☼ ◗ Z3–8 H8–1 ‡80ft (25m) ↔70ft (20m)
A large tree best suited to parks and golf courses. The large, spiny fruit can be a problem when mowing. 'Baumannii' is smaller, with double flowers and no fruit.

Betula pendula
EUROPEAN WHITE BIRCH
☼ ☼ ◊ Z2–7 H7–1 ‡80ft (24m) ↔30ft (9m)
Leafs out early and tends to hold its leaves late in fall, when they turn yellow-green. It transplants easily and grows quickly. Very susceptible to miners and borers.

Cornus kousa
KOUSA DOGWOOD
☼ ☼ ◊ Z5–8 H8–5 ‡22ft (7m) ↔15ft (5m)
A conical tree that grows best on sandy, organic, slightly acidic soils. Early summer flowers are followed by edible red fruit. Leaves turn red in fall.

Gleditsia triacanthos cultivars
HONEYLOCUST

Ⓝ ☀ ◐◑ Z3–7 H7–1 ↕70ft (20m) ↔50ft (15m)

Very adaptable trees that grow in most soils. Many named forms have different growth habits or foliage colors. All are very salt-tolerant and easy to grow.

Carya ovata
SHAGBARK HICKORY

Ⓝ ☀ ◑ ◐ Z4–8 H8–1
↕80ft (25m) ↔50ft (15m)

Deep-rooted tree that needs a rich soil to grow and fruit well. Attractive bark peels in long, thin strips attached at the center. Good yellow fall color and very tasty nuts.

MORE CHOICES

- *Populus deltoides* Z3–9 H9–1
- *Pyrus ussuriensis* Z4–9 H9–1
- *Quercus rubra* Z5–9 H9–5
- *Sorbus aucuparia* Z2–7 H7–1
- *Tilia cordata* Z3–8 H8–1
- *Ulmus parvifolia* Z5–9 H9–5

Gymnocladus dioica
KENTUCKY COFFEE TREE

Ⓝ ☀ ◐ Z5–9 H9–5 ↕70ft (20m) ↔50 ft (15m)

Spreading tree with pink-edged young leaves, then yellow foliage in fall. Clusters of white flowers bloom in early summer, followed by hanging pods on females.

Nyssa sylvatica
SOUR GUM

Ⓝ ☀ ◐ ◑ Z4–9 H9–2 ↕70ft (20m) ↔30ft (9m)

Slow-growing, pyramidal tree that spreads and becomes more irregular with maturity. Leaves emerge late in spring. Females produce black fruit that birds devour.

Robinia pseudoacacia
BLACK LOCUST

Ⓝ ☀ ◐ Z4–9 H9–3 ↕80ft (24m) ↔50 ft (15m)

Very fragrant flowers in late spring to early summer are followed by flat brown pods. Bees are very attracted to the flowers, producing a rich honey.

Ginkgo biloba
MAIDENHAIR TREE

☀ ◐ Z5–9 H9–3 ↕100ft (30m) ↔25ft (8m)

Narrow to spreading young tree becomes umbrella-shaped. Slow-growing, tolerant of pollution and heat, and free of pests. Outstanding yellow fall foliage.

Salt-tolerant shrubs

Salt, whether it arrives on winds from the coast or as spray from winter roads, can be lethal to many plants. By altering the chemistry of the soil as it washes through, it interferes with the uptake of minerals the plant may need to survive. The plants shown here are able to cope with this change and seem to show no ill effects from salt.

Lespedeza thunbergii
BUSHCLOVER
☼ ◊ Z6–8 H8–6 ↕6ft (2m) ↔10ft (3m)
Although this is often killed almost to the ground in winter, it is fast growing and soon regains its size. The flowers open in late summer on arching stems.

Clethra alnifolia
SUMMERSWEET
Ⓝ ☼ ● ᵖᴴ Z3–9 H9–1 ↕ 8ft (2.5m) ↔8ft (2.5m)
Grow in highly organic soil. Late to leaf out in spring, the foliage turns golden in fall. Very fragrant flowers open in summer and last about a month.

Berberis thunbergii 'Helmond Pillar'
HELMOND PILLAR JAPANESE BARBERRY
☼ ☼ ◊ Z4–8 H8–1 ↕5ft (1.5m) ↔24in (60cm)
A narrowly upright variety that turns bright red in fall. Yellow spring flowers give red berries.

Myrica pensylvanica
BAYBERRY

Ⓝ ☀ ☀ ◐ Z3–6 H6–1 ↕9ft (2.5m) ↔5–12ft (1.5–4m)

Bears yellowish green male catkins in spring before the leaves. Waxy gray fruit produced in autumn last through winter. Works well in a seashore garden.

MORE CHOICES

- *Caragana arborescens* Z2–8 H8–1
- *Chaenomeles speciosa* Z5–9 H9–1
- *Cytisus scoparius* Z6–8 H8–6
- *Euonymus alatus* Z4–9 H9–1
- *Hypericum* spp. Z7–9 H9–7
- *Juniperus horizontalis* Z3–9 H9–1
- *Lespedeza bicolor* Z5–8 H8–5
- *Ligustrum* spp. Z6–10 H9–1
- *Lonicera tatarica* Z3–9 H9–1
- *Microbiota descussata* Z3–7 H7–1
- *Pinus mugo* Z2–7 H7–1
- *Prunus maritima* Z3–6 H6–1
- *Rhamnus frangula* 'Aslpenifolia' Z3–8 H8–1
- *Ribes alpinum* Z2–6 H6–1
- *Spiraea* spp. Z4–9 H10–2

Aronia arbutifolia
RED CHOKEBERRY

Ⓝ ☀ ◐ ◌ Z5–9 H9–4 ↕↔10ft (3m)

The spring flowers become very astringent, decorative, shiny red fruits that last well into winter. Leaves turn glowing red to purple in fall.

Caryopteris x *clandonensis* 'Arthur Simmonds'
BLUE MIST SHRUB

☀ ◐ ◌ Z6–9 H9–1 ↕3ft (1m) ↔5ft (1.5m)

A rounded shrub that grows best in poor soil and may becomes rampant in rich soil. Late summer flowers are on the new growth, so cut back hard in late winter.

Hydrangea macrophylla 'Blue Wave'
BLUE WAVE BIGLEAF HYDRANGEA

☀ ◐ ◌ ◐ Z6–9 H9–6 ↕5–6ft (1.5–2m) ↔6–8ft (2–2.5m)

Flowers grown in acidic soil are blue or purple; flowers grown in neutral or alkaline soil are pink or red. Dried flowerheads are good for arrangements.

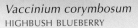

Vaccinium corymbosum
HIGHBUSH BLUEBERRY

Ⓝ ☀ ◐ ◌ ◐ ⊛ Z3–7 H7–1 ↕↔5ft (1.5m)

Clusters of cylindrical white flowers appear from late spring to early summer. The blueberries that follow are blue-black with a white bloom (powdery coating).

Hippophae rhamnoides
SEA BUCKTHORN

☀ ◌ Z3–8 H8–1 ↕↔20ft (6m)

Male and female are on different plants, and you need one male (with conical flower buds) to every six females (with rounded flower buds) to get fruit.

Rosa rugosa
RUGOSA ROSE, JAPANESE ROSE
☼ ◊ Z2–9 H9–1 ↕3–6ft (1–2m)
A vigorous, spiny species with leathery leaves and round, red fruit in winter. Flowers open from early summer to fall. There are many named forms.

Calluna vulgaris 'Firefly'
FIREFLY SCOTCH HEATHER
☼ ◊ pH Z5–7 H7–5 ↕to 24 in (60cm) ↔20in (50cm)
Heathers grow best in a moist, sandy soil with good organic content. Intolerant of drought and need a site sheltered from drying winds. They flower in summer.

MORE CHOICES

- *Syringa* spp. Z3–8 H8–3
- *Tamarix ramosissima* Z3–8 H8–1
- *Vaccinium angustifolium* Z2–8 H8–1
- *Vaccinium macrocarpon* Z2–7 H7–1
- *Vitex rotundifolia* Z6–9 H9–5

Potentilla fruticosa 'Abbotswood'
ABBOTSWOOD SHRUBBY CINQUEFOIL
Ⓝ ☼ ◊ Z3–7 H7–1 ↕3ft (1m) ↔5ft (1.5m)
These compact, deciduous shrubs have pinnate leaves composed of 5–7 dark green leaflets. Flowers from spring to midfall. Grows well in dry, sunny sites.

Vaccinium vitis-idaea
COWBERRY
Ⓝ ☼ ☼ ◊ pH Z2–6 H6–1 ↕3/4–10in (2–25cm) ↔indefinite
Spreading, evergreen groundcover. Leaves turn dull red in winter. Summer blooms produce dark red fruits.

Buddleja davidii 'Empire Blue'
EMPIRE BLUE BUTTERFLY BUSH
☼ ◊ Z6–9 H10–4 ↕10ft (3m) ↔15ft (5m)
Dense cones of lilac to purple flowers are 12in (30cm) in length. Attracts insects, especially bees and butterflies. Cut back hard in spring for more flowers.

Erica carnea 'Springwood Pink'
SPRINGWOOD PINK SPRING HEATH

☼ ◊ ᵖᴴ Z5–7 H7–5 ↕12in (30cm) ↔18in

There are many different species of heath, but all need the same soil type as Heather (left). Many named forms have flowers shading from white to dark red.

Cotoneaster dammeri
BEARBERRY COTONEASTER

☼ ◊ Z6–8 Hx–x ↕8in (20cm) ↔6ft (2m)

A low, evergreen shrub with branches that root where they touch the soil. It flowers in late spring, and berries ripen to red in early fall.

Prunus x cistena
PURPLELEAF SANDCHERRY

☼ ◊ Z3–8 H8–1 ↕↔5ft (1.5m)

An upright shrub that flowers in spring as the leaves unfurl. Edible black fruit are produced in late summer but are hard to find among the purple foliage.

Hypericum cerastioides
BALKAN ST. JOHN'S WORT

☼ ◊ Z6–9 H9–6 ↕6in (15cm) or more ↔16–20in (40–50cm)

Flowering starts in late spring. Leaves have a curry odor when crushed. Needs a deep soil.

Hypericum frondosum
GOLDEN ST. JOHN'S WORT

Ⓝ ☼ ☼ ◊ ◖ Z6–8 H8–4 ↕↔2–4ft (60–120cm)

An erect, deciduous shrub with thick, flaking stems. Flowers from mid- to late summer on the current season's growth. Prefers moderately fertile soil.

Hibiscus syriacus 'Blue Bird'
BLUE BIRD ROSE OF SHARON

☼ ◊ Z5–9 H9–5 ↕10ft (3m) ↔6ft (2m)

Flowers in late summer on new growth, so prune hard in early spring. Makes a good border plant or hedge. Species also flowers in white, mauve, or pink.

Trees tolerant of shady conditions

In general, trees are climax vegetation, the plants that provide shade for others, but sometimes there is the need to plant trees in the permanent shade of buildings or beneath the canopy of large trees that may be showing signs of age. The trees illustrated here will thrive in these conditions, providing they are given sufficient water until established.

WOODY PLANTS

Acer palmatum
JAPANESE MAPLE
☀ ◊ Z5–8 H8–2 ↕↔20ft (6m)
Leaves vary greatly in color and shape, and habit ranges from upright to weeping. Can be grown as a single-stemmed tree or multistemmed large shrub.

Acer rufinerve
SNAKEBARK MAPLE
☀ ◊ Z6–9 H9–6
↕↔50ft (15m)
A deciduous tree with bluish new shoots and white to pale tan striping on older bark. The fruit is red with widespread wings. Fall color can be a bright red.

Acer palmatum 'Sangokaku'
CORALBARK MAPLE
☀ ◊ Z5–8 H8–2 ↕↔20ft (6m)
Upright tree with brightly colored stems. Best used as a specimen or accent plant; also nice in a group or border. Like all Japanese maples, it has few problems.

Acer shirasawanum 'Aureum'
GOLDEN FULLMOON MAPLE
☀ ◊ Z5–7 H7–5 ↕↔30ft (10m)
Upright clusters of small pink/cream spring flowers produce pink-tinged fruits. Foliage turns red in fall but may scorch in sun. Closely related to Japanese maple.

Acer griseum
PAPERBARK MAPLE
☀ ◊ Z4–8 H8–1 ↕↔30ft (10m)
This oval-headed tree grows well in most soils and bears leaves that turn red late in fall. The main beauty, however, is in the attractive flaking bark shown here.

Acer circinatum
VINE MAPLE
Ⓝ ☀ ◐ ◊ Z6–9 H9–4 ↕15ft (5m) ↔20ft (6m)
Attractive white flowers open from red buds in spring and give red fruits later. Foliage turns yellow and orange in fall. Often grown as a multistemmed tree/large shrub.

MORE CHOICES

- *Acer capillipes* Z5–7 H7–5
- *Acer japonicum* Z5–7 H7–1
- *Acer pseudosieboldianum* Z5–7 H7–5
- *Acer tegmentosum* Z4–7 H7–1
- *Amelanchier canadensis* Z3–7 H7–1
- *Amelanchier x grandiflora* Z3–7 H7–1
- *Carpinus caroliniana* Z3–9 H9–1
- *Catalpa speciosa* Z5–9 H9–5
- *Cornus alternifolia* Z4–8 H8–1

Acer pensylvanicum
MOOSEWOOD

Ⓝ ☼ ◊ Z3–7 H7–1 ↕↔50ft (15m)

This has smooth, bright green bark with white stripes. Flowers are yellow in drooping clusters. 'Erythrocladum' features carmine red twigs with white markings.

Carpinus caroliniana
AMERICAN HORNBEAM

Ⓝ ☼ ☼ ◊ Z3–9 H9–1 ↕↔30ft (9m)

Slow grower with smooth gray bark that is sinewy and fluted, much like muscles. Leaves change to yellow, orange, and red in fall. Tolerates seasonal flooding.

Stewartia pseudocamellia
JAPANESE STEWARTIA

☼ ◊ ⌖ Z5–8 H8–4 ↕↔50ft (15m)

A Japanese tree valued for its red to purple fall color, distinctive sinewy and peeling bark, and its pyramidal shape, as well as its summer flowers.

Halesia diptera var. magniflora
TWO-WINGED SILVERBELL

Ⓝ ☼ ☼ ◊ Z5–9 H8–4 ↕20ft (6m) ↔30ft (10m)

Larger flowers than the species. Winged green fruit appear after the flowers. Foliage on this rounded tree turns yellow in autumn. Protect from wind.

Halesia monticola
MOUNTAIN SILVERBELL

Ⓝ ☼ ◊ Z6–9 H9–6 ↕↔50ft (15m)

Spring flowers become pendulous fruit in early fall. Best in a rich, slightly acidic soil; may appear chlorotic in alkaline soils. 'Rosea' has pale pink flowers.

Stewartia monadelpha
TALL STEWARTIA

☼ ◊ ⌖ Z6–9 H9–6 ↕↔50ft (15m)

This pyramidal-rounded, shrubby tree displays deep red fall color on leaves that hang on into winter. Flowers appear for at least a month. Native to Japan.

WOODY PLANTS

Cornus kousa
KOUSA DOGWOOD
☼ ☀ ◊ Z5–8 H8–5 ↕22ft (7m) ↔15ft (5m)
A slow-growing tree with almost horizontal branches.
White bracts are held above the branches in spring;
edible red fruit hang down in fall. Good fall color.

Amelanchier arborea
COMMON SERVICEBERRY
Ⓝ ☼ ☀ ◊◊ Z4–9 H9–4 ↕30ft (10m) ↔40ft (12m)
White spring flowers produce edible red to purple-
black fruit. Fall color is bright yellow to red. Suitable
for most soils, it forms a rounded, densely brached tree.

Amelanchier laevis
ALLEGHENY SERVICEBERRY
Ⓝ ☼ ◊ Z5–9 H9–3 ↕↔30ft (10m)
A small tree or large shrub, this is
similar to the Common Serviceberry
(left) but has young foliage that is
tinged bronze. Fruit and fall color
are just as good.

Ptelea trifoliata
HOP TREE
Ⓝ ☼ ◊ Z5–9 H9–5 ↕↔22ft (7m)
Flowers are small and greenish white, but the flat,
papery fruit borne in late summer are the reason to
grow this. Suckering, large shrub or rounded tree.

Viburnum prunifolium
BLACKHAW VIBURNUM
Ⓝ ☼ ☀ ◊ Z3–9 H9–1 ↕12–15ft (4–5m)
Creamy, flat-topped heads of flowers produce pink fruits
that change to blue-black as they ripen. An adaptable
small tree or large shrub that grows on most soils.

Clethra barbinervis
SUMMERSWEET

☼ ◊ Ꝋ Z5–8 H8–6 ↕↔10ft (3m)

Long clusters of fragrant flowers open in late summer. Foliage turns red and yellow in fall, and attractive peeling brown bark adds winter interest. Deciduous.

Magnolia virginiana
SWEET BAY MAGNOLIA

Ⓝ ☼ ◐ ◊ Z6–9 H9–6 ↕28ft (9m) ↔20ft (6m)

Flowering from late spring through to fall, this has 3in (8cm) lemon-scented blooms that fade to yellow with age. Sometimes evergreen, it needs a deep, acidic soil.

Cornus florida 'Cherokee Chief'
CHEROKEE CHIEF DOGWOOD

Ⓝ ☼ ◐ ◊ Z5–8 H8–3 ↕20ft (6m) ↔25ft (8m)

Grow in a slightly acidic soil, with plenty of organic matter, and mulch to retain summer moisture. There are many named forms of Flowering Dogwood.

Alnus glutinosa 'Imperialis'
IMPERIAL BLACK ALDER

☼ ◊ ◐ Z3–7 H7–1 ↕30ft (10m) ↔12ft (4m)

The glossy, dark green foliage is deeply cut to give a lacy appearance. A good choice for poor, infertile soils. It can be grown as a multistemmed tree.

Laburnum x watereri
GOLDEN CHAIN TREE

☼ ◊ Z6–8 H8–3 ↕↔25ft (8m)

An adaptable tree that grows in most soils, except very wet. Needs midday shade in the southern parts of its hardiness range. Seeds are poisonous.

MORE CHOICES

- *Cornus florida* Z5–8 H8–5
- *Halesia carolinina* Z5–8 H8–4
- *Halesia tetraptera* Z5–8 H8–4
- *Halesia tetraptera* 'Rosea' Z5–8 H8–4
- *Maackia amurensis* Z5–7 H7–5
- *Magnolia sieboldii* Z6–9 H9–6
- *Ostrya virginiana* Z5–9 H9–2
- *Parrotia persica* Z4–7 H7–1
- *Prunus virginiana* Z3–8 H8–1
- *Ptelia trifoliata* Z5–9 H9–5
- *Stewartia koreana* Z5–8 H8–4
- *Styrax japonicus* Z6–8 H8–6

Shrubs tolerant of shady conditions

The shady north side of a building and the area under large trees are often considered being problem places in which to grow plants. In fact, they extend the range of plants you can grow by providing a specialized habitat. Many of the plants on these two pages will not survive if planted in full sun and require the reflected light or dappled shade to thrive.

Aesculus parviflora
BOTTLEBRUSH BUCKEYE
Ⓝ ☼ ☼ ◊ ◖ Z5–9 H9–4 ‡10ft (3m) ↔15ft (5m)
Young bronze leaves turn dark green in summer and yellow in fall. Sometimes slow to establish. Best grown in a large or medium-sized garden.

Clethra alnifolia
SUMMERSWEET
Ⓝ ☼ ◖ ᵖᴴ Z3–9 H9–1 ‡↔8ft (2.5m)
The fragrant, bell-shaped white flowers of this shrub form elegant spires. Upright shrub often increases through suckering. Leaves turn yellow in fall.

Calycanthus floridus
CAROLINA ALLSPICE, COMMON SWEETSHRUB
Ⓝ ☼ ◊ Z5–9 H9–1 ‡8ft (2.5m) ↔10ft (3m)
A spreading shrub that is tolerant of most soils and of sun. The fragrant flowers are produced from late spring into summer. Foliage is also fragrant when crushed.

MORE CHOICES

- *Clethra acuminata* Z5–8 H8–3
- *Dirca palustris* Z4–9 H9–1
- *Hamamelis mollis* 'Pallida' Z5–9 H9–5
- *Hamamelis vernalis* Z4–8 H8–1
- *Hydrangea arborescens* Z4–9 H9–1
- *Hydrangea serrata* Z6–9 H9–6
- *Kerria japonica* Z4–9 H9–1
- *Rhododendron mucronulatum* Z5–8 H8–5
- *Rhododendron dauricum* Z4–8 H8–1
- *Symphoricarpos albus* Z3–7 H7–1

Hydrangea quercifolia
OAKLEAF HYDRANGEA
Ⓝ ☼ ☼ ◊ Z5–9 H9–1 ‡6ft (2m) ↔8ft (2.5m)
Bears flowers from midsummer through midfall that become pink-tinged with age. Leaves turn red and purple in fall. Distinctive, peeling, orange-brown bark.

Hamamelis virginiana
COMMON WITCHHAZEL

Ⓝ ☼ ◊ ⌘ Z3–8 H8–1
↕↔20ft (6m)

Bears small spidery yellow flowers in fall, unlike the rest of its spring-blooming relatves. Grows well in the shade of a wall or fence. Native to E North America.

Abelia x *grandiflora*
GLOSSY ABELIA

☼ ◊ Z6–9 H9–1 ↕10ft (3m) ↔12ft (4m)

Evergreen or semi-evergreen shrub. Fragrant flowers are borne from midsummer to fall. Irresistible to many butterflies. Also known as *A. rupestris*.

Hydrangea macrophylla 'Blue Wave'
BLUE WAVE BIGLEAF HYDRANGEA

☼ ◐ ◊ Z6–9 H9–3 ↕5–6ft (1.5–2m) ↔6–8ft (2–2.5m)

Flowers grown in acidic soil are blue or purple; flowers grown in neutral or alkaline soil are pink or red. Dried flowerheads are good for arrangements.

Enkianthus campanulatus
REDVEIN ENKIANTHUS

☼ ◐ ◊ ◖ ⌘ Z4–7 H7–3 ↕↔12–15ft (4–5m)

Creamy yellow, bell-shaped flowers with pink or red veins bloom in late spring to early summer. Dull green leaves turn orange to red in fall. Native to Japan.

Aronia arbutifolia
RED CHOKEBERRY

Ⓝ ☼ ◐ ◖ Z5–9 H9–4 ↕10ft (3m) ↔5ft (1.5m)

An upright, suckering shrub that thrives on most soils and also in sun. In fall, the foliage turns bright crimson, while the scarlet, bitter fruit persist well into winter.

Cornus alba 'Elegantissima'
VARIEGATED RED TWIG DOGWOOD

☼ ◊ Z2–8 H8–1 ↕↔10ft (3m)

Gray-green leaves have an irregular white margin. White flowers appear in late spring and early summer, followed by white fruit. Shoots are bright red in winter.

Lindera benzoin
SPICE BUSH

Ⓝ ◐ ◖ ◖ ⌘ Z4–9 H8–1 ↕↔10ft (3m)

Grown for its aromatic foliage, which turns yellow in fall. It bears tiny, yellow-green, star-shaped flowers, followed by red berries on female plants.

Evergreen trees for shady conditions

Evergreens fulfill a vital role in the landscape by providing focal points during the long winter period then most trees are reduced to bare branches. Although the number of evergreen trees that will grow well in shade is limited, the ones shown here will thrive under these conditions and amply repay their cultivation.

Ilex opaca
AMERICAN HOLLY
Ⓝ ☼ ◑ ☀ ◊ Z5–9 H9–5
↕45ft (14m) ↔4ft (1.2m)
Crimson (sometimes yellow, or orange) berries in winter. Like most hollies, spiny leaves are occasionally smooth-edged. May be pruned hard once established.

MORE CHOICES

- *Sciadopitys verticillata* Z5–9 H9–4
- *Torreya nucifera* Z6–10 H10–6
- *Torreya taxifolia* Z6–11 H12–6

Ilex x *altaclerensis* 'Golden King'
GOLDEN KING ALTACLARA HOLLY
☼ ◑ ◊ Z7–9 H9–7 ↕to 70ft (20m) ↔40–50ft (12–15m)
A vigorous tree with almost spineless leaves. Pollution- and salt-tolerant; use as a specimen plant or windbreak. Female plant; a male must be nearby to produce berries.

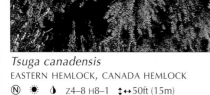

Tsuga canadensis
EASTERN HEMLOCK, CANADA HEMLOCK
Ⓝ ☼ ◊ Z4–8 H8–1 ↕↔50ft (15m)
Grows on both alkaline and acidic soils, but not in wet soils or exposed locations. Excellent hedging plant. Many cultivars that are upright, dwarf, or weeping.

Tsuga chinensis
CHINESE HEMLOCK
☼ ◑ ◊ Z5–9 H9–5 ↕140ft (45m) ↔100ft (30m)
Conical; peeling, pale brown bark. Needs organic-rich soil, preferably slightly acidic. Intolerant of pollution and salt. New growth pale yellow; turns greenish gray.

Tsuga caroliniana
CAROLINA HEMLOCK
Ⓝ ☼ ◑ ◊ Z3–8 H7–3 ↕50ft (15m) ↔25ft (8m)
An upright tree with short, often pendulous branches, and a fissured, scaly, brown bark. This is intolerant of drought and needs protection from strong winds.

Cryptomeria japonica
JAPANESE CEDAR

☼ ◑ Z6–9 H9–4 ‡70ft (20m) ↔25ft (8m)

Cryptomeria is one of the few conifers that can be successfully coppiced (cut back severely). Normally a conical or columnar tree, it is a moderately fast grower.

Thuja occidentalis
AMERICAN WHITE CEDAR

Ⓝ ☼ ◑ Z2–7 H7–1 ‡30–60ft (9–18m) ↔15ft (5m)

Remains very full to the ground as it matures. Growth rate is slow to moderate. Some especially columnar cultivars are 'Pyramidalis' and 'Hetz Wintergreen'.

Magnolia grandiflora 'Little Gem'
LITTLE GEM SOUTHERN MAGNOLIA

Ⓝ ☼ ◑ ◑ Z7–9 H9–3 ‡20ft (6m) ↔10ft (3m)

More compact and upright than the species, with smaller, very fragrant flowers. Prefers well-drained soil. Prone to leaf spots, cankers, mildew, and scale insects.

Chamaecyparis nootkatensis
WEEPING ALASKAN CEDAR

Ⓝ ☼ ◑ ◑ Z4–7 H7–1 ‡50ft (15m) ↔20ft (6m)

Brown-gray bark peels in large plates. Small green female cones ripen in spring.

Ilex aquifolium
ENGLISH HOLLY

☼ ◑ ◑ ◑ Z7–9 H9–7 ‡70ft (20m) ↔20ft (6m)

Upright evergreen with dense foliage and gray bark. Berries are prized for winter decorations. Grows best in well-drained soil. Native to Europe, N Africa, Asia.

WOODY PLANTS

Evergreen shrubs for shady conditions

The range of evergreen shrubs is much wider than with evergreen trees and includes both coniferous and flowering plants. Some flowering shrubs are so worth establishing an area of shade just to be able to grow them. *Camellia* and mountain laurel (*Kalmia*), listed in the More Choices boxes, have many forms with flowers in different shades and shapes.

Hedera helix
ENGLISH IVY

☼ ◑ ● ◊ z5–11 H12–6 ↕30ft (10m) ↔15ft (5m)
Normally a self-clinging climber, there are some cultivars ('Congesta', 'Conglomerata') that are shrubby. Best grown in fertile, organic soil.

Aucuba japonica
JAPANESE LAUREL

☼ ◑ ◊ z6–15 H12–6 ↕10ft (3m) ↔10ft (3m)
Glossy-leaved evergreen shrub produces small, red-purple flowers in midspring. In fall, female plants produce red berries. Disliked by rabbits.

Microbiota decussata
SIBERIAN CYPRESS, RUSSIAN ARBORVITAE

☼ ◑ ◊ z3–7 H7–1 ↕20in (50cm) ↔6–10ft (2–3m)
A vigorous, spreading groundcover that needs careful locating to avoid having to prune severely each year. Winter coloration is usually brownish.

Cephalotaxus harringtonia
COW'S-TAIL PINE

☼ ◊ z6–9 H9–3 ↕15ft (5m) ↔10ft (3m)
Can be a large shrub or small tree as it ages. Female plants produce small, egg-shaped, olive green fruit in fall. Prefers fertile soil. Tolerates severe cutting back.

Osmanthus heterophyllus
FALSE HOLLY

☼ ◑ ◊ z7–9 H9–7 ↕↔15ft (5m)
Grows best on acidic soils; also okay in soils that are close to neutral. Young leaves are hollylike; on mature plants they are oval and spineless. Good hedge plant.

MORE CHOICES

- *Camellia japonica* 'Betty Sette' z6–9 H8–7
- *Camellia oleifera* z6–9 H8–7
- *Camellia sasanqua* 'Mist Maiden' z7–8 H8–7
- *Camellia* x 'Snow Flurry' z6–10 H8–7
- *Camellia* x 'Winter's Beauty' z6–10 H8–7
- *Cephalotaxus harringtonia* z6–9 H9–3
- *Euonymus fortunei* cultivars z5–9 H9–5
- *Illicium floridanum* z7–9 H9–4
- *Kalmia latifolia* z5–9 H9–5

Pieris floribunda
FETTERBUSH

Ⓝ ☼ ◐ ⊕ Z5–8 H8–5 ↕↔10ft (3m)

A low, rounded shrub with stiff branches. The flowers open in early spring. Grows in slightly alkaline soils. Native from Virginia to Georgia.

Rhododendron 'Olga Mezitt'
OLGA MEZITT RHODODENDRON

☼ ◐ ⊕ Z4–8 H8–1 ↕4ft (1.2m) ↔5–6ft (1.5–2m)

One of a group of small-leaved rhododendrons, of which 'P.J.M.' is the best known. They don't suffer the winter leaf-burn that afflicts many large-leaved hybrids.

Pieris japonica
JAPANESE PIERIS

☼ ◐ ⊕ Z6–8 H8–6 ↕↔20ft (6m)

This species needs a slightly acidic soil with additional organic matter. New leaves are usually bronze, and some cultivars have been selected for this trait.

Rhododendron atlanticum
COAST AZALEA

Ⓝ ☼ ◐ ⊕ Z6–9 H9–4 ↕↔3–6ft (1–2m)

A small shrub with fragrant white or pink flowers in spring. It is native to coastal pine woods from Delaware to South Carolina.

Rhododendron 'Solidarity'
SOLIDARITY RHODODENDRON

☼ ◐ ⊕ Z5–9 H9–5 ↕3ft (1m) ↔3–4ft (1–1.2m)

One of an incredible number of rhododendron hybrids of varying hardiness, size, and flower color. Spectacular in flower, and a good background plant when not.

MORE CHOICES

- *Mahonia* x *media* Z8–9 H9–8
- *Pachysandra terminalis* Z4–8 H8–1
- *Prunus laurocerasus* Z6–9 H9–6
- *Sarcococca hookeriana* var. *digyna* Z6–9 H9–6
- *Sarcococca hookeriana* var. *humilis* Z6–9 H9–6
- *Taxus baccata* 'Repandens' Z7–8 H8–7
- *Vinca minor* Z4–9 H9–1

Leucothoe fontanesiana 'Girard's Rainbow'
RAINBOW FETTERBUSH

Ⓝ ☼ ◐ ◐ ⊕ Z5–8 H8–5 ↕5ft (1.5m) ↔10ft (3m)

Grown for its attractive foliage and white spring flowers, this need an organic soil that is not allowed to become dry, and protection from drying winds.

Mahonia japonica 'Bealei'
LEATHERLEAF MAHONIA

☼ ◐ Z7–8 H8–7 ↕↔10ft (3m)

Mildly fragrant, pale yellow flowers appear in early spring. Fruits ripen to blue-purple. Prefers moderately fertile, organic soil. Oldest leaves turn orange in fall.

WOODY PLANTS

Lilacs: the genus *Syringa*

What would our gardens be like without lilacs? Although their flowers are often fleeting, they are one of the essential plants of spring and fill the air with their perfume. If you have room for more than one, plant lilacs of different types to extend the flowering season and to experience the subtle differences in their fragrance.

Syringa vulgaris 'Président Grévy'
PRESIDENT GREVY LILAC

☼ ◊◑ Z4–8 H8–1 ↕↔22ft (7m)

Very fragrant, double flowers open from red-violet buds. Clusters can reach 10in (25cm) long. Can be cut back severely to control its size.

Syringa meyeri 'Palibin'
DWARF KOREAN LILAC

☼ ◊ Z4–7 H7–1 ↕↔5ft (1.5m)

Dense clusters of single, lilac-pink flowers bloom in late spring and early summer. Deadhead recently planted lilacs. Older plants can be cut back hard.

Syringa vulgaris 'Charles Joly'
CHARLES JOLY LILAC

☼ ◊◑ Z4–8 H8–1 ↕↔22ft (7m)

Conical clusters of sweetly scented, dark purple-red, double flowers. Requires little pruning, although it may grow to be treelike.

Syringa vulgaris 'Madame Lemoine'
MADAME LEMOINE LILAC

☼ ◊ Z4–8 H8–1 ↕↔22ft (7m)

Double, sweetly scented flowers in spring. An older variety, introduced in 1890, but still very popular and readily available. Sometimes sold as a miniature tree.

Syringa vulgaris 'Sensation'
SENSATION LILAC

☼ ◊◑ Z4–8 H8–1 ↕↔22ft (7m)

Flowers are very fragrant. Deadhead the plant for the first few years, and cut out weak shoots in winter. Suitable for heavy clay soils.

MORE CHOICES

- *Syringa* x *chinensis* Z3–8 H8–1
- *Syringa* x *hyacinthiflora* 'Assessippi' Z3–7 H7–1
- *Syringa* x *hyacinthiflora* 'Mount Baker' Z2–7 H7–1
- *Syringa* x *hyacinthiflora* 'Pocohontas' Z3–7 H7–1
- *Syringa microphylla* 'Superba' Z5–8 H8–5
- *Syringa* 'Minuet' Z2–7 H7–1
- *Syringa oblata* Z4–7 H7–1
- *Syringa patula* 'Miss Kim' Z3–8 H8–1
- *Syringa* x *josiflexa* 'Royalty' Z4–7 H7–1
- *Syringa* x *prestoniae* 'Donald Wyman' Z2–7 H7–1
- *Syringa* x *prestoniae* 'James MacFarlane' Z2–7 H7–1
- *Syringa reticulata* 'Ivory Silk' Z4–8 H8–1
- *Syringa vulgaris* 'Katherine Havemeyer' Z4–8 H8–1
- *Syringa vulgaris* 'Michel Buchner' Z4–8 H8–1
- *Syringa vulgaris* 'President Lincoln' Z4–8 H8–1
- *Syringa vulgaris* 'Primrose' Z3–8 H8–3

Evergreen rhododendrons

The large, ball-like heads of bloom on hybrid rhododendrons are recognized by anyone with the slightest interest in gardening. There are hundreds of species and hybrids in a great range of flower colors and of hardiness, but they all need an acidic, organic soil, ample moisture during the summer, and dappled shade. Given these conditions, they will thrive.

Rhododendron yakushimanum
YAKU RHODODENDRON

☀ ◑ pH Z5–9 H9–5 ↕3ft (1m) ↔4ft (1.2m)
Makes a small, dense, compact, rounded shrub that flowers in late spring. Leaf undersides are covered with an off-white down. Widely used in hybridizing.

MORE CHOICES

- *Rhododendron carolinianum* Z5–9 H9–5
- *Rhododendron* 'Chionoides' Z5–9 H9–4
- *Rhododendron* 'Delaware Valley White' Z6–8 H8–6
- *Rhododendron* 'Hershey Red' Z5–9 H9–5
- *Rhododendron impeditum* Z5–8 H8–1
- *Rhododendron keiskii* Z6–9 H9–6

Rhododendron 'Yaku Princess'
YAKU PRINCESS RHODODENDRON

☀ ◑ pH Z5–9 H9–5 ↕↔5ft (1.5m)
This has a similar habit of growth to *R. yakushimanum*, but the leaves lack the white reverse. Flowers fade to white at maturity.

Rhododendron maximum
GREAT LAUREL, ROSEBAY RHODODENDRON

Ⓝ ☀ ◑ pH Z4–9 H9–1 ↕12ft (4m) ↔15ft (5m)
Flowering in early summer after most other rhododendrons, the color can vary from purple-pink to near white.
It requires a cool, moist soil to grow well.

Rhododendron 'Olga Mezitt'
OLGA MEZITT RHODODENDRON

☀ ◑ pH Z4–8 H8–1 ↕4ft (1.2m) ↔5–6ft (1.5–2m)
The individual flower clusters are small but are produced in abundance. Spring flowering. Foliage turns a copper color in cold weather.

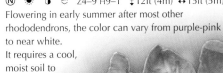

Rhododendron 'Solidarity'
SOLIDARITY RHODODENDRON

☀ ◑ pH Z5–9 H9–5 ↕3ft (1m) ↔3–4ft (1–1.2m)
Dense, well-shaped plant that flowers in late spring. Free-flowering, with clusters about 4in (10cm) in diameter. Leaves have whitish down on the undersides.

Deciduous azaleas

A division of the genus *Rhododendron*, these enjoy similar conditions but are generally hardier and less prone to winter injury in the northern parts of our region. Their flowers are more delicate, in small clusters rather than large heads, and often have a sweet or spicy fragrance. Several are native to this region, and the large number of hybrids gives added choice.

Rhododendron atlanticum
COAST AZALEA

Ⓝ ☀ ◐ 💧 ꝑ Z6–9 H9–4 ↕↔3–6ft (1–2m)

This makes an attractive shrub that suckers slowly. Fragrant flowers open in early spring before the blue-green leaves. Native from Delaware to South Carolina.

Rhododendron calendulaceum
FLAME AZALEA

Ⓝ ☀ ☀ ◐ 💧 ꝑ Z5–8 H9–4 ↕↔6–10ft (2–3m)

Produces yellow, scarlet, or orange flowers in early summer, with or just after the leaves. Midgreen leaves are softly hairy both above and underneath.

Rhododendron yedoense var. *poukhanense*
KOREAN AZALEA

☀ ◐ 💧 ꝑ Z5–9 H9–5 ↕↔6ft (2m)

Slightly fragrant flower in clusters of 2 or 3 are freely produced in late spring. The dark green foliage turns orange to red in fall.

Rhododendron prunifolium
PLUMLEAF AZALEA

Ⓝ ☀ ◐ 💧 ꝑ Z6–9 H9–5 ↕10ft (3m) ↔8ft (2.5m)

A hairless shrub with medium-sized, elliptic leaves. Orange-red to red flowers blossom in summer, much later than most azaleas. Sometimes semi-evergreen.

Rhododendron arborescens
SWEET AZALEA

Ⓝ ☀ ◐ 💧 ꝑ Z5–9 H9–4 ↕↔20ft (6m)

Forms an upright shrub with scented flowers in early summer. The dark green, shiny leaves turn red in fall. Native from Pennsylvania to Georgia.

Rhododendron dauricum
DAHURIAN AZALEA

☀ ◐ 💧 ꝑ Z4–8 H8–1 ↕↔5ft (1.5m)

This species flowers in very early spring on the tips of the branches. The glossy, dark green leaves turn purplish in late fall. There is also a white-flowered form.

Rhododendron schlippenbachii
ROYAL AZALEA
☼ ◐ ◊ ꝑ Z5–8 H8–5 ↕↔8ft (2.5m)
Unlike most rhododendrons, this spring-flowering species grows well in neutral soils. Give protection from late frosts. Good fall color if grown in part sun.

Rhododendron 'Fireball'
FIREBALL AZALEA
☼ ◊ ꝑ Z5–9 H9–3 ↕↔3ft (1m)
An Exbury hybrid raised in England, this vigorous plant has bronze colored new foliage that turns green when mature and yellow in fall. Best in cooler climates.

Rhododendron mucronulatum
SNOW AZALEA
☼ ◊ ꝑ Z5–8 H8–5 ↕↔4–5ft (1.2–1.5m)
In addition to the form seen here, the fragrant, late spring flowers may be of various pink shades. Dome-shaped plants have grayish green foliage.

MORE CHOICES

- *Rhododendron bakeri* Z5–7 H9–7
- *Rhododendron canescens* Z6–9 H9–4
- *Rhododendron* 'Hershey Red' Z5–9 H9–5
- *Rhododendron* 'Gibraltar' Z5–8 H8–5
- *Rhododendron* 'Homebush' Z5–8 H8–5
- *Rhododendron japonicum* Z5–9 Hx9–5
- *Rhododendron kaempferi* Z6–9 H9–6
- *Rhododendron* 'Klondyke' Z5–8 H8–4
- *Rhododendron luteum* Z7–9 H9–7
- *Rhododendron* 'My Mary' Z5–9 H9–5
- *Rhododendron* 'Narcissiflorum' Z5–8 H8–5
- *Rhododendron* 'Northern Lights' hybrids
  Z3–7 H7–1
- *Rhododendron* 'Oxydol' Z5–8 H8–5
- *Rhododendron prinophyllum* Z4–9 H9–3
- *Rhododendron prinophyllum* 'Album'
  Z4–9 H9–3
- *Rhododendron* 'Strawberry Ice' Z4–8 H8–1
- *Rhododendron vaseyi* Z5–8 H8–4
- *Rhododendron vaseyi* 'White Find'
  Z5–8 H8–4
- *Rhododendron viscosum* Z3–9 H9–1

Rhododendron periclymenoides
PINXTERBLOOM AZALEA
Ⓝ ☼ ◊ ꝑ Z4–9 H9–5 ↕6ft (2m) ↔10ft (3m)
Flowers open before the leaves in mid- to late spring and vary from white to violet. Grows well in sandy, rocky soil. Native from Massachusetts to North Carolina.

Trees tolerant of moist conditions

Sometimes a garden can be wet without actually having swamplike conditions. If the water table is close to the surface, many deep-rooted trees can suffer. Those shown here will grow well in these conditions or in a garden where spring runoff creates wet soil for a limited time. They will also grow well beside a river or stream.

Acer saccharinum
SILVER MAPLE

Ⓝ ☼ ◑ Z4–8 H8–1 ↕80ft (20m) ↔50ft (15m)

Fast-growing and widely adaptable riverbottom species that may, however, prove to be too large for many gardens. Variable fall color.

Chamaecyparis pisifera
SAWARA FALSE CYPRESS

☼ ◑ Z4–8 H8–3 ↕70ft (20m) ↔15ft (5m)

The species is not commonly grown, but its many named forms are. These may have yellow or silver-blue foliage, branches that are stringlike and pendulous, or foliage that is reduced to small needles.

Betula alleghaniensis
YELLOW BIRCH

Ⓝ ☼ ◑ Z4–7 H7–1 ↕40ft (12m) ↔10ft (3m)

Grows best where summers are cool and moist. Foliage turn yellow in fall. Amber bark peels loose in large plates. Native from Newfoundland to Tennessee.

MORE CHOICES

- *Acer negundo* Z5–8 H8–3
- *Acer rubrum* Z3–9 H9–1
- *Alnus* sp. Z2–6 H6–1
- *Carya laciniosa* Z6–9 H9–6
- *Magnolia virginiana* Z6–9 H9–6
- *Metasequoia glypostroboides* Z4–11 H12–1
- *Nyssa aquatica* Z5–9 H9–5
- *Platanus occidentalis* Z5–8 H8–5
- *Pterocarya fraxinifolia* Z6–9 H9–6
- *Pterocarya x rehderiana* Z6–9 H9–6
- *Quercus bicolor* Z4–8 H8–1
- *Taxodium ascendens* Z5–11 H12–5

Fraxinus pennsylvanica
GREEN ASH

Ⓝ ☼ ◑ Z3–9 H9–4 ↕↔70ft (20m)

Upright and spreading tree with age. Shiny foliage turns yellow in autumn. Avoid seedling-grown trees; many bear nuisance fruit. Prone to borers and scale.

Chamaecyparis nootkatensis
ALASKA CEDAR, NOOTKA CYPRESS

Ⓝ ☼ ◑ Z4–7 H7–1 ↕100ft (30m) ↔25ft (8m)

Brown-gray bark peels in large plates. Small green female cones, with a recurved central hook on each of the 4-6 scales, ripen in spring.

Amelanchier laevis
ALLEGHENY SERVICEBERRY

Ⓝ ☼ ◗ Z5–9 H9–3 ↕↔30ft (10m)

Sweet purple-black fruits, relished by birds and animals, follow the spring flowers. May be grown in large containers. Leaves turn orange-red to bright red in fall.

Chamaecyparis thyoides
WHITE FALSE CYPRESS, ATLANTIC WHITE CEDAR

Ⓝ ☼ ◗ Z3–8 H8–1 ↕50ft (15m) ↔12ft (4m)

This prefers a soil on the acidic side and will not grow in competition with deciduous trees. Its cultivars are usually grown. Native in swamps from Maine to Florida.

Betula nigra
RIVER BIRCH

Ⓝ ☼ ◗◗ Z4–9 H9–1 ↕60ft (18m) ↔40ft (12m)

Tolerates dry soil in summer, providing the soil is wet in spring. 'Heritage' has attractive, flaking bark and shows resistance to leaf miners and borers.

Taxodium distichum
BALD CYPRESS

Ⓝ ☼ ◗◗ Z5–11 H12–5 ↕80ft (24m) ↔25ft (8m)

The needles turn rust-brown in fall before dropping. Distinctive aerial roots ("knees") form around the base of the tree in wet sites. Moderate growth rate.

Quercus palustris
PIN OAK

Ⓝ ☼ ◗ Z5–8 H8–5 ↕70ft (20m) ↔40ft (12m)

Very striking growth form, with a clearly pyramidal outline and horizontal branching habit. Fall color can be an outstanding red. Tolerant of city conditions.

Nyssa sylvatica
SOUR GUM

Ⓝ ☼ ◗ Z4–9 H9–2 ↕70ft (20m) ↔30ft (9m)

Slow-growing, pyramidal tree that spreads and becomes more irregular with maturity. Leaves emerge late in spring. Females produce black fruit that birds devour.

WOODY PLANTS

Shrubs tolerant of moist conditions

Naturally wet areas, or the overflow of ornamental pools and ponds following rain, often produces permanently moist areas in the garden. Many plants will not survive in these areas, but the shrubs shown here, along with the perennials on pages 218–219, will grow well under such conditions and provide color and interest all summer long.

Aralia spinosa
DEVIL'S WALKING STICK, HERCULES CLUB
Ⓝ ☼ ☀ ◊ Z4–9 H9–1 ↕30ft (10m) ↔15ft (5m)
A very spiny, large shrub or small tree with leaves up to 5ft (1.5m) long. An adaptable species, it will also grow in dry, rocky soils and tolerates pollution.

Aronia arbutifolia
RED CHOKEBERRY
Ⓝ ☼ ☀ ◊ Z5–9 H9–4 ↕10ft (3m) ↔5ft (1.5m)
This upright, slow-growing, multistemmed shrub has bitter, bright red berries in fall that birds don't eat until spring. Foliage turns bright red to purple in fall.

Calluna vulgaris 'Firefly'
FIREFLY SCOTCH HEATHER
☼ ◊ ♨ Z5–7 H7–5 ↕18in (45cm) ↔30in (75cm)
Grow this summer flowering, dwarf shrub in sandy soil with plenty of organic matter. The many cultivars have white, pink, or red flowers and a range of foliage colors.

Enkianthus campanulatus
RED VEIN ENKIANTHUS
☼ ☀ ◊◊ ♨ Z5–8 H8–4 ↕↔12–15ft (4–5m)
Creamy yellow, bell-shaped flowers with pink or red veins bloom in late spring to early summer. Dull green leaves turn orange to red in fall. Native to Japan.

MORE CHOICES

- *Andromeda polifolia* Z2–6 H6–1
- *Baccharis halimifolia* Z3–9 H7–1
- *Cephalanthus occidentalis* Z5–11 H12–3
- *Cornus amomum* Z5–9 H8–4
- *Cornus stolonifera* 'Baileyi' Z2–8 H8–1
- *Cyrilla racemiflora* Z6–9 H9–5
- *Ilex decidua* Z5–9 H9–1
- *Ilex serrata* Z5–7 H7–5
- *Ilex verticillata* Z5–8 H8–1
- *Kalmia angustifolia* Z7–8 H8–7
- *Rhododendron vaseyi* Z5–8 H8–4

Chaenomeles speciosa 'Moerloosei'
MOERLOOSE FLOWERING QUINCE
☼ ☀ ◊ Z5–9 H9–1 ↕8ft (2.5m) ↔15ft (5m)
A small shrub with prickly branches. Spring flowers produce yellowish fruit with black spots. Although too tart to eat raw, they make good jellies and preserves.

Erica carnea 'Vivellii'
VIVELLII SPRING HEATH
☼ ◊ ♨ Z5–7 H7–5 ↕6in (15cm) ↔18in (45cm)
Heaths and heathers need similar conditions, but heaths flower from late winter on in the same range of colors as the heathers. Some have golden foliage.

Ilex verticillata
WINTERBERRY

Ⓝ ☼ ◊ Z5–8 H8–5 ↕↔15ft (5m)
Deciduous shrub bears bright
green, saw-toothed leaves. White
flowers are followed by fruit that
may be dark red to scarlet, or
sometimes orange or yellow.

Hamamelis virginiana
COMMON WITCH HAZEL

Ⓝ ☼ ◊ pH Z3–8 H8–1 ↕↔20ft (6m)
Bears small, fragrant, spidery yellow flowers in fall, unlike the rest of its
spring-blooming relatives. Grows well in the shade of a wall or fence.
Native to much of eastern North America.

Lindera benzoin
SPICE BUSH

Ⓝ ☼ ◊ pH Z4–9 H8–1 ↕↔10ft (3m)
Grown for its aromatic foliage, which turns yellow in
fall. It bears tiny, yellow-green, star-shaped flowers,
followed by red berries on female plants.

Itea virginica
VIRGINIA SWEETSPIRE

Ⓝ ☼ ◊ Z6–9 H10–7 ↕↔5ft (1.5m)
Fragrant white flowers bloom in dense, elongated
clusters. Open shrub grows upright, then arching.
Dark green leaves turn red to purple in fall.

Deutzia gracilis
SLENDER DEUTZIA

☼ ◊ Z4–8 H8–1 ↕↔3ft (1m)
Grow this toward the back of a mixed border, where
the spring flowers are effective but other plants help
mask its rather straggly habit as it matures.

Myrica pensylvanica
BAYBERRY

Ⓝ ☼ ☀ ◊ Z3–6 H6–1 ↕9ft (2.5m) ↔5–12ft (1.5–4m)
Bears yellowish green male catkins in spring before
the leaves. Waxy gray fruit produced in autumn persist
through winter. Good choice for a seaside garden.

WOODY PLANTS

MORE CHOICES

- *Rhododendron viscosum* z3–9 H9–1
- *Salix discolor* z4–8 H8–2
- *Vaccinium* sp. z5–9 H9–5
- *Viburnum nudum* z5–9 H9–5

Viburnum opulus
'Roseum'
SNOWBALL BUSH
☼ ☼ ◐ ◊ z3–8 H8–1
↕15ft (5m) ↔12ft (4m)
An easy-to-grow plant, tolerant of most conditions. Globe-shaped flowers open in early summer and turn pink as they age.

Calycanthus floridus
COMMON SWEETSHRUB
Ⓝ ☼ ◊ z5–9 H9–1 ↕8ft (2.5m) ↔10ft (3m)
A spreading plant with leaves that have a spicy fragrance when crushed and turn yellow in fall. The flowers open from midsummer onward and can be dried.

Sambucus nigra
BLACK ELDER, EUROPEAN ELDER
☼ ☼ ◊ z6–8 H8–6 ↕↔20ft (6m)
An upright, bushy shrub. The flat heads of white, early summer flowers have a strange odor. Edible black berries can be used for pies or wine.

Leucothoe fontanesiana
DROOPING LEUCOTHOE
Ⓝ ☼ ☼ ◊ ᵖᴴ z5–8 H8–5 ↕5ft (1.5m) ↔10ft (3m)
Evergreen shrub produces clusters of flowers from mid- to late spring. Glossy, leathery leaves have sharp teeth. Makes a nice hedge.

Zenobia pulverulenta
DUSTY BLUE HONEYCUPS
Ⓝ ☼ ◊ z5–8 H8–5 ↕6ft (2m) ↔5ft (1.5m)
Pendent, bell-shaped, fragrant white flowers bloom in early to midsummer. Blue-green to dark green leaves have a bluish white underside when young.

Cornus stolonifera 'Flaviramea'
YELLOWTWIG DOGWOOD

Ⓝ ☼ ◐ ◊ ◊ ◉ Z3–8 H8–1 ↕6ft (2m) ↔12ft (4m)

A good choice to plant where it can be seen from inside the house. Cut it back almost to the ground every couple of years; new growth has the brightest color.

Cornus stolonifera 'Isanti'
ISANTI RED OSIER DOGWOOD

Ⓝ ☼ ◐ ◊ ◊ ◉ Z2–8 H8–1 ↕6ft (2m) ↔12ft (4m)

A dwarf, twiggy form with very bright red winter twigs that make a dense, compact bush. White berries give color in early fall, before the leaves turn.

Cornus alba 'Aurea'
GOLDEN TATARIAN DOGWOOD

☼ ◊ ◉ Z2–8 H8–1 ↕↔10ft (3m)

Golden in spring, this becomes greener as summer progresses and then turns bright yellow in fall. The new shoots are not as bright red as on other cultivars.

Clethra alnifolia
SUMMERSWEET

Ⓝ ☼ ◉ ᵖᴴ Z3–9 H9–1 ↕↔8ft (2.5m)

An upright shrub with oval, toothed leaves. Spikes of white flowers bloom in late summer and early fall. Can be planted in a woodland garden or mixed border.

Amelanchier canadensis
SHADBLOW, SHADBUSH

Ⓝ ☼ ◐ ◉ ᵖᴴ Z3–7 H7–1 ↕20ft (6m) ↔10ft (3m)

A suckering shrub with brilliant orange and red fall color. Edible black fruit. Flowering occurs when shad are spawning in spring, hence the common name.

Shrubs for fall color

One of the glories of the Northeast is the wonderful fall color of our native trees. Many of the shrubs we can grow may be equally brilliant, although on a smaller scale, while others have more subtle copper and bronze tones. Plant these in full sun to obtain the best color, since plants grown in only part sun seldom color up as brightly.

Amelanchier x grandiflora 'Autumn Brilliance'
AUTUMN BRILLIANCE APPLE SERVICEBERRY
☼ ☀ ◑ ◌ Z3–7 H7–1 ‡25ft (8m) ↔30ft (10m)
Large shrub or small tree with new leaves tinged pink, then remaining green until fall. White spring flowers produce sweet, edible fruits.

Fothergilla gardenii
WITCH ALDER
Ⓝ ☼ ☀ ◑ ◌ Z4–9 H9–1 ‡↔3ft (1m)
Bears spikes of fragrant flowers in spring, before the leaves. Dark blue-green leaves turn orange, red, and purple in fall. Good for a woodland garden.

Hamamelis x intermedia 'Jelena'
JELENA HYBRID WITCHHAZEL
☼ ☀ ◑◑ Z5–9 H9–1 ‡↔12ft (4m)
Bright green leaves turn orange and red in fall and drop off before blossoms appear in early to midwinter. Dislikes dry soils and very windy sites.

MORE CHOICES

- *Aesculus parviflora* Z5–9 H9–4
- *Clethra alnifolia* Z3–9 H9–1
- *Aronia arbutifolia* 'Brilliantissima' Z5–9 H9–4
- *Calycanthus floridus* Z5–9 H9–1
- *Cornus florida* Z5–8 H8–3
- *Deutzia gracilis* 'Nikko' Z4–8 H8–1
- *Enkianthus campanulatus* 'Hollandia' Z5–7 H7–5
- *Enkianthus campanulatus* 'Red Bells' Z6–8 H8–6
- *Euonymus alatus* Z4–9 H9–1
- *Fothergilla major* Z4–8 H9–2
- *Hamamelis virginiana* Z3–8 H8–1

Spiraea japonica 'Flaming Globe'
FLAMING GLOBE JAPANESE SPIREA
☼ ◌ Z3–9 H9–1 ‡↔1ft (30cm)
Red-tipped new foliage turns yellow with age, then is bright crimson in fall. Flat heads of pink flowers are carried above the leaves from midsummer until frost.

Cotinus 'Grace'
GRACE SMOKEBUSH
☼ ☀ ◌ Z5–8 H8–3 ‡↔15ft (5m)
A vigorous, tall, deciduous hybrid smokebush with conical purplish flowers in summer. The pinkish flower stems later give the effect of pink smoke.

Acer tataricum subsp. ginnala
AMUR MAPLE

☼ ☼ ◐ ◊ Z3–7 H7–1 ↕30ft (10m) ↔25ft (8m)

A large shrub, sometimes grown as a small tree, with pink-tinged leaves in spring. Pendent, fragrant white flowers in spring produce red-tinged fruit in summer.

Cornus obliqua
SILKY DOGWOOD

Ⓝ ☼ ◐ ◊ Z5–8 H8–5 ↕6ft (2m) ↔5ft (1.5m)

Deciduous shrub with dull orange branches. Leaves, dull green above, have silky, gray-white hairs underneath. White flowers produce bluish fruit in late summer.

Diervilla lonicera
BUSH HONEYSUCKLE

Ⓝ ☼ ◐ ◊ Z5–8 H8–5 ↕↔3ft (1m)

A spreading, suckering plant that grown as an understory plant in dry soils. Midgreen oval leaves. Yellow flowers occur in groups of three in summer in the leaf joints.

Rosa 'John Davis'
JOHN DAVIS ROSE

☼ ◊ Z3–9 H9–1 ↕8ft (2.5m) ↔4ft (1.5m)

A climbing or trailing rose with good resistance to blackspot and powdery mildew. Clusters of medium pink, double flowers with a spicy fragrance appear in summer.

Rhus typhina
STAGHORN SUMAC

Ⓝ ☼ ◊ Z3–8 H8–1 ↕15ft (5m) ↔20ft (6m)

A thicket-forming shrub that spreads by underground runners. It thrives on poor soil and will often turn color in late summer in a dry year. Felty new shoots.

MORE CHOICES

- Hydrangea quercifolia 'Snow Queen' Z5–9 H9–5
- Itea virginica 'Henry's Garnet' Z6–9 H10–7
- Itea virginica 'Merlot' Z5–9 H10–7
- Itea virginica 'Saturnalia' Z5–9 H10–7
- Lindera benzoin Z4–9 H8–1
- Ptelia trifoliata Z5–9 H9–5
- Rhus aromatica Z2–8 H8–1
- Rhus copallina Z5–9 H9–4
- Rhododendron luteum Z7–9 H9–7
- Ribes alpinum Z2–6 H6–1
- Spiraea japonica Z4–9 H9–1
- Stephanandra incisa Zx–x Hx–x
- Vaccinium corymbosum Z3–7 H7–1
- Viburnum acerifolium Z4–8 H8–1
- Viburnum dilatatum Z5–8 H8–5
- Viburnum nudum Z5–9 H9–5

Aronia melanocarpa
BLACK CHOKEBERRY

Ⓝ ☼ ◐ ◊ Z3–8 H8–1 ↕6ft (2m) ↔10ft (3m)

A small, upright shrub with glossy, dark green leaves in summer. Small clusters of slightly fragrant white flowers in spring produce tart black berries.

WOODY PLANTS

Shade trees for large spaces

The trees that are illustrated here are large and best suited to rural properties, parks, or public planting. They need space in order to develop properly, but when mature they can become imposing specimens and often live to a great age. Many are slow growing; plant them for future generations to enjoy fully.

Larix decidua
EUROPEAN LARCH

☼ ◊ Z3–6 H6–1 ‡100ft (30m) ↔15–50ft (5–15m)

An attractive deciduous specimen conifer intolerant of very alkaline soils or pollution. New growth is bright green, and fall color is a brilliant yellow.

Acer saccharinum
SILVER MAPLE

Ⓝ ☼ ◐ ◊ Z3–8 H8–1 ‡↔30ft (10m) or more

A fast-growing tree with a silvery reverse to the leaves. Young, silvery gray bark becomes furrowed and in long strips. Brittle and subject to storm damage.

Aesculus hippocastanum
HORSE CHESTNUT

☼ ◊ Z3–8 H8–1 ‡100ft (30m) ↔75ft (22.5)

Easy to grow in most soils, but avoid very dry locations. The flowers open in late spring and produce spiny fruit containing 2–3 large, brown, inedible nuts that cause litter. The cultivar 'Baumannii' has double flowers and no fruit.

Larix kaempferi
JAPANESE LARCH

☼ ◊ Z3–6 H6–1

‡80ft (24m) ↔30ft (9m)

A conical tree with scaly, rust-brown to gray bark. Needles are shed in fall, revealing purplish red winter shoots covered in a waxy bloom. Also known as L. leptolepis.

Juglans nigra
BLACK WALNUT

Ⓝ ☼ ◊ Z5–9 H9–5 ‡100ft (30m) ↔75ft (23m)

Oval to rounded habit. Huge taproot makes it difficult to transplant. Many plants are affected by chemicals emitted from this tree and cannot grow under it.

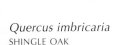

Quercus alba
WHITE OAK

☼ ☼ ◊ ⌂ Z5–9 H8–1 ↕↔60–100ft (30m) (18–30m)

A handsome oak with majestic, wide-spreading branches at maturity. Foliage turns a rich wine red in fall. Its acorns are relished by birds and mammals.

Quercus muehlenbergii
CHINKAPIN OAK

☼ ☼ ◊ Z4–8 H8–2 ↕50 ft (15m) ↔40ft (12m)

Open, rounded head with a spread greater than its height at maturity. Yellow to orange-brown color in fall. Flaking gray bark and a massive trunk. Pest-free.

Quercus imbricaria
SHINGLE OAK

☼ ☼ ◊ Z5–8 H8–4 ↕70ft (20m) ↔50ft (15m)

Reddish unfurling leaves turn russet-red in autumn and hang on through winter. Tolerates heavy pruning and so makes a good large hedge plant.

Quercus macrocarpa
BUR OAK, MOSSYCUP OAK

☼ ☼ ◊ Z3–9 H9–1 ↕50ft (15m) ↔30ft (9m)

Develops a massive trunk and widely spreading habit with age. Foliage turns yellow in fall. Acorns are oval and distinctly fringed on the caps.

Liriodendron tulipifera
TULIP TREE

☼ ☼ ⌂ Z5–9 H9–1 ↕100ft (30m) ↔50 ft (15m)

Fast-growing tree with golden yellow foliage in fall. Aphids are a big problem, as are scale, powdery mildew, and leaf spot. Native to the eastern US.

WOODY PLANTS

WOODY PLANTS

Platanus occidentalis
BUTTONWOOD, SYCAMORE

Ⓝ ☼ ◊ Z5–8 H8–3 ‡80ft (24m) ↔70ft (20m)

Wide-spreading tree with very attractive, flaking brown, gray, and cream bark. Produces green, then brown, fruit clusters that hang on in fall and winter.

Betula lenta
SWEET BIRCH, CHERRY BIRCH

Ⓝ ☼ ◊ Z3–7 H7–2 ‡50ft (15m) ↔40ft (12m)

Pyramidal tree that does best in a deep, slightly acidic soil. Weeping yellow catkins appear in late winter, and foliage turns yellow in fall. Attractive red-brown bark.

Betula alleghaniensis
YELLOW BIRCH

Ⓝ ☼ ◊ Z4–7 H7–1 ‡40ft (12m) ↔10ft (3m)

The common name comes from the bark, which is yellowish, turning bronze at maturity. Fall color is a good yellow. Native from Newfoundland to Georgia.

Magnolia acuminata
CUCUMBERTREE MAGNOLIA

Ⓝ ☼ ◊ Z4–8 H8–2 ‡70ft (20m) ↔30ft (9m)

Wide-spreading branches and freedom from pests make this tree perfect for parks, estates, and golf courses. Pinkish red, cucumber-like fruit in fall.

Robinia pseudoacacia 'Frisia'
GOLDEN BLACK LOCUST

Ⓝ ☼ ◊ Z4–9 H9–4 ‡50ft (15m) ↔25 ft (8m)

The golden-leaved form of the common Black Locust also features orange-yellow fall foliage. Afternoon shade in summer helps preserve the golden color.

WOODY PLANTS

Zelkova serrata
JAPANESE ZELKOVA

☼ ☀ ● Z5–9 H9–5 ‡100ft (30m) ↔60ft (18m)

As it matures, smooth gray bark flakes off to reveal orange patches. Rough-textured, elmlike leaves have toothed edges. Native to Japan, Taiwan, and South Korea.

Ulmus parvifolia
CHINESE ELM

☼ ◊ Z5–9 H9–5 ‡↔50ft (15m)

Spreading tree with flaking orange and brown bark. Very small red flowers appear in late summer, followed by green fruit and yellow to red leaves in late fall.

Castanea mollissima
CHINESE CHESTNUT

☼ ☀ ◊ Z4–8 H8–1 ‡↔70ft (20m)

A tough tree that thrives in hot, dry sites, providing the soil is a bit acidic. Foliage turns yellow in fall. Fruit are edible nuts, but the prickly cases can be a nuisance.

MORE CHOICES

- *Aesculus flava* Z3–8 H8–1
- *Carya illinoinensis* Z4–9 H9–1
- *Carya tomentosa* Z5–8 H8–1
- *Larix laricina* Z5–7 H7–5
- *Platanus x acerifolia* Z5–8 H8–3
- *Pterocarya fraxinifolia* Z6–9 H9–6
- *Pterocarya x rehderiana* Z6–9 H9–6
- *Quercus prinus* Z4–8 H8–3
- *Tetradium hupehensis* Z5–8 H8–5
- *Tilia mongolica* Z3–7 H7–1
- *Tilia tomentosa* Z6–9 H9–6
- *Ulmus carpinifolia* Z5–8 H8–5
- *Ulmus parvifolia* Z5–9 H9–5

Tetradium danielli
BEE TREE, KOREAN EVODIA

☼ ◊ Z5–8 H8–5 ‡↔50ft (15m)

Spreading, deciduous tree that grows well in most soils. Flat clusters of white flowers in midsummer produce black-seeded fruits . May be offered as *Evodia*.

Fagus sylvatica
EUROPEAN BEECH

☼ ☀ ◊ ● Z5–7 H7–5 ‡80ft (24m) ↔50 ft (15m)

Very formal, pyramidal tree that branches to the ground. Produces triangular nuts inside a bristly, woody husk. Bronze-russet fall color.

Tilia americana
AMERICAN LINDEN, BASSWOOD

Ⓝ ☼ ☀ ◊ Z2–8 H8–1 ‡80ft (25m) ↔40ft (12m)

Easy to grow on most soils, but tends to be shallow rooted unless they are deep. Fragrant, pale yellow summer flowers are attractive to bees and butterflies.

Deciduous screens and hedges

Hedges strongly influence the microclimate within the garden by reducing the wind and giving shelter. Deciduous trees and shrubs provide less winter protection, but the range of suitable plants is large, giving the gardener a greater choice of heights and textures. They may be closely trimmed as formal hedges or be allowed to grow informally, depending on the species.

Euonymus alatus
BURNING BUSH

☼ ☀ ◊ Z4–9 H9–1 ↕6ft (2m) ↔10ft (3m)

A deciduous shrub with dark green leaves that turn red in fall. Also produces orange fruit. Tolerant of many soil types. 'Compacta' is more compact, with pinker fall color.

Carpinus betulus
EUROPEAN HORNBEAM

☼ ☀ ◊ Z4–8 H8–1

↕80ft (25m) ↔70ft (20m)

The smooth gray bark is fluted and muscly-looking. Leaves are yellow in fall and unusually free of pests. Excellent as a screening plant, as a hedge, or in large planters.

Forsythia x intermedia
BORDER FORSYTHIA

☼ ☀ ◊ Z6–9 H9–3 ↕↔5ft (1.5m)

Profuse flowers are produced in early and midspring, before the leaves. Remove oldest stems after flowering to rejuvenate the plant. Useful as a hedge or screen.

MORE CHOICES

- *Chaenomeles speciosa* Z5–9 H9–1
- *Hibiscus syriacus* Z5–9 H9–5
- *Lonicera nitida* 'Baggesen's Gold' Z6–9 H9–6
- *Poncirus trifoliata* Z5–9 H9–5
- *Prinsepia sinensis* Z3–7 H7–1
- *Rosa* spp. Z4–9 H9–3
- *Physocarpus opulifolius* Z3–7 H7–1
- *Shepherdia argentea* Z3–6 H6–1

Acer campestre
HEDGE MAPLE

☼ ☀ ◊ Z6–8 H8–4 ↕↔25–55ft (8–17m)

Slow-growing, very adaptable tree. Often used as a street tree in urban areas: it tolerates compaction around the roots, heavy pruning, and air pollution.

Viburnum prunifolium
BLACKHAW VIBURNUM

Ⓝ ☼ ☀ ◊◊ Z3–9 H9–1 ↕15ft (5m) ↔12ft (4m)

Shrub or small tree. Fruits persist through winter and attract cedar waxwings and other birds. Creamy white flowers in late spring. Best in moderately fertile soil.

Evergreen screens and hedges

Because evergreen hedges keep their leaves all year round, they make a better choice if your garden is in a windy location. On the downside, in northern regions, snow tends to pile up more on the lee side than it would with a deciduous hedge and may cause damage by its weight. Always remove snow carefully by brushing upward and before it freezes together.

Ilex glabra 'Compacta'
DWARF INKBERRY
Ⓝ ☀ ◑ ◖ Z5–9 H9–3 ↕↔4–6ft (1.2–2m)
The upright habit makes this a good choice for hedging. Spreads slowly by underground runners, forming a dense thicket. Trim in late fall.

MORE CHOICES

- *Buxus sempervirens* Z6–8 H8–6
- *Buxus sempervirens* 'Handsworthiensis' Z6–8 H8–6
- x *Cupressocyparis leylandii* Z6–7 H9–3
- *Ilex crenata* Z5–7 H7–5
- *Ilex opaca* Z5–9 H9–5
- *Juniperus chinensis* Z3–9 H9–1
- *Osmanthus heterophyllus* Z7–9 H9–4
- *Pinus koraiensis* Z4–7 H7–1
- *Taxus baccata* 'Repandens' Z7–8 H8–7
- *Thuja plicata* Z6–8 H8–6
- *Thuja occidentalis* Z2–7 H7–1

Berberis julianae
WINTER BARBERRY
☀ ◖ Z6–9 H9–4 ↕↔10ft (3m)
Dense, bushy shrub. Leaves are dark green and glossy above and pale green underneath. Yellow or red-tinged flowers are followed by egg-shaped black fruits.

Tsuga canadensis
EASTERN HEMLOCK, CANADA HEMLOCK
Ⓝ ☀ ◑ ◖ Z4–8 H8–1 ↕↔50ft (15m)
An excellent hedge, it also makes a good specimen plant or can be used in foundation plantings. Tolerant of most soils, it needs shelter from strong winter winds.

Prunus laurocerasus
CHERRY LAUREL
☀ ◖ Z6–9 H9–6 ↕20ft (6m) ↔30ft (10m)
Spreading shrub that is best used as an informal hedge. Hand-prune in fall, removing only the shoots that are growing away from the general shape.

Small to medium-sized flowering trees

While city dwellers have a limited space in their gardens, they still have the need for shade and the desire to plant trees. Many trees become too large for small city lots, but the ones shown here are suitable for these locations. Remember: they need room to mature, so don't plant them near a corner of the garden or if a neighbor already has a tree on the other side of the fence.

Albizia julibrissin
SILK-TREE, MIMOSA
☼ ◊ Z6–9 H9–6 ↕↔30ft (10m)
Light gray-brown seedpods persist through the winter. Grows quickly and normally is not long-lived. Very susceptible to wilt and webworm. Self-sows strongly.

Franklinia alatamaha
FRANKLIN TREE
Ⓝ ☼ ◊ Z6–9 H9–6 ↕↔15ft (5m)
Flowers from mid-summer onward. Needs an acidic to neutral soil. Native to Georgia, it was collected in 1770 and has not been found in the wild since.

MORE CHOICES

- *Cornus x rutgersensis* Z5–8 H8–3
- *Crataegus laevigata* 'Crimson Cloud' Z5–8 H8–3
- *Crataegus punctata* 'Ohio Pioneer' Z4–7 H7–1
- *Crataegus x mordenensis* 'Snowbird' Z3–8 H8–1
- *Crateagus laevigata* 'Paul's Scarlet' Z5–8 H8–3
- *Euscaphis japonica* Z7–8 H8–7
- *Lagerstroemia x* 'Tuskeegee' Z7–9 H9–7
- *Magnolia* 'Ann' Z3–8 H8–1
- *Malus* 'Prariefire' Z5–8 H8–4
- *Prunus serrulata* 'Snowgoose' Z6–8 H8–6
- *Prunus x* 'Hally Jolivette' Z6–8 H8–3

Prunus cerasifera 'Thundercloud'
THUNDERCLOUD PLUM
☼ ◊ Z4–9 H9–1 ↕↔30ft (10m)
One of many named forms of cherry plum, this has foliage that keeps its purple color all summer. Keep well fertilized to encourage strong growth.

Davidia involucrata
DOVE TREE, HANDKERCHIEF TREE
☼ ☼ ◊ Z6–8 H8–6 ↕50ft (15m) ↔30ft (10m)
Plant this in a soil rich in organic matter. A very showy tree when in flower, with leaves that persist until hard frost. Does not flower at a young age.

Cercis chinensis 'Avondale'
AVONDALE CHINESE REDBUD
☼ ☼ ◊ Z6–9 H9–3 ↕↔10ft (3m)
Flowering just before the native redbud (*C. canadensis*), this is an upright, often multistemmed tree with glossy leaves. This cultivar has darker flowers than the species.

Sorbus aucuparia
EUROPEAN MOUNTAIN ASH
☼ ☼ ◊ Z2–7 H7–1 ↕50ft (15m) ↔22ft (7m)
Growing best on acidic soils, this has flat clusters of white flowers with a strange scent in early summer. There are several named forms with fruit in other colors.

Aesculus parviflora
BOTTLEBRUSH BUCKEYE

Ⓝ ☼ ◐ ◊ Z5–9 H9–4 ↕15ft (5m) ↔10ft (3m)

Flowering in early summer, this is a favorite food source for swallowtail butterflies. Leaves turn yellow in fall. Usually grown as a tall, spreading thicket.

Laburnum x waterei 'Vossii'
VOSS'S GOLDENCHAIN TREE

☼ ◊ Z5–8 H8–3 ↕↔30ft (10m)

Has a denser habit and longer flower clusters than its hybrid parent, plus olive green, fissured bark. Benefits from siting in a protected spot near a building.

Crataegus x lavallei
LAVALLE HAWTHORN

☼ ◐ ◊ Z5–7 H7–4 ↕22ft (7m) ↔30ft (9m)

Red to orange-red, brown-speckled fruit follow the flowers in late fall and hang on into winter. Oval-crowned and dense. Not as plagued by rust as others.

Halesia monticola
MOUNTAIN SILVERBELL

Ⓝ ☼ ◊ Z6–9 H9–6 ↕↔50ft (15m)

A conical tree with larger flowers than the more common Carolina silverbell (*H. carolina*). Native from North Carolina to Georgia at altitudes over 3,000ft. (900m.).

Magnolia x soulangiana 'Lennei Alba'
WHITE SAUCER MAGNOLIA

☼ ◐ ◊ Z6–9 H9–6 ↕22ft (7m) ↔15ft (5m)

Low-branched tree or a large shrub. The flowers open in early spring; there are often scattered flowers again in fall, especially when warmth follows a cold spell.

Magnolia x loebneri 'Ballerina'
BALLERINA MAGNOLIA

☼ ◐ ◊ Z4–9 H9–1 ↕30ft (10m) ↔22ft (7m)

Fragrant flowers have more than 30 petals and open after the other Loebner magnolia varieties, escaping late frost damage. Grows best in a slightly acidic soil.

WOODY PLANTS

Shrubs for flowers in winter and early spring

Winters are long in much of the Northeast, and plants that bloom while the rest of the garden is dormant are very desirable. A few shrubs have this ability and can do much to lift the spirits and convince us that spring is on the way. Many of the shrubs shown here are sweetly scented and also provide food for bees while little else is in flower.

Chimonanthus praecox
WINTERSWEET
☼ ◐ ◌ Z7–9 H9–7 ‡8ft (2.5m) ↔10ft (3m)
In winter, this shrub produces fragrant, pendent, cup-shaped flowers. Leaves are lance shaped and glossy, arranged in opposite pairs. Provide protection.

Rhododendron dauricum
DAHURIAN AZALEA
☼ ◐ ◌ Z4–8 H8–1 ‡↔5ft (1.5m)
A deciduous to semi-evergreen shrub with dark green foliage that turns purple in winter. Flowers appear on the previous year's growth in late winter.

Corylopsis pauciflora
BUTTERCUP WINTER HAZEL
☼ ◐◌◌ ◌ Z3–9 H9–1 ‡ 5ft (1.5m) ↔8ft (2.5m)
Fragrant flowers are produced in pendent clusters in midspring. This dense, bushy shrub has bright green leaves with bristlelike teeth.

MORE CHOICES

- *Cornus officianalis* Z5–8 H8–3
- *Corylopsis spicata* Z5–8 H8–5
- *Daphne caucasica* Z6–8 H8–6
- *Daphne x burkwoodii* Z4–8 H9–2
- *Hamamelis mollis* Z5–9 H9–1
- *Hamamelis vernalis* Z4–8 H8–1
- *Jasminum nudiflorum* Z6–9 H9–6
- *Mahonia bealei* Z5–8 H8–3
- *Mahonia x media* Z8–9 H9–8
- *Rhododendron mucronulatum* Z5–8 H8–5
- *Stachyurus praecox* Z7–9 H9–7

Erica carnea 'Springwood Pink'
SPRINGWOOD PINK SPRING HEATH
☼ ◌ ◌ Z5–7 H7–5 ‡12in (30cm) ↔18in (45cm)
This is one of the spring heaths that set their flower buds in late summer and bloom early the following spring. 'Springwood White' is a white-flowered cultivar.

Daphne mezereum
FEBRUARY DAPHNE
☼ ◊ Z5–8 H8–5 ↕↔5ft (1.5m)
A sweet-smelling small shrub that is deciduous in the northern part of the Northeast. The flowers produce poisonous red fruits in summer.

Viburnum farreri
FRAGRANT VIBURNUM
☼ ◊ Z6–8 H8–6 ↕↔10ft (3m)
Flowers so early the first blooms are often cold-damaged. Plant where it will be protected from winter winds, and never in a frost pocket.

Lonicera fragrantissima
WINTER HONEYSUCKLE
☼ ☼ ◊ Z4–8 H8–3 ↕6ft (2m) ↔12ft (4m)
Very fragrant, short-tubed flowers are produced during winter and early spring and are welcomed by bees. Berries are dull red.

Mahonia aquifolium
OREGON GRAPE HOLLY
Ⓝ ☼ ◊ Z6–9 H9–6 ↕↔5ft (1.5m)
Evergreen shrub with glossy, bright green leaves. Flowers are followed by round, blue-black berries Can be grown as a hedge or screen.

Abeliophyllum distichum
WHITE FORSYTHIA, KOREAN ABELIA LEAF
☼ ◊ Z5–9 H9–1 ↕↔4ft (1.2m)
Flowers bloom in late winter or early spring but may be damaged by hard frosts. Grows well when provided the shelter and warmth of a wall. Native to Korea.

Cornus mas
CORNELIAN CHERRY
☼ ☼ ◊ Z5–8 H8–4 ↕↔15ft (5m)
Star-shaped flowers on bare branches precede edible, egg-shaped, bright red fruit that entice birds into the garden. Dark green leaves turn reddish purple in fall.

Hamamelis x intermedia 'Jelena'
JELENA HYBRID WITCHHAZEL
☼ ☼ ◊ Z5–9 H9–1 ↕↔12ft (4m)
Fragrant yellow, dark red, or orange flowers appear on bare branches. Bright green leaves turn yellow in fall. Grows well in acidic soil.

WOODY PLANTS

Low-maintenance shrub roses

Unlike their more popular cousins, the hybrid tea and floribunda roses, these roses are easy-care. They are mostly disease-free and very hardy, needing no winter protection even in the north of our region. Many are repeat bloomers, and some have attractive winter fruits. They are all suited to mixing with other shrubs or being grown in a mixed border.

MORE CHOICES

- *Rosa* 'Ausmas' Z5–9 H9–1
- *Rosa* 'Champlain' Z3–9 H9–1
- *Rosa* 'Cuthbert Grant' Z3–9 H9–1
- *Rosa* 'Hansa' Z3–9 H9–1
- *Rosa* 'John Franklin' Z3–9 H9–1
- *Rosa* 'Meipotal' Z4–9 H9–1
- *Rosa* 'Morden Centennial' Z2–9 H9–1
- *Rosa* 'Thérèse Bugnet' Z2–9 H9–1

Rosa 'Harwelcome'
FELLOWSHIP ROSE
☼ ◊ Z4–11 H12–1 ↕5ft (1.5cm) ↔6ft (2m)
A modern floribunda rose. The cultivar name is the patent name, and the name under which the rose is sold is different, here "Fellowship" or "Livin' Easy".

Rosa woodsii
WESTERN WILD ROSE
☼ ◊ Z5–9 H9–6 ↕6ft (2m) ↔4ft (1.2m)
A prairie species that forms an upright shrub with few thorns, especially on the flowering shoots. The fruit (hips) are small, round, and bright red. Foliage turns dark red in fall.

Rosa pimpinellifolia 'Glory of Edzell'
GLORY OF EDZELL SCOTCH ROSE
☼ ◊ Z3–9 H9–1 ↕5ft (1.5m) ↔4ft (1.2m)
An upright, suckering, spiny rose that is one of the first to flower. Not repeat flowering but very prolific when in bloom. Resistant to rose diseases.

Rosa glauca
REDLEAF ROSE
☼ ◊ Z2–8 H8–1 ↕6ft (1.8m) ↔5ft (1.5m)
An eyecatching rose with arching stems and foliage tinged dark red. The smallish flowers are followed by round, bright red hips that last through winter but don't seem attractive to birds.

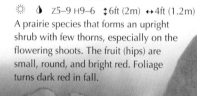

Rosa gallica 'Versicolor'
ROSA MUNDI ROSE

☼ ◊ Z3–9 H9–1 ↕4ft (1.2m)
↔3ft (1m)

The oldest of roses with striped
flowers, it makes a small, prickly
bush that suckers freely. Flowers
vary greatly in the amounts of pink
and white. Said to be named for
Rosamund, mistress of King Henry II.

Rosa 'Meidomonac' ('Bonica')
BONICA ROSE

☼ ◊ Z5–9 H9–1 ↕3ft (1m) ↔3½ft (1.1m)

A justifiably popular rose with arching stems and
glossy, coppery green foliage. It is very free-flowering
and continues to bloom up to frost.

Rosa rugosa 'Alba'
WHITE RUGOSA ROSE

☼ ◊ Z2–9 H9–1 ↕↔3–6ft (1–2m)

Fast-growing, beach-loving shrub with fragrant flowers in
spring, followed by bright red fruit (hips) ripening in late
summer to fall. Yellow to orange to red fall foliage.

Rosa foetida 'Persiana'
PERSIAN YELLOW ROSE

☼ ◊ Z3–9 H9–1 ↕5ft (1.5m) ↔4ft (1.2m)

The erect, arching canes are covered with flowers in
late spring. The related Austrian Copper rose (R.f.
'Bicolor') is similar but with copper-red flowers.

Rosa 'The Fairy'
THE FAIRY ROSE

☼ ◊ Z5–9 H9–5 ↕↔36in (1m)

A Dwarf Polyantha rose that can be used as a groundcover, in containers, or in the front of a border. Repeat
flowering, shade tolerant, and an excellent cut flower.

Rosa rugosa
RUGOSA ROSE

☼ ◊ Z2–9 H9–1 ↕↔3–6ft (1–2m)

Produces fragrant flowers from spring to fall, followed
by bright red hips. One of the easiest roses to grow and
is resistant to most fungal diseases.

WOODY PLANTS

Deciduous groundcover shrubs and climbers

In areas that don't take a lot of foot traffic, grass can be replaced with a groundcover to reduce garden maintenance. To eliminate the need for weeding, first cover the area with landscape fabric (geotextile), then cut slits to plant through it. The fabric will decompose in time, unless you cover it with a mulch of shredded bark or something similar.

Cotoneaster salicifolius 'Scarlet Leader'
SCARLET LEADER WILLOWLEAF COTONEASTER
☼ ◑ ◊ Z6–8 ↕3ft (1m) ↔8ft (2.4m)
Although the species grows 15ft (5m) tall, this variety hugs the ground. Excellent for covering banks, it may be evergreen except at the northern limits of hardiness.

MORE CHOICES

- *Cornus stolonifera* 'Isanti' Z2–8 H8–1
- *Cotoneaster adpressus* 'Praecox' Z6–8 H8–1
- *Cotoneaster dammeri* 'Lowfast' Z6–8 H8–6
- *Cotoneaster horizontalis* Z4–7 H7–3
- *Genista tinctoria* Z2–8 H8–1

Vaccinium angustifolium
LOWBUSH BLUEBERRY
Ⓝ ☼ ◑ ◑ ᵖᴴ Z2–8 H8–1 ↕↔4–24in (10–60cm)
Plant this where soil is poor, acidic, and dry. Leaves have a bluish sheen, and the white spring flowers produce edible, commercial blueberries.

Xanthorhiza simplicissima
YELLOWROOT
Ⓝ ☼ ◑ ◑ Z3–9 H9–1 ↕24in (60cm) ↔5ft (1.5m)
A mat-forming plant that does well in both wet and dry soils, providing they are not very alkaline. Early spring flowers are not very showy. Gold to orange fall color.

Ribes alpinum 'Aureum'
GOLDEN ALPINE CURRANT
☼ ◊ Z2–6 H6–1 ↕24in (60cm) ↔36in (1m)
A mounded, spreading shrub that grows in most soils and conditions. Yellow flowers are in short, drooping clusters in spring are followed by tasteless black fruit.

Hypericum calycinum
AARON'S BEARD, ROSE OF SHARON
☼ ◊ Z5–9 H9–4 ↕24in (60cm) ↔indefinite
A semi-evergreen shrub that thrives in sandy soil, spreads by underground shoots, and forms a dense carpet. Flowers from midsummer onward.

Cotoneaster adpressus 'Little Gem'
LITTLE GEM COTONEASTER

☼ ☀ ◊ Z4–7 H7–3 ‡2ft (60cm) ↔6ft (2m)

The dark green leaves of this shrub turn red in fall. Five-petaled, red-tinged white flowers appear in summer. The numerous berries are ¼in (6mm) long.

Stephanandra incisa 'Crispa'
LACE SHRUB

☼ ☀ ◊ Z3–8 H9–4 ‡24in (60cm) ↔10ft (3m)

This form, which has crinkly leaves, is lower- growing than the species and makes a tangled mat of stems. Early summer flowers are not very showy, but the leaves turn purplish in fall.

MORE CHOICES

- *Sorbaria sorbifolia* Z2–9 H9–1
- *Symphoricarpos* x *chenaultii* 'Hancock' Z4–7 H7–1
- *Vaccinium vitis-idaea* Z2–6 H6–1
- *Vaccinium myrtillus* Z5–7 H7–5
- *Vitex rotundifolia* Z6–9 H9–5

Parthenocissus tricuspidata
BOSTON IVY, JAPANESE IVY

☼ ◊ Z4–8 H8–1 ‡to 70ft (20m)

A vigorous climber that makes a good groundcover. Foliage is glossy, dark green all summer; inconspicuous flowers produce small grapelike fruits in fall.

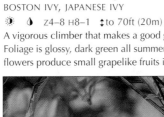

Clematis tangutica
RUSSIAN VIRGIN'S BOWER

☼ ☀ ◊ Z6–9 H9–6 ‡20ft (6m) ↔10ft (3m)

A vigorous climber that will also make a goodground cover, forming a thick carpet of intertwining stems. Flowers from summer to fall produce fluffy seedheads.

Cotoneaster apiculatus
CRANBERRY COTONEASTER

☼ ◊ Z5–7 H7–5 ‡3ft (1m) ↔8ft (2.5m)

This species has vigorous, prostrate growth. Solitary, red- tinged white flowers are borne in summer, followed by abundant fruit in fall. Prefers moderately fertile soil.

Cornus canadensis
BUNCHBERRY

Ⓝ ☼ ☀ ◊ Z2–7 H7–1 ‡ 6in (15cm) ↔indefinite

This needs a fairly acidic soil with lots of organic matter. The showy flowers produce bright red berries in late summer that remain until eaten by wildlife.

WOODY PLANTS

Evergreen shrubs for groundcover

Frequently planted for the color they give to the winter garden, these evergreen shrubs vary greatly in spread. Individual heaths and heathers will seldom grow more than 2ft (60cm) across, while the Russian arborvitae (*Microbiota*) easily grows to five times this spread. Keep the ultimate spread in mind when deciding on a species to plant to avoid needing to prune later.

Gaultheria procumbens
CHECKERBERRY, WINTERGREEN
Ⓝ ☀ ◐ Z3–8 H8–1 ↕6in (15cm) ↔3ft (1m)
This needs an organic soil. Pale pink flowers in summer produce berries that persist until the following year and are a source of wintergreen oil. Leaves turn red in fall.

Juniperus conferta 'Blue Pacific'
SHORE JUNIPER
☀ ☀ ◊ Z5–9 H9–1 ↕12in (30cm)
This cultivar is more trailing than the species and has a deeper blue cast to the foliage. Produces black fruit with a silvery white coating. Growth rate is moderate.

Pachysandra terminalis 'Green Sheen'
GREEN SHEEN JAPANESE SPURGE
☀ ☀ ◊◊ Z4–8 H8–1 ↕8in (20cm) ↔indefinite
This cultivar's leaves are a glossier and darker green than the species'. Tiny white flowers are produced on short spikes in early summer. Grows well on most soils.

Erica carnea 'Vivelli'
VIVELLII SPRING HEATH
☀ ◊ ᵖᴴ Z5–7 H7–5 ↕10in (25cm) ↔14in (35cm)
Providing the soil is high in organic matter, this will grow well in a slightly alkaline soil but better in acidic. There are many named forms of Spring Heath.

Pachysandra procumbens
ALLEGHANY SPURGE
Ⓝ ☀ ☀ ◊◐ Z5–9 H8–3 ↕12in (30cm) ↔indefinite
Grow this in an organic soil. It may be only semi-evergreen at the northern limits of hardiness. Fragrant white flowers open in spring with the new foliage.

Arctostaphylos uva-ursi
BEARBERRY, KINNIKINICK
Ⓝ ☀ ☀ ◊ Z2–6 H6–1 ↕4in (10cm) ↔20in (50cm)
Mat-forming shrub. Flowers precede bright scarlet berries. Suitable for use in a rock garden. Grows in very sandy soil and withstands sea winds and salt spray.

Microbiota decussata
RUSSIAN ARBORVITAE

☼ ◐ ◊ Z3–7 H7–1 ‡3ft (1m) ↔indefinite

An adaptable plant that will thrive in most soils. Don't be fooled by the small plant you buy: it needs to be planted where it has room to spread freely.

Sarcococca hookeriana var. digyna
SLENDER SWEETBOX

☼ ◊◊ Z6–9 H9–6 ‡5ft (1.5m) ↔6ft (2m)

Dense, clump-forming evergreen groundcover. Sweetly scented white flowers are succeeded by round black fruits. Male flowers have cream anthers.

Juniperus procumbens 'Nana'
JAPANESE GARDEN JUNIPER

☼ ◊ Z3–9 H9–1 ‡6–8in (15–20cm) ↔30in (75cm)

A dwarf, compact form of an already procumbent shrub results in a low, mat-forming plant. Foliage turns slightly purple in winter. Growth rate is slow.

MORE CHOICES

- *Gaultheria shallon* Z6–8 H8–6
- *Juniperus horizontalis* 'Blue Chip' Z3–9 H9–1
- *Juniperus horizontalis* 'Wiltoni' Z4–9 H9–1
- *Pachysandra terminalis* Z4–8 H8–1
- *Pachysandra terminalis* 'Green Carpet' Z4–8 H8–1
- *Sarcococca hookeriana* var. *humilis* Z6–9 H9–6
- *Vaccinium macrocarpon* Z2–7 H7–1

Mahonia repens
CREEPING BARBERRY

Ⓝ ☼ ☀ ◊ Z5–8 H8–3 ‡1ft (30cm) ↔6ft (2m)

An upright, suckering plant. Dark yellow flowers bloom from mid to late spring. Blue-black berries follow. Best if grown in moderately fertile, organic soil.

Vinca minor 'Variegata'
VARIEGATED PERIWINKLE

☼ ☀ ◊◊◊ Z5–9 H9–1 ‡8in (20cm) ↔indefinite

Flowers from midspring to autumn. A mat-forming plant that makes a good groundcover and grows well in most soils. Cut back in spring to control growth.

Vaccinium vitis-idaea
COWBERRY

Ⓝ ☼ ☀ ◊ pH Z2–6 H6–1 ‡10in (25cm) ↔indefinite

A very prostrate, evergreen plant. The flowers are followed by dark red berries that have a bitter taste.

Calluna vulgaris cultivars
SCOTCH HEATHER

☼ ◊ pH Z5–7 H7–5 ‡24in (60cm) ↔30in (75cm)

Requiring similar conditions to spring heath, it flowers in summer. The many cultivars come in a range of flower and foliage colors, adding year-round interest.

WOODY PLANTS

Large broad-leaved evergreen shrubs

Not all of the shrubs shown here are literally broad-leafed; the term is used to differentiate between cone-bearing plants (conifers) and other evergreens. Some of these have quite fine foliage, but they will all grow into large plants and need to be given ample space at planting time. You can interplant with annuals for the first few years until the shrubs mature.

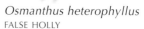

Osmanthus heterophyllus
FALSE HOLLY
☼ ☼ ◊ Z7–9 H9–4 ↕↔15ft (5m)
An adaptable plant that prefers an acidic soil but will grow in neutral soils also. It prunes well and can be used for hedges and screens. Spiny leaves repel intruders.

MORE CHOICES

- *Buxus handsworthiensis* Z6–8 H8–6
- *Camellia japonica* cultivars Z7–11 H8–7
- *Kalmia latifolia* Z5–9 H9–5
- *Prunus laurocerasus* Z6–9 H9–6
- *Rhododendron catawbiense* Z4–8 H8–1
- *Viburnum* x *rhytidophylloides* 'Alleghany' Z5–8 H8–5

Pyracantha coccinea 'Lalandei'
LALAND SCARLET FIRETHORN
☼ ☼ ◊ Z6–9 H9–6 ↕↔12ft (4m)
A stiff, spiny, upright shrub that needs slightly acidic soil and withstands dry soil once established. White flowers in small, flat-topped clusters in spring.

Ilex pedunculosa
LONGSTALK HOLLY
☼ ☼ ◊ Z6–9 H9–6 ↕30ft (10m) ↔22ft (7m)
An attractive shrub for acidic soils, with a dense habit of growth. The fruit persist into winter or until eaten by birds. Late spring white flowers on the new growth.

Viburnum 'Pragense'
PRAGUE VIBURNUM
☼ ☼ ◊ Z6–8 H8–6 ↕↔10ft (3m)
Thin, spreading shoots on an upright-oval plant. Flowers are pink in bud and produce black fruit in late summer. A hybrid raised in Prague in 1955.

Viburnum rhytidophyllum
LEATHERLEAF VIBURNUM
☼ ☼ ◊ Z5–8 H8–5 ↕15ft (5m) ↔12ft (4m)
A fast-growing, upright shrub that needs protection from strong winds. It may be deciduous at the northern limits of its range. Fruit are red, turning black.

Pieris japonica 'Mountain Fire'
JAPANESE ANDROMEDA, MOUNTAIN FIRE PIERIS

☼ ◐ ◊ pH Z6–8 H8–6 ↕↔10ft (3m)

Evergeen leaves are brilliant red when young, turning chestnut brown as they mature. Produces abundant clusters of flowers. Deer find this shrub unappealing.

Pieris floribunda
FETTERBUSH

Ⓝ ☼ ◐ ◊ pH Z5–8 H8–5 ↕6ft (2m) ↔10ft (3m)

Forms a rounded bush with stiff branches and dense foliage. Grows in more alkaline soils that other *Pieris*. Fragrant flowers open in spring and can last a month.

Cotoneaster salicifolius
WILLOWLEAF COTONEASTER

☼ ☼ ◊ Z6–8 ↕↔15ft (3m)

A spreading, arching shrub with shiny foliage that turns purplish in winter. Small white flowers in flattened heads in early summer produce berries that persist all winter.

Rhododendron maximum
ROSEBAY RHODODENDRON

Ⓝ ☼ ◊◊ Z4–9 H9–1 ↕to 15ft (5m) ↔indefinite

In the wild this can form impenetrable thickets with intertwined, twisted stems. The flowers open in late spring/early summer. Native from Nova Scotia to Georgia.

Berberis julianae
WINTER BARBERRY

☼ ◊ Z6–9 H9–4 ↕↔10ft (3m)

A durable shrub that survives in exposed, windy sites. Flowers borne in late spring and early summer are followed ovoid black berries. Silvery leaf undersides.

WOODY PLANTS

Medium to large street trees

Where streets are wide, large trees can be planted and will grow to provide shade and a canopy of branches over the street. Some of the trees shown here, especially the maples, may not grow well in high-traffic areas, where pollution levels are high. Do not plant these under utility wires: as they grow, they will need to be pruned, and their shape may well be ruined.

Tilia tomentosa
SILVER LINDEN
☼ ☀ ◊ Z6–9 H9–6 ‡100ft (30m) ↔70ft (20m)
A broadly pyramidal tree for a moist, fertile soil, but tolerant of drought when established. The flowers are fragrant and can stupefy bees in summer.

MORE CHOICES

- *Fraxinus pennsylvanica* Z3–9 H9–4
- *Liquidambar styraciflua* 'Rotundiloba' Z6–9 H9–1
- *Platanus x acerifolia* Z5–8 H8–3
- *Ulmus americana* Z3–9 H9–1
- *Zelkova serrata* Z5–9 H9–5

Gymnocladus dioica
KENTUCKY COFFEE TREE
Ⓝ ☼ ◊ Z5–9 H9–2 ‡70ft (20m) ↔50 ft (15m)
An underused tree with bark raised in vertical ridges and, on female trees, long, leathery pods that persist all winter. Seeds were once used as a coffee substitute.

Celtis occidentalis
COMMON HACKBERRY, SUGARBERRY
Ⓝ ☼ ◊ Z2–9 H9–1 ‡70ft (20m) ↔50 ft (15m)
Very adaptable to soils and locations. Mature trees have a shape reminiscent of American elm. Spring flowers are not showy, but the brown-red fall fruit are sweet.

Fraxinus americana
WHITE ASH

Ⓝ ☼ ◊ Z6–9 H9–6 ↕80ft (24m) ↔50 ft (15m)

Develops an open, rounded head at maturity, with yellow to red to dark purple foliage in early fall. Excellent for lawns and other large spaces.

Liriodendron tulipifera
TULIP TREE

Ⓝ ☼ ☼ ♈ Z5–9 H9–1 ↕100ft (30m) ↔50 ft (15m)

Greenish yellow flowers in late spring are followed by conical seedheads that persist into winter. Yellow fall color brightens large spaces, where this tree does best.

Quercus phellos
WILLOW OAK

Ⓝ ☼ ☼ ◊ Z6–9 H9–3 ↕70ft (20m) ↔50ft (15m)

Fast-growing, with a cone-shaped growth habit. Smooth gray bark later develops shallow ridges. In warmer areas, dead leaves hang on through winter.

Quercus rubra
RED OAK

Ⓝ ☼ ☼ ◊ ♈ Z5–9 H9–5 ↕80ft (24m) ↔70ft (20m)

Fast-growing, round-headed, symmetrical tree with pinkish red unfurling leaves and red fall foliage. Deep ridges add interest on old bark. Tolerates pollution.

Quercus palustris
PIN OAK

Ⓝ ☼ ☼ ◊ Z5–8 H8–3 ↕70ft (20m) ↔40ft (12m)

Very striking growth form, with a clearly pyramidal outline and horizontal branching habit. Fall color can be an outstanding red. Tolerant of city conditions.

Corylus colurna
TURKISH FILBERT

☼ ☼ ◊ Z5–7 H7–5 ↕70ft (20m) ↔22ft (7m)

Heavy-textured, very leathery leaves turn yellow to purple in autumn. Aging bark flakes off to reveal orange-brown patches beneath. Needs room.

WOODY PLANTS

Medium-sized street trees

These trees are suitable for most urban locations and are widely planted by some municipalities. On many new subdivisions, it is left to the home-owner to plant street trees. If this is your situation, try to diversify the planting by choosing something different from your neighbors. Over-planting a single tree type often leads to pest and disease problems.

Acer campestre
HEDGE MAPLE

☼ ◐ ◊ Z6–8 H8–4 ↕↔25–55ft (8–17m)

Slow-growing, very adaptable tree. Often used as a street tree in urban areas: it tolerates compaction around the roots, heavy pruning, and air pollution.

Ostrya virginica
AMERICAN HOP HORNBEAM

Ⓝ ☼ ◐ ◊ Z5–9 H9–2 ↕50ft (15m) ↔40ft (12m)

Pyramidal when young, this develops a rounded outline with age. Small catkins in winter and spring produce hoplike fruit. May be slow to establish.

MORE CHOICES

- *Acer* x *freemanii* Cultivars Z4–7 H7–1
- *Aesculus hippocastanum* 'Baumannii' Z3–8 H8–1
- *Carpinus betulus* 'Fastigiata' Z4–8 H8–3
- *Corylus colurna* Z5–7 H7–5
- *Koelreuteria paniculata* Z6–9 H9–1

Prunus cerasifera 'Newport'
NEWPORT CHERRY PLUM

☼ ◊ Z4–9 H9–1 ↕↔30ft (10m)

Early flowering. New foliage darkens to purple as it ages. A round-headed tree tolerant of most soils. Like all cherries, it is attacked by many pests and diseases.

Prunus sargentii
SARGENT CHERRY
☼ ◊ z5–9 H9–5 ‡70ft (20m) ↔50ft (15m)
Red-tinged new leaves turn shiny, dark green, and then bronze in fall. Spring flowers produce dark red fruit that birds devour. The bark is glowing orange-brown and peeling. 'Columnaris' is more upright.

Prunus x *subhirtella* 'Pendula Plena Rosea'
WINTER-FLOWERING CHERRY
☼ ◊◊ z6–8 H8–6 ‡↔25 ft (8m)
Single flowers in early spring, before the leaves, which turn yellow in fall. There may be scattered flowers in fall also. Fruit are red cherries, becoming black.

Prunus serrula
ORIENTAL CHERRY
☼ ◊ z6–8 H8–6 ‡↔30ft (10m)
A rounded tree with white flowers in spring as the foliage unfurls, followed by unshowy red fruit. Leaves turn yellow in fall. The highly polished, lined winter bark is the best feature. Susceptible to the usual cherry pests and diseases.

Pyrus calleryana 'Bradford'
BRADFORD PEAR
☼ ◊ z5–8 H8–3 ‡50ft (15m) ↔40ft (12m)
Pyramidal tree that grows quickly, tolerates pollution, and is adaptable to many soil types. Tight branch crotches are weak and break easily. Often overused.

MORE CHOICES

- *Maackia amurensis* z5–7 H7–5
- *Quercus robur* 'Fastigiata' z5–8 H8–3
- *Sophora japonica* z5–9 H9–1

Prunus mume
JAPANESE APRICOT
☼ ◊◊ z6–8 H8–6 ‡↔28ft (9m)
Fragrant flowers are borne singly or in pairs in late winter to early spring before the leaves. Round yellow fruits follow. A range of cultivars is available.

Tilia cordata 'Greenspire'
GREENSPIRE LITTLELEAF LINDEN
☼ ☼ ◊ z4–8 H8–1 ‡50ft (15m) ↔22ft (7m)
A pollution-tolerant tree that will grow in a wide variety of soils and transplants easily. Fragrant flowers appear in midsummer. Other cultivars have broader outlines.

Phellodendron amurense
AMUR CORK TREE
☼ ◊ z4–7 H8–5 ‡47ft (14m) ↔50ft (15m)
Broad, spreading tree with yellow fall foliage. Notable for its deeply ridged, corklike, gray-brown bark on mature trees. Requires a large space to do well.

WOODY PLANTS

Trees for difficult urban sites

Where traffic is heavy, producing high pollution levels, where frequent industrial smog gives a poor air quality, or where soil is thin, poor, and lacking in nutrients, a plant needs to be tough to survive and grow well. The trees shown here are adapted to difficult sites. Given care until established, they will thrive despite poor growing conditions.

MORE CHOICES

- *Catalpa* spp. Z5–9 H9–5
- *Celtis* spp. Z2–9 H9–1
- *Crataegus* spp. Z5–8 H8–1
- *Ginkgo biloba* Z5–9 H9–3
- *Gleditsia triacanthos* v. *inermis* Z3–7 H7–1
- *Platanus* x *acerifolia* Z5–8 H8–3
- *Prunus virginiana* Z3–8 H8–1
- *Styphnolobium* (*Sophora*) *japonica* Z5–9 H9–1
- *Tilia* spp. Z4–7 H7–1
- *Ulmus americana* & hybrids Z3–9 H9–1
- *Zelkova serrata* Z5–9 H9–5

Carpinus caroliniana
AMERICAN HORNBEAM

Ⓝ ☼ ☀ ◊ Z3–9 H9–1 ↕↔30ft (9m)

Because there appear to be muscles flexing beneath the undulating surface of blue-gray, smooth bark, this tree acquired the common name of Musclewood.

Taxodium distichum
BALD CYPRESS

Ⓝ ☼ ☀ ◊ ◑ Z5–11 H12–5 ↕80ft (24m) ↔25ft (8m)

The needles turn rust-brown in fall before dropping. Distinctive aerial roots ("knees") form around the base of the tree in wet sites. Moderate growth rate.

Carpinus betulus
EUROPEAN HORNBEAM

☼ ☀ ◊ Z4–8 H8–1 ↕80ft (25m) ↔70ft (20m)

The smooth gray bark is fluted and muscly-looking. Leaves are yellow in fall and unusually free of pests. Excellent as a screening plant, as a hedge, or in planters.

Aesculus hippocastanum
HORSE CHESTNUT

☼ ◊ Z3–8 H8–1 ↕100ft (30m) ↔75ft (22.5)

Easy to grow in most soils, including alkaline ones, but avoid very dry locations. Each spiny fruit contains 2–3 large, brown, inedible nuts.

Phellodendron amurense
AMUR CORK TREE

☼ ◊ Z3–7 H7–1 ↕45ft ↔50 ft (15m)

Broad, spreading tree with yellow fall foliage. Notable for the deeply ridged, corklike, gray-brown bark on mature trees. Requires a large space.

Maackia amurensis
AMUR MAACKIA

☼ ◊ Z5–7 H7–5 ↕50 ft (15m) ↔30ft (9m)

Shiny, curling bronze-colored bark and late summer flowers offer outstanding landscape appeal. Use as a street tree or grow in large containers. Pest-free.

Koelreuteria paniculata
PANICLED GOLDEN RAIN TREE

☼ ◊ Z6–9 H9–1 ↕↔30ft (10m)

Opening leaves are purplish red, become bright green, then turn golden yellow in fall. Yellow flowers appear in midsummer and become inflated fruit.

Acer tataricum subsp. ginnala
AMUR MAPLE

☼ ◐ ◊ Z3–7 H7–1 ↕30ft (10m) ↔25ft (8m)

A good small tree or large shrub with yellow flowers in spring, red-tinged fruit in summer, and excellent fall color. Cultivars have brighter fruit and fall color.

Nyssa sylvatica
SOUR GUM

Ⓝ ☼ ◐ ● Z5–9 H9–7 ↕70ft (20m) ↔30ft (9m)

Has a cone-shaped head with straight trunk and horizontal branches. Useful as a street tree or specimen. Tolerates coastal conditions, but not shade.

Gymnocladus dioica
KENTUCKY COFFEE TREE

Ⓝ ☼ ◊ Z5–9 H9–2 ↕70ft (20m) ↔50 ft (15m)

Of greatest interest is the dark brown, scaly, curly bark, found even on young branches. Very late to leaf out in spring. Thick, leathery pods hang on through winter.

Pinus nigra
AUSTRIAN PINE, BLACK PINE

☼ ◊ Z5–8 H8–4 ↕to 100ft (30m) ↔25ft (8m)

This makes a flat-topped tree with spreading branches at maturity. The mottled, ridged bark is various shades of brown. Makes a good specimen tree or windbreak.

Liquidambar styraciflua
AMERICAN SWEET GUM

Ⓝ ☼ ◊ Z6–9 H9–6 ↕100ft (30m) ↔75ft (23m)

This species has fleshy roots and is slow to establish. Does not do well where root space is restricted. Named forms have superior fall color.

Trees unlikely to be browsed by deer

While it is fairly easy to protect the trunks of young trees from deer browsing by wrapping them in chicken wire or a tree wrap, the branches are more difficult to protect. Even when the lower branches are above deer height, occasional deep snowfalls give them access and the chance to cause severe damage. Damage can be reduced by planting species they do not find tasty.

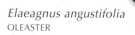

Elaeagnus angustifolia
OLEASTER
☼ ◊ Z2–8 H8–1 ‡↔20ft (6m)
Fragrant, creamy yellow flowers appear in summer, followed by edible yellow fruit. Branches are red-tinted with silvery scales. Deciduous.

Liquidambar styraciflua 'Palo Alto'
PALO ALTO SWEET GUM
Ⓝ ☼☀ ◑ Z6–9 H9–1 ‡80ft (25m) ↔40ft (12m)
Transplant in spring into a slightly acidic soil. Fleshy roots take time to become established. This cultivar has bright orange-red leaves in fall.

Pinus nigra
AUSTRIAN PINE, BLACK PINE
☼ ◊ Z5–8 H8–4 ‡to 100ft (30m) ↔25ft (8m)
A tough tree that will withstand city conditions, salt, and most soils except very dry. Makes a good specimen tree, with attractive bark. Also useful for windbreaks.

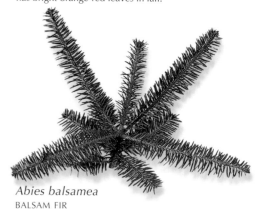

Magnolia grandiflora
SOUTHERN MAGNOLIA
Ⓝ ☼☀ ◊ Z7–9 H9–1 ‡↔30ft (9m)
Wonderfully fragrant white flowers in late spring to early summer are followed by conelike fruit ripening in fall to expose red seeds. Normally pest-free.

Larix decidua 'Pendula'
WEEPING EUROPEAN LARCH
☼ ◊ Z3–6 H6–1 ‡100ft (30m) ↔20ft (4m)
Young foliage is bright green, becoming glowing yellow in late fall after most trees have shed. Grows in wet soils but is intolerant of very alkaline soils and pollution.

Abies balsamea
BALSAM FIR
Ⓝ ☼ ◑ Z3–6 H6–1 ‡↔3ft (1m)
A shallow-rooted species that prefers an acidic soil and will grow in swampy ground. It forms a narrow, upright tree that makes an attractive specimen.

Picea glauca
WHITE SPRUCE

Ⓝ ☼ ◊ Z3–6 H6–1 ↕30–50ft (9–15m) ↔15ft (5m)
A narrowly or broadly conical tree. Bark is ash gray
and becomes scaly with age. Growth rate is moderate.
'Densata' grows more slowly.

Ilex opaca
AMERICAN HOLLY

Ⓝ ☼ ◐ ● ◊ Z5–9 H9–5 ↕45ft (14m) ↔4ft (1.2m)
In old age, the habit becomes more open and irregular.
Fragrant white flowers in early summer are followed
by small, persistent red fruit. Not for dry, windy areas.

Picea glauca 'Conica'
DWARF ALBERTA SPRUCE

Ⓝ ☼ ◊ Z3–6 H6–1 ↕6–15ft (2–5m) ↔3–6ft (1–2m)
A dwarf variety that maintains a neat, conical shape.
Growth is slow, and be watchful of reverted growth.
Also known as *P. glauca* var. *albertiana* 'Conica'.

MORE CHOICES

- *Acer negundo* Z5–8 H8–3
- *Arbutus menziesii* Z7–9 H9–7
- *Cryptomeria japonica* Z6–9 H9–4
- *Elaeagnus angustifolius* Z2–8 H8–1
- *Populus nigra* 'Italica' Z3–9 H9–1
- *Robinia pseudoacacia* Z4–9 H9–3
- *Thuja plicata* Z6–8 H8–6

Picea omorika
SERBIAN SPRUCE

☼ ◊ Z4–8 H8–1 ↕100ft (30m) ↔75ft (22m)
Brown bark cracks into square patches. Bears oblong
red-brown cones that turn brown. Growth rate is slow.
Tolerates alkaline soil.

Fraxinus pennsylvanica 'Summit'
SUMMIT GREEN ASH

☼ ◊ Z4–9 H9–1 ↕45ft (14m) ↔25ft (8m)
A very adaptable tree, often planted in boulevards
and parking lots because of its vigor and pollution
resistance. Good color, but leaves drop early in fall.

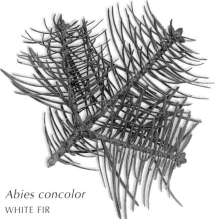

Abies concolor
WHITE FIR

Ⓝ ☼ ◊ Z3–7 H7–1 ↕100ft (30m) ↔25ft (8m)
Columnar tree that maintains its foliage to the ground.
Slow to moderate growth. Cylindrical cones measure
up to 5in (25cm) and disintegrate before falling.

Ilex x aquipernyi 'Brilliant'
BRILLIANT AQUIPERN HOLLY

☼ ◐ ◊ Z6–8 H8–6 ↕20ft (6m) ↔12ft (4m)
A conical, small, dense evergreen tree with shiny
leaves that are almost spineless. This cultivar sets
fruit without having a male tree nearby.

WOODY PLANTS

Deciduous shrubs unlikely to be deer-browsed

Being comparatively low-growing, shrubs are easily eaten by deer, and the high populations of this animal found in many suburban and rural areas make damage almost inevitable. Even the shrubs shown here may be browsed in severe weather when the deer are hungry and food is in short supply, but the damage should be minimal.

Vitex agnus-castus
CHASTE TREE

☼ ◊ Z6–9 H9–6 ↕↔8ft (2.5m)

Fragrant flowers appear through much of summer. Deadhead to encourage repeat bloom. Prefers hot weather. Native to southern Europe and western Asia.

MORE CHOICES

- *Cotinus coggygria* Z5–9 H9–3
- *Daphne mezereum* Z5–8 H8–5
- *Forsythia ovata* Z5–7 H7–5
- *Potentilla fruiticosa* Z3–7 H7–1

Hypericum 'Hidcote'
HIDCOTE ST. JOHN'S WORT

☼ ◊ Z6–9 H9–6 ↕↔5ft (1.5m)

Flowers from midsummer to early autumn This dense and bushy hybrid bears evergreen to semi-evergreen foliage and prefers moderately fertile soil.

Euonymus alatus
BURNING BUSH

☼ ☼ ◊ Z4–9 H9–1 ↕6ft (2m) ↔10ft (3m)

Corky wings decorate green shoots. Leaves are dark green in spring and summer. Bears yellowish fruit that split open to reveal orange seeds. Rabbits avoid it, too.

Caryopteris x clandonensis 'Arthur Simmonds'
BLUE MIST SHRUB

☼ ☼ ◊ Z6–9 H9–1 ↕3ft (1m) ↔5ft (1.5m)

Rounded shrub with flowers in late summer on new growth. Cut back hard in late winter. Grow this in lean soil to prevent excessive leafiness.

Myrica pensylvanica
BAYBERRY

Ⓝ ☼ ☼ ◊◊ Z3–6 H6–1 ↕9ft (2.5m) ↔12ft (4m)

Bears yellow-green catkins in spring before the leaves. Waxy layer on the outside of the berries is used to make candles. Nice hedge or screen.

Abelia 'Edward Goucher'
EDWARD GOUCHER ABELIA

☼ ◐ ◊ Z6–9 H9–1 ↕10ft (3m) ↔12ft (4m)

Evergreen or semi-evergreen shrub. Fragrant flowers are borne from midsummer to fall. Irresistible to many butterflies. Also known as *A rupestris*.

Clerodendrum trichotomum
HARLEQUIN GLORYBOWER

☼ ◊ Z7–9 H9–7 ↕↔20ft (6m)

At the limits of hardiness, treat this as a perennial, cutting it back to live wood in spring. Fragrant flowers open from midsummer to fall; when fruit appear with the later flowers.

Buddleja davidii 'White Bouquet'
WHITE BOUQUET BUTTERFLY BUSH

☼ ◊ Z5–9 H9–2 ↕10ft (3m) ↔15ft (3m)

Flowering from midsummer until frost, the sweetly scented blooms are a magnet to butterflies. Very easy to grow, it can become almost a weed. Can be cut back almost to the ground in early spring.

Viburnum farreri
FRAGRANT VIBURNUM

☼ ◊ Z6–8 H8–6 ↕↔10ft (3m)

Flowering from late winter to early spring, this needs a sheltered location to prevent the open flowers from being damaged by late frost. New foliage emerges with later flowers.

Potentilla fruticosa 'Goldfinger'
GOLDFINGER POTENTILLA

Ⓝ ☼ ◊ Z3–7 H7–1 ↕3ft (1m) ↔4ft (1.2m)

Flowers up to 2in (5cm) across blossom profusely among the leaves, composed of five narrowly oblong leaflets. Potentillas can be cut to the ground in spring to keep them neat.

WOODY PLANTS

Evergreen shrubs resistant to deer

Although deer will eat almost anything in the winter when they are hungry, evergreen foliage is their favorite; it contains more food value than dry twigs and branches. Eastern white cedar, or arborvitae (*Thuja occidentalis*), often used for hedging, is a favorite food, as shown by the browse line on many plants. However, the plants shown here should be almost damage-free.

Mahonia aquifolium
OREGON GRAPE HOLLY
Ⓝ ☼ ◑ ◊ Z6–9 H9–6 ‡↔5ft (1.5m)
Slow-growing, upright, evergreen shrub turns purplish bronze in fall. Blue-black, wax-coated berries ripen in early fall and hang on through winter.

Pyracantha 'Mohave'
MOHAVE FIRETHORN
☼ ◊ Z6–9 H9–6 ‡12ft (4m) ↔15ft (5m)
Upright grower with white flowers in spring giving way to the fruit, which ripen in early fall and hang on through winter. Resistant to scab and fireblight.

MORE CHOICES

- *Buxus* spp. Z5–9 H10–4
- *Mahonia bealei* Z5–8 H8–3
- *Pyracantha coccinea* Z6–9 H9–6
- *Kalmia latifolia* Z5–9 H9–5
- *Sarcoccoca hookeriana* v. *humilis*
  Z6–9 H9–6

Berberis x *gladwynensis* 'William Penn'
WILLIAM PENN HYBRID BARBERRY
☼ ◑ ◊ Z6–9 H9–4 ‡↔4ft (1.2m)
Clusters of bright yellow flowers in spring produce purple fruit on a dense mound. Introduced by the Henry Foundation of Gladwyne, PA.

Berberis verruculosa
WARTY BARBERRY
☼ ◑ ◊ Z6–9 H9–4 ‡↔5ft (1.5m)
A spiny, dense, compact shrub with leaves that are whitish beneath and turn dark red during winter. The late spring flowers produce dark purple fruits.

Berberis julianae
WINTER BARBERRY

☼ ◊ Z6–9 H9–4 ↕↔10ft (3m)

Dense, bushy shrub. Leaves are dark green and glossy above and pale green underneath. Yellow or red-tinged flowers are followed by egg-shaped black fruits.

Juniperus x 'Pfitzeriana'
PFITZER CHINESE JUNIPER

☼ ◐ ◊ Z4–9 H9–1 ↕5ft (1.5m) ↔20ft (6m)

Probably the most widely planted juniper and tolerant of most soils, except overly wet. There are many named forms with yellow-tinged or bluish foliage. May be offered as a variety of *J. chinensis* at nurseries.

Juniperus horizontalis
CREEPING JUNIPER

☼ ◐ ◊ Z3–9 H9–1 ↕12in (30cm) ↔indefinite

A very adaptable plant that will grow in most soils, including dry and alkaline. Named varieties may have blue or bright green needles and grow to varying heights.

Ilex x meservae cultivars
BLUE HOLLY

☼ ◐ ◊ Z5–9 H9–5 ↕15ft (5m) ↔10ft (3m)

The names of the cultivars reveal the sex of the plant, for example 'Blue Prince' and 'Blue Princess'. One male must be planted as pollinator for berries to form.

Pieris japonica
JAPANESE ANDROMEDA, JAPANESE PIERIS

☼ ◐ ◊ pH Z6–8 H8–6 ↕12ft (4m) ↔10ft (3m)

Grow this in well enriched with organic matter. New foliage is bronze, and the flowers open in early spring. There are many named forms, some with pink flowers.

Juniperus procumbens 'Nana'
JAPANESE GARDEN JUNIPER

☼ ◊ Z3–9 H9–1 ↕6–8in (15–20cm) ↔30in (75cm)

A dwarf, compact form of an already procumbent shrub resulting in a low, mat-forming plant. Foliage turns slightly purple in winter. Growth rate is rather slow.

WOODY PLANTS

Trees and shrubs for protected sites

Most of these plants are at the limit of their hardiness in our region. Do not try these in a garden that is exposed to winter winds or where frost occurs late in spring. In a sheltered garden, especially one with high hedges to add protection, they are worth the extra effort. Give winter protection, such as a burlap screen, for at least the first year until they are well established.

MORE CHOICES

- *Camellia japonica* 'April Kiss' Z7–8 H10–7
- *Camellia japonica* 'Spring Promise' Z7–8 H10–7
- *Camellia* x 'Winter Beauty' Z6–10 H8–7
- *Camellia* x 'Winter Star' Z6–10 H8–7
- *Hydrangea aspera* ssp. *sargentiana* Z7–9 H9–7

Ilex x altaclerensis 'Golden King'
GOLDEN KING ALTACLARA HOLLY
☼ ◐ ◊ Z7–9 H9–7 ‡70ft (20m) ↔50ft (15m)
Grow in an organic soil and protect from strong winds. This is a female form, so a male needs to be nearby to produce berries.

Ilex aquifolium
ENGLISH HOLLY
☼ ◐ ◓ ◊ Z7–9 H9–7 ‡70ft (20m) ↔20ft
A popular species that is available in a wide range of cultivars that were selected for their leaf and fruit color as well as for their leaf and overall plant shape.

Musa basjoo
JAPANESE BANANA
☼ ◊ Z8–11 H12–1 ‡15ft (5m) ↔12ft (4m)
This needs a sheltered location in a rich soil, with protection from strong winds that damage the foliage. Yellow flowers in summer produce small, inedible fruits.

WOODY PLANTS

Daphne odora
WINTER DAPHNE

☼ ☽ ◊ Z7–9 H9–7 ‡↔4ft (1.2m)

Very fragrant flowers blossom from midwiner to early spring and are followed by fleshy red fruit. Also try the yellow-edged 'Aureomarginata'.

MORE CHOICES

- *Ilex cornuta* 'Burfordii' Z6–9 H9–1
- *Ilex x koehneana* Z7–9 H9–7
- *Lagerstroemia x* 'Hopi' Z5–9 H9–5
- *Lagerstroemia x* 'Tuskegee' Z7–9 H9–7
- *Stachyurus chinensis* Z8–9 H9–8

Lagerstroemia 'Natchez'
NATCHEZ CRAPE MYRTLE

☼ ◊ Z6–9 H9–6 ‡↔25ft (8m)

Glossy, dark green leaves turn red and orange in fall. From midsummer to fall, clusters of pure white flowers open in arching sprays. The bark is attractive year-round.

Camellia japonica 'Bette Sette'
BELLE SETTE CAMELLIA

☼ ◊ ᴾᴴ Z6–9 H8–7 ‡15ft (4m) ↔10ft (3m)

Flowers open in late winter and may be damaged by cold, which turns them brown, but unopened buds are normally unaffected. Grow in an organic soil, and mulch annually to ptotect the shallow root system.

Chimonanthus praecox
WINTERSWEET

☼ ◊ Z7–9 H9–7 ‡8ft (2.5m) ↔10ft (3m)

In winter, this shrub produces fragrant, pendent, cup-shaped flowers. Leaves are lance shaped and glossy, arranged in opposite pairs.

Skimmia japonica
JAPANESE SKIMMIA

☼ ◊ Z7–9 H9–7 ‡↔5ft (1.5m)

Has slightly fragrant leaves as well as fragrant red- or pink-tinged white flowers. If both sexes are present, female plant bears red fruit.

Buddleja lindleyana
LINDLEY BUTTERFLY BUSH

☼ ◊ Z8–9 H9–8 ‡↔6ft (2m)

An unusual deciduous shrub, with arching then hanging stems and leaves in a single plane, rather than around the branchlets. It flowers from mid- to late summer.

Spreading evergreens

Many of these plants are commonly used for foundation planting, but they are also make good groundcovers, especially on slopes, where their fibrous root system binds the soil. Some of the spreading junipers can become very large in time and may outgrow their location or need severe pruning to keep them within bounds.

Chamaecyparis obtusa
HINOKI CYPRESS
☼ ☼ ◊ ◊ Z4–8 H8–3 ↕70ft (20m) ↔15ft (5m)
An open, irregular shrub to small tree, depending on the cultivar. Small cones start green and turn brown as they ripen in fall. Growth rate is moderate.

MORE CHOICES

- *Buxus* 'Green Mound' z6–9 H9–6
- *Buxus* 'Green Mountain' z6–9 H9–6
- *Buxus* 'Vardar Valley' z6–9 H9–6
- *Cephalotaxus harringtonia* 'Duke Gardens' z6–9 H9–3
- *Cephalotaxus harringtonia* 'Prostrata' z6–9 H9–6
- *Juniperus* 'Blauuw' z3–9 H9–1
- *Juniperus* 'Gold Coast' z3–9 H9–1
- *Juniperus* 'Pfitzeriana Glauca' z4–9 H9–1
- *Juniperus* 'Robusta Green' z5–9 H9–1

Cephalotaxus harringtonia
COW'S-TAIL PINE
☼ ◊ Z6–9 H9–3 ↕15ft (5m) ↔10ft (3m)
Can be a large shrub or small tree as it ages. Female plants produce small, egg-shaped, olive green fruit in fall. Prefers fertile soil. Tolerates severe cutting back.

Torreya nucifera
JAPANESE TORREYA, KAYA
☼ ☼ ◊ Z6–10 H10–6 ↕50ft (15m) ↔25ft (8m)
A small tree or large shrub with aromatic, yewlike foliage and whorled branches. The fruits, which resemble a nutmeg, take two years to develop.

Taxus baccata 'Repandens'
DWARF SPREADING ENGLISH YEW

☼ ☼ ☼   ◊   Z7–8 H8–7   ‡24in (60cm)
↔15ft (5m)

A wide shrub with drooping branch tips.
New growth is as shown, darkening later in
summer to a midgreen. It grows equally
well on alkaline and acidic soils.

Leucothoe fontanesiana 'Girard's Rainbow'
RAINBOW FETTERBUSH

☼ ☼ ☼   ◊   ⊞   Z5–8 H8–3   ‡↔5ft (1.5m)

Although the fragrant spring flowers are
attractive, this shrub is grown more for the
decorative foliage. While most striking in
spring, it is colorful for most of the summer.

Ilex glabra 'Compacta'
DWARF INKBERRY

Ⓝ ☼ ☼   ◊   ⊞   Z5–9 H9–5   ‡10ft (3m)   ↔6ft (2m)

Grow this in an acidic soil; it will not thrive
in alkaline ones. Late spring flowers
are white and are followed
by black berries that last
through winter until
new flowers open.

Juniperus chinensis
CHINESE JUNIPER

☼ ☼   ◊   Z3–9 H9–1
‡70ft (20m)   ↔20ft (6m)

This species can be either an ovoid-
conical tree or spreading shrub. Growth rate is
moderate to slow. Many cultivars are available.

Prunus laurocerasus
CHERRY LAUREL

☼ ☼   ◊   Z6–9 H9–6   ‡25ft (8m)   ↔30ft (10m)

A dense shrub with fragrant white flowers in upright
spikes in spring, followed by red fruit that ripen to black
in summer. 'Otto Luyken' is smaller and readily available.

Chamaecyparis pisifera
SAWARA FALSE CYPRESS

☼   ◊   Z4–8 H8–1   ‡70ft (20m)   ↔15ft (5m)

This grows best in areas with high humidity, and the
soil should be kept moist in summer, especially while
the plant is young. There are many named forms.

WOODY PLANTS

Conifers for large spaces

The trees illustrated here will all grow large in time, often with wide-spreading branches. They are best suited to parks or large estates and are not good choices for most city gardens. Several have blue or silvery needles and make good specimen plants while others, white pine for example, make excellent windbreaks.

Abies balsamea
BALSAM FIR
Ⓝ ☼ ◑ ⚘ Z3–6 H6–1 ‡50ft (15m) ↔15ft (5m)
Grow this in areas that are pollution-free. It forms a narrow pyramid with the foliage smelling of balsam. Found in the wild from swamps to mountain tops.

MORE CHOICES

- *Abies nordmanniana* Z4–6 H6–4
- *Cedrus atlantica* Z6–9 H9–6
- *Cedrus libani* Z6–9 H9–3
- *Picea mariana* Z3–6 H6–1
- *Picea orientalis* Z5–8 H8–5
- *Pinus koraiensis* Z4–7 H7–1
- *Pinus virginiana* Z3–7 H7–1
- *Pseudotsuga menziesi* Z4–7 H7–1
- *Thuja plicata* Z6–8 H8–6

Pinus wallichiana
BHUTAN PINE, HIMALAYAN PINE
☼ ◊ Z6–9 H9–5 ‡to 120 ft (35m)
A broadly conical tree that keeps its branches to the ground. Plant in sandy, acidic soil as a small tree, larger ones don't transplant well.

Cedrus atlantica 'Glauca'
BLUE ATLAS CEDAR
☼ ◊ Z6–9 H9–3 ‡100ft (30m) ↔75ft (22m)
Scrawny when young but fills out as it matures with horizontally spreading branches. Moderate growth rate. Also known as *C. libani* subsp. *atlantica* f. *glauca*.

Abies concolor
WHITE FIR
Ⓝ ☼ ◊ Z3–7 H7–1 ‡100ft (30m) ↔25ft (8m)
Columnar tree that maintains its foliage to the ground. Slow to moderate growth. Cylindrical cones measure up to 5in (25cm) and disintegrate before falling.

Picea pungens
COLORADO SPRUCE
Ⓝ ☼ ◊ Z3–8 H8–1 ‡50ft (15m) ↔15ft (5m)
Gray-green needles are less prominent in the landscape than those of the bluer cultivars. Very tough and adaptable.

Picea omorika
SERBIAN SPRUCE

☼ ◐ ◊ Z4–8 H8–1 ‡100ft (30m) ↔75ft (22m)

Brown bark cracks into square patches. Bears oblong red-brown cones that turn brown. Growth rate is slow. Tolerates alkaline soil.

Picea abies
NORWAY SPRUCE

☼ ◊ Z3–8 H8–1 ‡to 130ft (40m) ↔20ft (6m)

The spreading root system makes this an easy species to transplant. A good shelter belt or hedge. 'Nidiformis', the bird's nest spruce, is good for small gardens.

Picea engelmannii
ENGLEMANN SPRUCE

Ⓝ ☼ ◊ Z3–8 H8–1 ‡to 130ft (40m) ↔15ft (5m)

A densely pyramidal tree with almost horizontal branches best planted in deep soils. The foliage has a disagreeable odor when crushed.

Picea glauca
WHITE SPRUCE

Ⓝ ☼ ◊ Z3–6 H6–1 ‡30–50ft (9–15m) ↔15ft (5m)

A narrowly or broadly conical tree. Bark is ash-gray becoming scaly with age. Growth rate is moderate. 'Densata' grows more slowly.

Pinus strobus
EASTERN WHITE PINE

Ⓝ ☼ ◊ Z4–9 H9–1 ‡to 100 ft (30m) ↔25ft (8m)

Conical when young, this pine becomes irregular and flat-topped with age. The smooth gray bark becomes black and cracked.

Evergreens for small spaces

Modern townhouses and garden homes often have very small lots, creating a challenge for the enthusiastic gardener who wants to grow a diversity of plants in the tiny space available. The evergreens that are shown here are suitable for these locations or for growing in a rock or raised garden where small-scale plants are needed.

Abies balsamea 'Nana'
DWARF BALSAM FIR

Ⓝ ☼ ◐ Z3–6 H6–1 ↕↔3ft (1m)

A slow-growing plant that does best in acidic soils. The species is often found growing in swamps in the wild. Needles are green above, whitish beneath.

MORE CHOICES

- Abies koreana 'Aurea' z5–6 H6–5
- Chamaecyparis lawsoniana 'Ellwood's Pillar' z4–8 H8–3
- Picea abies 'Pygmea' z3–8 H8–1
- Pinus densiflora 'Globosa' z4–7 H7–1

Chamaecyparis lawsoniana 'Lane'
LANE LAWSON FALSE CYPRESS

☼ ◐ Z5–9 H9–5 ↕to 130ft (40m) ↔to 15ft (5m)

There are many cultivars: some are pyramidal, like this, others spreading and not suitable for small gardens. 'Ellwoodii' is a miniature variety.

Chamaecyparis lawsoniana 'Columnaris'
COLUMNAR LAWSON FALSE CYPRESS

Ⓝ ☼ ◐ Z5–9 H9–5 ↕30ft (10m) ↔3ft (1m)

A slender variety with almost vertical branches and dense foliage. These plants grow best in a neutral to slightly acidic soil with shelter from winter winds.

Picea pungens 'Glauca Globosa'
GLOBE BLUE SPRUCE

Ⓝ ☼ ◊ Z2–8 H8–1 ↕↔3ft (1m)

This is a truly dwarf cultivar of the blue gray form of *P. pungens*. It can be found grafted onto a standard trunk. Growth rate is slow.

Juniperus scopulorum 'Blue Star'
BLUE STAR ROCKY MOUNTAIN JUNIPER

☼ ◐ ◊ Z4–8 H8–1 ↕16in (40cm) ↔3ft (1m)

Most of the Rocky Mountain Junipers are upright trees, but a few selections are dwarf, slowly spreading plants, such as this, suitable for small spaces.

Pinus sylvestris 'Watereri'
WATERER SCOTCH PINE

☼ ◊ Z3–7 H7–1 ‡to 100ft (30m) ↔40ft (12m)

One of several dwarf forms, this is not the slowest growing, but is fairly easy to find commercially. Young trees are upright but become more rounded with time.

Pinus mugo 'Mops'
MOPS MUGO PINE

☼ ◊ Z3–7 H7–1 ‡8ft (2.5m) ↔15ft (3m)

An almost spherical form that grows very slowly. Un-named selections of dwarf mugo pine are available; those with the shortest shoots are the slowest growing.

Picea glauca var. albertiana 'Conica'
DWARF ALBERTA SPRUCE

Ⓝ ☼ ◊ Z3–6 H6–1 ‡6–20ft (2–8m) ↔3–8ft (1–2.5m)

This dwarf form was found by the then director of the Arnold Arboretum, while waiting for a train in Alberta. It makes a compact, slow growing cone.

Thuja occidentalis 'Holmstrup'
HOLMSTRUP EASTERN ARBORVITAE

☼ ◊ Z2–7 H7–1 ‡12ft (4m) ↔10ft (3m)

There are many dwarf varieties, round, columnar, or conical. Most are green, but some have golden yellow foliage. This variety originated in Denmark.

Taxus x media 'Hicksii'
HICK'S HYBRID YEW

☼ ☼ ☼ ◊ Z5–7 H7–5 ‡25ft (8m) ↔10ft (3m)

A cross between the English and Japanese yews, these are slightly hardier than either one. This forms a narrow column when young, widening later.

Taxus baccata 'Repandens'
DWARF SPREADING ENGLISH YEW

☼ ☼ ☼ ◊ Z7–8 H8–7 ‡24in (60cm) ↔15ft (5m)

A good groundcover with horizontal main branches and branchlets that hang like a curtain. This female form will set red berries in fall if a male clone is nearby.

WOODY PLANTS

Conifers with weeping or pendulous habits

These are the oddities of the plant world, but they are quite eye-catching and make good specimen plants for many gardens. Some of these conifers can be trained across archways where their weeping branches form a fringe, others are upright but with a narrow silhouette, making them suitable for small gardens such as a city garden.

Cedrus atlantica 'Glauca'
BLUE ATLAS CEDAR
☼ ◊ Z6–9 H9–3 ↕100ft (30m) ↔75ft (22m)
Somewhat difficult to transplant, it should be bought container-grown, not balled-and-burlapped. A good blue accent for the garden with pendulous branchlets. 'Glauca Pendula' weeps even more.

Cedrus deodara 'Pendula'
WEEPING DEODAR CEDAR
☼ ◊ Z7–9 H9–6 ↕to 130ft (40m) ↔30ft (10m)
An excellent specimen tree, it can be grown as a low shrublike plant with branches that spread along the ground. As a standard the branches hang gracefully.

Cedrus libani 'Pendula'
WEEPING CEDAR OF LEBANON
☼ ◊ Z7–9 H9–6 ↕30in (75cm) ↔13ft (5m)
This requires a deep, rich soil and location away from pollution. It is mostly grafted to a tall rootstock so the branches can hang, but can be trained sideways.

MORE CHOICES

- *Juniperus chinensis* 'Horstmann' Z3–9 H9–1
- *Picea abies* 'Repens' Z3–8 H8–1
- *Picea omorika* 'Pendula' Z4–8 H8–1
- *Picea pungens* 'Glauca Globosa' Z2–8 H8–1
- *Pinus densiflora* 'Pendula' Z4–7 H7–1
- *Pinus flexilis* 'Glauca Pendula' Z3–7 H7–1
- *Pinus thunbergii* 'Arakawa' Z5–8 H7–6

Picea abies 'Pendula'
WEEPING NORWAY SPRUCE
☼ ◊ Z2–8 H8–1 ↕80ft (25m) ↔6ft (2m)
A variable form that may be as shown, or upright with weeping branches as in 'Pendula Major' and 'Inversa'. There are other forms with pendulous branches.

Picea breweriana
BREWER SPRUCE
Ⓝ ☼ ◊ Z6–8 H8–6 ↕50ft (15m) ↔12ft (4m)
An upright tree with branches that curve downwards and weeping branchlets that can grow to 7ft (2m) long. It will grow in most soils but is not widely available.

Chamaecyparis nootkatensis 'Pendula'
WEEPING ALASKA CEDAR,
WEEPING NOOTKA CYPRESS

☼ ◐ ◊ Z4–7 H7–1 ↕to 100ft (30m) ↔25ft (8m)

A graceful, pendulous tree that will grow in most soils and is often available in nurseries. There are two forms of this, one with a dense, somewhat spreading habit (seen here), the other more slender.

Pinus strobus 'Pendula'
WEEPING WHITE PINE

Ⓝ ☼ ◊ Z4–9 H9–1 ↕to 120 ft (35m) ↔20–25ft (6–8m)

Twisted, hanging branches give this cultivar a very distinctive outline. Makes a striking specimen tree. This horizontally growing sport of P. strobus is usually grown as a standard. Smooth gray bark turns black and cracked with age.

Pinus wallichiana
BHUTAN PINE, HIMALAYAN PINE

☼ ◊ Z6–9 H9–5 ↕to 120 ft (35m) ↔40ft (12m)

Best moved while young, this does best in a sandy, acidic soil. It forms a wide pyramid and keeps its branches to the ground.

Pinus densiflora 'Pendula'
WEEPING JAPANESE RED PINE

☼ ◊ Z4–7 H7–1 ↕65ft (20m) ↔6ft (2m)

An interesting form that is normally grafted as a standard but as a low plant it will trail over a wall or down a steep bank. Best in a slightly acidic soil.

Tsuga canadensis 'Pendula'
WEEPING CANADA HEMLOCK

Ⓝ ☼ ◑ ◊ Z4–8 H8–1 ↕12ft (4m) ↔25ft (8m)

A somewhat variable form that may make a spreading green mound or may be more upright. It is adaptable and will grow in both acidic and slightly alkaline soils.

WOODY PLANTS

Conifers with yellow or gold foliage

During the summer, the yellow foliage of these conifers stands out against other shrubs, but it is during winter, when many plants have lost their foliage, that these conifers are at their visual best. The bright yellow and golden shades gleam in winter sunshine, or help brighten a dull day. Try to position these plants where they can be seen from inside the house.

Chamaecyparis lawsoniana 'Hillieri'
HILLIER LAWSON FALSE CYPRESS
☀ ◑ Z5–9 H9–5 ‡60ft (18m) ↔20ft (6m)
A narrowly conical, variety with feathery branches that becomes a bright gold in the sun. This is one of several yellow forms of Lawson False Cypress.

Chamaecyparis 'Sungold'
SUNGOLD FALSE CYPRESS
☀ ◑ Z4–8 H8–1 ‡8ft (2.5m) ↔15ft (4.5m)
A thread-leaved form that is more sun-tolerant than most of the yellow varieties. Easy to grow in most soils except highly alkaline. It does well in humid climates.

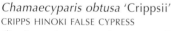

Chamaecyparis obtusa 'Crippsii'
CRIPPS HINOKI FALSE CYPRESS
☀ ◑ Z4–8 H8–1 ‡50ft (15m) ↔25ft (8m)
A conical form with spreading branches and nodding, fanlike sprays of foliage. It stays yellow on the branch tips, but reverts to green inside the plant, in shade.

MORE CHOICES

- *Cedrus deodara* 'Goldcone' Z7–9 H9–6
- *Cephalotaxus harringtonia* 'Ogon' Z6–9 H9–3
- *Chamaecyparis thyoides* 'Aurea' Z3–8 H8–1
- *Chamaecyparis pisifera* 'Plumosa Aurea' Z5–8 H8–1
- *Chamaecyparis pisifera* 'Filifera Aurea Nana' Z5–8 H8–1
- *Chamaecyparis obtusa* 'Verdon' Z5–8 H8–2
- *Cryptomeria japonica* 'Elegans Aurea' Z6–9
- *Juniperus chinensis* 'Gold Coast' Z3–9 H9–1
- *Pinus densiflora* 'Oculis-draconis' Z4–7 H7–1

Cryptomeria japonica 'Sekkan-sugi'
SEKKAN-SUGI JAPANESE CEDAR
☀ ☀ ◐◑ Z6–9 H8–6 ‡80ft (25m) ↔20ft (6m)
A slow-growing variety with short branches bearing stiff needles. Grow this in deep, rich, acidic soil, that does not dry out in summer. It needs midday shade.

x *Cupressocyparis leylandii* 'Robinson's Gold'
ROBINSON'S GOLD LEYLAND CYPRESS
☀ ☀ ◑ Z6–9 H9–6 ‡to 120ft (35m) ↔15ft (3m)
A rapidly growing conifer that is frequently used for hedging. Named selections make good specimen plants. Foliage is a bronzy yellow in spring, becoming gold.

Thuja occidentalis 'Rheingold'
AMERICAN ARBORVITAE

Ⓝ ☼ ◊ Z2–7 H7–1 ‡10–12ft (3–4m) ↔6–12ft (2–4m)
This cultivar is smaller and shrubbier than the species.
Foliage is pink tinted when young, and the growth rate
is slow. Also called *T. o.* 'Ellwangeriana Aurea'.

Thuja plicata 'Collyer's Gold'
WESTERN RED CEDAR

Ⓝ ☼ ◊ Z6–8 H8–6 ‡6ft (2m) ↔3ft (1m)
A dense, upright shrub form of the species. Young
shoots are gold, so prune older plants to encourage
more new growth. Growth rate is slow

Juniperus x media 'Pfitzeriana Aurea'
GOLDEN PFITZER JUNIPER

☼ ☼ ◊ Z4–9 H9–1 ‡7ft (2m) ↔15ft (4m)
A widely planted juniper that is large at maturity and
needs room to develop. It does well in clay soils. The
color of new growth is intense in spring and summer.

Pinus sylvestris 'Gold Coin'
GOLD COIN SCOTS PINE

☼ ◊ Z3–7 H7–1 ‡↔6ft (2m)
Slower-growing than the species, with a golden cast
replacing the typical blue-green leaves. Bark peels off
in thin flakes. Works well in a mixed border.

Juniperus chinensis 'Gold Lace'
GOLD LACE JUNIPER

☼ ☼ ◊ Z3–9 H9–1 ‡4ft (1.2m) ↔6ft (1.8m)
Like all Chinese junipers, this has prickly branches and
should not be planted close to a walkway. A recent
introduction, selected for a restrained growth habit.

Taxus baccata 'Standishii'
STANDISH COMMON YEW

☼ ☼ ☼ ◊ Z7–8 H8–7 ‡7ft (5m) ↔5ft (1.5m)
Columnar and slow growing, this makes a good accent
tree. It grows well on both acidic and alkaline soils but
must have good drainage. Wet soils are lethal.

WOODY PLANTS

Climbers for sunny sites

Climbing plants can play a large role in the garden. They give gardeners the opportunity to make use of normally ignored surfaces, walls, fences, and arbors, increasing the range of plants we can grow. Some need support, a trellis or wires around which to twine, while others have modified leaf tips or tendrils and can anchor themselves to most surfaces.

Parthenocissus quinquefolia
FIVE-LEAVED IVY, VIRGINIA CREEPER

Ⓝ ☼ ☼ ◊ Z7–9 H9–1
↕ 50ft (15m) or more
Grows vigorously and climbs over and onto anything in its path. Brilliant red fall foliage and dark blue fruits are additional virtues.

Wisteria sinensis
CHINESE WISTERIA

☼ ☼ ◊ Z5–8 H8–5 ↕ 28ft (9m)
Dense, pendent clusters bear fragrant blooms in early spring. In the wild, wisterias climb trees, but in gardens we can train them up walls and on pergolas.

Wisteria sinensis 'Alba'
WHITE CHINESE WISTERIA

☼ ◊ Z5–8 H8–5 ↕ to 28ft (9m)
This cultivar makes a wonderful color contrast when grown with Wisteria sinensis 'Purpurea' (see left). The flower clusters of this species open up all at once.

Wisteria floribunda 'Macrobotrys'
JAPANESE WISTERIA

☼ ◊ Z5–8 H8–3 ↕ to 28ft (9m)
Early spring flowers clusters open from the base down to the tips. This cultivar has flowers that are four times as long as the species, which is only 1ft (30cm) long.

Parthenocissus tricuspidata
BOSTON IVY, JAPANESE IVY

☼ ◊ Z4–8 H8–1 ↕ to 70ft (20m)
Red to purple color appears in fall. In warmer regions, Boston Ivy may hold its leaves through winter. Makes a good substitute for English Ivy in colder regions.

MORE CHOICES

- *Actinidia arguta* Z3–8 H8–1
- *Bignonia capreolata* Z6–9 H9–6
- *Bignonia capreolata* 'Atrosanguinea' Z6–9 H9–3
- *Bignonia capreolata* 'Tangerine Beauty' Z6–9 H9–1
- *Campsis radicans* 'Flamenco' Z5–8 H8–3
- *Gelsemium sempervirens* 'Pride of Augusta' Z6–9 H9–4

Wisteria sinensis 'Prolific'
PROLIFIC CHINESE WISTERIA

☼ ☀ ◐ z6–8 H8–6 ↕28ft (9m)

Chinese wisteria differs from the more common Japanese wisteria in several ways, the most visible being it twines counter-clockwise. The heavy vine needs a strong trellis.

Parthenocissus tricuspidata 'Lowii'
LOW'S BOSTON IVY

Ⓝ ☼ ☀ ☀ ◐ z4–8 H8–1 ↕70ft (20m)

Less vigorous than the species, their dissected, feathery leaves are green in summer. A tough vine that climbs by adhesive tendrils and clings to almost any surface.

MORE CHOICES

- *Humulus lupulus* 'Aureus' z4–8 H8–1
- *Lonicera sempervirens* 'John Clayton' z5–8 H8–1
- *Lonicera sempervirens* 'Alabama Crimson' z4–9 H9–1
- *Lonicera sempervirens* 'Blanche Sandman' z5–8 H8–1
- *Lonicera* x *heckrottii* 'Goldflame' z6–9 H9–6
- *Wisteria floribunda* z5–9 H9–3
- *Wisteria floribunda* 'Alba' z5–9 H9–5
- *Wisteria floribunda* 'Ivory Tower' z5–9 H9–3
- *Wisteria floribunda* 'Pink Ice' z5–8 H8–3
- *Wisteria floribunda* 'Snow Showers' z5–8 H8–1
- *Wisteria frutescens* z6–9 H9–6
- *Wisteria macrostachys* z6–9 H9–6
- *Wisteria macrostachys* 'Clare Mack' z5–8 H8–5
- *Wisteria sinensis* 'Purpurea' z5–8 H8–1
- *Wisteria venusta* var. *violacea* 'White Silk' z5–9 H9–5

Lonicera x heckrottii 'Gold Flame'
GOLD FLAME HONEYSUCKLE

☼ ☀ ◐ z6–9 H9–6 ↕15ft (5m)

This is easy-to-grow, long-flowering, and starts to bloom in late spring It continues until late summer. The flowers have a faint fragrance. Fruit is rarely produced.

Parthenocissus tricuspidata 'Fenway Park'
FENWAY PARK BOSTON IVY

Ⓝ ☼ ☀ ☀ ◐ z4–8 H8–1 ↕70ft (20m)

The golden foliage retains its color throughout the summer and becomes overlaid with red in fall. Just as vigorous and easy to grow as the regular Boston ivy.

Campsis radicans 'Flava'
YELLOW TRUMPET CREEPER

Ⓝ ☼ ☀ ◐ z5–9 H9–5 ↕30ft (10m)

Not quite as vigorous or invasive as the species, this is as easy to grow. Both leaf out late in spring and the foliage turns yellow in fall. Prune hard in spring.

Campsis radicans
TRUMPET CREEPER

Ⓝ ☼ ☀ ◐ z5–9 H9–3 ↕30ft (10m)

A rampant climber that can strangle trees. The bright orange-red flowers are borne from midsummer onward. Grows anywhere; a good hummingbird plant.

Lonicera x brownii 'Dropmore Scarlet'
DROPMORE SCARLET TRUMPET HONEYSUCKLE

☼ ☀ ◐ z3–9 H9–1 ↕12ft (4m)

A vigorous vine that flowers from midsummer until hard frost. It is slow to get established, but after the first year grows quickly. It originated in Manitoba, Canada.

WOODY PLANTS

Climbers for shady sites

The climbers illustrated here can be used to clothe the north side of a house or fence or to climb into a tree. Although the range of species is not as large as those for sunny sites, many have attractive flowers and fruit. Several of the clematis shown on pages 214–215 will also grow well in shade, especially when growing through a tree.

MORE CHOICES

- *Actinidia* 'Arctic Beauty' z3–11 H12–1
- *Actinidia kolomikta* z3–11 H12–1
- *Celastrus scandens* z3–8 H8–1
- *Clematis alpina* 'Willy' z6–9 H9–6
- *Euonymus fortunei* z4–9 H9–5
- *Hedera helix* 'California Gold' z5–11 H12–6
- *Schizophragma hydrangeoides* 'Brookside Littleleaf' z6–9 H9–6
- *Schizophragma hydrangeoides* 'Roseum' z5–7 H9–6

Humulus lupulus 'Aureus'
GOLDEN HOPS
Ⓝ ☼ ◊ Z4–8 H8–1 ↕to 20ft (6m)
Foliage is more golden in partial shade. In summer, female plants bear fragrant green flower spikes that turn straw-colored and are used to flavor beer.

Clematis 'Nelly Moser'
NELLY MOSER CLEMATIS
☼ ☀ ◊ Z4–9 H9–1 ↕3ft (1m)
A compact, deciduous climber that flowers in early summer on the previous year's growth, as well as in late summer on the current season's growth.

Clematis viticella 'Madame Julia Correvon'
MADAME JULIA CORREVON CLEMATIS
☼ ☀ ◊ Z4–9 H9–1 ↕8–11ft (2.5–3.5m)
This summer-flowering clematis climbs by twining leaf stalks; provide thin supports. Prune almost to the ground in spring, or remove only dead stems for more height.

Akebia quinata
CHOCOLATE VINE
☼ ◊ z5–9 H9–5 ↕30ft (10m) or more
Spicily scented flowers appear in early spring, followed by sausage-shaped, purple-fleshed fruits. Prefers fertile soil. Prune after flowering to restrict growth.

Hydrangea anomala subsp. *petiolaris*
CLIMBING HYDRANGEA

☼ ◐ ◊ Z4–9 H9–1 ‡50ft (15m)

The midsummer flowers and attractive cinnamon bark in winter make this desirable. Climbing by rootlike holdfasts, it can cover almost any building, stump, or eyesore. Grow on an east-facing wall where winters are harsh.

Actinidia arguta
HARDY KIWI VINE, TARA VINE

☼ ◊ Z3–8 H8–1 ‡22ft (7m)

A vigorous twining vine with fragrant flowers in early summer. Male and female flowers are on separate plants; both are usually needed to produce the edible fruit. 'Issai', however, is self-fertile.

Hedera helix 'Golden Heart'
GOLDEN HEART ENGLISH IVY

☼ ◐ ◊ Z5–11 H12–6 ‡20ft (6m)

Ivy grows best in organic soils, either acidic or alkaline, but is tolerant of poorer soils. Ivies climb by small rootlike growths that can eventually damage walls.

Hedera colchica 'Sulphur Heart'
SULPHUR HEART PERSIAN IVY

☼ ◐ ◊ Z6–11 H12–1 ‡15ft (5m) ↔10ft (3m)

Similar to *Hedera helix* in requirements, this and its related cultivars have larger leaves and a coarser texture overall. All make good groundcovers.

Schizophragma hydrangeoides
JAPANESE HYDRANGEA VINE

☼ ◐ ◊ Z6–9 H9–6 ‡to 40ft (12m)

Slightly fragrant, creamy white, midsummer flowers are in flattened heads, with conspicuous, large sterile flowers around the edge. They climb by aerial roots.

Climbers for seashore environments

Gardening can be very difficult where salt spray is a problem. Many plants will not grow well in soil that has been contaminated by salt, especially near the sea where winds, laden with salt, can occur at any time of year. The plants illustrated here are those that are salt-tolerant and are therefore able to grow in this difficult environment.

Wisteria sinensis
CHINESE WISTERIA

☼ ☀ ◊ Z5–8 H8–5 ↕28ft (9m)

Dense, pendent clusters bear fragrant blooms in early spring. Int the wild, wisterias climb trees, but in gardens they can be trained up walls or on pergolas.

MORE CHOICES

- *Actinidia arguta* Z3–8 H8–1
- *Lonicera x heckrotii 'Goldflame'* Z6–9 H9–6
- *Parthenocissus quinquefolia* Z4–9 H9–5
- *Schizophragma hydraneoides* Z6–9 H9–6

Clematis 'Ernst Markham'
ERNST MARKHAM CLEMATIS

☼ ◊ Z4–9 H9–1 ↕10–12ft (3–4m)

Prune this in spring for a concentrated display Either cut back to the first strong buds for early bloom, with some rebloom, or almost to the ground for later flowers.

Clematis 'Nelly Moser'
NELLY MOSER CLEMATIS

☼ ☀ ◊ Z4–9 H9–1 ↕3ft (1m)

A very popular variety that should be pruned the same as 'Ramona'. Like all clematis, it grows best with a cool root system. Plant a spreading ground cover to keep the root zone shaded.

Clematis 'Ramona'
RAMONA CLEMATIS

☼ ☀ ◊ Z4–9 H9–1 ↕10ft (3m) ↔3ft (1m)

This variety should not be cut back hard. Remove dead growth and cut back to the first strong buds. This will flower in early summer followed by a second flush.

Lonicera x brownii 'Dropmore Scarlet'
DROPMORE SCARLET TRUMPET HONEYSUCKLE

☼ ☀ ◊ Z3–9 H9–1 ↕↔12ft (4m)

A vigorous, deciduous vine once established, although it may take a year to get growing. It is adaptable and grows in most soils. Good for covering chain-link fencing.

Climbing roses

Although we call them climbing roses, in fact they don't really climb. These roses are sprawlers that, in nature, would grow up through other plants and hang on with their backward-pointing thorns. In the garden, however, we must provide these plants with a trellis or pergola of some kind and be prepared to tie them to it.

MORE CHOICES
- *Rosa 'Altissimo'* ('*Delmur*') Z5–9 H9–1
- *Rosa 'America'* ('*JACclam*') Z5–9 H9–1
- *Rosa 'American Pillar'* Z5–9 H9–5
- *Rosa 'Eden Climber'* ('*Meiviolin*') Z6–9 H9–1
- *Rosa 'Fourth of July'* ('*Wekroalt*') Z5–9 H9–5
- *Rosa 'John Davis'* Z3–9 H9–1
- *Rosa 'Dorothy Perkins'* Z5–9 H9–5
- *Rosa 'William Baffin'* Z2–9 H9–1

Rosa 'New Dawn'
NEW DAWN ROSE

☼ ◊ Z5–9 H9–5 ‡10ft (3m) ↔8ft (2.5m)

The fragrant flowers are produced from early summer into late fall. One of the longest-blooming climbers Introduced in 1930, this is still a very popular variety.

Rosa 'Korwest'
WESTERLAND™ ROSE

☼ ◊ Z4–11 H12–1 ‡8ft (2.5m) ↔4ft (1.2m)

A floribunda rose that is also available in a climbing form. Be sure you are getting the correct plant when you buy this. The trademark name is the one that it is sold under.

Rosa 'Dublin Bay'
DUBLIN BAY ROSE

☼ ◊ Z5–9 H9–5 ‡ ↔7ft (2.2m)

This free-flowering rose is possibly even brighter than the popular 'Blaze'. It is slightly smaller, a bonus in city gardens. Continual flower throughout the summer.

Rosa 'John Cabot'
JOHN CABOT ROSE

☼ ◊ Z3–9 H9–1 ‡5ft (1.5m) ↔4ft (1.2m)

One of the excellent "Exploror" disease-resistant roses introduced from Canada. It has a main flush of flowers in midsummer and reblooms in late summer and early fall.

Rosa 'Golden Showers'
GOLDEN SHOWERS ROSE

☼ ◊ Z5–9 H9–5 ‡10ft (3m) ↔6ft (2m)

This variety can be grown as either a climber or a large shrub. The rather open flowers bloom throughout the summer. This is one of the best yellow-flowered cultivars.

Climbers: the genus *Clematis*

Justifiably called "the Queen of Climbers," clematis can find a home in every garden. There is such a wide range of species and cultivars that it is easy to have them in flower from early spring until hard frost strikes in late fall. The large flowered hybrids are well known but others are equally worth growing. Many have attractive seed heads that persist into winter.

Clematis montana var. *rubens*
PINK ANEMONE CLEMATIS
☀ ◐ ◊ Z6–9 H9–6 ↕30ft (10m) ↕10ft (3m)
A very vigorous climber that does not require pruning. This will cover a house wall or climb high into a tree and cover itself with flowers in late spring.

Clematis 'Jackmanii'
JACKMAN CLEMATIS
☀ ◐ ◊ Z4–9 H9–1 ↕10ft (3m)
This large-flowering, fast-growing variety flowers on the current season's shoots, so prune in spring. Blooms in late summer and continues lightly into fall.

Clematis 'The President'
THE PRESIDENT CLEMATIS
☀ ◐ ◊ Z4–9 H9–1 ↕10ft (3m) ↔3ft (1m)
If lightly pruned, removing only dead growth, this will flower in early summer on the old wood and then again in late summer on the new growth. There is a silvery bar on the petal reverse.

Clematis 'Niobe'
NIOBE CLEMATIS
☀ ◐ ◊ Z4–9 H9–1 ↕10ft (3m) ↔3ft (1m)
Prune ack to a little above ground level to promote new growth that will flower in late summer. Like all clematis, it needs cool roots; mulch with flat rocks.

MORE CHOICES

- *Clematis macropetala* Z6–9 H9–6
- *Clematis texensis* 'Gravetye Beauty' Z5–9 H9–5
- *Clematis virginiana* Z5–9 H9–5
- *Clematis vitalba* Z5–9 H9–5

Clematis viticella 'Betty Corning'
BETTY CORNING VIRGIN BOWER
☀ ◐ ◊ Z4–9 H9–1 ↕6ft (2m) ↔3ft (1m)
Cut back hard in late winter or early spring. A vigorous grower that flowers freely in summer. It was introduced into England during the reign of Elizabeth I.

Clematis 'Comtesse de Bouchaud'
COMTESSE DE BOUCHAUD CLEMATIS

☼ ☀ ◊ Z4–9 H9–1 ‡6–10ft (2–m)

A very strong-growing, deciduous climber with mid-green leaves. Flowers bloom on current season's shoots from summer to late autumn.

Clematis tangutica
RUSSIAN VIRGIN'S BOWER

☼ ☀ ◊ Z6–9 H9–6 ‡20ft (6m) ↔10ft (3m)

A vigorous clematis that can climb a tree, be trained over an archway, or used as groundcover. It does not need pruning and flower from midsummer on.

Clematis terniflora
SWEET AUTUMN CLEMATIS

☼ ☀ ◊ Z4–9 H9–1 ‡20ft (6m) ↔10ft (3m)

Masses of hawthorn-scented blooms open in late summer and early fall. It does not need pruning. It may be sold as C. maximowicziana, or C. paniculata

Clematis 'Ernst Markham'
ERNST MARKHAM CLEMATIS

☼ ◊ Z4–9 H9–1 ‡10–12ft (3–4m)

Flowers in summer on the current year's growth. Best if grown in a fertile, organic soil. A vigorous, deciduous choice for covering a pergola or trellis.

Clematis alpina
ALPINE CLEMATIS

☼ ☀ ◊ Z6–9 H9–6 ‡10ft (3m) ↔5ft (1.5m)

An early flowering species that does not need pruning. It is not as rampant as the Anemone Clematis, but can climb into a small tree.

Clematis 'Elsa Späth'
ELSA SPÄTH CLEMATIS

☼ ☀ ◊ Z4–9 H9–1 ‡10ft (3m) ↔3ft (1m)

This can be left almost un-pruned for early flowers, or cut back hard to flower in late summer. Early flowers are large; the later smaller ones are more prolific.

Clematis montana f. grandiflora
LARGE-FLOWERED ANEMONE CLEMATIS

☼ ☀ ◊ Z6–9 H9–6 ‡30ft (10m) ↔12ft (4m)

A very vigorous and free-flowering species that seldom needs pruning. It can climb high into a tree or cover the side of a house. Late spring flowers are large.

HERBACEOUS PLANTS

Herbaceous plants – by definition, those that die down to ground level each year – are the multifaceted components of almost every gardener's palette. Whatever the size of your garden, you can use them to produce infinite combinations of colors, textures, scents, and shapes and to provide interest throughout most of the year (all year, in the case of evergreen herbaceous plants). They often require more time investment than woody plants but repay rich dividends.

The backbone of the herbaceous garden is often the bulbs – the crocuses and snowdrops, narcissus and tulips. Among the first and most dependable harbingers of spring, some bloom well into summer. Many bulbous plants last for years, often naturalizing and, in many cases, spreading well beyond the area where they were originally planted.

At the other end of the spectrum are the decorative grasses, whose leaves and seedheads remain until they are pruned back in spring. Some of these grasses can be used on the edge of a pond or if you have a particularly damp area.

Rudbeckia species and cultivars
The black-eyed Susan and its relatives bloom from late summer through midfall. Many can be grown as biennials or short-lived perennials.

Another group of perennials well suited to difficult growing conditions are the alpine plants, those that are native to regions of high altitude. They do well in dry, windy sites and are often used in rock gardens because of their small size and creeping habit.

Regardless of any limitations of your garden, you will be able to find many herbaceous plants to provide a kaleidoscope of color and texture.

Hemerocallis 'Red Rum'
Most daylilies are summer bloomers, providing color for a few to several weeks, mostly in summer. As their name suggests, each flower lives only a single day.

Tulipa 'Pink Beauty'
Available in nearly every color and many differnt forms beyond the simple goblet shape shown above, tulips are excellent in a bed or border.

Aquilegia McKana hybrids
The characteristic spurred blossoms of this white example could be the centerpiece of a perennial bed or grown for use as a cut flower.

Viola x wittrockiana Ultima Series (Pansies)
A bed of these colorful small perennials remains in bloom from winter throughout spring.

Perennials for moist, sunny sites or wetlands

These plants grow best in soil that is permanently moist, or even wet. While most will not suffer from the occasional brief dry spell, they will not survive a prolonged drought, and a few will resent even a brief period of dryness. Grow them on the banks of a small stream or where the overflow from a garden pond keeps the soil from drying out.

Iris pseudacorus
YELLOW FLAG
Ⓝ ☼ ◗ Z5–8 H8–3 ‡6ft (2m) ↔indefinite
A vigorous iris that blooms from mid- to late summer. Ripe seeds fall from the capsule and then float away and spread to new locations.

Aster novae-angliae 'Barr's Pink'
BARR'S PINK NEW ENGLAND ASTER
Ⓝ ☼ ☼ ◗ Z4–8 H8–1 ‡54in (1.3m) ↔24in (60cm)
Indispensable for the fall border, this is one of a large number of named forms in shades of white, pink, red, mauve, and blue. They also vary in height from 3ft (1m) to almost 6ft (2m).

Hibiscus coccineus
SCARLET HIBISCUS
Ⓝ ☼ ◗ Z6–15 H12–1 ‡10ft (3m) ↔4ft (1.2m)
An uncommon perennial with lobed leaves. Flowers are on the tops of the stems in summer and early fall. The base of the plant becomes woody. Native in the SE.

Iris versicolor
BLUE FLAG, WILD IRIS
Ⓝ ☼ ◗◗ Z3–9 H9–1
‡2ft (60cm) ↔indefinite
Blooms in early to midsummer. Prefers fertile, well-drained, loamy soil. Susceptible to aphids and mealybugs, especially when in bloom.

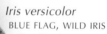

Pontederia cordata
PICKEREL WEED
Ⓝ ☼ ◗ Z3–11 H12–1 ‡30in (75cm) ↔18in (45cm)
Flowers are borne from late spring to fall. When grown in an aquatic container, the soil should be loamy and fertile. Can also be grown in water-filled barrels.

Saururus cernuus
LIZARD'S TAIL
Ⓝ ☼ ◗ Z5–11 H12–5 ‡9in (23cm) ↔12in (30cm)
Flowers appear in early summer. The group of nutlets that forms along the stem resembles a lizard's tail, giving the plant its common name. Spreads by runners.

Asclepias incarnata
SWAMP MILKWEED

Ⓝ ☼ ◑ Z3–8 H8–1 ↕4ft (1.2m) ↔24in (60cm)

Blooms midsummer to early autumn. Prefers fertile, well-drained, loamy soil. Susceptible to aphids and mealybugs, especially when in bloom.

Nuphar lutea
YELLOW POND LILY

Ⓝ ☼ ◑ Z3–9 H9–1 ↔5ft (1.5m)

Produces peculiar-smelling flowers in summer among mid- to deep green leaves with wavy edges. Divide plants regularly to promote flowering.

Sagittaria latifolia
WAPATO, DUCK POTATO

Ⓝ ☼ ◑ Z5–11 H12–5 ↕5ft (1.2m) ↔2ft (60cm)

Similar in appearance and growth habits to the Japanese arrowhead (*S. sagittifolia*). Susceptible to leaf spots, leaf smut, spider mites, and aphids.

Chelone glabra
WHITE TURTLEHEAD

Ⓝ ☼ ☼ ◑ Z3–8 H9–1 ↕3ft (1m) ↔18in (45cm)

Erect with square stems and long-lasting flowers tinged with pink or red, in late summer. This will tolerate dry soils in the north, but needs moisture in the south.

Eupatorium perfoliatum
BONESET

Ⓝ ☼ ☼ ◑ Z3–9 H8–1 ↕to 5ft (1.5m) ↔3ft (1m)

White flower heads are often purple tinged and provide nectar to bees and butterflies. This clump-forming perennial prefers moderately fertile soil.

Caltha palustris
MARSH MARIGOLD

Ⓝ ☼ ◑ Z3–7 H7–1 ↕16in (40cm) ↔18in (45cm)

Less compact than some of its cultivars. Prefers rich soil and open sites. Does best if water level is less than 2in (5cm). Widespread in Northern Hemisphere.

Lobelia siphilitica
BLUE CARDINAL FLOWER

Ⓝ ☼ ☼ ◑ Z4–8 H8–1 ↕4ft (1.2m) ↔12in (30cm)

Upright stems bear long-lasting flowers in late summer. Short-lived; divide every 2–3 years. Botanical name comes from an old-time medicinal use.

MORE CHOICES

- *Aster novi-belgii* Z4–8 H9–1
- *Butomus umbellatus* Z3–11 H8–5
- *Eupatorium fistulosum* Z4–8 H8–2
- *Lobelia cardinalis* Z2–8 H8–1
- *Mimulus ringens* Z4–9 H9–4
- *Solidago sempervirens* Z3–10 H9–6
- *Vernonia noveboracensis* Z4–8 H8–3

HERBACEOUS PLANTS

Perennials for dry, sunny sites

These are plants that thrive in full sun and on well-drained soils. Some of these will make good groundcovers for a sandy bank while others can be used to soften the edges of gravel paths or between dry-stone paving. Because of their dry habitat, growth is very rarely lush and even tall plants seldom need staking.

Sedum 'Autumn Joy'
AUTUMN JOY STONECROP

☼ ◊ Z4–9 H12–1 ↕↔to 2ft (60cm)
This hybrid is a very upright, clumping perennial that blooms early autumn. Prefers moderately fertile soil. Also sold under the name 'Herbsfreude'.

Yucca filamentosa 'Ivory Tower'
IVORY TOWER YUCCA

Ⓝ ☼ ◊ Z4–9 H12–1 ↕22in (55cm) ↔5ft (1.5m)
This cultivar's flower face outward, unlike the species', which droop. Prefers well-drained soil and tolerates drought. Makes a bold statement.

Rudbeckia fulgida 'Goldsturm'
GOLDSTURM CONEFLOWER

Ⓝ ☼ ◐ ◊ Z4–9 H9–1 ↕24in (60cm) ↔18in (45cm)
Blooms freely from late summer to midautumn. Prefers moderately fertile, heavy soil. More drought-tolerant than some in the genus.

Aster oblongifolius 'Fanny'
FANNY AROMATIC ASTER

Ⓝ ☼ ◊ Z4–8 H8–1 ↕3ft (1m) ↔2ft (60cm)
A prairie species with slightly sticky stems that forms a stiff, bushy plant. It grows well on alkaline soils. Native from Minnesota and Pennsylvania southward.

Eryngium bourgatii
MEDITERRANEAN SEA HOLLY

☼ ◊ Z5–9 H9–5 ↕6–18in (15–45cm)
↔12in (30cm)
The gray leaves are divided into 5 fingers, each with a white vein. The flowers, on stiff stems, open in summer and dry well.

Lychnis coronaria
ROSE CAMPION

☼ ◐ ◊ Z4–8 H8–1 ↕32in (80cm) ↔18in (45cm)
A branching plant with gray, wooly stems and leaves, that flowers in summer. It is fairly short-lived, but will leave behind a multitude of seedlings that are easy to remove while small.

Baptisia australis
FALSE INDIGO

Ⓝ ☼ ◊ Z3–9 H9–1 ↕30in (75cm)
↔24in (60cm)
Blooms in early summer. Seedpods are ornamental. Best used in the back of a border or as a specimen plant. It attracts birds.

Salvia x nemerosa 'Ostfriesland'
EAST FRIESLAND SAGE

☼ ☼ ◐ Z5–9 H9–5 ‡30in (75cm) ↔18in (45cm)

A multibranched plant with stiff spikes of bloom in early summer. Flowers are produced for most of the summer providing old spikes are removed. Other varieties have darker flowers.

Asclepias tuberosa
BUTTERFLY WEED

Ⓝ ☼ ◐ Z4–9 H9–2 ‡30in (75cm) ↔18in (45cm)

Blooms in midsummer. Prefers fertile, well-drained, loamy soil. Susceptible to aphids and mealybugs when in bloom.

Knautia macedonica
MACEDONIAN SCABIOUS

☼ ◐ Z5–9 H9–5 ‡32in (80cm) ↔18in (45cm)

The slender stems grow from long basal leaves with a lobed tip. Flowers appear from mid-to late summer and are long lasting. They can be dried for later use.

Echinops ritro
SMALL GLOBE THISTLE

☼ ◐◐ Z3–9 H12–1 ‡to 24in (60cm) ↔18in (45cm)

Flowers in late summer. Prefers marginally fertile soil and self-sows freely. Good for large borders. Attracts insects and birds but is unpalatable to deer.

Dianthus deltoides
MAIDEN PINK

☼ ◐ Z3–10 H10–1 ‡6in (15cm) ↔12in (30cm)

Scentless flowers borne in summer. Flower colors can range from white, to deep pink and red. A mat-forming plant that makes a good groundcover. Self-sows.

Coreopsis verticillata
THREAD-LEAVED TICKSEED

Ⓝ ☼ ☼ ◐ Z4–9 H9–1 ‡32in (60cm) ↔18in (45cm)

The finely divided, threadlike foliage make this an attractive plant all summer. Dead-head after the first flush of flowers, for re-bloom in fall.

HERBACEOUS PLANTS

Allium aflatunense
PERSIAN ONION

☼ ◊ Z4–8 H8–1 ↕3ft (1m) ↔4in (10cm)

A good species to dot through other plants in a border, rather than planting in a group. They may rot in heavy soils. The heads of flowers are large in late spring.

Kniphofia 'Strawberries and Cream'
STRAWBERRIES AND CREAM RED-HOT POKER

☼ ☼ ◊ Z6–9 H9–4 ↕24in (60cm) ↔12in (30cm)

This is one of the many named forms of red-hot poker. It flowers in early summer. After flowers fade, the spikes should be cut off to prevent seed formation.

Allium cristophii
STAR OF PERSIA, DOWNY ONION

☼ ◊ Z3–9 H9–5 ↕24in (60cm) ↔7in (19cm)

In early summer, the large flower heads may contain 100 individual flowers. A very striking plant with strap-shaped leaves covered in fine hairs, hence Downy Onion.

Echinacea purpurea
PURPLE CONEFLOWER

Ⓝ ☼ ◊ Z3–9 H9–1 ↕to 5ft (1.5m) ↔18in (45cm)

Flowers from midsummer to early autumn and prefers deep, organic soil. The cultivars bred from this native plant are often more suitable for the garden border.

Monarda fistulosa
WILD BEE BALM

Ⓝ ☼ ◊ Z4–9 H9–2 ↕4ft (1.2m) ↔18in (45cm)

Flowers from midsummer through early fall in light pink to lilac-purple. Spicily aromatic leaves are reminiscent of thyme and oregano. Clump-forming.

Valeriana officinalis
COMMON VALERIAN, ALL HEAL

☼ ☼ ◊ ◊ Z4–9 H9–1 ‡6ft (2m) ↔16–32in (40–80cm)
A very fragrant flower that scents the summer garden. It flowers for many weeks. The roots were used for the treatment of a wide range of illnesses, hence All Heal.

Gaura lindheimeri
WHITE GAURA

Ⓝ ☼ ◊ Z6–9 H9–6 ‡5ft (1.5m) ↔3ft (1m)
In a rich soil this is free-flowering, especially in the south of this region. It is very drought tolerant. In the north, it may be an annual but can self-seed.

Oenothera speciosa
SHOWY EVENING PRIMROSE

Ⓝ ☼ ◊ Z5–8 H8–1 ‡↔12in (30cm)
If grown in a rich soil, the spreading roots make this plant invasive. It is less so in poor soils. The summer flowers turn pale pink as they age. There is also a form with light pink blooms.

MORE CHOICES

- *Agastache mexicana* Z7–11 H12–7
- *Amsonia tabernaemontana* Z3–9 H9–1
- *Centaurea macrocephala* Z3–7 H7–1
- *Inula magnifica* Z5–8 H8–5
- *Leucanthemum x superbum* Z6–9 H9–6
- *Nepeta grandiflora* Z3–8 H8–1
- *Paeonia tenuiflolia* Z3–8 H8–1
- *Papaver alpinum* Z5–8 H8–3
- *Phlomis fruticosa* Z8–9 H9–8
- *Platycodon grandiflorus* Z4–9 H9–1
- *Potentilla atrosanguinea* Z5–8 H8–5
- *Ratibida pinnata* Z3–9 H12–1
- *Rudbeckia maxima* Z4–8 H8–1
- *Sedum spectabile* Z4–9 H9–1
- *Sedum telephium* Z4–9 H9–1
- *Solidago* spp. Z3–10 H9–6
- *Stachys* spp. Z4–9 H9–1
- *Stokesia laevis* 'Purple Parasols' PPAF Z5–8 H9–4
- *Veronica* spp. Z4–8 H8–2

Euphorbia chariacas subsp. *wulfenii*
WULFEN'S SPURGE

☼ ◊ Z7–11 H12–7 ‡↔4ft (1.2m)
An upright, evergreen with a woody base that may become shrublike in a warm climate. The flowers are tiny; it is the bracts surrounding them that are showy.

Geranium sanguineum
BLOODY CRANESBILL

☼ ◊ Z4–8 H8–1 ‡10in (25cm) ↔12in (30cm)
Blooms during summer. Prefers moderately fertile soil, so do not over fertilize. Divide in spring every few years to keep plants vigorous and healthy.

Achillea 'Taygetea'
TAYGETEA YARROW

☼ ◊ ◊ Z3–8 H8–1 ‡24in (60cm) ↔18in (45cm)
This hybrid yarrow has gray-green foliage and forms a low mound. The flowers open in early summer and are continuous until fall if old flowers are removed.

Perovskia atriplicifolia
RUSSIAN SAGE

☼ ◊ Z6–9 H9–6 ‡4ft (1.2m) ↔3ft (1m)
The aromatic foliage and flowers make this attractive all summer. Cut back to 6in (15cm) in early spring. The stems are woody and break out from the lower part.

Perennials for average shade conditions

These are plants that will grow well in a regular garden bed that is shaded during the hottest part of the day. They will take early morning or late afternoon sun, but their foliage may scorch badly if exposed to full, strong, hot sunlight. Other than this, they need no special care and should be treated like most perennials.

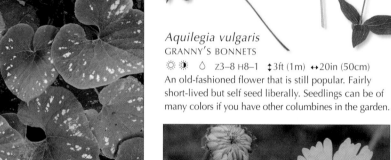

Tiarella cordifolia
FOAMFLOWER

☀ ◑ ◊ Z3–8 H7–1 ↕8in (20cm) ↔12in (30cm) or more
Free-spreading plant that makes a good groundcover, flowering a long time in summer. Foliage often takes on bronze fall tints. 'Marmorata' has purple-tinged leaves.

Brunnera macrophylla 'Langtrees'
LANGTREES SIBERIAN BUGLOSS

☀ ◑ ◊ Z3–7 H7–1 ↕12–18in (30–45cm) ↔20in (50cm)
Although grown mainly for its foliage effect, the blue flowers in spring are also effective. Rigorously remove any shoots that revert to plain green; they will take over.

Phlox divaricata
BLUE PHLOX

Ⓝ ☀ ◊ Z4–8 H8–1 ↕12in (30cm) ↔8in (20cm)
A slowly spreading, low plant with creeping stems. Spring flowers are on upright stems that rise above the mats. Cultivars have flowers in white, pale blue, and purple.

Aquilegia vulgaris
GRANNY'S BONNETS

☀ ◑ ◊ Z3–8 H8–1 ↕3ft (1m) ↔20in (50cm)
An old-fashioned flower that is still popular. Fairly short-lived but self seed liberally. Seedlings can be of many colors if you have other columbines in the garden.

Doronicum orientale 'Frühlingspacht'
SPRING BEAUTY LEOPARD'S BANE

☀ ◑ ◊ Z5–8 H8–5 ↕18in (45cm) ↔12in (30cm)
This flowers in early spring with spring bulbs and spreads slowly by underground rhizomes. Tolerant of summer drought. Wilts during the day if planted in sun.

Pulmonaria longifolia
LONGLEAF LUNGWORT

☀ ◑ ◊ Z3–8 H8–4 ↕12in (30cm) ↔18in (45cm)
Early spring flowers on a slowly spreading, clump-forming plant. Provide organic soil. 'Bertram Anderson' has narrower leaves with more prominent markings.

MORE CHOICES

- *Alchemilla mollis* Z4–7 H7–1
- *Dicentra spectabilis* Z3–9 H9–1
- *Digitalis purpurea* Z4–8 H9–1
- *Heuchera* (hybrids) Z4–8 H8–1
- *Hosta* cvs Z3–8 H8–1

Cimicifuga racemosa
BLACK BUGBANE, BLACK COHOSH

Ⓝ ☀ ◑ ◊ Z3–8 H12–1 ‡4–7ft (1.2–2.2m) ↔24in (60cm)
A clump-forming perennial that blooms in mid-summer. Flowers are scented, but many people find them disagreeable. Prefers moist, fertile, organic soil.

Astrantia major
MASTERWORT

☀ ◊ Z4–7 H7–1 ‡24in (60cm) ↔18in (45cm)
An upright plant with a rosette of lobed basal leaves. Grows best in moist soil. Flowers appear from mid- to late-summer. Cultivars have pink or red flowers.

Dicentra spectabilis
BLEEDING HEART

☀ ◊ Z3–9 H9–1 ‡30in (75cm) ↔20in (50cm)
A very showy plant when in flower. Foliage lasts all summer in cooler climates and moist soil, but dies down soon after flowering in hotter regions or drier soil.

Asarum canadense
CANADIAN WILD GINGER

Ⓝ ☀ ◑ ◊ Z2–8 H8–1 ‡↔6in (15cm)
Spreads by rhizomes and makes a good ground cover. The interesting but inconspicuous flowers appear in late spring. Stems smell of ginger if crushed.

Astilbe chinensis 'Pumila'
DWARF FALSE GOATSBEARD

☀ ◑ ◊ Z4–8 H8–1 ‡12in (30cm) ↔8in (20cm)
Flowers in late summer. Grow in fertile, organic soil. Astilbes are easy to propagate by division, which should be done in spring just as the new growth emerges.

HERBACEOUS PLANTS

Large perennials for shade or partial shade

The majority of shade-loving perennials are low to medium in height, but the plants shown here will grow tall and can serve a useful purpose in the back of a shaded border or under trees. Their growth habit is often fairly soft and they may need to be supported to keep them from flopping over in rain or a high wind, but they amply repay this extra bit of attention.

Kirengeshoma palmata
YELLOW WAX-BELLS

☀◐ ◌ ♨ Z5–8 H8–5 ‡3ft (1m) ↔2ft (60cm)
This clump-forming perennial flowers from late summer to early fall. Prefers highly organic soil. Young plants are susceptible to slugs and snails.

MORE CHOICES

- *Aconitum* x *cammarum* Z3–7 H7–1
- *Aquilegia* 'Spring Song' Z4–7 H7–1
- *Campanula lactiflora* Z5–7 H7–5
- *Chelone lyonii* Z3–9 H9–3
- *Digitalis purpurea* Z4–8 H9–1
- *Gentiana asclepiadea* Z6–9 H9–6
- *Meconopsis betonicifolia* Z7–8 H8–7
- *Polygonatum odoratum* Z3–8 H9–1
- *Rodgersia aesculifolia* Z5–8 H8–5

Anemone x *hybrida* 'Honorine Jobert'
HONORINE JOBERT ANEMONE

☀ ◌ ♨ Z4–8 H8–5 ‡5ft (1.5m) ↔2ft (60cm)
Flowers appear from late summer to midautumn in shades of white, pink, and purple. This garden hybrid is also called *A.* x *elegans* and *A. japonica*.

Aruncus dioicus
GOATSBEARD

Ⓝ ☀ ◌ Z3–7 H7–1 ‡6ft (2m) ↔4ft (1.2m)
Blooms from early to midsummer and make good cut flowers. Fernlike, alternately pinnate, midgreen leaves can grow 3ft (1m) long. Best grown in fertile soil.

Rodgersia pinnata
RODGERSIA, RODGER'S FLOWER

☀◐ ◌ Z3–7 H7–1 ‡to 4ft (1.2m) ↔30in (75cm)
Blooms in mid- to late summer. Flowers can also be found in white and pink. Leaf and flower stalks are reddish green. Grow in soil rich in organic matter.

Aconitum x *cammarum* 'Bicolor'
BICOLOR MONKSHOOD

☀ ◌ Z3–8 H8–3 ‡4ft (1.2m) ↔20in (50cm)
Blooms from mid- to late summer. Prefers fertile soil but is fairly tolerant of other soil types. All parts of monkshoods are highly poisonous.

Arisaema triphyllum
JACK-IN-THE-PULPIT

Ⓝ ☀ ◌ Z4–9 H9–1 ‡24in (60cm) ↔6in (15cm)
A tuberous plant that increases slowly and needs a woodland-type soil. The spring flowers give showy red berries in fall. Native to eastern woodlands.

Astrantia major
MASTERWORT

☼ ◑ ◐ ◆ Z4–7 H7–1 ↕3ft (1m) ↔18in (45cm)

A clump-forming plant that spreads slowly by underground runners. The flowers opening late spring and make an excellent cut flower. Red-flowered varieties and one with variegated foliage are available.

Rheum palmatum
CHINESE RHUBARB, ORNAMENTAL RHUBARB

☼ ◑ ◐ ◆ Z5–9 H9–1 ↕8ft (2.5m) ↔6ft (2m)

A large plant that needs space to develop properly. Plants are intolerant of drought and must be kept moist to survive. The variety 'Atrosanguineum' has purple leaves and darker flowers.

Cimicifuga racemosa
BLACK BUGBANE, BLACK COHOSH

Ⓝ ◐ ◆ Z3–8 H12–1 ↕4–7ft (1.2–2.2m) ↔24in (60cm)

A clump-forming perennial that blooms in mid-summer. Flowers are scented, but many people find them disagreeable. Prefers moist, fertile, organic soil.

Chelone glabra
WHITE TURTLEHEAD

Ⓝ ◐ ◐ ◆ Z3–8 H9–1 ↕3ft (1m) ↔18in (45cm)

With their tubular, double-lipped blossoms and their toothed leaves, these will add emphasis to a late summer border Mulch in midspring with well-rotted compost.

Perennials for moist shade

Damp shade can occur on the north side of buildings or fences, in low-lying areas shaded by trees, or under shrubs planted in a heavy soil. The plants shown on these pages include a number of native woodland plants as well as some introduced species that are commonly available. Many of the hostas (*see* pp.294–295) will also grow well in these conditions.

Trillium grandiflorum
WAKE ROBIN

Ⓝ ☀☀ ◐◑ Z4–7 H7–3 ↕18in (45cm) ↔12in (30cm)
Flowers bloom in midspring and often turn pink as they age. Prefers acidic to neutral soil rich in organic matter. Mulch in fall with leaf mold.

Actaea rubra
RED BANEBERRY

Ⓝ ☀ ◐ Z4–8 H8–1 ↕20in (50cm) ↔12in (30cm)
Oval white flower clusters appear from mid-spring to early summer, followed by berries. A clump forming perennial, it prefers moderately fertile, organic soil.

Chelone lyonii
PINK TURTLEHEAD

Ⓝ ☀☀ ◐ Z3–9 H9–3 ↕4ft (2m) ↔24in (60cm)
Given adequate moisture this will form a large clump in 3–4 years; in dryer soil it grows slowly. Flowers produced in late summer. Native in SE mountains.

Corydalis flexuosa
FUMEWORT

☀ ◐ Z6–8 H8–6 ↕12in (30cm) ↔8in (20cm)
Blooms appear from late spring to summer and may repeat if deadheaded. It prfers moderately fertile, organic, well-drained soil.

Astilbe x arendsii 'Fanal'
FANAL ASTILBE

☼ ◐ ◊ Z3–9 H9–1 ↕24in (60cm) ↔18in (45cm)

Flowers appear in midsummer above very dark green, pinnate foliage. Prefers organic, rich soil. Divide every 4 years to maintain bloom quality.

Tiarella wherryi
WHERRY'S FOAMFLOWER

◐ ◑ ◊ Z3–7 H7–1 ↕8in (20cm) ↔6in (15cm)

A clump-forming species more refined than *T. cordifolia* and flowers earlier, in late spring. Named forms have pink flowers and bronze-mottled leaves.

Lobelia cardinalis
CARDINAL FLOWER

Ⓝ ☼ ◊ Z2–8 H8–1 ↕3ft (1m) ↔9in (23cm)

Flowers from summer to early autumn. Foliage is lance-shaped, bright green, and tinged with bronze. Best if grown in fertile, organic soil. Short-lived.

Aruncus dioicus
GOATSBEARD

Ⓝ ☼ ◊ Z3–7 H7–1 ↕6ft (2m) ↔4ft (1.2m)

An imposing plant that needs plenty of space. It will take some sun in the north but leaf margins burn if given too much. Flowers in early summer.

Mertensia virginica
VIRGINIA BLUEBELLS

Ⓝ ☼ ◊ Z3–7 H7–1 ↕24in (60cm) ↔18in (45cm)

Flowers open from pink-tinted buds in mid- to late spring. Grow in well-drained, organic soil. Prone to problems but usually outgrows them.

MORE CHOICES

- *Bergenia cordifolia* Z3–8 H8–1
- *Hosta sieboldiana* Z3–9 H9–1
- *Ligularia stenocephala* Z4–8 H8–1
- *Lobelia siphilitica* Z4–8 H8–1
- *Osmunda regalis* Z2–10 H9–1
- *Primula bulleyana* Z5–8 H8–5
- *Primula denticulata* Z2–8 H8–1
- *Primula japonica* Z4–8 H8–1
- *Rheum palmatum* Z5–9 H9–1
- *Rodgersia aesculifolia* Z5–8 H8–5
- *Rodgersia pinnata* Z3–7 H7–1
- *Sanguinaria canadensis* Z3–9 H8–1
- *Trollium x cultorum* Z5–8 H8–5

Polygonatum odoratum
FRAGRANT SOLOMON'S SEAL

◐ ◑ ◊ Z3–8 H9–1 ↕34in (85cm) ↔12in (30cm)

Spreading by creeping rhizomes, this forms a large clump with flowers that perfume the garden on a spring evening. 'Variegatum' has white-edged leaves.

Perennials for dry shade

In addition to being shaded, the soil under shallow-rooted trees such as maples is often dry, because the tree roots absorb moisture from the soil and the leafy canopy overhead sheds rain. The perennials shown here will grow well in these conditions, as long as they are given additional water for the first summer until they are established. Some hostas (*see* p.294) and ferns (*see* p. 290) will also grow under these conditions.

Geranium macrorrhizum
SCENTED CRANESBILL

☼ ◑ ◊ Z4–8 H8–1 ↕20in (50cm) ↔24in (60cm)
Early summer blooms mature into distinctive seedheads. Prefers moderately fertile, organic soil. Self sows freely and is attractive to beneficial insects and birds.

Heuchera americana
AMERICAN ALUMROOT

Ⓝ ◑ ◊ Z4–8 H8–1 ↕18in (45cm) ↔12in (30cm)
An evergreen perennial with young foliage mottled with purple, becoming green, then turning purple again in fall. This is a parent of many modern hybrids.

MORE CHOICES

- *Aster cordifolius* Z3–8 H8–1
- *Aster divaricatus* Z4–8 H8–1
- *Dicentra eximia* Z3–8 H10–1
- *Epimedium sp.* Z5–9 H9–5
- *Eupatorium coelestinum* Z5–11 H9–1
- *Eupatorium rugosum* Z4–8 H8–2

Liriope muscari
BIG BLUE LILYTURF

☼ ◊ Z6–10 H21–1 ↕12in (30cm) ↔18in (45cm)
Flowers of this evergreen perennial's cultivars range from white to violet. Prefers a light moderately fertile, well-drained soil. Moisture is welcome.

Aquilegia vulgaris
GRANNY'S BONNETS

☼ ◊ z3–8 H8–1 ‡3ft (1m) ↔20in (50cm)

Very adaptable, this grows in most conditions and seeds itself freely without becoming invasive. An old-fashioned flower that has been overshadowed the new.

Eupatorium rugosum
WHITE SNAKEROOT

Ⓝ ☼ ◊ z4–8 H8–2 ‡4ft (1.2m) ↔18in (45cm)

The late summer flowers last well into fall. It grows best in an alkaline soil supplemented with organic matter. Native to woods from Quebec to Texas.

Iris cristata
DWARF CRESTED IRIS

Ⓝ ☼ ◖ z4–10 H10–1 ‡4in (10cm) ↔indefinite

Grows from a shallow rhizome that creeps on the surface and spreads fairly rapidly. Blooms in spring. There is a white-flowered form, plus other color variants.

Epimedium grandiflorum 'Rose Queen'
ROSE QUEEN BISHOP'S HAT

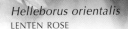

☼ ◊ z4–8 H8–2 ‡↔12in (30cm)

The young leaves are dark bronze-purple. Other cultivars have flowers in shades of white, yellow, and pink. All prefer fertile, organic soil.

Epimedium x youngianum 'Niveum'
WHITE YOUNG'S BARRENWORT

☼ ◊ z5–9 H9–5 ‡↔12in (30cm)

Leaves are divided into nine leaflets, stained with red when young, and turning deep crimson in fall. Makes a good groundcover that competes well with tree roots.

Sedum ternatum
WOODLAND STONECROP

Ⓝ ☼ ◊ z4–9 H9–1 ‡4in (10cm) ↔12in (30 cm)

Although individual shoots die after flowering in spring, offshoots persist and remain green over winter. A good choice for rocky slopes where little else will survive.

Helleborus orientalis
LENTEN ROSE

☼ ◖ z4–8 H8–3 ‡↔to 18in (45cm)

An elegant plant with leathery, deep green overwintering leaves. Flowers, most often white or greenish cream aging to pink, bloom from midwinter to midspring.

Phlox divaricata
BLUE PHLOX

Ⓝ ☼ ◖ z4–8 H8–1 ‡12in (30cm) ↔8in (20cm)

Spreading slowly by creeping rhizomes, this makes a good edging for a woodland path. Upright flower stems appear in spring. There are several named forms.

MORE CHOICES

- *Euphorbia amygdaloides v. robbiae* z6–9 H9–6
- *Galium odoratum* z5–8 H8–5
- *Geranium maculatum* z4–8 H8–1
- *Helleborus orientalis* z4–8 H8–3
- *Lamium galeobdolon* z4–8 H8–1
- *Phlox stolonifera* z4–8 H8–1
- *Polygonatum odoratum* z3–8 H9–1
- *Saxifraga stolonifera* z7–9 H9–5
- *Solidago* 'Golden Fleece' z5–9 H9–5
- *Symphytum grandiflorum* z3–9 H9–1

Salt-tolerant perennials

Gardening by the sea can be a challenge. Even in summer, salt-laden winds can sweep across the garden leaving in their wake a fine deposit of salt on leaves and stems. The seashore is the native habitat for some of the plants shown here, but most are inland plants that just happen to be able to withstand a higher salt concentration.

Campanula persicifolia
PEACH-LEAVED BELLFLOWER
☼ ◐ ◊ Z3–8 H8–1 ‡36in (90cm) ↔12in (30cm)
Available in several shades of blue, plus white, this is a somewhat floppy plant and needs some support. It flowers in summer and will repeat if dead-headed.

Monarda didyma 'Marshall's Delight'
MARSHALL'S DELIGHT BEE BALM
Ⓝ ☼ ◐ ◊ Z4–8 H8–1 ‡3ft (1m) ↔24in (60cm)
Blooms from mid- to late summer. Prefers moderately fertile, organic, well-drained soil. Highly resistant to powdery mildew. Susceptible to leaf spots and rust.

Armeria maritima 'Vindictive'
VINDICTIVE SEA THRIFT
☼ ◊ Z3–9 H9–1 ‡8in (20cm) ↔12in (30cm)
From tufts of grasslike foliage, stiff stems of flowers appear in late spring. Good for rock gardens, this variety is shorter, with darker flowers than the species.

Arabis blepharophylla 'Spring Charm'
SPRING CHARM EYELASH ARABIS
☼ ◊ Z5–8 H8–5 ‡4in (10cm) ↔8in (20cm)
A mat-forming plant with the basal leaves having a fringe of hairs, like an eyelash. A good rock garden or border-front plant that flowers in early summer.

Aster novae-angliae 'Barr's Pink'
BARR'S PINK NEW ENGLAND ASTER
Ⓝ ☼ ◐ ◊ Z4–8 H8–1 ‡4½ft (1.3m) ↔24in (60cm)
One on the mainstays of the fall border, the varieties of this aster come in a range of heights and colors. Tall varieties should be staked to fully enjoy them.

Aster novi-belgii 'Snowsprite'
SNOWSPRITE NEW YORK ASTER
Ⓝ ☼ ◊ Z4–8 H8–1 ‡15in (38cm) ↔24in (60cm)
Generally shorter than New England asters, these are for the middle-to-front of the border that rarely need staking. Divide them every 3 years to keep clumps small.

Oenothera speciosa
SHOWY EVENING PRIMROSE

Ⓝ ☼ ◊ Z5–8 H8–1 ↕↔12in (30cm)

On poor soils this plant is restrained and spreads slowly. On rich moist soils, it will cover a large area in one season. Flowers open white and change color with age.

Aquilegia McKana hybrids
MCKANA COLUMBINE

☼ ☼ ◊ Z4–7 H7–1 ↕30in (75cm) ↔24in (60cm)

Flowers come in a variety of colors and are spectacular in late spring. Grows well in dappled shade and is a good plant to attract hummingbirds.

Lilium 'Black Beauty'
BLACK BEAUTY LILY

☼ ◊ Z3–8 H8–1 ↕6ft (18.m) ↔x

A fragrant trumpet lily that is the result of genetic engineering; two formerly incompatible species made this strong lily that grows well in all but heavy clay soils.

MORE CHOICES

- *Achillea millefolium* Z3–9 H9–1
- *Alcea* sp. Z3–9 H10–3
- *Astilbe* sp. Z3–8 H8–2
- *Crambe maritima* Z6–9 H9–6
- *Hemerocallis* sp. Z3–8 H12–1
- *Iris sibirica* Z3–9 H9–1
- *Nepeta* sp. Z3–9 H12–2
- *Paeonia lactiflora* Z3–8 H8–1

Penstemon pinifolius 'Mersea Yellow'
MERSEA YELLOW PINELEAF PENSTEMON

Ⓝ ☼ ◊ Z4–10 H10–1 ↕16in (40cm) ↔10in (25cm)

A long-lived plant with narrow needlelike foliage, that flowers over several months in summer. It has bright red flowers and is often raised from seed. Color may vary.

Phlox paniculata 'Eventide'
EVENTIDE GARDEN PHLOX

Ⓝ ☼ ☼ ◊ Z4–8 H8–1
↕ ↔3ft (1m)

Deliciously fragrant plants that attract butterflies and hummingbirds. They are prone to mildew; clumps should be small to allow air circulation.

Hemerocallis 'Stella de Oro'
STELLA DE ORO DAYLILY

☼ ◊ Z3–9 H12–1 ↕12in (30cm) ↔18in (45cm)

This plant is vigorous and free flowering and blooms early, repeating throughout the season. It prefers fertile soil. Arguably it is the finest of all daylilies.

HERBACEOUS PLANTS

Perennials tolerant of urban or polluted sites

The soil in older, city gardens can be very poor. In addition, traffic and industrial pollution may contaminate the air, and rain washes these contaminants into the ground. By adding compost and nutrients the gardener can do much to improve the soil (*see* "Get to know your soil," p.16), but these plants will grow even in poor soils.

see "Get to know your soil," p.16

Aster novae-angliae 'Barr's Pink'
BARR'S PINK NEW ENGLAND ASTER
Ⓝ ☀☀ ◊ Z4–8 H8–1 ‡5ft (1.5m) ↔24in (60cm)
This is just one of a large number of named forms of this species. They are excellent garden plants with an upright habit, and add color to the border in fall.

Sedum 'Ruby Glow'
RUBY GLOW STONECROP
☀ ◊ Z5–9 H9–1 ‡10in (25cm) ↔18in (45cm)
A low, spreading plant that adds a bright splash of color to the front of a border from late summer to early fall. It roots easily but does not become invasive.

Potentilla nepalensis 'Miss Willmott'
NEPAL CINQUFOIL
☀ ◊ Z4–7 H9–4 ‡↔12–36in (30–90cm)
A mounded plant that flowers over a long period during summer. Often short-lived, it should be divided every 2–3 years.

Liatris spicata
DENSE GAYFEATHER
Ⓝ ☀ ◊ Z4–9 H9–5 ‡24in (60cm) ↔12in (30cm)
Long-lasting flowers bloom from late summer to early fall. Prefers light, moderately fertile, well-drained, organic soil. In cooler areas, mulch during winter.

Silphium perfoliatum
CUP PLANT
Ⓝ ☀☀ ◊ Z5–9 H9–5 ‡8ft (2.5m) ↔3ft (1m)
The leaves of this upright plant encircle the stem and hold water after rain – hence "cup plant." Blossoms in late summer. Native from Ontario to Georgia.

Asclepias tuberosa
BUTTERFLY WEED
Ⓝ ☀ ◊ Z4–9 H9–2 ‡30in (75cm) ↔18in (45cm)
Blooms in midsummer. Prefers fertile, well-drained, loamy soil. Susceptible to aphids, mealybugs, rust, and bacterial and fungal leaf spots.

MORE CHOICES

- *Achillea millefolium* Z3–9 H9–1
- *Agastache* spp. Z4–11 H12–5
- *Amsonia* spp. Z3–9 H8–4
- *Coreopsis* spp. Z4–9 H12–1
- *Geum* spp. Z3–7 H7–1
- *Hemerocallis* spp. Z3–8 H12–1
- *Leucanthemum* spp. Z6–9 H9–6
- *Lupinus* spp. Z4–7 H7–1
- *Rudbeckia* spp. Z4–9 H9–2
- *Solidago* spp. Z3–10 H9–6
- *Veronica spicata* Z3–8 H8–1

HERBACEOUS PLANTS

Geranium sanguineum 'Album'
WHITE CRANESBILL
☼ ◊ Z4–8 H8–1 ‡12in (30cm) ↔16in (40cm)
Blooms freely throughout summer. Prefers
moderately fertile, organic, well-drained soil.
Prone to the same problems as the species.

Malva moschata
MUSK MALLOW
☼ ◊ Z4–8 H8–1 ‡3ft (1m) ↔24in (60cm)
A woody-based perennial with heart-shaped lower leaves
that has become naturalized in the northeast. It flowers for
most of the summer. There is also a white-flowered variety.

Stachys byzantina
LAMBS' EARS
☼ ◊ Z4–8 H8–1 ‡18in (45cm) ↔24in (60cm)
An excellent edging plant that makes a good foil for
brighter flowers. The flowers detract from the foliage;
the flowerless variety 'Silver carpet' may be preferable.

Agastache rupestris
SUNSET HYSSOP, LICORICE MINT
☼ ◊◊ Z7–9 H9–7 ‡24in (60cm) ↔18in (45cm)
Easy to grow in moist to dry soil, this blooms in mid-
summer, and the flower spikes are good for drying.
The foliage can be used for teas or on salads.

Gaillardia x *grandiflora* 'Kobold'
KOBOLD BLANKET FLOWER
☼ ◊ Z3–8 H8–1 ‡3ft (1m) ↔18in
(45cm)
Although often short-lived, these are
very popular plants because of their
heat-tolerance and long flowering
season. This cultivar may also be sold
as 'Goblin'.

Echinacea purpurea
PURPLE CONEFLOWER
Ⓝ ☼ ◊ Z3–9 H9–3 ‡to 5ft (1.5m) ↔18in (45cm)
Flowers from midsummer to early autumn. Prefers deep, organic
soil. Cultivars of this native plant are often more suitable for the
border than the species.

Nepeta x *faassenii*
CATMINT
☼ ◊ Z4–8 H8–1 ‡↔18in (45cm)
Flowers from early summer to early autumn. Cut back
scented foliage after flowering to keep plants tight and
encourage repeat flowering. Also known as *N. mussinii*.

HERBACEOUS PLANTS

Summer perennials with white flowers

The shape of solid white flowers, like lilies and phlox, catches the eye and makes them more visible. Conversely, plants with tiny white flower, such as gypsophila, create a misty effect that is bright without being intrusive and other colors, when seen through them, almost shimmer. Pure white flowers are rare; many may have spots, stripes, or centers of another shade.

HERBACEOUS PLANTS

Astilbe japonica 'Deutschland'
DEUTSCHLAND ASTILBE
☼ ☼ ◊ ◊ ◊ Z4–9 H8–2 ‡20in (50cm) ↔12in (30cm)
The lacy foliage makes these attractive even when not in flower in late spring. There are several other *Astilbe* hybrids with flower in red, pink and salmon shades.

Iris 'Silver Years'
SILVER YEARS IRIS
☼ ☼ ◊ Z3–9 H9–1 ‡3ft (1m)
This is one of many bearded irises with white flowers, although they also come in many other colors. There are also white selections of smaller bearded irises.

Geranium sanguineum 'Album'
WHITE CRANESBILL
☼ ◊ Z4–8 H8–1 ‡12in (30cm) ↔16in (40cm)
Blooms freely throughout summer. Prefers moderately fertile, organic, well-drained soil. Prone to the same problems as the species..

Gaura lindheimeri 'Whirling Butterflies'
WHIRLING BUTTERFLIES GAURA
Ⓝ ☼ ☼ ◊ ◊ Z6–9 H9–6 ‡30in (75cm) ↔3ft (1m)
This native from Louisiana and Texas adapts well to cultivation in the Northeast, being heat- and humidity-tolerant. Blooms almost continuously through summer.

Leucanthemum x superbum 'Alaska'
ALASKA SHASTA DAISY
☼ ☼ ◊ Z5–8 H8–5 ‡36in (90cm) ↔24in (60cm)
Easy and reliable, Shasta daisies may have single or double flowers and bloom in summer. They need to be divided every 2–3 years to keep growing vigorously.

Phlox paniculata 'David'
DAVID GARDEN PHLOX
Ⓝ ☼ ☼ ◊ Z4–8 H8–1
↕↔42in (1.2m)
This robust variety blooms from midsummer to early autumn and is mildew resistant, which is unusual for this species. Grows best in fertile soil.

Lysimachia clethroides
GOOSENECK LOOSESTRIFE
☼ ☼ ◊ Z4–9 H9–1 ↕36in (90cm) ↔24in (60cm)
A somewhat invasive plant that soon makes a large clump and should be divided regularly to keep it under control. It will also seed freely.

Baptisia alba
WHITE WILD INDIGO
Ⓝ ☼ ◊ Z3–9 H9–2 ↕4ft (1.2m) ↔24in (60cm)
An easy, long-lived plant that should be better known. It will tolerate some shade and needs regular watering until established. The seed pods are also attractive.

MORE CHOICES

- *Aruncus dioicus* Z3–7 H7–1
- *Asclepias* 'Ice Ballet' Z3–9 H10–2
- *Asclepias verticillata* Z4–9 H9–2
- *Baptisia lactaea* Z4–8 H8–1
- *Campanula carpatica* 'White Clips' Z4–7 H7–1
- *Campanula persicifolia* 'Alba' Z3–7 H7–1

Gypsophila paniculata
BABY'S BREATH
☼ ◊ Z5–9 H9–1 ↕8–12in (20–30cm) ↔6in (15cm)
Much used by florists as a summer filler, this should have a place in every garden. It needs an alkaline soil. 'Bristol Fairy' is the commonly grown double form,

Campanula lactiflora 'White Pouffe'
WHITE POUFFE MILKY BELLFLOWER
☼ ☼ ◊ Z3–9 H9–1 ↕10in (25cm) ↔18in (45cm)
An erect plant that doesn't need staking, this does well in part shade in the south of this region. Established plants don't move easily

Gypsophila repens 'Alba'
CREEPING BABY'S BREATH
☼ ◊ Z4–7 H7–1 ↕4in (20cm) ↔20in (50cm)
A good edging plant or suitable to hang down a rock wall, not tolerant of wet soil. The species is pale pink but there are named forms with darker flowers as well.

Achillea ptarmica 'Ballerina'
BALLERINA SNEEZEWORT
☼ ◊ Z3–8 H8–1 ↕24in (60cm) ↔12in (30cm)
An upright plant that spreads by runners. It is good as a cut flower and can also be dried. Dried leaves cam be used as a substitute for snuff.

HERBACEOUS PLANTS

HERBACEOUS PLANTS

Paeonia 'Candy Fluff'
CANDY FLUFF PEONY
☼ ☼ ◊ Z3–8 H8–1 ↕32in (80cm) ↔3ft (1m)
Peonies will grow for many years undisturbed. If moved and divided, plant with the buds 1–3in (3–7cm) below soil level.

MORE CHOICES

- *Centranthus ruber* 'Albus' Z4–9 H9–2
- *Corydalis sempervirens* 'Alba' Z6–9 H9–6
- *Dianthus deltoides* 'Albus' Z3–10 H10–1
- *Echinacea purpurea* 'White Swan' Z3–9 H9–1
- *Eremurus himalaicus* Z5–8 H8–5
- *Eupatorium maculatum* 'Bartered Bride' Z3–7 H7–1
- *Lamium maculatum* 'White Nancy' Z4–8 H8–1

Iris sibirica 'White Swirl'
WHITE SWIRL SIBERIAN IRIS
☼ ☼ ◊ Z4–9 H9–1 ↕3ft (1m)
These do not have the "beard" of the more common irises and flower a little later. They are more clump-forming, without the stout rhizomes.

Echinacea purpurea 'White Lustre'
WHITE LUSTRE PURPLE CONEFLOWER
Ⓝ ☼ ◊ Z3–9 H9–1 ↕32in (80cm) ↔18in (45cm)
A tough plant that withstands heat and drought well, but is inclined to self-seed. Blooms from mid-summer until fall if the plants are dead-headed.

Penstemon digitalis 'Husker Red'
HUSKER RED PENSTEMON
Ⓝ ☼ ☼ ◊ Z3–8 H8–1 ↕30in (75cm) ↔12in (30cm)
Blooms from early to late summer. Tolerant of high humidity. Prone to foliage diseases and slugs and snails.

Boltonia asteroides 'Snowbank'
CHRISTMAS ROSE
Ⓝ ☼ ☼ ◊ Z4–9 H9–1 ↕5ft (1.5m) ↔3ft (1m)
A strong-stemmed plant with blue-green leaves and flowers from late summer into early fall in white, lilac, or pinkish purple. Divide every few years.

Yucca filamentosa 'Ivory Tower'
IVORY TOWER YUCCA

Ⓝ ☀ ◊ z5–9 H12–1 ‡22in (55cm) ↔5ft (1.5m)

This cultivar's flower face outward, unlike the species', which droop. Prefers well-drained soil and tolerates drought. Makes a bold statement.

Lilium martagon var. album
WHITE MARTAGON LILY

☀ ◊ z3–7 H7–1 ‡6ft (18.m)

A very adaptable lily that tolerates a wide range of soil and light conditions. The early summer flowers have a strange odor. Hybrids in yellow and pink shades.

Thalictrum delavayi 'Album'
WHITE YUNNAN MEADOW RUE

◑ ◊ z4–7 H7–1 ‡4ft (1.2m) ↔24in (60cm)

The soft stems, with fern-like foliage, need supporting to stop them blowing over in a wind. Flowers appear in summer and are good when cut.

MORE CHOICES

- *Kalimeris pinnatifida* z4–8 H8–1
- *Lavandula* 'Coconut Ice' z5–8 H8–3
- *Liatris scariosa* 'White Spires' z5–9 H9–1
- *Liatris spicata* 'Floristan White' z3–9 H8–1
- *Oenothera speciosa* 'Woodside White' z5–8 H8–4

Hemerocallis 'Gentle Shepherd'
GENTLE SHEPHERD DAYLILY

☀ ◑ z3–10 H12–2

‡26in (65cm)

There is no pure white daylily, but this cultivar comes very close. This semi-evergreen variety blooms in early summer on a branched flower scape.

Cimicifuga racemosa
BLACK BUGBANE, BLACK COHOSH

Ⓝ ☀ ◊ z3–8 H12–1 ‡7ft (2.2m) ↔ 24in (60cm)

Clump-forming; blooms in midsummer. Many dislike the flower scent. Prefers moist, fertile, organic soil.

HERBACEOUS PLANTS

Tall white perennials for sunny conditions

The most relaxing of colors, white and cream flowers create a sense of harmony when grown adjacent to brighter blooms. They are almost luminous in evening light and stand out when brighter flowers have disappeared into the dusk. At the back of a border, these tall, pale colored plants recede and seem to give an added depth.

HERBACEOUS PLANTS

Macleaya cordata
PLUME POPPY

☼ ◊ Z4–8 H9–1 ‡8ft (2.5m) ↔3ft (1m)
An invasive plant with fleshy roots that quickly outgrows its allotted space and needs frequent division to keep in within bounds. Blooms during summer.

Crambe cordifolia
COLEWORT

☼ ◊ Z6–9 H9–6 ‡to 6ft (2m) ↔4ft (1.2m)
This plant makes a bold statement with spectacular blooms rising above the foliage from late spring to midsummer. Best if sited toward the back of a border.

MORE CHOICES

- *Clematis recta* Z3–7 H7–1
- *Eremurus himalaicus* Z5–8 H8–5
- *Physostegia virginiana* 'Summer Snow' Z4–8 H8–1
- *Yucca filamentosa* Z4–11 H12–5

Veronicastrum virginicum f. *album*
WHITE CULVER'S ROOT

Ⓝ ☼ ☼ ◊ Z4–8 H8–3 ‡6ft (2m) ↔18in (45cm)
An imposing plant that seldom needs staking. The lance-shaped leaves are in whorls around the stem. The late summer flowers are long-lasting.

Delphinium 'Olive Poppleton'
OLIVE POPPLETON DELPHINIUM
☀ ◊ Z3–7 H7–1 ↕8ft (2.5m)
↔24in (60cm)
Named varieties of delphinium, grown
from cuttings, have larger flower
spikes and are more robust than the
more commonly available varieties
grown from seed.

Aruncus dioicus
GOATSBEARD
Ⓝ ☀ ◊ Z3–7 H7–1 ↕6ft (2m) ↔4ft (1.2m)
Flowers appear from early to midsummer and make
good cut flowers. Fernlike, alternately pinnate, midgreen
leaves can grow 3ft long. Best grown in fertile soil.

Phlox paniculata 'David'
DAVID GARDEN PHLOX
Ⓝ ☀ ☀ ◊ Z4–8 H8–1 ↕↔42in (1.2m)
This robust variety blooms from midsummer to early
autumn and is mildew resistant, which is unusual for
this species. Grows best in fertile soil.

Eryngium giganteum
MISS WILLMOTT'S GHOST, GIANT SEA HOLLY
☀ ◊ Z4–9 H12–1 ↕36in (90cm) ↔12in (30cm)
A short-lived plant easy to grow from seed. Upper
leaves are spiny, lower ones are not. Miss Willmott
sprinkled seeds of this wherever she traveled.

Lilium martagon var. *album*
WHITE MARTAGON LILY
☀ ◊ Z3–7 H7–1 ↕3–6ft (1–2.m)
A vigorous lily with 3–4 whorls of leaves on the stem.
The flowers are fragrant and bloom in early summer.
The species has purple-red flowers.

Cimicifuga racemosa
BLACK BUGBANE, BLACK COHOSH
Ⓝ ☀ ◊ Z3–8 H12–1 ↕4–7ft (1.2–2.2m) ↔24in (60cm)
A clump-forming perennial that blooms in mid-
summer. Flowers are scented, but many people find
them disagreeable. Prefers moist, fertile, organic soil.

HERBACEOUS PLANTS

Perennials with yellow or orange flowers

Yellow brings a cheerfulness to the garden, but it should be used with discretion or it may conflict with other strong colors. Paler yellows, or yellow with a touch of green, are less demanding and appear cooler in midsummer when the sun is high overhead. While pale yellow can be cool, orange is a warm color and they tone well together.

Achillea 'Coronation Gold'
CORONATION GOLD YARROW
☼ ◊ Z3–9 H9–1 ‡3ft (1m) ↔18in (45cm)
A stiff, well-branched, upright hybrid. Flowering begins in early summer and continues for many weeks. Dries well, keeping its color.

Oenothera fruticosa 'Fyrverkeri'
FIREWORKS SUNDROPS
Ⓝ ☼ ◊ Z4–8 H8–1 ‡3ft (1m) ↔12in (30cm)
This differs from the species by having red-tinged stems, larger flowers, and not growing as tall. A good border plant with leaves that turn red in fall.

Asclepias tuberosa
BUTTERFLY WEED
Ⓝ ☼ ◊ Z4–9 H9–2 ‡30in (75cm) ↔18in (45cm)
Blooms in midsummer. Prefers fertile, well-drained, loamy soil. Susceptible to aphids, mealybugs, rust, and bacterial and fungal leaf spots.

Trollius x *cultorum* cultivar
GLOBE FLOWER
☼ ☼ ● Z5–8 H8–5 ‡36in (90cm) ↔18in (45cm)
The many named varieties of globe flower come in various shades of yellow. They make good border plants and will take part shade if the soil is moist.

Achillea millefolium 'Paprika'
PAPRIKA YARROW
Ⓝ ☼ ◊ Z3–9 H8–2 ‡↔24in (60cm)
Blooms from early to late summer. Seedheads persist through the winter if not cut back, but yarrows tend to self sow, producing possibly unwanted "volunteers."

MORE CHOICES

- *Achillea* 'Moonshine' Z3–9 H9–1
- *Centaurea macrocephala* Z3–7 H7–1
- *Cephalaria gigantea* Z3–7 H7–1
- *Euphorbia polychroma* Z5–9 H9–5
- *Helenium autumnale* Z4–8 H8–1
- *Hemerocallis citrina* and cultivars Z3–10 H12–2
- *Helianthus* x 'Capenoch Star' Z5–9 H9–5
- *Ligularia stenocephala* Z4–8 H8–1
- *Lysimachia punctata* Z4–8 H9–3
- *Thermopsis villosa* Z4–8 H9–1

Coreopsis grandiflora 'Early Sunrise'
EARLY SUNRISE TICKSEED

Ⓝ ☼ ☀ ◊ Z3–9 H9–1 ↕↔18in (45cm)

Flowers appear from late spring to late summer and make good cut flowers. This cultivar blooms the first year from seed and is sometimes treated as an annual.

Coreopsis verticillata 'Zagreb'
ZAGREB THREAD-LEAVED TICKSEED

☼ ☀ ◊ Z4–9 H9–1 ↕↔12in (30cm)

If the first flush of flowers in summer is trimmed off, this variety will bloom again in early fall. It forms an attractive mound with threadlike foliage.

Rudbeckia nitida
SHINING CONEFLOWER

Ⓝ ☼ ◊ Z3–7 H7–1 ↕6ft (2m) ↔3ft (1m)

Coneflowers are very popular. They need support to keep from blowing over in storms, but are otherwise undemanding plants.

Coreopsis verticillata 'Moonbeam'
MOONBEAM TICKSEED

Ⓝ ☼ ☀ ◊ Z3–8 H9–1 ↕↔18in (45cm)

Flowers freely from early summer to autumn. Deaheading helps extend the bloom period. This cultivar has an upright habit and is drought resistant.

Rudbeckia fulgida 'Deamii'
DEAMII CONEFLOWER

Ⓝ ☼ ☀ ◊◊ Z4–9 H9–1 ↕3ft (1m) ↔2ft (60cm)

A free-flowing form that is more drought-tolerant than the speces. Blooms from late summer to midfall. Prefers moderately fertile soil.

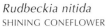

HERBACEOUS PLANTS

Summer perennials with red flowers

Red can dominate everything around it, but used sparingly, it can inspire a planting and bring it to life. Red flower seem brightest when viewed against a green backdrop and some shades of red are very difficult to place close to another color. Remember, red stands for danger and this color should not be used to excess.

Kniphofia 'Atlanta'
ATLANTA RED-HOT POKER
☼ ☀ ◊ Z6–9 H9–4 ‡4ft (1.2m) ↔30in (75cm)
Although justifiably popular in Europe, red-hot pokers are still rare in North American gardens. At the northern limits of hardiness, mulch in the first winter.

MORE CHOICES

- *Alcea rosea* Z3–9 H10–3
- *Aquilegia canadensis* Z3–8 H8–1
- *Aster novi-belgii* 'Winston Churchill' Z4–8 H8–1
- *Crocosmia* 'Lucifer' Z6–9 H9–6
- *Dianthus* 'Brympton Red' Z5–9 H8–1
- *Epimedium* x *rubrum* Z4–8 H8–1
- *Euphorbia griffithii* Z4–9 H9–2

Heuchera x *brizoides* 'Firefly'
CORAL BELLS
☼ ☀ ◊ Z4–8 H8–1 ‡30in (75cm) ↔18in (45cm)
Flowers bloom from late spring to early summer on mound-forming plants. Highly attractive to hummingbirds, and resistent to slugs.

Astilbe x arendsii 'Fanal'
FANAL ASTILBE
☼ ◑ ◊ Z3–9 H9–1 ↕24in
(60cm) ↔18in (45cm)
Strong-stems bear tapering panicles
of tiny flowers that turn brown and
keep their shape in winter. Broad
leaves divided into leaflets. Prefers
organic soil.

Centranthus ruber
JUPITER'S BEARD, RED VALERIAN
☼ ◊ Z5–8 H8–5 ↕3ft (1m) ↔2ft (60cm)
A tough plant that will seed itself into the tops of walls,
and cliff faces, it grows best on poor, alkaline soils. It
flowers in spring and occasionally in summer.

MORE CHOICES

- *Gaillardia* x *grandiflora* Z3–8 H8–1
- *Geum chiloense* 'Mrs. Bradshaw'
  Z5–9 H9–5
- *Heuchera sanguinea* 'Pluie de Feu'
  Z4–8 H8–1
- *Lobelia cardinalis* Z2–8 H8–1
- *Lychnis chalcedonica* Z4–8 H8–1
- *Mimulus* 'Whitecroft Scarlet' Z8–9 H9–8
- *Paeonia tenuifolia* Z3–8 H8–1
- *Penstemon piniifolius* Z4–10 H10–1
- *Potentilla* 'Gibson's Scarlet' Z5–8 H8–5
- *Pulmonaria montana* 'Redstart' Z5–8 H8–3
- *Sedum* 'Ruby Glow' Z5–9 H9–1

Hemerocallis 'Pardon Me'
PARDON ME DAYLILY
Ⓝ ☼ ◊ Z5–11 H12–1 ↕↔18in (45cm)
A free-flowering repeat bloomer bearing fragrant 3in
(7cm) flowers in summer. Attractive arching foliage
is deciduous.

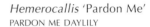

Phlox paniculata 'Starfire'
STARFIRE GARDEN PHLOX
☼ ☼ ◊ Z4–8 H8–1 ↕3ft (1m) ↔24–40in (60cm–1m)
Bronzy green foliage shows off vivid flowers that
bloom from summer to early fall. Grows best in fertile
soil. Attracts hummingbirds and butterflies.

Kniphofia 'Royal Standard'
ROYAL STANDARD RED-HOT POKER
☼ ◊ Z5–8 H9–4 ↕3ft (1m) ↔24in (60cm)
Flowers are borne on thick stems from mid- to late
summer. Good hummingbird plant. Prefers sandy soil
that is deep, fertile, and high in organic content.

Papaver orientale 'Turkish Delight'
ORIENTAL POPPY
☼ ◊ Z4–9 H9–1 ↕↔3ft (1m)
Blooms from late spring to midsummer. Large flowers
may require staking. Reasonably long-lived, but best if
divided every four years or so.

Monarda didyma 'Jacob Cline'
JACOB CLINE BEE BALM
☼ ☼ ◊◊ Z4–9 H9–1 ↕18in (45cm) ↔2ft (60cm)
Blooms from mid- to late summer. Grow in moderately
fertile, organic, well-drained soil. More resistant to
powdery mildew and rust than the species.

HERBACEOUS PLANTS

Tall perennials for sunny conditions

Yellow and gold are the brightest colors in the garden but they can overwhelm more subtle pale shades if used to excess. Pale yellow, on the other hand, blends well with white, silver, and gray. Red is the most dominant of the colors and bright red shades need to be used with care lest they become overpowering.

Patrinia scabiosifolia
EASTERN VALERIAN

☀ ☀ ◐ ◊ Z5–8 H8–5 ‡to 7ft (2.2m) ↔24in (60cm)
A clump-forming perennial that needs an organic-rich soil and is intolerant of drought. It also does well in part shade. Blooms from late summer to fall.

Lilium superbum
TURKSCAP LILY

Ⓝ ☀ ◊ Z4–8 H8–1 ‡↔5–10ft (1.5–3m)
Flowers in mid- to late summer. Puple-mottled stems bear lance-shaped leaves that spiral around the stem. Prefers organic soil.

Belamcanda chinensis
BLACKBERRY LILY

☀ ☀ ◊ Z5–9 H9–5 ‡36in (90cm) ↔8in (20cm)
This has foliage like an iris but the flowers appear in summer. The common name comes from the showy fruit in fall, which resemble blackberries.

Thalictrum flavum
YELLOW MEADOW RUE

☀ ◊ Z3–10 H9–1 ‡3ft (1m)
A stately perennial that seldom needs staking. The fragrant flowers are light and move in the slightest breeze. Variety glaucum has blue tinged foliage.

Centaurea macrocephala
GIANT KNAPWEED

☀ ◊ Z3–7 H7–1 ‡5ft (1.5m) ↔24in (60cm)
A stiff, upright plant with crinkled, deep green leaves. The summer flowers last well in water, and the seed heads can be dried for winter arrangements.

MORE CHOICES

- *Hibiscus moscheutos* 'Lord Baltimore' Z5–11 H12–1
- *Helenium autumnale* Z4–8 H8–1
- *Hemerocallis dumortieri* Z5–9 H9–1
- *Phlox paniculata* 'Prince of Orange' or 'Orange Fire' Z4–8 H8–1
- *Senecio doria* Z4–7 H7–1
- *Silphium laciniatum* Z5–9 H9–5
- *Thermopsis caroliniana* Z4–8 H9–1
- *Verbascum olympicum* Z5–9 H9–5

Phlox paniculata 'Starfire'
STARFIRE GARDEN PHLOX

☼ ☼ ◑ Z4–8 H8–1 ‡3ft (1m) ↔24–40in (60cm–1m)

Bronzy green foliage shows off vivid flowers, which bloom from summer to early fall. Grows best in fertile soil.

Helianthus angustifolius
SWAMP SUNFLOWER

Ⓝ ☼ ◑ Z6–9 H9–4 ‡6ft (1.8m) ↔4ft (1.2m)

Despite the common name, these will grow well in ordinary soil if it is not too dry. An upright plant, it flowers freely in late summer and fall.

Rudbeckia maxima
GREAT CONEFLOWER

Ⓝ ☼ ☼ ◑ Z4–8 H8–1 ‡5–6ft (1.5–2m) ↔2ft (60cm)

Flowers appear in late summer. An erect and stiff plant with oval, gray-green leaves. Prefers moderately fertile soil. Good for the back of a border.

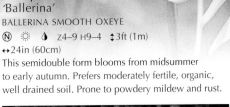

Heliopsis helianthoides 'Ballerina'
BALLERINA SMOOTH OXEYE

Ⓝ ☼ ◑ Z4–9 H9–4 ‡3ft (1m) ↔24in (60cm)

This semidouble form blooms from midsummer to early autumn. Prefers moderately fertile, organic, well drained soil. Prone to powdery mildew and rust.

Silphium perfoliatum
CUP PLANT

Ⓝ ☼ ☼ ◑ Z5–9 H9–5 ‡8ft (2.5m) ↔3ft (1m)

A prairie species that flowers into fall. Basal leaves are long-stalked, but the ones on the flower stems encircle the stems, forming a cup that catches rain.

Perennials with purple or magenta flowers

Purple and magenta are close to the edge of our visible spectrum and border into the ultraviolet. Many insects can detect ultraviolet, therefore these colors are very attractive to bees and other honey collectors. Bright magenta is hard and clashes with other bright shades, however, so plant this near white, pale yellow or light pink, but violet and purple are softer and blend well.

Aster x frikartii
MICHAELMAS DAISY, FRIKART'S ASTER

☼ ◑ ◊ Z4–8 H8–1 ‡28in (70cm) ↔18in (45cm)

Flowers from late summer to early fall. This hybrid of *A. amellus* and *A. thomsonii* prefers moderately fertile soil. Susceptible to *Verticillium* wilt and other diseases.

Astilbe chinensis
FALSE GOATSBEARD, CHINESE ASTILBE

☼ ◑ ◊ ◊ Z4–8 H8–2 ‡↔24in (60cm)

Flowers in late summer. Grow in fertile, organic soil. Easy to propagate by division, which should be done in spring, just as the new growth emerges.

Geranium sanguineum 'New Hampshire Purple'
NEW HAMPSHIRE PURPLE BLOODY CRANESBILL

☼ ◐ ◊ Z3–8 H8–1 ‡↔12in (30cm)

An excellent species for the front of a border, this also comes in several shades of mauve, pink and white. The roots have a red sap when broken.

Veronica 'Royal Candles'
ROYAL CANDLES SPEEDWELL

☼ ◑ ◊ Z3–8 H8–1 ‡16in (40cm) ↔18in (45cm)

A new hybrid speedwell that flowers over a long period in summer, especially if old flowers are removed.Good cut flower with few disease problems.

Campanula persicifolia
PEACH-LEAVED BELLFLOWER

☼ ◑ ◊ Z3–8 H8–1 ‡3ft (1m) ↔12in (30cm)

One of the best bellflowers for the garden, this has an upright growth habit but needs staking. A good cut flower that blooms in summer.

Baptisia australis
FALSE INDIGO

Ⓝ ☼ ◊ Z3–9 H9–1 ↕30in (75cm) ↔24in (60cm)

Blooms in early summer. Seedpods are ornamental. Best used in the back of a border or as a specimen plant. This member of the pea family attracts birds.

Liatris spicata 'Kobold'
KOBOLD GAYFEATHER

☼ ◊ Z4–9 H8–1 ↕↔16–20in (40–50cm)

An excellent cut flower that lasts well. Flowers open from the top down. Plants may need some support in windy locations. There is a white-flowered cultivar.

MORE CHOICES

- *Campanula lactiflora* 'Prichard's Variety' Z5–7 H7–5
- *Campanula* x 'Kent Belle' Z5–8 H8–5
- *Delphinium* cvs. Z3–8 H6–1
- *Geranium* 'Patricia' Z4–7 H7–1
- *Geranium clarkei* 'Kashmir Purple' Z5–8 H8–5
- *Iris sibirica* 'Ruffled Velvet' Z3–9 H9–1
- *Liatris spicata* 'Floristan Violet' Z4–9 H9–5
- *Limonium latifolium* Z4–9 H9–x1
- *Monarda* 'Claire Grace' Z3–11 H12–1
- *Monarda* 'Violet Queen' Z3–9 H9–1
- *Nepeta* x *faassenii* Z4–8 H8–1
- *Phlox* 'Russian Violette' Z4–8 H8–1
- *Stokesia* x 'Purple Parasols' Z5–8 H9–4
- *Vernonia fasciculata* Z3–8 H8–1
- *Veronicastrum virginicum* 'Lavendelturm' Z3–8 H8–1

Lychnis coronaria
ROSE CAMPION

☼ ◑ ◊ Z4–8 H8–1 ↕32in (80cm) ↔18in (45cm)

Felt-covered stems. This is a short lived species, often dying after the second year, but leaving a multitude of seedlings. Second-year plants flower better than first.

Iris 'Purple Pepper'
PURPLE PEPPER BEARDED IRIS

☼ ◑ ◊ Z3–9 H9–1 ↕3ft (1m)

The central upright petals on irises are called standards, the outer drooping ones, falls. The dotted two-tone pattern on the falls of this flower is known as plicata.

Iris sibirica 'Caesar's Brother'
CAESAR'S BROTHER SIBERIAN IRIS

☼ ◑ ◊ Z4–9 H9–1 ↕30in (75cm)

Flowering after the more widely grown bearded iris, this is an older variety that has been much used to produce modern hybrids. Foliage turns yellow in fall.

HERBACEOUS PLANTS

Summer perennials with pink flowers

Pink is the most complex of colors. It ranges from the palest of off-whites to almost red and, given a hint of blue, toward the pale purples and magentas. This wide range of shades makes it difficult to give color combinations, although white and pale yellow are always safe choices. Pinks from opposite ends of the scale do not necessarily harmonize.

Asclepias incarnata
SWAMP MILKWEED

Ⓝ ☼ ◊ Z3–8 H8–1 ↕4ft (1.2m) ↔24in (60cm)
Blooms midsummer to early autumn. Prefers fertile, well-drained, loamy soil. Susceptible to aphids and mealybugs, especially in bloom.

Geranium sanguineum 'Striatum'
STRIPED BLOODY CRANESBILL

☼ ◊ Z3–8 H8–1 ↕4–6in (10–15cm) ↔12in (30cm)
This more compact form of the species prefers the same conditions and is prone to the same problems as the species (see above).

Geranium sanguineum
BLOODY CRANESBILL

☼ ◊ Z3–8 H8–1 ↕10in (25cm) ↔12in (30cm)
Blooms during summer. Prefers moderately fertile soil, so do not over fertilize. Divide in spring every few years to keep plants vigorous and healthy.

Monarda didyma 'Marshall's Delight'
MARSHALL'S DELIGHT BEE BALM

Ⓝ ☼☼ ◊ Z4–8 H8–1 ↕3ft (1m) ↔24in (60cm)
Blooms from mid- to late summer. Prefers moderately fertile, organic, well-drained soil. Highly resistant to powdery mildew. Susceptible to leaf spots and rust.

MORE CHOICES

- *Achillea millefolium* 'Heidi' Z3–9 H9–1
- *Achillea* 'Ortel's Rose' Z3–9 H9–1
- *Achillea* 'Terra Cotta' Z3–9 H9–1
- *Aethionema* 'Warley Rose' Z6–8 H8–6
- *Astilbe chinensis* 'Visions' Z4–8 H8–2
- *Astrantia major* 'Rosea' Z4–7 H7–1
- *Centaurea dealbata* Z3–9 H9–1
- *Centranthus ruber* 'Roseus' Z5–8 H8–1
- *Coreopsis rosea* Z4–8 H8–1

Lavatera thuringiaca 'Kew Rose'
KEW ROSE TREE MALLOW

☼ ◊ Z8–10 H9–7 ↕↔6ft (2m)
Flowers profusely in summer Rounded leaves have heart-shaped bases. Protect from cold, drying winds. Prone to scale, root rot, rust, and leaf spot.

Dianthus alpinus 'Joan's Blood'
JOAN'S BLOOD ALPINE PINK

☼ ◊ Z4–8 H8–1 ‡6in (15cm) ↔12in (30cm)

Alpine pinks form a loose clump that eventually can cover a large area. It grows best in an alkaline soil. The scentless, early summer flowers almost hide the foliage.

Dianthus gratianopolitanus 'Mountain Mist'
MOUNTAIN MIST CHEDDAR PINK

☼ ◊ Z4–8 H8–1 ‡↔12in (30cm)

If constantly dead-headed, this will produce flowers for most of the summer. Forms small hummocks that gradually spread into a mat of fine, tight grayish foliage.

Liatris spicata
DENSE GAYFEATHER

Ⓝ ☼ ◊ Z4–9 H9–5 ‡24in (60cm) ↔12in (30cm)

Long-lasting flowers bloom from late summer to early fall. Prefers light, moderately fertile, well-drained, organic soil. In cooler areas, mulch during winter.

Dianthus 'Brympton Red'
BRYMPTON RED BORDER PINK

☼ ◊ Z5–9 H8–1 ‡24in (60cm) ↔12in (30cm)

Hybrids, with several species in the parentage, of border pinks are ideal edging plants. The fragrant flowers open in summer and are good cut flowers.

Eupatorium fistulosum
JOE PYE WEED

Ⓝ ☼ ☼ ◊ Z3–8 H8–2 ‡5ft (1.5m) ↔3ft (1m)

A compact, upright plant with wine-colored stems and whorls of lance-shaped leaves. Flowers from summer to fall. An excellent source of nectar for butterflies.

Filipendula rubra
QUEEN OF THE PRAIRIE

Ⓝ ☼ ◐ Z3–9 H9–1 ‡6–8ft (2–2.5m) ↔4ft (1.2m)

Fragrant flowers in midsummer. A spreading plant, it forms large clumps of irregularly cut, pinnate leaves. Prefers moderately fertile, leafy soil.

HERBACEOUS PLANTS

Paeonia 'Lady Alexander Duff'
LADY ALEXANDER DUFF PEONY

☼ ☼ ◊ Z3–8 H8–1 ↕↔3ft (1m)

A midseason variety with large, fragrant flowers, borne in small clusters. The plant is very free-flowering and the strong stems support the flowers well.

Astilbe chinensis 'Pumila'
DWARF FALSE GOATSBEARD

☼ ◊ Z4–8 H8–1 ↕12in (30cm) ↔8in (20cm)

Flowers in late summer. Grow in fertile, organic soil. They are easy to propagate by division, which should be done in spring just as the new growth emerges.

Oenothera speciosa
SHOWY EVENING PRIMROSE

Ⓝ ☼ ◊ Z5–8 H8–1 ↕↔12in (30cm)

The flowers open one evening and then last all the following day, turning pink as they age. Spread by underground runners and become invasive in rich soil.

Echinacea purpurea
PURPLE CONEFLOWER

Ⓝ ☼ ◊ Z3–9 H9–3 ↕to 5ft (1.5m) ↔18in (45cm)

Flowers from midsummer to early autumn and prefers deep, organic soil. The cultivars bred from this native plant are often more suitable for the garden border.

MORE CHOICES

- *Corydalis sempervirens* z6–8 H8–6
- *Eremurus robustus* z5–8 H8–5
- *Eupatorium dubium* z0–0
- *Eupatorium maculatum* z5–11 H9–1
- *Eupatorium purpureum* z3–9 H9–1
- *Filipendula rubra* 'Venusta' z3–9 H9–1
- *Filipendula vulgaris* 'Kahome' z4–9 H9–1
- *Fragaria* 'Pink Panda' z5–9 H9–5
- *Fragaria* 'Wildfire' z5–9 H9–5
- *Gaura* 'Siskiyou pink' z6–9 H9–6
- *Geranium* 'Claridge Druce' z4–8 H8–1
- *Geum rivale* z3–7 H7–1

Paeonia lactiflora 'Sarah Bernhardt'
SARAH BERNHARDT PEONY

☼ ☼ ◊ Z3–8 H8–1 ↕↔3ft (1m)

A free-flowering variety with slight fragrance and large flower. This is a late bloomer, when most other peonies have finished. The large flowers are on stiff stems, well above the leaves.

Chrysanthemum 'Clara Curtis'
CLARA CURTIS CHRYSANTHEMUM

☼ ◐ ◊ Z5–9 H9–1 ↕30in (75cm) ↔24in (60cm)
A showy border plant that is very free flowering in late summer, before the fall 'mums. Will thrive in most soils. The fragrant flowers are good for cutting.

Chelone obliqua
ROSE TURTLEHEAD

Ⓝ ☼ ◐ ◐ Z3–9 H9–3 ↕24in (60cm) ↔12in (30cm)
Smooth leaves have prominent veins and are toothed. Flowers open in late summer and fall and blend well with fall asters. Native to wetlands in central and SE US.

Iris 'Beverley Sills'
BEVERLEY SILLS IRIS

☼ ◐ ◊ Z3–9 H9–1 ↕36in (90cm)
A very popular variety, this won the top award from the American Iris Society in 1985. Like all bearded iris, rhizomes should be planted with their tops slightly above soil level.

Physostegia virginiana 'Rosy Spire'
ROSY SPIRE OBEDIENT PLANT

Ⓝ ☼ ◐ ◐ Z4–8 H8–1 ↕4ft (1.2m) ↔3ft (1m)
A very vigorous plant that need to be thinned frequently to keep it within bounds. It tends to be weak-stemmed in rich soils and requires staking.

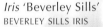

MORE CHOICES

- *Gypsophila* 'Pink Fairy' Z3–9 H9–3
- *Hemerocallis* 'Becky Lynn' Z3–11 H12–1
- *Heuchera* 'Strawberry Swirl/Candy' Z3–8 H8–1
- *Incarvillea delavayi* Z6–10 H9–3
- *Iris sibirica* 'Pink Haze' Z3–9 H9–1
- *Lathrus rotundifolius* Z5–10 H10–1
- *Liatris spicata* Z4–9 H9–1
- *Lychnis flos-jovis* Z4–8 H8–1
- *Macleaya micorcarpa* 'Kelway's Coral Plume' Z4–9 H9–1
- *Nepeta* 'Dawn to Dusk' Z4–8 H8–1
- *Papaver orientale* 'Queen Alexander' Z4–9 H9–1
- *Phlox paniculata* 'Eva Cullum' Z4–8 H8–1
- *Phlox paniculata* 'Lizzy' Z4–8 H8–1
- *Phlox paniculata* 'Bright Eyes' Z4–8 H8–1
- *Thalictrum aquilegifolium* 'Roseum' Z5–7 H9–5
- *Tradescantia* x *andersoniana* 'Pauline' Z5–8 H8–2

HERBACEOUS PLANTS

Summer perennials with blue flowers

Blue gives the impression of space and distance – blue sky and blue water that go on forever. It blends well with all other colors, especially with paler shades like violets, pinks, and pale yellows, while its coolness tones down the brightness of hot reds and yellows. Blues are especially valuable in shade where their cool color is most welcome.

Scabiosa columbaria 'Butterfly Blue'
BUTTERFLY BLUE PINCUSHION FLOWER
☀ ◊ Z3–8 H8–1 ↕20in (50cm) ↔3ft (1m)
Flowers from mid- to late summer. More compact than the species. Prefers moderately fertile soil. Deadhead to extend bloom. Nectar source for bees and butterflies.

Echinops ritro
SMALL GLOBE THISTLE
☀ ◊◊ Z3–9 H12–1 ↕to 24in (60cm) ↔18in (45cm)
Flowers in late summer. Prefers marginally fertile soil and self-sows freely. Good for large borders. Attracts insects and birds but is unpalatable to deer.

Campanula carpatica 'Blue Clips'
BLUE CLIPS CARPATHIAN BELLFLOWER
☀ ☀ ◊ Z4–7 H7–1 ↕9in (23cm) ↔24in (60cm)
Useful in the front of a border, a rock garden, or trailing over a wall, but grows best in a cool soil, so mulch in summer, especially in the south of this region.

Platycodon grandiflorus 'Mariesii'
MARIESII BALLOON FLOWER
☀ ☀ ◊ Z4–9 H9–3 ↕18in (45cm) ↔12in (30cm)
In late summer, large, balloonlike buds precede the flowers, which reach 2in (5cm) wide. This semi-dwarf subspecies prefers deep, fertile, loamy soil.

MORE CHOICES

- *Amsonia* spp. *(hubrichtii, salicifolia, ciliata,* cvs.)* Z3–9 H8–4
- *Campanula carpatica* 'Deep Blue Clips' Z4–7 H7–1
- *Campanula cochlearifolia* 'Bavaria Blue' Z5–7 H7–5
- *Centaurea montana* Z3–9 H9–1
- *Gentiana* spp., e.g. *G. septemfida* Z6–8 H8–6
- *Iris sibirica* 'Borboleta' Z3–9 H9–1
- *Iris sibirica* 'Orville Fay' Z3–9 H9–1
- *Knautia arvensis* Z5–9 H9–5
- *Lavandula* 'Hidcote' Z5–8 H8–5
- *Monarda* 'Blue Stocking' Z4–9 H9–2
- *Nepeta* x *faassenii* 'Blue Wonder' Z4–8 H8–1

Gentiana septemfida
CRESTED GENTIAN
☀ ◊ Z6–8 H8–6 ↕8in (20cm) ↔12in (30cm)
A clump-forming plant with erect stems becoming lax later. The flowers may have six or seven petals. This is one of the easiest gentians to grow and is long-lived.

Amsonia tabernaemontana
WILLOW BLUE-STAR

Ⓝ ☼ ◊ Z3–9 H9–1 ↕18–24in (45–60cm) ↔12in (30cm)
An erect, clump-forming perennial. Will grow in most soil types but prefers sandy soil. Cut plant back by one-third after it finishes flowering in spring.

Nepeta x *faassenii*
CATMINT

☼ ◊ Z4–8 H8–1 ↕↔18in (45cm)
Flowers from early summer to early autumn. Cut back scented foliage after flowering to keep plants tight and encourage repeat flowering. Also known as *N. mussinii*.

Eryngium bourgatii
MEDITERRANEAN SEA HOLLY

☼ ◊ Z5–9 H9–5 ↕6–18in (15–45cm) ↔12in (30cm)
A good choice for maritime gardens or those liable to winter road salt, they also grow well in poor, dry soils. The spiky flowers dry well.

Perovskia atriplicifolia
RUSSIAN SAGE

☼ ◊ Z6–9 H9–6 ↕4ft (1.2m) ↔3ft (1m)
Flowers from summer to early autumn. Bloom period can be extended by deadheading older flowers. Grows well in minimally to moderately fertile soil.

Salvia nemorosa 'Ostfriesland'
EAST FRIESLAND SAGE

☼ ◑ Z5–9 H9–5 ↕18in (45cm) ↔24in (60cm)
Mature plant puts on a spectacular show of flowers, blooming from late spring well into summer, especially if dead-headed. Does well in hotter areas.

Geranium x 'Johnson's Blue'
JOHNSON'S BLUE CRANESBILL

☼ ◊ Z4–8 H8–1 ↕12in (30cm) ↔24in (60cm)
This interspecific hybrid blooms in summer. Prefers moderately fertile, organic, well-drained soil. Prone to problems that affect others in the genus (see opposite).

Lobelia siphilitica
BLUE CARDINAL FLOWER

Ⓝ ☼ ◐ ◊ Z4–8 H8–1 ↕4ft (1.2m) ↔12in (30cm)
An upright plant with un-branched spikes of flowers in late summer. Short-lived; should be divided every 2–3 years. Will self-seed freely if conditions are right.

HERBACEOUS PLANTS

Delphinium x *belladonna* 'Wendy'
WENDY BELLADONNA DELPHINIUM

☼ ◊ Z3–7 H6–1 ‡4ft (1.2m) ↔18in (45cm)

This group name is given to the hybrids from a specific cross that are usually raised from seed. This particular selection, however, is propagated from cuttings.

Delphinium 'Fanfare'
FANFARE DELPHINIUM

☼ ◊ Z3–7 H7–1 ‡7ft (2.2m) ↔24in (60cm)

Named forms of delphinium, raised from cuttings, are far superior to the normal seed-grown plants. Thin new growth in spring for larger flowers, and stake and tie.

Delphinium grandiflorum 'Blue Beauty'
BLUE BEAUTY DELPHINIUM

☼ ◊ Z3–8 H8–1 ‡20in (50cm) ↔12in (30cm)

This short-lived species is sometimes grown as an annual or biennial. A soft plant without stiff, upright spikes, and long-lasting flowers from early summer.

Baptisia australis
FALSE INDIGO

Ⓝ ☼ ◊ Z3–9 H9–1 ‡30in (75cm) ↔24in (60cm)

Blooms in early summer. Seedpods are ornamental. Best used in the back of a border or as a specimen plant. This member of the pea family attracts birds.

Campanula portenschlagiana
DALMATION BELLFLOWER

☼ ◑ ◊ Z4–7 H7–1 ‡6in (15cm) ↔20in (50cm)

A trailing plant that is well suited for rock walls or alpine gardens and demands excellent drainage. It can also be used as a groundcover or edging plant.

MORE CHOICES

- *Nepeta* x *faassenii* 'Dropmore' Z4–8 H8–1
- *Nepeta* x *faassenii* 'Six Hills Giant' Z4–8 H8–1
- *Nepeta* 'Walker's Low' Z4–8 H8–1
- *Nepeta* 'Subsessilis' Z4–8 H8–1
- *Phlox paniculata* 'Franz Schubert'
  Z4–8 H8–1
- *Phlox paniculata* 'Katherine' Z4–8 H8–1
- *Platycodon grandiflorus* 'Double Blue'
  Z4–9 H9–1
- *Platycodon grandiflorus* 'Sentimental Blue'
  Z3–8 H8–1
- *Sisyrinchium angustifolium* 'Lucerne'
  Z5–8 H8–5
- *Veronica spicata* 'Goodness Grows'
  Z3–8 H8–1

Phlox paniculata 'Eventide'
EVENTIDE GARDEN PHLOX

Ⓝ ☼ ◗ ◊ Z4–8 H8–1 ‡ ↔3ft (1m)

Very fragrant plants, loved by butterflies and hummingbirds. One of a many named forms in a range of pastel shades, some with variegated foliage.

Agastache foeniculum 'Blue Fortune'
BLUE FORTUNE HYSSOP

☼ ◊ Z7–10 H12–7 ‡3ft (1m) ↔24in (60cm)

The stiff, upright stems have licorice-scented foliage and the flowers appear from early summer onward. A new introduction, this does well in dry locations.

Iris sibirica 'Dragonfly'
DRAGONFLY SIBERIAN IRIS

☼ ◗ ◊ Z3–9 H9–1 ‡4ft (1.2m) ↔18in (45cm)

Equally at home in wet soil, these iris begin to bloom just after the tall bearded type. They are easy care plants and can go several years without being divided.

Stokesia laevis
STOKES' ASTER

Ⓝ ☼ ◊ 🕿 Z5–9 H9–5 ‡24in (60cm) ↔18in (45cm)

Flowers appear from midsummer to early autumn above the rosettes of oval-shaped to lance-shaped, evergreen elaves. Prefers light, fertile soil.

Veronica spicata 'Sunny Border Blue'
SUNNY BORDER BLUE SPEEDWELL

☼ ◗ ◊ Z3–8 H8–1 ‡20in (50cm) ↔12in (30cm)

A hybrid whose variety name says it all. Flowering from midsummer, it will continue to bloom for several weeks if the old flower spikes are cut off.

HERBACEOUS PLANTS

Tall pink or purple perennials

The hot shades of purple and pink may not always go together, magenta-pink and bright purple can clash, but the cooler shell-pinks, and lilac-purples generally blend well with each other and with blue flowers. One beauty of growing perennials is that they move readily and a poor color combination is easy to cure. These plants all grow well in sunny conditions.

Alcea rosea
HOLLYHOCK

☼ ◊ Z3–9 H10–3 ‡6ft (2m) ↔24in (60cm)

Hollyhocks are easy to grow from seed. They can be attacked by a rust disease that disfigures the foliage but is not fatal. Good sanitation in fall helps control this.

Lavatera thuringiaca 'Barnsley'
BARNSLEY TREE MALLOW

☼ ◊ Z6–8 H8–6 ‡↔6ft (2m)

This cultivar has a more extended bloom season than the species. Blooms from summer until frost. Best when grown in moderately fertile soil.

MORE CHOICES

- *Aster tataricus* Z3–9 H9–1
- *Clematis* x *durandii* Z4–9 H9–5
- *Thalictrum delavayi* Z4–7 H7–1
- *Verbascum* 'Cotswold Queen' Z5–9 H9–5

Campanula persicifolia
PEACH-LEAVED BELLFLOWER

☼ ☼ ◊ Z3–8 H8–1 ‡36in (90cm) ↔12in (30cm)

An upright perennial that may need support in exposed locations. It flowers in early summer over a long period and makes a good cut flower.

Eupatorium purpureum
PURPLE JOE PYE WEED

Ⓝ ☼ ◐ ◍ ◑ ⬤ Z3–9 H9–1 ↕7ft (2.2m) ↔3ft (1m)
Blooms from midsummer to early autumn. Leaves
smell like vanilla when bruised. Prone to rust,
powdery mildew, white smut, and leaf spots.

Filipendula rubra
QUEEN OF THE PRAIRIE

Ⓝ ☼ ◑ ⬤ Z3–9 H9–1 ↕6–8ft (2–2.5m) ↔4ft (1.2m)
Fragrant flowers in midsummer. A spreading plant, it
forms large clumps of irregularly cut, pinnate leaves.
Prefers moderately fertile, leafy soil.

Verbena bonariensis
BRAZILIAN VERBENA

☼ ⬤ Z7–11 H12–7 ↕6ft (2m) ↔18in (45cm)
Dainty, upright stems grow from a cluster of basal
leaves. Makes an excellent accent plant when grown
singly. Probably a self-seeding annual in the north.

Allium giganteum
GIANT ORNAMENTAL ONION

☼ ⬤ Z3–9 H9–5 ↕6ft (2m) ↔12–14in (30–35cm)
Amazingly dense flowerheads bloom in summer.
Strap-shaped leaves wither before the plant blooms.
Grows best in fertile soil. Excellent cut flower.

Phlox paniculata 'Eventide'
EVENTIDE GARDEN PHLOX

Ⓝ ☼ ◑ ⬤ Z4–8 H8–1 ↕ ↔3ft (1m)
These fragrant, summer-flowering, phlox are prone to
powdery mildew; lift and divide every 2–3 years to
keep the clumps small and allow good air circulation.

Vernonia noveboracensis
IRONWEED

Ⓝ ☼ ◑ ⬤ Z4–8 H8–3 ↕to 6ft (2m) ↔24in (60cm)
An upright, branching plant with toothed leaves.
Blooms from late summer into fall. The common name
comes from the rusty color of the old flowers.

Thalictrum rochebrunianum
JAPANESE MEADOW RUE

◑ ⬤ Z5–9 H9–5 ↕3ft (1m) ↔12in (30cm)
Upright with fernlike foliage. It will grow in most soils.
The summer flowers are good for cutting. The variety
'Lavender Mist' has darker flowers and purple stems.

HERBACEOUS PLANTS

Late-blooming perennials

Normally, one thinks of trees and shrubs to provide color late in the year, but these perennials can also help by providing a richer pallet of color. The blues and whites show up particularly well against bright fall foliage while the pinks and lavenders blend with ornamental grasses. Many of these plants have interesting seed pods or heads that add winter interest.

Aconitum carmichaelii 'Arendsii'
ARENDS AZURE MONKSHOOD

☼ ☼ ◑ ◊ Z3–8 H8–3 ‡6ft (1.8m) ↔16in (40cm)

A strong plant that seldom needs staking, with dark green, leathery leaves. Grow in an organic rich soil and afternoon shade. The flowers last well into fall.

Begonia grandis
HARDY BEGONIA

☼ ☼ ◊ Z6–9 H9–5 ‡3ft (1m) ↔4ft (1.2m)

A bulbous begonia that needs a slightly acidic soil rich in organic matter. Where not hardy, lift in fall after frost has killed stems and overwinter in a frost-free place.

Chelone glabra
WHITE TURTLEHEAD

Ⓝ ☼ ☼ ◑ Z3–8 H9–1 ‡3ft (1m) ↔18in (45cm)

This genus can be propagated by soft-tip cuttings in summer or by diviion or seed in fall or spring. Flowers may be tinged with pink or red *in late summer*.

Tricyrtis formosana
TOAD LILY

☼ ☼ ◑ ◊ Z6–9 H9–6 ‡3ft (1m) ↔18in (45cm)

This plan blooms in early fall. It has leaves that are dark green with purple-green spots. Slugs and snails attack soft young growth.

Tradescantia x andersoniana 'Iris Pritchard'
IRIS PRITCHARD SPIDERWORT

☼ ☼ ◑ ◊ Z3–10 H12–1 ‡↔24in (60cm)

Spiderworts need to be divided every 2–3 years. Although each flower only lasts a day, the plant continues to flower for almost 2 months.

Cimicifuga simplex 'White Pearl'
KAMCHATKA BUGBANE

☀ ◐ ◊ ◔ Z4–8 H12–1 ↕3ft (1m) ↔24in (60cm)

Clump-forming perennial with light green to purplish green, irregularly lobed leaves. Grow this plant in fertile, organic soil. Excellent plant for a woodland garden.

Anemone x hybrida 'Honorine Jobert'
HONORINE JOBERT JAPANESE ANEMONE

☀ ◐ ◊ Z4–8 H8–1 ↕5ft (1.5m) ↔indefinite

A good plant for a woodland garden with an organic-rich soil. This is an old variety but still one of the best whites and widely available. The flowers are tinged pink on the reverse.

Anemone x hybrida 'Coupe d'Argent'
CUP OF GOLD JAPANESE ANEMONE

☀ ◐ ◊ Z4–8 H8–1 ↕5ft (1.5m) ↔3ft (90cm)

A modern hybrid that brings a new color into these plants. There are many named forms with single and double flowers in shades of pink to rose.

Sedum 'Ruby Glow'
RUBY GLOW STONECROP

☀ ◊ Z5–9 H9–1 ↕10in (25cm) ↔18in (45cm)

This groundcover plant is excellent for the front of a border or as path edging. The red-tinged foliage is attractive and the flowers last for weeks.

Solidago rugosa 'Fireworks'
FIREWORKS GOLDENROD

Ⓝ ☀ ◐ ◊ Z4–9 H9–1 ↕4ft (1.2m) ↔3–4ft (1–1.2m)

Late-summer blooming. Flowers are attractive to bees and butterflies. Grow in marginal to moderately fertile soil. Prone to powdery mildew, leaf spots, and rust.

MORE CHOICES

- *Aconitum fischerii* Z3–8 H8–3
- *Aster laevis* 'Bluebird' Z4–8 H8–4
- *Aster tataricus* Z3–9 H9–1
- *Dendranthema* 'Sheffield Pink' Z4–10 H12–1
- *Gentiana andrewsii* Z3–7 H8–1
- *Gentiana saponaria* Z4–7 H8–1
- *Gentiana scabra* Z4–8 H8–1
- *Heuchera villosa* 'Autumn Bride' Z5–9 H9–5
- *Sedum* 'Autumn Joy' Z4–9 H12–1
- *Vernonia* spp. Z5–9 H9–5

HERBACEOUS PLANTS

Perennials with variegated foliage

The wide range of color combinations and patterns found in these plants make this a fascinating aspect of gardening. Some form of variegation is found in many species of both woody and perennial plants, and some gardeners become so enamored with them that they grow little else. Probably the greatest range of variegation is found in hostas (*see* p.294).

Aegopodium podagraria 'Variegatum'
VARIEGATED GOUTWEED, BISHOP'S WEED
☀ ◐ ◊ Z4–9 H9–1 ↕4in (10cm) ↔indefinite
An aggressive, spreading groundcover that will survive in the most inhospitable conditions. It should be grown only where it cannot spread into other plants.

Iris pallida 'Variegata'
VARIEGATED DALMATIAN IRIS
☀ ◐ ◊ Z4–9 H9–2 ↕3ft (1m) or more ↔indefinite
The fragrant flowers can't compare with most modern hybrids, but this iris deserves a place in the garden for its striped foliage that is attractive all summer.

Hosta 'Francee'
FRANCEE HOSTA
☀ ◐ ◊ Z3–8 H8–1 ↕22in (55cm) ↔3ft (1m)
An excellent landscape plant, with funnel-shaped lavender flowers on thin 42in (1.1m) stems in summer. Won a top American Hosta Society award.

Pulmonaria longifolia 'Bertram Anderson'
BERTRAM ANDERSON LONGLEAF LUNGWORT
☀ ◐ ◊ Z3–8 H8–1 ↕12in (30cm) ↔18in (45cm)
The narrow leaves can be up to 18in (45cm.) long and are spotted with white. Has brighter flowers than the species and flowers after many other lungworts.

Phlox paniculata 'Norah Leigh'
NORAH LEIGH GARDEN PHLOX
Ⓝ ☼ ◐ ◌ Z4–8 H8–1 ↕4ft (1.2m) ↔2ft (60cm)
Plant this where it will receive some shade during the middle of the day. An excellent choice for the middle to front of the border, where its foliage can be admired.

Liriope spicata 'Silver Dragon'
SILVER DRAGON LILYTURF
☼ ◐ ◌ Z6–10 H12–1 ↕↔12–15in (30–38cm)
Similar to the species, except the foliage is white-striped, and it is slower-growing. The light purple flowers appear in late summer. Spreads determinedly.

Brunnera macrophylla 'Variegata'
VARIEGATED SIBERIAN BUGLOSS
☼ ◌ Z3–7 H7–1 ↕12–18in (30–45cm) ↔20in (50cm)
Plants spread and form a mound of foliage. A location with morning sun is ideal, but soil must not be overly dry. Spring flowers last for several weeks if well grown.

MORE CHOICES

- *Gaura lindheimeri* 'Corrie's Gold' Z6–9 H9–6
- *Heuchera* 'Silver Scrolls' Z4–8 H8–1
- *Heuchera* 'Pewter Veil' Z4–9 H9–1
- *Heuchera* 'Cathedral Windows' Z4–8 H8–1
- *Lamium galeobdolon* 'Variegatum' Z4–8 H8–1
- *Lamium galeobdolon* 'Herman's Pride' Z4–8 H8–1
- *Mentha suaveolans* 'Variegata' Z6–9 H9–6
- *Polygonatum falcatum* 'Variegatum' Z4–8 H8–1
- *Polygonatum odoratum* 'Variegatum' Z4–8 H8–1
- *Pulmonaria longifolia* ssp. *cevennensis* Z3–8 H8–4
- *Rumex acetosa* 'Rhubarb Pie' Z4–7 H7–1
- *Sisyrinchium striatum* 'Aunt May' Z7–8 H8–7
- *Symphytum* x *uplandicum* 'Variegatum' Z5–9 H9–4
- *Veronica gentianoides* 'Variegata' Z4–7 H7–1

Polemonium caeruleum 'Bris d'Anjou'
BRIS D'ANJOU JACOB'S LADDER
Ⓝ ☼ ◐ ◌ Z4–8 H8–1 ↕18in (45cm) ↔12in (30cm)
Plant in organic soil and, in southern areas, in shade. Grown primarily for its foliage; the summer flowers are not as freely produced as in the species.

Lysimachia punctata 'Alexander'
ALEXANDER WHORLED LOOSESTRIFE
☼ ◐ ◌ Z4–8 H9–3 ↕24in (60cm) ↔12in (30cm)
This will grow in most situations. When established, cut back hard after the first flowering in early summer to encourage new shoots with brighter foliage.

Lamium maculatum 'Beacon Silver'
BEACON SILVER DEADNETTLE
◐ ☼ ◌ Z4–8 H8–1 ↕8in (20cm) ↔24in (60cm)
A creeping plant with stems that root easily and form a dense mat that will take light foot traffic. Pink flowers from early to midsummer. Can be a bit invasive.

Perennials with gold foliage

Eye-catching from a distance, the plants described here tend to draw you into the garden to discover their identity. Most need to be grown in full sun to retain their brightness, turning greenish in shade, but even the yellow-leaved hostas, normally a shade loving species, need protection only from the hot midday sun.

Campanula garganica 'Dickson's Gold'
DICKSON'S GOLD ADRIATIC BELLFLOWER
☼ ☼ ◊ Z4–7 H7–1 ‡2in (5cm) ↔12in (30cm)
The flowers appear in late spring and last for several weeks. A good rock garden plant, it needs to be divided often to control its spread.

Tanacetum vulgare 'Isla Gold'
ISLA GOLD TANSY
☼ ◊ Z4–8 H8–1 ‡24–36in (60–90cm) ↔indefinite
A vigorous, easy-to-grow plant that self-seeds freely, although seedlings will probably revert to green. Small, buttonlike yellow flowers appear in summer.

Centaurea montana 'Gold Bullion'
GOLD BULLION MOUNTAIN BLUET
☼ ◊ Z0–0 ‡18in (45cm) ↔24 (60cm)
The species can be a weed, taking over large areas with underground shoots, but this cultivar is more refined and spreads slowly. Flowers from spring into summer.

Lysimachia nummularia 'Aurea'
GOLDEN CREEPING JENNY
☼ ◊ Z4–8 H8–1 ‡2in (5cm) ↔indefinite
A very vigorous, stem-rooting evergreen that can cover a fairly large area in just one season. Bright yellow, cup-shaped flowers in summer add interest.

Hosta 'Midas Touch'
MIDAS TOUCH HOSTA
☼ ☼ ◊ Z3–9 H9–2 ‡20in (50cm) ↔45in (1.1m)
Pleated leaves have an almost metallic sheen. Like most yellow-leaved hostas, this will take more sun than the blue-leaved varieties.

Carex elata 'Aurea'
BOWLES' GOLDEN SEDGE
☼ ◐ ◊ ◑ Z5–9 H9–3 ‡28in (70cm) ↔18in (45cm)
Narrow yellow leaves have a thin green stripe. Color is best in the new spring foliage but remains good for summer. Foliage burns badly if soil is too dry.

Aquilegia 'Mellow Yellow'
MELLOW YELLOW COLUMBINE
☼ ◐ ◊ Z4–7 H7–1 ‡30in (75cm)
↔24in (60cm)
A recent introduction that will mostly come true from seed, although there may the occasional green seedling. White or very pale blue flowers appear in late spring.

Tradescantia x andersoniana 'Blue and Gold'
BLUE AND GOLD SPIDER FLOWER
☼ ◐ ◊ Z5–9 H9–5 ‡↔24in (60cm)
Recently introduced from England, this is a breakthrough in spiderwort foliage. The plants bloom over a long period. Divid every third year to keep them vigorous.

Lamium maculatum 'Cannon's Gold'
CANNON'S GOLD DEADNETTLE
◐ ☼ ◊ Z4–8 H8–1 ‡8in (20cm) ↔3ft (1m)
A low, spreading plant with stems that root easily. It quickly forms a wide mat. The leaves are without the white markings characteristic of the species.

Stachys byzantina 'Primrose Heron'
PRIMROSE HERON LAMBS' EARS
☼ ◊ Z4–8 H8–1 ‡18in (45cm) ↔24in (60cm)
An excellent edging plant with yellow foliage in spring that gradually turns silver-gray during summer. The purple flowers in woolly spikes are not attractive.

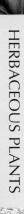

Melissa officinalis 'All Gold'
ALL GOLD LEMON BALM
☼ ◊ Z3–7 H7–1 ‡3ft (1m) ↔18in (45cm)
A tough, drought-resistant plant with lemon scented foliage used for teas and potpourri. White flowers, with a hint of lilac, open throughout summer.

MORE CHOICES

- *Dicentra spectabilis* 'Gold Heart' Z3–9 H9–1
- *Filipendula ulmaria* 'Aurea' Z3–9 H9–1
- *Hosta* 'Piedmont Gold' Z3–9 H9–2
- *Pleioblastus auricoma* Z7–15 H12–1
- *Valeriana phu* 'Aurea' Z5–9 H9–5

Perennials with blue or silver foliage

The cool foliage appearance of these plants makes then a perfect foil for brighter colors. Low-growing and spreading species are ideal at the front of the border and are especially effective in front of dark flowers or foliage. Taller plants can be utilized as a buffer between bold colors. Ornamental grasses with blue foliage are another good source of cool color (*see*.316–317).

Rudbeckia maxima
GREAT CONEFLOWER
Ⓝ ☼ ☼ ◊ Z4–8 H8–1 ‡5–6ft (1.5–2m) ↔2ft (60cm)
Flowers appear in late summer. An erect and stiff plant with oval, gray-green leaves. Prefers moderately fertile soil. Good for the back of a border.

Dianthus gratianopolitanus 'Mountain Mist'
MOUNTAIN MIST CHEDDAR PINK
☼ ◊ Z4–8 H8–1 ‡to 6in (15cm) ↔to 16in (40cm)
When not in flower, this is an attractive gray-green hummock. The flowers start to open in late spring and will continue well into summer if deadheaded.

Artemisia arborescens 'Powis Castle'
POWIS CASTLE WORMWOOD
☼ ◊ Z7– 9 H12–8 ‡2ft (60cm) ↔3ft (1m)
Low, mound-forming, evergreen shrub with aromatic foliage. Cut it back hard to keep it compact. Bears sparse clusters of yellow-tinged silver flowers in summer.

Hosta sieboldiana
SIEBOLD'S HOSTA
☼ ◊ Z3–9 H9–1 ‡3ft (1m) ↔4ft (1.2m)
Possibly the very first hosta exported from Japan, this is the parent of many hybrids. The puckered leaves and elegant flower spikes are loved by flower arrangers.

MORE CHOICES

- *Anthemis marschalliana* Z7–9 H9–7
- *Perovskia atriplicifolia* Z6–9 H9–6
- *Stachys byzantinus* 'Helen von Styne' Z4–8 H8–1

Sedum 'Vera Jameson'
VERA JAMESON STONECROP
☼ ◊ Z4–9 H9–1 ‡12in (30cm) ↔18in (45cm)
This hybrid blooms on purple stems from late summer to early autumn. Like most sedums, it prefers moderately fertile soil but is tolerant of poorer ones.

Perennials with purple or black foliage

Dark foliage tends to be gloomy, so its use should be kept to a minimum; use it as individual plants or in small groups. This color shows off pale colored flowers well, and some red shades go with plants with reddish purple foliage, but not with the blue-purples. This is a color for planting in bright light, because it disappears in a shaded location.

Euphorbia dulcis 'Chameleon'
CHAMELEON SPURGE

☀ ◊ ◊◊ Z3–8 H10–1 ‡↔12in (30cm)
Greenish yellow flowers with purple-tinged bracts appear in early summer. Foliage changes from purple in spring to burgundy, then finally red. Self-sows.

Heuchera 'Palace Purple'
PALACE PURPLE HEUCHERA

☼ ☀ ◊ Z4–8 H8–1 ‡↔18in (45cm)
The original selection has deep purple foliage that fades to a bronzy purple in time. Plants are now often grown from seed and may lack that color intensity.

Ophiopogon planiscapus 'Nigrescens'
BLACK MONDO GRASS

☼ ☀ ◊ ⌖ Z6–11 H12–1 ‡8in (20cm) ↔12in (30cm)
A wonderful contrast plant that makes paler plants stand out. Grow this under white-barked trees like Himalayan white birch, or with light green hostas such as 'Lemon Lime'.

Cimicifuga ramosa 'Brunette'
BRUNETTE AUTUMN SNAKEROOT

☀ ◊ Z3–9 H9–1 ‡4ft (1.2m)
↔3ft (1m)
A clump-forming plant that prefers an organic soil. The foliage is attractive all summer, and the flowers appear in fall. Variety *atropurpurea* is similar, but taller.

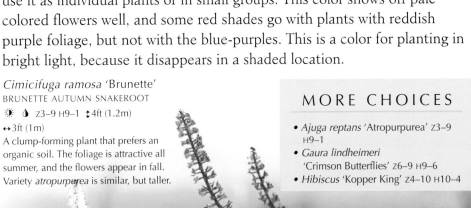

MORE CHOICES

- *Ajuga reptans* 'Atropurpurea' z3–9 H9–1
- *Gaura lindheimeri* 'Crimson Butterflies' z6–9 H9–6
- *Hibiscus* 'Kopper King' z4–10 H10–4

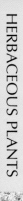

HERBACEOUS PLANTS

Perennials with fine or dissected foliage

Although the shape of perennial foliage differs greatly, most plants have broad to lance-shaped leaves. These may be entire or divided into leaflets, but the overall effect is similar. The plants shown here have narrow to lacy leaves that make a contrast with surrounding plants, especially when they are not in bloom. The differences in texture add interest to the garden.

HERBACEOUS PLANTS

Helleborus multifidus subsp. *hercegovinus*
BOSNIAN HELLEBORE

☀ ◐ ◊ Z7–9 H9–7 ‡12in (30cm) ↔18in (45cm)
A clump-forming perennial for a woodland border with neutral to alkaline soil. The new foliage is tinted brown, and the flowers appear in late winter to early spring.

Corydalis flexuosa
FUMEWORT

☀ ◐ ◊ Z6–8 H8–6 ‡12in (30cm) ↔8in (20cm)
The spring to summer flowers grow from a rootstock that produces small bulbils and goes dormant after flowering. There are several named varieties.

MORE CHOICES

- *Amsonia ciliata* Z5–9 H9–5
- *Astilbe* x *arendsii* 'Fanal' Z3–9 H9–1
- *Dianthus gratianopolitanus* 'Firewitch' Z4–9 H9–1
- *Echinacea tennesseensis* Z3–9 H9–1
- *Perovskia atriplicifolia* 'Filagran' Z6–9 H9–6

Corydalis lutea
YELLOW CORYDALIS

☀ ◊ Z5–8 H8–4 ‡↔8–12in (20–30cm)
A beautiful evergreen plant that flowers from late spring to early fall. Self-sows readily but can be controlled. Best in fertile to moderately fertile soil.

Artemisia arborescens 'Powis Castle'
POWIS CASTLE WORMWOOD

☼ ◊ Z7– 9 H12–8 ‡2ft (60cm) ↔3ft (1m)
Low, mound-forming, evergreen shrub with aromatic foliage. Bears sparse clusters of yellow-tinged silver flowers in summer. Cut back to keep compact.

Paeonia tenuifolia
FERNLEAF PEONY

☼ ☼ ◊ Z3–8 H8–1 ‡↔28in (70cm)
This is among the first peonies to flower. The flowers are short-lived, but the foliage makes this an attractive plant all summer. There is also a double-flowered form.

Santolina rosmarinifolia
GREEN LAVENDER COTTON

☼ ◊ Z6–9 H9–6 ‡24in (60cm) ↔36in (90cm)
This is a good front-of-the-border plant with bright green foliage. A very small shrub sometimes grown as a perennial, it is often best treated as an annual.

Iberis sempervirens
CANDYTUFT

☼ ◊ Z5–9 H9–3 ‡12in (30cm) ↔24in (60cm)
Flowers appear from late spring to early summer on this spreading evergreen perennial. Prefers marginally to moderately fertile soil; does well in a rock garden.

Dicentra eximia
TURKEY CORN, FRINGED BLEEDING HEART

Ⓝ ☼ ◊ Z3–8 H10–1 ‡24in (60cm) ↔18in (45cm)
A mound-shaped plant that flowers in early spring. Grow this in a woodland location. Several named forms have white or darker pink flowers.

Amsonia hubrectii
NARROW-LEAF BLUE-STAR

Ⓝ ☼ ☼ ◊ Z6–8 H8–5 ‡3ft (1m) ↔4ft (1.2m)
Flowers in late spring. Willowlike midgreen leaves turn bright yellow in fall. Tolerant of most soil types. Equally at home in a wildflower garden or border.

Adiantum pedatum
MAIDENHAIR FERN

Ⓝ ☼ ◊ Z3–8 H8–1 ‡↔12–16in (30–40cm)
A popular, easy-to-grow, deciduous fern that is worth a place in every shady garden. Spreads slowly by under-ground stems. Native to eastern North America.

Perennials with attractive fruits or seedheads

Showy as flowers may be, many of them are fleeting, and it is the long-term effect of form and foliage that makes a garden interesting. Plants such as the ones shown here that are still attractive once the flowers have fallen are a bonus. If left to stand in fall, when the rest of their fellow perennials are cut down, many of these can add winter interest as well.

Iris foetidissima
GLADWIN, STINKING IRIS
☼ ◐ ◊ Z4–9 H9–2 ↕3ft (1m) ↔indefinite
This summer-blooming beardless iris gets its name from the foliage, which smells rank when bruised. Prefers moderately fertile, well-drained soil.

MORE CHOICES

- *Centaurea macrocephala* Z3–7 H7–1
- *Cornus canadensis* Z2–7 H7–1
- *Dictamnus albus* Z3–8 H8–1
- *Paeonia japonica* Z3–8
- *Paeonia obovata* Z3–8 H8–1
- *Physalis alkekengi* Z3–9 H8–1
- *Rudbeckia* spp. Z4–9 H9–2

Mitchella repens
PARTRIDGE BERRY
Ⓝ ☼ ◊ Z4–9 H9–1 ↕2in (5cm) ↔indefinite
Mat-forming, prostrate stems root at the nodes (joints). White or pink-flushed flowers appear in early summer, followed in fall by colorful berries. Best in organic soil.

Panicum virgatum
SWITCH GRASS
Ⓝ ☼ ◊ Z5–9 H9–1 ↕3ft (1m) ↔30in (75cm)
One of the major tall-grass prairie grasses, this is clump forming with blue-green summer foliage. It will grow in most soils, from boggy to dry.

Echinacea purpurea 'White Lustre'
WHITE LUSTRE PURPLE CONEFLOWER
Ⓝ ☼ ◊ Z3–9 H12–1 ↕32in (80cm) ↔18in (45cm)
The seedheads of this attractive garden plant can be dried when the petals fade. Hang them in bunches in a cool, sun-free place.

Iris sibirica cultivars
SIBERIAN IRIS
☼ ◐ ◊ Z3–9 H9–1 ↕to 48 in (120cm) ↔2ft (60cm)
An adaptable iris that will grow in most soils. There are many cultivars available with flowers in different colors. Seedpods can be left for winter interest.

Echinops ritro
SMALL GLOBE THISTLE
☼ ◊ ◐ Z3–9 H12–1 ↕to 24in (60cm) ↔18in (45cm)
Flowers in late summer. Prefers marginally fertile soil. Good for large borders. Attracts insects and birds but is unpalatable to deer.

Chasmanthium latifolium
RIVER OATS

Ⓝ ☼ ☀ ◐ ◊ Z5–9 H9–5 ‡3ft (1m) ↔24in (60cm)

Upright clumps of foliage have feathery flower spikes in summer that produce pendulous, oatlike seed heads. They hang on into winter, surviving fall rains.

Actaea rubra
RED BANEBERRY

Ⓝ ☼ ◊ Z4–8 H8–1 ‡20in (50cm) ↔12in (30cm)

Oval white flower clusters appear from midspring to early summer, followed by berries. A clump-forming perennial, it prefers moderately fertile, organic soil.

Arum italicum
LORDS AND LADIES

☼ ☀ ◊ Z7–9 H9–3 ‡12in (30cm) ↔6in (15cm)

Pale greenish white spathes surround early summer blooms. Red fruit clusters appear in fall. Arrow-shaped leaves have silvery white veins. Prefers organic soil.

Arisaema triphyllum
JACK-IN-THE-PULPIT

Ⓝ ☀ ◐ ◊ Z4–9 H9–1 ‡6–24in (15–60cm) ↔6in (15cm)

Once the well-known spring flowers have faded, clusters of small green fruit enlarge and turn bright red by fall.

Belamcanda chinensis
BLACKBERRY LILY

☼ ☀ ◊ Z5–9 H9–5 ‡36in (90cm) ↔8in (20cm)

The showy flowers bloom in summer and are followed by seedpods that split when ripe to show clusters of hard, shiny, black fruit resembling blackberries.

Allium cernuum
NODDING ONION

Ⓝ ☼ ◊ Z3–9 H9–5 ‡28in (70cm) ↔5in (12cm)

A vigorous, bulbous plant with strap-shaped, dark green basal leaves. Flowers are borne in summer. Plant the bulbs in fertile soil in fall.

Perennials for meadows or prairies

Wildflower meadows and prairie habitats are popular garden projects (*see* Tenet 6, Regional Habitats. p.54). While the purist would only include plants native to that particular area, most gardeners are content with a more eclectic mix and the plants illustrated here are frequently grown in such areas. Many of the grasses on pp.324–325 can also be used.

Hemerocallis fulva
COMMON DAYLILY, TIGER LILY

☼ ◊ Z3–9 H12–1 ‡3ft (1m) ↔4ft (1.2m)

This is the common daylily that has naturalized itself. Almost impossible to kill, it is still widely grown and thrives under many soil and moisture conditions.

Asclepias tuberosa
BUTTERFLY WEED

Ⓝ ☼ ◊ Z4–9 H9–2 ‡30in (75cm) ↔18in (45cm)

Blooms in midsummer. Prefers fertile, well-drained, loamy soil. This species is susceptible to aphids, mealybugs, rust, and bacterial and fungal leaf spots.

Echinacea purpurea
PURPLE CONEFLOWER

Ⓝ ☼ ◊ Z3–9 H9–1 ‡to 5ft (1.5m) ↔18in (45cm)

Flowers from midsummer to early autumn. Prefers deep, organic soil. Cultivars of this native plant are often more suitable for the border than the species.

MORE CHOICES

- *Achillea millefolium* Z3–9 H9–1
- *Aslcepias incarnata* Z3–9 H9–2
- *Aster oblongifolius* Z4–8 H8–1
- *Daucus carota* Z3–9 H9–1
- *Helenium autumnale* Z4–8 H8–1
- *Hemerocallis flava* Z3–9 H12–1
- *Lupinus* spp. Z4–7 H7–1
- *Solidago* spp. Z3–10 H9–6
- *Vernonia noveboracencis* Z4–8 H8–3

Baptisia australis
FALSE INDIGO

Ⓝ ☼ ◊ Z3–9 H9–1 ‡30in (75cm) ↔24in (60cm)

Blooms in early summer. Seedpods are ornamental. Best used in the back of a border or as a specimen plant. This member of the pea family attracts birds.

Filipendula rubra
QUEEN OF THE PRAIRIE

Ⓝ ☼ ● Z3–9 H9–1 ‡6–8ft (2–2.5m) ↔4ft (1.2m)

Fragrant flowers in midsummer. A spreading plant, it forms large clumps of irregularly cut, pinnate leaves. Prefers moderately fertile, leafy soil.

Liatris pycnostachya
CAT-TAIL GAYFEATHER

Ⓝ ☼ ◊ Z3–9 H9–2 ‡5ft (1.5m) ↔18in (45cm)

Flowers from midsummer to early fall above densely clustered, basal leaves. 'Alexander' is less likely to need staking. Prefers moderately fertile soil.

Helianthus angustifolius
SWAMP SUNFLOWER

Ⓝ ☼ ◐ Z6–9 H9–4 ↕6ft (1.8m) ↔4ft (1.2m)

One of the best plants for adding color to a meadow in fall. Plants are well branched and stand up well, but need feeding to achieve maximum height. Native to eastern U.S.

Liatris spicata
DENSE GAYFEATHER

Ⓝ ☼ ◊ Z4–9 H9–4 ↕24in (60cm) ↔12in (30cm)

Long-lasting flowers bloom from late summer to early fall. Prefers light, moderately fertile, well-drained, organic soil. In cooler areas, mulch during winter.

Eupatorium purpureum
PURPLE JOE PYE WEED

Ⓝ ☼ ◐ ◊ Z3–9 H9–1 ↕7ft (2.2m) ↔3ft (1m)

Blooms from midsummer to early autumn. Leaves smell like vanilla when bruised. Prone to rust, powdery mildew, white smut, and leaf spots.

Achillea millefolium
YARROW

Ⓝ ☼ ◊ Z3–9 H9–1 ↕↔24in (60cm)

Blooms from early to late summer. Tolerates a wide range of soil conditions. Will self-sow, so cut back flowers after blooming if you don't want volunteers.

Monarda fistulosa
WILD BEE BALM

Ⓝ ☼ ◐ Z4–9 H9–2 ↕4ft (1.2m) ↔18in (45cm)

Flowers from midsummer through early fall vary from light pink to lilac purple. Spicily aromatic leaves are reminiscent of thyme and oregano. Clump-forming.

HERBACEOUS PLANTS

Perennials for rock gardens

Rock gardening is a very intensive and addictive form of gardening. It is ideal for the avid gardener who has limited space, enabling a wide variety of interesting and sometimes challenging plants to be grown in a small area. The number of possible plants is enormous, and there are national and local rock garden societies able to give advice (*see* p.385).

Aethionema armenum 'Warley Rose'
WARLEY ROSE STONECRESS
☼ ◊ Z6–8 H8–6 ↕ ↔6in (15cm)
A spreading, woody perennial that flowers profusely in late spring. It may be short-lived but will self-seed without becoming invasive, especially into rock crevices.

Papaver alpinum
ALPINE POPPY
☼ ◊ Z5–8 H8–3 ↕8in (20cm) ↔4in (10cm)
A short-lived plant that is easy to grow from seed. Sow in place; seedlings do not transplant easily. Flowering is in early summer; deadheading will prolong blooming.

Gentiana sino-ornata
FALL GENTIAN
☼◑ ◊ Z5–7 H7–5 ↕3in (8cm) ↔12in (30cm)
A creeping plant with erect stem tips, which spreads by runners to form a mat. It needs an acidic, fertile soil. If grown from seed, the flowers may vary in color from pale blue to purple.

Gypsophila repens
CREEPING BABY'S BREATH
☼ ◊ Z4–7 H7–1 ↕8in (20cm) ↔20in (50cm)
A trailing plant that can tumble over a rock face or make a carpet. The flowers open in summer and last for several weeks. There is also a white form.

Armeria maritima
SEA THRIFT
Ⓝ ☼ ◊ Z3–9 H9–1 ↕4in (10cm) ↔6in (15cm)
Flowers from late spring to summer. Prefers marginally to moderately fertile soil and will tolerate almost pure sand. Divide every 4–5 years as the center dies out.

Anemone sylvestris
SNOWDROP WINDFLOWER
☼◑ ◊ Z3–9 H9–1 ↕20in (50cm) ↔12in (30cm)
A plant for an alkaline soil that is native to open woods in western Asia. Spring flowers are followed by conical seedheads that open to release woolly-covered seeds.

Lewisia cotyledon

LEWISIA

Ⓝ ☼ ◊ Z5–8 H8–1 ‡12in (30cm) ↔10in (25cm)

An evergreen plant with fleshy leaves that is intolerant of moisture in the crown. Plant this in a vertical crevice or mulch with gravel to give perfect drainage. Well worth the effort.

Iberis sempervirens

CANDYTUFT

☼ ◊ Z5–9 H9–3 ‡12in (30cm) ↔24in (60cm)

Flowers from late spring to early summer on a spreading, evergreen mound. Prefers marginally to moderately fertile soil.

Dianthus gratianopolitanus 'Mountain Mist'

MOUNTAIN MIST CHEDDAR PINK

☼ ◊ Z4–8 H8–1 ‡10in (25cm) ↔12in (30cm)

A mat-forming, summer-flowering gem. If deadheaded, flowering can be prolonged for several weeks.

Sedum spurium

TWO-ROW STONECROP

☼ ◊ Z4–9 H9–1 ‡4in (10cm) ↔24in (60cm)

A mat-forming, evergreen plant with branching stems and vigorous growth. The flowers open in late summer, a time when rock gardens are lacking flowers. It thrives in most soils.

MORE CHOICES

- *Anacyclus pyrethrum* v. *depressus* Z6–8 H8–6
- *Anthemis marschalliana* Z7–9 H9–7
- *Arenaria montana* Z3–5 H5–1
- *Draba aizoides* Z4–6 H6–1
- *Lychnis alpina* Z4–7 H7–1
- *Penstemon* spp. Z3–9 H9–1
- *Saxifraga* spp. Z6–9 H9–6
- *Sempervivum* spp. Z5–8 H8–5
- *Silene* spp. Z4–8 H9–3
- *Verbascum* spp. Z5–9 H7–2

Campanula carpatica

CARPATHIAN BELLFLOWER

☼ ◑ ◊ Z4–7 H7–1 ‡12in (30cm) ↔24in (60cm)

Clump-forming, this has upright, branching flower stems in summer. Several named forms have flowers from white to dark blue.

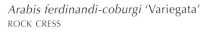

Arabis ferdinandi-coburgi 'Variegata'

ROCK CRESS

☼ ◑ ◊ ◊ Z5–8 H8–3 ‡↔3–4in (7.5–19cm)

Flowers are borne from spring to early summer. This mat-forming perennial is good as a groundcover in the open garden. Also called *A. procurrens* 'Variegata'.

HERBACEOUS PLANTS

Perennials for rock walls & cracks

Many rock garden plants have a trailing habit and are seen at their best when planted at the top of, or between the stones of, a rock wall. Others with a spreading habit can be planted in the crevices between uncemented stone paving, where they will soften the harshness of the stone, survive light foot traffic, and provide bright splashes of color.

Sedum acre
GOLDEN CARPET STONECROP

Ⓝ ☼ ◊ Z3–8 H8–1
↕2in (5cm) ↔indefinite
Blooms in late spring to early summer. Prefers moderately fertile, well drained, soil and moderate to little water. Susceptible to mealybugs, scale insects, slugs, and snails.

Saxifraga burseriana
BURSER'S SAXIFRAGE

☼ ◊ Z6–8 H8–6 ↕2in (5cm) ↔6in (15cm)
This is one example of the encrusted saxifrages, with stiff, silvery foliage. They need an alkaline soil with excellent drainage and protection from hot midday sun.

Saponaria ocymoides
ROCK SOAPWORT

☼ ◊ Z4–8 H8–1 ↕3in (8cm) ↔18in (45cm)
Easy to grow, this vigorous grower should be sheared back hard after its midsummer flowering to stop seed production and to keep the plant within bounds.

Arabis caucasica 'Variegata'
VARIEGATED ROCK CRESS

☼ ◊ Z4–8 H8–1 ↕6in (15cm) ↔20in (50cm)
A very easy plant that can form a large clump in time. Cut back after the spring flowers fade to encourage new growth, which has the brightest variegation.

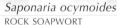

Lewisia cotyledon
LEWISIA

Ⓝ ☼ ◊ Z5–8 H8–1 ↕12in (30cm) ↔10in (25cm)
Given perfect drainage, this will form a large, evergreen rosette. Long-lasting spikes of blooms appear in early summer. Modern hybrids come in a range of shades.

Saxifraga oppositifolia
PURPLE MOUNTAIN SAXIFRAGE

☼ ◑ Z1–7 H7–1 ↕1in (2.5cm) ↔8in (20cm)
Here the leaves are in pairs and not as silvery as in the species above. This needs a woodland type of soil, but still alkaline and very well drained.

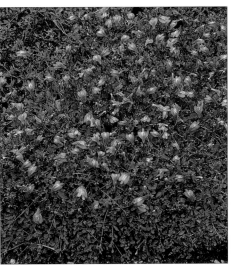

Sempervivum tectorum 'Pacific Hawk'
PACIFIC HAWK HOUSELEEK

☀ ◊ Z4–9 H8–1 ‡6in (15cm) ↔20in (50cm)
There are several hundred named varieties of houseleek that differ in size, color, and leaf shape. The individual rosettes die after flowering, but before making offsets.

MORE CHOICES

- *Armeria caespitosa* Z5–7 H8–4
- *Campanula portenschlagiana* Z4–7 H7–1
- *Gypsophila repens* Z4–7 H7–1
- *Sedum sieboldii* Z6–9 H9–6

Mazus reptans
CREEPING MAZUS

☀ ◊ Z5–8 H8–5 ‡2in (5cm) ↔12in (30cm)
A very prostrate plant that forms a green carpet. The two-lipped flowers appear in late spring and continue for several weeks. It needs good drainage.

Phlox subulata 'Marjorie'
MOSS PHLOX

☀ ◊ Z3–8 H8–1 ‡6in (15cm) ↔20in (50cm)
This is one of many named forms of moss phlox that form low, ground-covering mats. If left untrimmed after flowering, they will self-seed with abandon.

Gentiana acaulis
SPRING GENTIAN

☀ ◊ Z5–8 H8–5 ‡3in (8cm)
↔12in (30cm)
Sometimes difficult species that needs an alkaline soil. Once established, it forms a low mat with many solitary flowers in spring. Native to the Alps and Carpathian mountains.

Euphorbia myrsinites
MYRTLE SPURGE

☀ ◊ Z5–8 H8–5 ‡4in (10cm) ↔12in (30cm)
The spirally arranged, blue-green leaves make this attractive even when not in flower. It makes a dense mat with prostrate stems that flower in spring.

HERBACEOUS PLANTS

Perennial groundcovers for sun

Some of these plants are quite vigorous spreaders, will withstand being walked on, and can be used in place of grass in some locations. Others are more refined and stay reasonably compact. They all make good edging plants for planting along paths to hide their edges, for the front of borders, or, in some cases, for planting at the "skirts" of shrubs and trees, providing they get filtered sunlight.

Santolina chamaecyparissus
LAVENDER COTTON
☼ ◊ Z6–9 H9–4 ‡20in (50cm) ↔3fim)
A woody perennial grown mainly for its aromatic gray foliage. It makes an excellent edging plant that can be trimmed to keep it to size. The flowers are a bonus.

Euphorbia myrsinites
MYRTLE SPURGE
☼ ◊ Z5–8 H8–5 ‡4in (10cm) ↔12in (30cm)
An evergreen plant with prostrate stems and spirally arranged blue-green foliage. The spring flowers are long-lasting. Cannot be walked on.

Liriope muscari
BIG BLUE LILYTURF
☼ ◊ Z6–10 H10–6 ‡12in (30cm) ↔18in (45cm)
Flowers of this evergreen perennial's cultivars range from white to violet. Prefers a light, moderately fertile soil. Plenty of moisture is welcome but not vital.

Alchemilla mollis
LADY'S MANTLE

Ⓝ ☼ ◐ ◊ Z4–7 H7–1 ↕↔20in (50cm)

Tiny flowers produced from early summer to early fall can be used in fresh and dried arrangements. A sturdy, drought- tolerant groundcover that prefers organic soil.

MORE CHOICES

- *Coreopsis rosea* Z4–8 H8–1
- *Delosperma* sp. Z8–10 H10–8
- *Fragaria hybrids* Z5–9 H9–5
- *Lysimachia nummularia* 'Aurea' Z4–8 H8–3
- *Ranunculus montanus* Z5–8 H8–5
- *Sedum ternatum* Z4–8 H9–1
- *Thymus serpyllum* Z4–9 H9–1

Cerastium tomentosum
SNOW IN SUMMER

☼ ◊ Z3–7 H7–1 ↕3in (8cm) ↔indefinite

A tough plant with woolly leaves and spreading, somewhat invasive stems. It should be cut back immediately after flowering to prevent seeding.

Ceratostigma plumbaginoides
LEADWORT, PLUMBAGO

☼ ◊ Z6–9 H9–6 ↕18in (45cm) ↔12 in (30cm)

Clusters of small, dark blue flowers bloom in late summer and fall. Leaves turn brilliant red in fall. Wiry reddish stems. Use as groundcover or in a rock garden.

Dianthus deltoides
MAIDEN PINK

☼ ◊ Z3–10 H10–1 ↕6in (15cm) ↔12in (30cm)

Scentless flowers borne in summer. Flower colors can range from white to deep pink and red. A mat-forming plant that makes a good groundcover. Self-sows.

Stachys byzantina
LAMBS' EARS

☼ ◊ Z4–8 H8–1 ↕18in (45cm) ↔24in (60cm)

An excellent edging plant, except for the floppy stems of minimally attractive flowers. 'Silver Carpet' is non-flowering; 'Primrose Heron' has yellow leaves in spring.

Geranium sanguineum 'Max Frei'
MAX FREI CRANESBILL

☼ ◊ Z4–8 H8–1 ↕6in (15cm) ↔9in (23cm)

A mounded plant that flowers from summer to fall, this is one of many named forms of this geranium with flowers of different shades. Some are more spreading.

Phlox subulata 'Candy Stripe'
CANDY STRIPE CREEPING PHLOX

Ⓝ ☼ ◐ ◊ Z3–8 H8–1 ↕6in (15cm) ↔20in (50cm)

Flowers from late spring to early summer, and sometimes again in fall. Evergreen. Prefers fertile soil. Creeping stems good for groundcover or rock gardens.

HERBACEOUS PLANTS

Perennial groundcovers for shade

These plant will survive in most shade densities and are useful for planting beneath well established shrubs or trees with a high canopy. Tall shade-tolerant bulbs like summer snowflake (*Leucojum*) and daffodils (*Narcissus*) can be planted beneath them and will grow up through, but small bulbs like snowdrops (*Galanthus*) would be smothered by the taller groundcovers.

Alchemilla mollis
LADY'S MANTLE

Ⓝ ☼ ◐ Z4–7 H7–1 ↕↔20in (50cm)

Tiny flowers produced from early summer to early fall can be used in fresh and dried arrangements. This sturdy, drought-tolerant groundcover prefers organic soil.

Asarum canadense
CANADIAN WILD GINGER

Ⓝ ☼ ◑ ◐ Z2–8 H8–1 ↕↔6in (15cm)

A creeping plant with dull, slightly woolly leaves, that spreads to form large clumps. Small, brown flowers are often overlooked. Stems smell of ginger when crushed.

Lamium maculatum 'Beacon Silver'
BEACON SILVER DEADNETTLE

☼ ◑ ◐ Z4–8 H8–1 ↕8in (20cm) ↔24in (60cm)

A rapidly spreading plant that is shallow rooting and easy to remove if invasive. Pink flower in spring, with repeat flowering in summer. It also spreads by seeds.

MORE CHOICES

- *Aegopodium podagraria* 'Variegatum' Z4–9 H9–1
- *Asarum europaeum* Z4–8 H8–1
- *Brunnera macrophylla* Z3–7 H7–1
- *Convallaria majalis* Z2–7 H7–1
- *Cyclamen hederifolium* Z8–9 H9–7
- *Dicentra eximea* Z3–8 H10–1
- *Galax urceolata* Z5–8 H8–5
- *Geranium macrorrhizum* Z4–8 H8–1
- *Lamium galeobdolon* Z4–8 H8–1
- *Liriope spicata* Z6–11 H12–1
- *Petasites fragrans* Z7–9 H9–7
- *Polygonatum multiflorum* Z4–8 H8–1

Mertensia virginica
VIRGINIA BLUEBELLS

Ⓝ ☼ ◐ Z3–7 H7–1 ↕24in (60cm) ↔18in (45cm)

Flowers open from pink-tinted buds in mid- to late spring. Grow in well-drained, organic soil. Prone to problems but usually outgrows them

Mazus reptans
CREEPING MAZUS

☼ ◐ Z5–8 H8–5 ↕2in (5cm) ↔12in (30cm)

Mat-forming plant that needs permanently-moist soil and is intolerant of drought. The flowers bloom from late spring to summer. Will grow in sun with moisture.

Phlox stolonifera 'Ariane'
ARIANE CREEPING PHLOX

Ⓝ ☀ ◊ Z4–8 H8–1 ‡6in (15cm) ↔12in (30cm)
The dark green foliage makes a low mat. Flowers arise on short, upright stems in spring. The species has purple blooms and other varieties are pink or blue.

Ajuga reptans
CARPET BUGLEWEED

☀ ◊ Z3–9 H9–1 ‡6in (15cm) ↔36in (90cm)
A tough plant that will survive under heavy foot traffic. It is equally at home in sun or shade and can invade a lawn. Varieties with variegated foliage are superior.

Galium odoratum
SWEET WOODRUFF

☀☀ ◊◊ Z5–8 H8–5 ‡18in (45cm) ↔indefinite
A charming creeper that spreads by rhizomes, but easy to remove. Flowers open in late spring. Foliage is scented when dried. This was used as a "strewing herb."

Epimedium x *warleyensis*
WARLEY BARRENWORT

☀ ◊ Z5–9 H9–5 ‡20in (50cm) ↔3ft (1m)
A slow-spreading, evergreen plant with leaves that are hairy beneath and tinted red in spring and fall. The flowers are produced in late spring.

Epimedium pubigerum
BALKAN BARRENWORT

☀ ◊ Z4–8 H8–1 ‡↔18in (45cm)
Spreading by underground stems, this will slowly colonize an area. The shiny leaves are hairy beneath and keep their color in fall. Flowers appear in spring.

Tiarella cordifolia
FOAMFLOWER

☀ ◊ Z3–8 H7–1 ‡8in (20cm) ↔12in (30cm)
A gently-spreading plant that makes an excellent ground cover. It flowers in late spring. T. wherryi is similar but has maroon-tinted leaves and pinkish flowers.

Epimedium x *versicolor* 'Sulphureum'
YELLOW BARRENWORT

☀ ◊◊ Z5–8 H8–5 ‡12in (30cm) ↔3ft (1m)
Other cultivars of this hybrid cross have pink to copper-red flowers. Prefers fertile, organic, well-drained soil. Susceptible to vine weevil and mosaic virus.

HERBACEOUS PLANTS

Perennials not likely to be browsed by deer

While it is terrible if trees and shrubs get eaten by deer during the winter, it seems worse still if these pests come and eat perennials in spring as they emerge, or in summer as they start to bloom. The plants listed here seem to escape being browsed and are a good choice where deer are a problem. Fortunately, there are enough choices to still make a good display.

Echinops ritro
SMALL GLOBE THISTLE

☼ ◐ ◊ Z3–9 H12–1 ‡to 24in (60cm)
↔18in (45cm)
Flowers in late summer. Prefers marginally fertile soil. and self-sows freely. Good for large borders. Attracts insects and birds but is unpalatable to deer.

Ajuga pyramidalis
PYRAMIDAL BUGLEWEED

☼ ◊ Z3–9 H9–1 ‡10in (25cm) ↔24in (60cm)
A semi-evergreen, clump-forming species that is not as invasive as Common Bugleweed, which is also deer-proof. It forms a dense carpet and blooms in late spring.

MORE CHOICES

- *Achillea sp.* Z4–9 H9–2
- *Aquilegia sp.* Z3–8 H8–1
- *Arisaema sikokiana* Z4–9 H9–3
- *Arisaema triphyllum* Z4–9 H9–1
- *Armeria maritima* Z3–9 H9–1
- *Asclepias sp.* Z3–9 H10–2
- *Aster sp.* Z3–9 H9–1
- *Astilbe sp.* Z3–8 H8–2

Asclepias tuberosa
BUTTERFLY WEED

Ⓝ ☼ ◊ Z4–9 H9–2 ‡30in (75cm) ↔18in (45cm)
Blooms in midsummer. Prefers fertile, well-drained, loamy soil. Susceptible to aphids, mealybugs, rust, and bacterial and fungal leaf spots.

Perovskia atriplicifolia
RUSSIAN SAGE

☼ ◊ Z6–9 H9–6 ‡4ft (1.2m) ↔3ft (1m)
Flowers from summer to early autumn. Bloom period can be extended by deadheading older flowers. Grows well in minimally to moderately fertile soil.

Eupatorium purpureum
PURPLE JOE PYE WEED

Ⓝ ☼ ◐ ◊ Z3–9 H9–1 ‡7ft (2.2m) ↔3ft (1m)
Blooms from midsummer to early autumn. Leaves smell like vanilla when bruised. Prone to rust, powdery mildew, white smut, and leaf spots.

MORE CHOICES

- *Baptisia* sp. Z3–9 H9–2
- *Centaurea macrocephala* Z3–7 H7–1
- *Cimicifuga* sp. Z3–8 H12–1
- *Coreopsis* sp. Z4–9 H12–1
- *Dicentra* sp. Z3–9 H9–1
- *Digitalis* sp. Z5–9 H10–1

Alchemilla mollis
LADY'S MANTLE

Ⓝ ☀ ◊ Z4–7 H7–1 ↕↔20in (50cm)
Tiny flowers produced from early summer to early fall can be used in fresh or dried arrangements. This sturdy, drought-tolerant groundcover prefers organic soil.

Hibiscus coccineus
SCARLET HIBISCUS

Ⓝ ☀ ◊ Z6–15 H12–1 ↕10ft (3m) ↔4ft (1.2m)
A woody perennial with lobed basal leaves. Cut back hard in spring. Solitary flowers are carried in the leaf joints in late summer. Native from Georgia to Florida.

Convallaria majalis
LILY-OF-THE-VALLEY

☀ ◊ Z2–7 H7–1 ↕6in (15cm) ↔indefinite
Bears sweetly scented spring flowers. A handful of cultivars show varying flower color and leaf variegation. Prefers moist, organic soil and leaf mold mulch.

Aconitum carmichaelii
CARMICHAEL'S MONKSHOOD

☀ ◊ Z3–8 H8–3 ↕6ft (2m) ↔16in (40cm)
An erect plant that is best suited to the back of the border. It will probably need staking to display well. The flowers are carried on branched stems and open in fall. A good cut flower.

Anemone x hybrida
JAPANESE WINDFLOWER

☀ ◊ Z4–8 H8–5 ↕5ft (1.5m) ↔2ft (60cm)
Flowers appaer from late summer to midautumn in shades of white, pink, and purple. prerfers fertile organic soil. Also called *A. x elegans* and *A. japonica*.

Asarum europaeum
EUROPEAN WILD GINGER

☀ ◐ ◊ Z4–8 H8–1 ↕3in (8cm) ↔12in (30cm)
Easy to tell from the native species by leaves that are shiny, rather than dull, and evergreen. It creeps slowly and forms compact carpets. This flowers in late spring.

Asarum canadense
CANADIAN WILD GINGER

Ⓝ ☀ ◐ ◊ Z2–8 H8–1 ↕↔6in (15cm)
A low, spreading, deciduous plant that seeds itself freely from flowers held almost on the soil. It grows in sun and shade. Native from New Brunswick to North Carolina.

HERBACEOUS PLANTS

Allium karataviense
TURKESTAN ONION

☼ ◊ Z3–9 H9–5 ‡10in (25cm)

An interesting species with decorative foliage that is almost as ornamental as the flowers. Leaves are in pairs, broad, and tinged purple at the base.

Geranium macrorrhizum 'Spessart'
SPESSART SCENTED CRANESBILL

☼ ◊ Z4–8 H8–1 ‡20in (50cm) 24in (60cm)

Blooms appear in early summer, followed by distinctive seedheads. Prefers moderately fertile, organic, well-drained soil.

Scabiosa columbaria
PINCUSHION FLOWER

☼ ◊ Z3–8 H8–1 ‡20in (50cm) ↔3ft (1m)

A long-flowering species, from summer into fall, with flowers in solitary heads but freely produced. It is a good cut flower. There is also a pink-flowered variety.

Limonium platyphyllum
SEA LAVENDER

☼ ◊ Z4–9 H9–1 ‡24in (60cm) ↔18in (45cm)

A broad plant that needs room to grow. It is subject to rot if crowded and without air circulation. Flowers are on multi-branched stalks and bloom in summer.

Chelone lyonii
PINK TURTLEHOOD

Ⓝ ☼ ☼ ◊ Z3–9 H9–3 ‡4ft (2m) ↔24in (60cm)

This upright species with square stems will grow in part-shade if soil is moist. Flowers, in dense clusters with a yellow beard on the outer petals, open in summer.

MORE CHOICES

- *Echinops ritro* Z3–9 H12–1
- *Epimedium spp.* Z5–9 H9–5
- *Eryngium planum* Z4–9 H9–1
- *Euphorbia spp.* Z6–10 H10–2
- *Gypsophila paniculata* Z4–9 H9–1
- *Helleborus spp.* Z4–9 H8–1
- *Heuchera spp.* Z0–0
- *Iris sibirica* Z3–9 H9–1
- *Lavandula angustifolia* Z6–9 H12–7
- *Limonium gmelinii* Z8–9 H9–3
- *Liriope spicata* Z6–11 H12–1
- *Lobelia spp.* Z3–9 H9–2
- *Monarda didyma* Z4–9 H9–2
- *Nepeta spp.* Z3–9 H12–2
- *Opuntia humifusa* Z11–12 H12–9
- *Origanum spp.* Z4–9 H10–2
- *Pulmonaria spp.* Z3–8 H8–1
- *Salvia spp.* Z4–10 H12–1
- *Solidago spp.* Z3–10 H9–6
- *Tradescantia spp.* Z3–10 H12–1
- *Veronica spicata* Z3–8 H8–1

Boltonia asteroides
WHITE DOLL'S DAISY

Ⓝ ☀ ☀ ◐ ◖ Z4–8 H9–1 ‡6ft (2m) ↔3ft (1m)

A strong-stemmed plant with blue-green leaves and flowers from late summer into early fall in white, lilac, or pinkish purple. Divide every few years.

Paeonia tenuifolia
FERNLEAF PEONY

☀ ☀ ◐ ◖ Z3–8 H8–1 ‡ ↔28in (70cm)

One of the first peonies to flower, the finely dissected foliage is attractive once the flowers are finished. Flowers of the double form, 'Plena', are longer lasting.

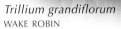

Trillium grandiflorum
WAKE ROBIN

Ⓝ ☀ ☀ ◐ ◖◖ Z4–7 H7–3 ‡18in (45cm) ↔12in (30cm)

Flowers bloom in midspring and often turn pink as they age. Prefers acidic to neutral soil rich in organic matter. Mulch in fall with leaf mold.

Amsonia tabernaemontana
WILLOW BLUE-STAR

Ⓝ ☀ ◖ Z3–9 H9–1 ‡18-24in (45-60cm) ↔12in (30cm)

An erect, clump-forming perennial. Will grow in most soil types but prefers sandy soil. Cut plant back by one-third after it finishes flowering in spring.

Paeonia lactiflora 'Sarah Bernhardt'
SARAH BERNHARDT PEONY

☀ ☀ ◐ ◖ Z3–8 H8–1 ‡↔20–28in (50–70cm)

A late bloomer with a slightly fragrant flower. It is free flowering with strong stems. Foliage turns a bronzy color in the fall. There are other deer-resistant named peonies.

Iberis sempervirens
CANDYTUFT

☀ ◖ Z5–9 H9–3 ‡12in (30cm) ↔24in (60cm)

Flowers appear from late spring to early summer on this spreading evergreen perennial. Prefers marginally to moderately fertile soil; does well in a rock garden.

Lychnis coronaria
ROSE CAMPION

☀ ☀ ◖ Z4–8 H8–1 ‡32in (80cm) ↔18in (45cm)

An easy-to-grow plant that is short lived but self-seeds freely. Seedlings are easy to weed while small. The stems and leaves are covered with a gray down.

Aruncus dioicus
GOATSBEARD

Ⓝ ☀ ◖ Z3–7 H7–1 ‡6ft (2m) ↔4ft (1.2m)

Flowers appear from early to midsummer and make good cut flowers. Fernlike, alternately pinnate, midgreen leaves can grow 3ft long. Best grown in fertile soil.

HERBACEOUS PLANTS

Perennials that attract hummingbirds

Everyone's favorite birds, hummingbirds are easy to attract into the garden by growing plants that are rich in nectar. A supplemental feeder will keep them coming even when their favored plants are not in bloom. Despite everything you may have read, hummingbirds do not feed only on red flowers, as the plants shown here demonstrate.

Agastache 'Blue Fortune'
BLUE FORTUNE HYSSOP

☼ ◊ Z7–10 H12–7 ↕3ft (1m) ↔24in (60cm)
A new introduction, this grows well in dry soils. Stiff, upright stems have licorice-scented foliage and flowers that open from early summer onward.

MORE CHOICES

- *Alcea* spp. Z3–9 H10–3
- *Asclepias* spp. Z3–9 H10–2
- *Campanula* spp. Z3–9 H9–1
- *Chelone lyonii* Z3–9 H9–3
- *Delphinium* spp. Z3–8 H6–1
- *Digitalis* spp. Z5–9 H10–1

Aster novae-angliae 'Barr's Pink'
BARR'S PINK NEW ENGLAND ASTER

Ⓝ ☼ ◑ ◊ Z4–8 H8–1 ↕4½ft (1.3m) ↔24in (60cm)
This is one of many named cultivars of this aster. They are mostly middle to back-of-the-border plants, and tall varieties may need staking to display well.

Lobelia cardinalis
CARDINAL FLOWER

Ⓝ ☼ ◊ Z2–8 H8–1 ↕3ft (1m) ↔9in (23cm)
Flowers from summer to early autumn. Foliage is lance-shaped, bright green, and tinged with bronze. Best if grown in fertile, organic soil. Short-lived.

Asclepias incarnata
SWAMP MILKWEED

Ⓝ ☼ ◊ Z3–8 H8–1 ↕4ft (1.2m) ↔24in (60cm)
Blooms midsummer to early autumn. Prefers fertile, well-drained, loamy soil. Susceptible to aphids and mealybugs, especially when in bloom.

Dicentra spectabilis
BLEEDING HEART

☼ ◐ ◊ Z3–9 H9–1 ‡to 4ft (1.2m) ↔18in (45cm)
A stately perennial with slightly arching stems of blooms. Prefers rich soil and may go dormant early if given too much sun, or in warmer parts of this region. There is also a white form.

Coreopsis verticillata
THREAD-LEAVED TICKSEED

Ⓝ ☼ ◑ ◊ Z4–9 H9–1 ‡32in (80cm) ↔18in (45cm)
A bushy plant that spreads slowly. The fine, light green foliage make it attractive even when not in flower. Blooms are in small clusters on slender stems in early summer. Deadheading will promote rebloom.

Lychnis coronaria
ROSE CAMPION

☼ ◑ ◊ Z4–8 H8–1 ‡32in (80cm) ↔18in (45cm)
A short-lived plant that is very showy in flower. The bright magenta color makes it hard to place in the border. It self-seeds freely and can become a nuisance.

Monarda didyma 'Jacob Cline'
JACOB CLINE BEE BALM

☼ ◑ ◊◊ Z4–11 H12–1 ‡18in (45cm) ↔2ft (60cm)
Blooms from mid- to late summer. Grow in moderately fertile, organic, well-drained soil. More resistant to powdery mildew and rust than the species.

Ajuga pyramidalis
PYRAMIDAL BUGLEWEED

☼ ◊ Z3–9 H9–1 ‡10in (25cm) ↔24in (60cm)
A mat-forming groundcover that spreads slowly and is not as invasive or tough as the Common Bugleweed. Do not grow where would it get much foot traffic.

MORE CHOICES

- *Echinacea* spp. Z3–9 H12–1
- *Echinops ritro* Z3–9 H12–1
- *Helianthus salicifolius* Z6–9 H9–6
- *Hemerocallis citrina* Z3–10 H12–2
- *Hosta plantaginea* Z3–9 H9–1
- *Lilium* sp. Z3–8 H8–1
- *Lobelia* sp. Z3–9 H9–2
- *Monarda didyma* Z4–9 H9–2
- *Penstemon* spp. Z3–9 H9–1
- *Phlox paniculata* Z4–8 H8–1

HERBACEOUS PLANTS

Perennials that attract butterflies

With the exception of the cabbage white, gardeners enjoy seeing butterflies flitting about the garden. Butterflies feed mainly on nectar, and the plants shown here are attractive to them for this reason. They also appreciate an area of wet sand or soil from which they can drink. To encourage butterflies, one must occasionally put up with the damage their caterpillars do.

HERBACEOUS PLANTS

Solidago 'Goldenmosa'
GOLDENMOSA GOLDENROD
☀ ◊ Z5–9 H9–5 ↕30in (75cm) ↔x18in (45cm)
Blooms in late summer. Other cultivars vary in height and flowering time. Although considered a weed by some, goldenrods are excellent butterfly plants.

Veronica spicata
SPIKE SPEEDWELL
☀ ◊ Z3–8 H8–1 ↕24in (60cm) ↔18in (45cm)
Early to late summer blooms can be used in fresh arrangements. Prefers moderately fertile soil. Resistant to deer browsing. Many good cultivars are available.

MORE CHOICES

- *Achillea millefolium* Z3–9 H9–1
- *Allium* spp. Z3–9 H9–5
- *Aster* spp. Z3–9 H9–1
- *Baptisia* spp. Z3–9 H9–2
- *Dianthus* 'Bath's Pink' Z5–8 H8–1
- *Echinacea purpurea* Z3–9 H9–1
- *Echinops ritro* Z3–9 H12–1

Agastache rupestris
SUNSET HYSSOP, LICORICE MINT
☀ ◊◑ Z7–9 H9–7 ↕24in (60cm) ↔18in (45cm)
Easy to grow; adaptable to soil and moisture. Midsummer blooms are good for drying, and the foliage can be used for teas or on salads. Attractive to hummingbirds.

Asclepias incarnata
SWAMP MILKWEED

Ⓝ ☼ ◖◗ Z3–8 H8–1 ‡4ft (1.2m) ↔24in (60cm)
Blooms midsummer to early autumn. Prefers fertile, loamy soil. Susceptible to aphids and mealybugs, especially when in bloom.

Asclepias tuberosa
BUTTERFLY WEED

Ⓝ ☼ ◗ Z4–9 H9–2 ‡30in (75cm) ↔18in (45cm)
Blooms in midsummer. Prefers fertile, well-drained, loamy soil. Susceptible to aphids, mealybugs, rust, and bacterial and fungal leaf spots.

Centaurea macrocephala
GIANT KNAPWEED

☼ ◗ Z3–7 H7–1 ‡5ft (1.5m) ↔24in (60cm)
A stiff, upright plant with long, wavy-edged, basal leaves. Seldom needs staking. The summer flowers are long-lasting. Seedheads can be used in winter arrangements.

Coreopsis verticillata
THREAD-LEAVED TICKSEED

Ⓝ ☼ ☼ ◗ Z4–9 H9–1 ‡32in (80cm) ↔18in (45cm)
A slowly spreading, bushy plant, with fine, light green foliage. Blooms are in small clusters on slender stems in early summer. Deadheading will promote a second flowering in early fall.

Digitalis purpurea
FOXGLOVE

☼ ◖ Z4–8 H9–1 ‡3–5ft (1–1.5m) ↔2ft (60cm)
Rosette-forming plant with a large flower spike that blooms in early summer. These variable plants can be biennial or perennial. Tolerates poor and dry soils.

MORE CHOICES

- *Eryngium planum* Z4–9 H9–1
- *Eupatorium* spp. Z4–8 H8–2
- *Heliopsis helianthoides* Z4–9 H9–1
- *Liatris spicata* Z4–9 H9–1
- *Lobelia cardinalis* Z2–8 H8–1
- *Lobelia siphilitica* Z4–8 H8–1
- *Monarda didyma* Z4–9 H9–2
- *Nepeta* spp. Z3–9 H12–2
- *Phlox paniculata* Z4–8 H8–1
- *Rudbeckia fulgida* Z4–9 H9–1

Oenothera missouriensis
OZARK SUNDROPS

Ⓝ ☼ ◗ Z5–8 H8–3 ‡6in (15cm) ↔20in (50cm)
Spreading plants with lax stems that are reddish at the tips. The summer flowers, often spotted with red, are up to 5in (12cm) across and are long-lasting.

HERBACEOUS PLANTS

Hemerocallis citrina
LEMON-SCENTED DAYLILY

☼ ◊ Z3–10 H12–2 ‡4ft (1.2m) ↔30in (75cm)

Slender, upright plants carry night-blooming flowers in midsummer. Although each flower only lasts a night, a mature clump can stay in flower for 6 weeks.

Hemerocallis fulva
COMMON DAYLILY, TIGER LILY

☼ ◊ Z3–9 H12–1 ‡3ft (1m) ↔4ft (1.2m)

The single- and double-flowered forms of this are very common. They thrive on neglect and grow almost anywhere. Flowers in midsummer.

Hemerocallis 'Gentle Shepherd'
GENTLE SHEPHERD DAYLILY

☼ ◊ Z3–10 H12–2
‡↔26in (65cm)

A good example of modern daylilies, this semi-evergreen cultivar thrives throughout the Northeast. The flowers are 5in (13cm) across, on branched stems, and are produced for several weeks.

MORE CHOICES

- *Scabiosa columbaria* 'Butterfly Blue' Z3–8 H8–1
- *Sedum spp.* Z6–9 H9–6
- *Tolmiea menziesii* Z6–9 H9–6
- *Verbena bonariensis* Z7–11 H12–7

Lavandula angustifolia 'Hidcote'
HIDCOTE LAVENDER

☼ ◊ Z5–8 H8–5 ‡24in (60cm) ↔30in (75cm)

A compact, woody-based, mound-forming cultivar slightly hardier than other named forms. Lavenders are worthy of a place in the perennial border.

Lilium auratum var. platyphyllum
LARGE-FLOWERED GOLDEN-RAY LILY

☼ ◊ Z3–8 H8–1 ‡8ft (2.4m) ↔3ft (90cm)

Best in a poor but open soil and grown without extra fertilizer or moisture. It makes an outstanding pot plant with a very strong fragrance.

Lilium 'Connecticut King'
CONNECTICUT KING LILY

☼ ◊ Z3–8 H8–1 ‡3ft (1m) ↔18in (45cm)

An Asiatic hybrid lily with up-facing flowers, this is an excellent border plant. Lift and divide every 4-5 years to keep the plants vigorous.

Lilium 'Magic Pink'
MAGIC PINK LILY

☼ ◊ Z3–8 H8–1 ‡4ft (1.2m) ↔18in (45cm)

An Oriental hybrid with slightly fragrant flowers in late summer. The large flowers tend to make the plants top-heavy; they need deep planting to withstand winds.

Lupinus albifrons
WHITE-WINGED LUPINE

Ⓝ ☼ ◑ ◊ ᵖᴴ Z0–0 ‡↔30in (75cm)

This upright, woody-based lupine needs excellent drainage. The spoon-shaped leaflets are covered with silver hairs. The spikes of flowers open in summer.

Salvia discolor
TWO-COLOR SAGE

☼ ◑ ◊ Z9–11 H12–3 ‡18in (45cm) ↔12in (30cm)

A very hairy species with the stems and undersides of the leaves covered with white, woolly hairs. The late summer flowers are in long spikes.

Iberis sempervirens
CANDYTUFT

☼ ◊ Z5–9 H9–3 ‡12in (30cm) ↔24in (60cm)

Flowers appear from late spring to early summer on this spreading, evergreen perennial. Prefers marginally to moderately fertile soil; does well in a rock garden.

Gaillardia x grandiflora 'Kobold'
KOBOLD BLANKET FLOWER

☼ ◊ Z3–8 H8–1 ‡3ft (1m) ↔18in (45cm)

A short-lived plant very widely grown for its heat tolerance and long flowering period. This may be sold as 'Goblin'. There are several other named forms.

Ferns that tolerate dry conditions

Many ferns are woodland plants, so it is not surprising that these are able to tolerate reasonably dry conditions. There are a few that grow in the open and in sunlight, but most are better suited to filtered shade. Most of these ferns die down in fall. Some are evergreen; a few evergreen only in he warmer parts of the Northeast.

MORE CHOICES

- *Adiantum pedatum* z3–8 H8–1
- *Cheilanthes lanosa* z5–9 H9–5
- *Cystopteris bulbifera* z4–8 H8–1
- *Dryopteris fragrans* z6–9 H9–6
- *Polystichum setiferum* z6–9 H9–6
- *Polypodium australe* z6–8 H8–6
- *Polystichum lonchitis* z3–8 H8–1
- *Polystichum polyblepharum* z6–8 H8–5
- *Woodsia obtusa* z4–7 H7–1

Polystichum aculeatum
HARD SHIELD FERN

☼ ◐ ◑ z3–8 H8–1 ‡24in (60cm) ↔30in (75cm)
This evergreen fern has pale, stiff, leathery new foliage, darkening later to a glossy green. It grows well on alkaline soils and also in moist ones.

Woodsia polystichoides
HOLLY-FERN WOODSIA

☼ ◑ ◐ z4–8 H8–1 ‡12in (30cm) ↔16in (40cm)
Deciduous new fronds appear in early spring. New growth is covered with hairs but becomes dark green with age. Grows well in acidic, rocky, organic soils.

Polystichum acrostichoides
CHRISTMAS FERN

Ⓝ ☼ ◐ z3–8 H8–1 ‡24in (60cm) ↔18in (45cm)
Shuttlecock-like, evergreen foliage emerges from clumping rhizomes as silvery fiddleheads . Clumps enlarge over time but do not spread aggressively.

Dryopteris erythrosora
JAPANESE SHIELD FERN

☀ ◑ Z5–9 H9–1 ↕18in (45cm) ↔12in (30cm)

Copper-colored, evergreen new foliage, which may be red in cool climates, appears in early fall. Establishes slowly and does well in containers.

Dryopteris x australis
DIXIE WOOD FERN

Ⓝ ☀ ☼ ◑ Z5–8 H8–5 ↕4ft (1.2m) ↔2ft (60cm)

A naturally occurring native hybrid with semi-evergreen fronds that mature to dark green. Tolerates dry soil. It is sterile (does not develop brown spores); propagate by division.

Dryopteris filix-mas
MALE FERN

Ⓝ ☀ ◑ Z4–8 H8–1 ↕4ft (1.2m) ↔3ft (1m)

Deciduous fronds emerge from the crown of a large rhizome. They open pale green and become darker and more leathery with age. Tolerant of many soil types.

Dryopteris affinis
GOLDEN MALE FERN

☀ ◑ Z6–8 H8–6 ↕↔3ft (1m)

Evergreen in more southern regions, newly emerging foliage is pale green with a golden midrib, and turns dark green with age. There are several named forms.

Dryopteris marginalis
MARGINAL WOOD FERN

Ⓝ ☀ ◑ Z3–8 H8–1 ↕24in (60cm) ↔12 (30cm)

An evergreen fern with blue-green summer foliage. It prefers an organic soil and is drought tolerant once established. Excellent groundcover for a shady hillside.

Ferns that tolerate moist conditions

These are ferns that are found growing on streamsides or in moist woods. They can generally take more sunlight than the ferns for dry locations, but some prefer shade. There are many named forms of the ferns shown here and on the previous pages that are available from nurseries specializing in this adaptable and ancient group of plants.

Osmunda regalis
ROYAL FERN
Ⓝ ☀ ◐ Z2–10 H9–1
↕6ft (2m) ↔3ft (1m)
An impressive deciduous fern that produces its ornamental fertile fronds in summer. Grow in fertile, organic soil. It is prone to rust. Rootstock is source of osmunda fiber. .

Osmunda cinnamomea
CINNAMON FERN
Ⓝ ☀ ◐ Z3–9 H9–1 ↕3ft (1m) ↔18in (45cm)
This upright fern's erect, fertile fronds bear cinnamon-colored sporangia in early spring. The deciduous sterile fronds turn yellow in fall.

Athyrium nipponicum 'Pictum'
JAPANESE PAINTED FERN
☀ ◐ Z5–8 H8–1 ↕12in (30cm) ↔indefinite
Showy, arching fronds increase slowly from spreading clumps on this deciduous fern. They color up best when the plants are grown in light shade. May show variation in color and may hybridize with other *Athyrium*.

MORE CHOICES

- *Dennstaedtia punctiloba* Z3–8 H8–1
- *Dryopteris clintoniana* Z6–8 H8–6
- *Polypodium virginianum* Z5–8 H8–5

Athyrium filix-femina 'Cristatum'
CRESTED LADY FERN
Ⓝ ☀ ◐ Z4–9 H9–1 ↕4ft (1.2m) ↔3ft (1m)
This is one of many named varieties of the Lady fern. Some have the ends of the pinnae (side fronds) greatly enlarged, while on others they are reduced to tufts.

Athyrium filix-femina
LADY FERN
Ⓝ ☀ ◐ Z4–9 H9–1 ↕4ft (1.2m) ↔3ft (1m)
The deciduous foliage radiates out from the center of the rhizome. Adaptable to many soil conditions, but it prefers fertile, highly organic soil.

HERBACEOUS PLANTS

Dryopteris marginalis
MARGINAL WOOD FERN
Ⓝ ☀ ◗ Z3–8 H8–1 ‡24in (60cm) ↔12 (30cm)
New fronds form in fall, uncurling in spring and
covered in brown scales that soon fall away. Evergreen
and prefers an organic, neutral to slightly acidic soil.

Matteuccia struthiopteris
OSTRICH FERN
N b f Z3–8 H8–1 h3ft (1m) s18in (45cm)
Here is a view of Ostrich Fern (also see right) in
autumn. Will survive on dry sites. An excellent
background fern that spreads slowly but sturdily.

Matteuccia struthiopteris
OSTRICH FERN
Ⓝ ☀ ◗ Z3–8 H8–1 ‡3ft (1m) ↔18in (45cm)
The edible, uncurling spring foliage ("fiddleheads")
appears later than most ferns. Fertile fronds, resembling
narrow brown brushes, appear in late summer.

Onoclea sensibilis
SENSITIVE FERN
Ⓝ ☀ ◗ Z4–9 H9–1 ‡↔18in (45cm)
This graceful fern produces both upright and arching ,
deciduous fronds. Fronds emerge in early spring and
are tinted pink to bronze. They collapse at first frost.

Blechnum spicant
DEER FERN
Ⓝ ☀ ◗ Z10–11 H12–10 ‡30in (75cm) ↔18in (45cm)
The older, sterile fronds lay out horizontally on this
tufted, evergreen fern that grows from short, creeping
rhizomes. Contrasts attractively with finer foliage.

HERBACEOUS PLANTS

Hostas: the genus *Hosta*

Hostas are the number-one plant for shade, although many of the yellow varieties do surprisingly well in almost full sun. While grown mainly for their foliage, which ranges from blue to yellow with a huge number of variegated forms, some hostas also have attractive and fragrant flowers. The American Hosta Society is dedicated to their culture.

Hosta 'Tokudama Aureonebulosa'
DAWN OF DAY HOSTA

☀ ◐ Z3–9 H9–2 ‡14in (35cm) ↔3ft (1m)

A very attractive hosta with infinite variations in the foliage. There are several named selections arising from this, such as 'Goldbrook Gift' and 'Winning Edge'.

Hosta 'Gold Standard'
GOLD STANDARD HOSTA

☀ ☀ ◐ Z3–8 H9–2 ‡30in (75cm) ↔3ft (1m)

Funnel-shaped, lavender-blue flowers are borne in midsummer. Can be used as an accent plant or ground-cover under deciduous trees. Best grown in fertile soil.

Hosta 'Frances Williams'
FRANCES WILLIAMS HOSTA

☀ ◐ Z3–9 H9–1 ‡24in (60cm) ↔3ft (1m)

First discovered in a bed of seedlings by Frances Williams in 1936, this is probably the most widely grown named cultivar. White flowers in late summer.

Hosta 'Sum and Substance'
SUM AND SUBSTANCE HOSTA

☀ ☀ ◐ Z3–8 H9–2 ‡↔3ft (1m)

Dense racemes of bell-shaped, pale lilac flowers appear in mid- to late summer. Puckering of leaves increases as the season progresses. Prefers fertile soil.

MORE CHOICES

- *Hosta* 'August Moon' Z3–8 H8–1
- *Hosta* 'Beatrice' Z3–9 H9–2
- *Hosta* 'Blue Umbrellas' Z3–9 H9–2
- *Hosta* 'Gold Drop' Z3–9 H9–1
- *Hosta sieboldiana* 'Elegans' Z4–8 H8–1

Hosta kikutii
WHITE-BACKED HOSTA

☀ ◐ Z3–9 H9–2 ‡18in (45cm) ↔12in (30cm)

A slow-growing plant with leaves that are white on the reverse. The flower spikes bear have dense heads of white flowers in late summer to fall.

Hosta 'June'
JUNE HOSTA

☼ ☀ ◐ Z3–8 H8–1 ↕16in (40cm) ↔28in (70cm)

A variegated sport of *H.* 'Halcyon', this bears gray-lavender flowers on a gray-green flower stalk in summer. Prefers fertile soil. Prone to slugs and snails.

Hosta 'Great Expectations'
GREAT EXPECTATIONS HOSTA

☼ ◐ Z3–8 H8–1 ↕22in (55cm) ↔34in (85cm)

The large leaves are yellow-centered in spring, going paler during summer. Tall spikes of white flowers bloom in late summer. Grows slowly but steadily.

Hosta undulata var. univittata
GREEN-EDGED WAVY HOSTA

☼ ☀ ◐ Z3–9 H9–2 ↕18in (45cm) ↔28in (70cm)

One of the first hostas brought back from Japan in 1829, this is a very common form, as is the variety with the colors reversed, *H.u.* var. *albomarginata*.

Hosta 'Royal Standard'
ROYAL STANDARD HOSTA

☼ ☀ ◐ Z4–8 H8–1 ↕24in (60cm) ↔4ft (1.2m)

A vigorous plant that will take quite a lot of sun without burning, providing the soil is moist. Tall spikes of fragrant white flowers are produced in late summer and fall.

Hosta sieboldii 'Kabitan'
KABITAN HOSTA

☼ ◐ Z3–9 H9–2 ↕8in (20cm) ↔10in (25cm)

A small plant that spreads by underground runners and makes a good container specimen. It needs sunlight in spring and dappled shade later. It declines in full shade.

Hosta 'Golden Tiara'
GOLDEN TIARA HOSTA

☼ ☀ ◐ Z3–9 H9–1 ↕12in (30cm) ↔20in (50cm)

It grows well but increases slowly in size. Purple-striped flowers appear in late summer. Won one of the top awards from the American Hosta Society in 1980.

Hosta 'Wide Brim'
WIDE BRIM HOSTA

☼ ◐ Z4–8 H8–1 ↕18in (45cm) ↔3ft (1m)

A showy plant with slightly puckered leaves, edged in yellow at first and turning white later. The flowers appear in late summer and last well in water.

HERBACEOUS PLANTS

Daylilies: the genus *Hemerocallis*

There are probably more varieties of daylily than any other plant, and the ones shown here are a minute representation of this genus. These plants are extremely tough and only demand lots of sunshine. Blooms on many modern varieties last more than a single day, especially on tetraploid varieties, and the flower scapes are branched with multiple blooms.

Hemerocalis 'Stella de Oro'
STELLA DE ORO DAYLILY
☼ ◑ Z3–9 H12–1 ‡12in (30cm)
↔18in (45cm)
Probably the most popular daylily, 'Stella' is vigorous and free-flowering, starting early and repeating throughout the season. Fragrant.

Hemerocalis 'Siloam Fairy Tale'
SILOAM FAIRY TALE DAYLILY
☼ ◑ Z3–10 H12–1 ‡18in (45cm) ↔12in (30cm)
One of many hybrid daylilies with "Siloam" in the name, raised by Pauline Henry and introduced in 1978. It is a deciduous, mid-season variety, with flowers that last for more than a day.

Hemerocalis citrina
LEMON-SCENTED DAYLILY
☼ ◑ Z3–10 H12–2 ‡6ft (1.8m) ↔5ft (1.5m)
Upright-growing with lemon-scented flowers, straplike petals, and a long blooming period. One of the first to flower, It has been used in breeding work to add scent.

MORE CHOICES

- *Hemerocallis dumortieri* Z5–9 H9–1
- *Hemerocallis fulva v. kwanso* Z3–9 H12–1
- *Hemerocallis lilio-asphodelus* Z3–10 H12–2
- *Hemerocallis middendorfii* Z3–9 H12–1
- *Hemerocallis multiflora* Z3–8 H12–1
- *Hemerocallis thunbergii* Z3–8 H12–1

Hemerocallis 'Brocaded Gown'
BROCADED GOWN DAYLILY
☼ ◑ Z3–10 H12–2 ‡26in (66cm)
↔18in (45cm)
An early flowering hybrid with repeat blooming and flowers that open early and last all day. Leaves stay partly green in winter, more so in warmer climates.

Hemerocallis 'Janice Brown'
JANICE BROWN DAYLILY
☼ ◑ Z3–11 H12–1 ‡21in (53cm) ↔18in (45cm)
This is an early to midseason variety with semi-evergreen foliage. The darker shading toward the middle of the flower is known as an eye zone.

Hemerocallis 'Pardon Me'
PARDON ME DAYLILY
☼ ◑ Z3–11 H12–1 ‡↔18in (45cm)
Free-flowering, bearing fragrant flowers in midseason and repeating reliably. Foliage is deciduous. Inroduced in 1982. Selected descendant of *H.* 'Little Grapette'.

Hemerocallis 'Eenie Weenie'
EENIE WEENIE DAYLILY

☀ ◐ ◊ z3–9 H12–1 ↕↔10in (25cm)

This is a compact cultivar with neat, mounded foliage. Very free-flowering, it usually blooms more than once during the season. Best when grown in fertile soil.

Hemerocallis 'Lavender Tonic'
LAVENDER TONIC DAYLILY

☀ ◊ z3–10 H12–2 ↕23in (58cm) ↔18in (45cm)

A semi-evergreen, mid-season bloomer with very pleated edges to the reflexed petals. The flowers are on branched scapes and each flower opens for almost a day.

Hemerocallis 'Condilla'
CONDILLA DAYLILY

☀ ◊ z3–11 H12–1 ↕20in (50cm) ↔15in (37cm)

A mid-season variety. Although not as numerous as the single flowered varieties, there are several named forms like this, with double flowers.

Hemerocallis 'Gentle Shepherd'
GENTLE SHEPHERD DAYLILY

☀ ◊ z3–10 H12–2 ↕29in (74cm) ↔18in (45cm)

A semi-evergreen, early to midseason variety. May take several years to form a large clump. This is about as close as it gets to white in daylilies.

Hemerocallis fulva
COMMON DAYLILY, TIGER LILY

☀ ◊ z3–9 H12–1 ↕50in (1.25m) ↔36in (90cm)

This is the common lily often seen growing in ditches. It is a parent of many modern varieties. The common name "Tiger Lily" is misleading.

Hellebores: the genus *Helleborus*

These plants are becoming better known and appreciated for their early blooms. The yellows, pinks, pale mauves, and chocolate shades of modern hybrid hellebores add a welcome touch of color at the end of winter. Generally evergreen, they may lose their foliage in the northern parts of the region over winter, and winter wind and sun can damage leaves.

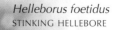

HERBACEOUS PLANTS

Helleborus foetidus
STINKING HELLEBORE

☼ ◑ ◊ Z6–9 H9–6 ↕↔18in (45cm)

Although the foliage is rank when bruised, the flowers can have a pleasant aroma. Makes a nice complement to spring-flowering bulbs. Often self-sows.

Helleborus niger
CHRISTMAS ROSE

☼ ◑ ◊ Z3–8 H8–1 ↕12in (30cm) ↔18in (45cm)

A clump-forming plant with overwintering, dark green, leathery leaves. Flowers can also be flushed with pink. Prefers fertile organic soil. Very early blooming.

Helleborus atrorubens
DARK RED HELLEBORE

☼ ◊ Z5–9 H9–5 ↕12in (30cm) ↔18in (45cm)

Stems and leaves may be tinged with purple, especially when young. Flowers before the leaves from late winter onward. Grows best in an alkaline soil.

MORE CHOICES

- *Helleborus multifidus* subsp *herzegovinus* Z7–9 H9–7
- *Helleborus niger* Blackthorn Strain Z6–9 H9–6
- *Helleborus odorus* Z4–9 H8–1
- *Helleborus torquatus* Wolverton Strain Z6–9 H9–6

Helleborus torquatus 'Dido'
DIDO HELLEBORE

☼ ◑ ◊ Z6–9 H9–6 ↕↔12in (30cm)

A clump-forming species with leaves hairy beneath. Grow in neutral to slightly alkaline soil. The flowers, tinged purple on the reverse, appear before the foliage.

Helleborus orientalis
LENTEN ROSE

☼ ◊ Z4–8 H8–3 ↕↔18in (45cm)

Elegant plant with leathery, deep green overwintering leaves. Flowers, most often white or greenish cream aging to pink, bloom from midwinter to midspring.

Helleborus argutifolius
CORSICAN HELLEBORE

☀ ◐ ◊ Z6–9 H9–6 ‡24in (60cm) ↔18in (45cm)

This species does well naturalized or in a woodland garden. Best if grown in highly organic soils. Also called *H. corsicus* (it is native to Corsica).

Helleborus purpurascens
PURPLISH HELLEBORE

☀ ◊ Z5–8 H8–5 ‡2–12in (5–30cm) ↔12in (30cm)

Blooms in late winter before the leaves appear. Prefers a slightly less shady location than most. The common name comes from the flowers, which often have a purple tinge.

Helleborus x sternii
STERN'S HELLEBORE

☀ ◐ ◊ Z6–9 H9–6 ‡↔12in (30cm)

A variable group of plants with several named forms. Foliage overwinters and has cream veins and purple stalks. Flowers borne in late winter and early spring.

Helleborus viridis
GREEN HELLEBORE

☀ ◐ ◊ Z6–8 H8–1 ‡8–16in (20–40cm) ↔18in (45cm)

Deciduous species with narrowly lobed, dark green leaves in a basal cluster. Paired flowers appear in late winter. Grows best in a slightly alkaline soil.

Helleborus x ballardiae
BALLARD'S HELLEBORE

☀ ◊ Z6–9 H9–6 ‡14in (35cm) ↔12in (30cm)

A clump-forming plant with evergreen leaves that live for two years. The flowers appear in early spring, and, as with many hellebores, their color darkens with age.

Barrenworts: the genus *Epimedium*

Justifiably popular, the many species and named forms of barrenwort bring color to the late spring shade garden. When flowering is finished, their red-tinged leaves keep them attractive until the foliage takes on russet tones in fall. Some barrenworts are best suited to the woodland garden while other species make good groundcovers in shade.

Epimedium acuminatum
SHARPLEAVED BARRENWORT

☀ ◐ ◑ Z5–9 H9–4 ‡12in (30cm) ↔18in (45cm)

Leaves are divided into three leaflets that taper to a narrow point, with toothed edges. The lower two leaflets have the characteristic uneven basal lobes. Flowers open in late spring.

Epimedium x *youngianum* 'Niveum'
WHITE YOUNG'S BARRENWORT

☀ ◐ Z5–9 H9–5 ‡↔12in (30cm)

The leaves are divided into 9 leaflets, splashed with red in spring, and turning crimson in fall. It flowers in spring. The variety 'Roseum' has pink to rose flowers.

MORE CHOICES

- *Epimedium alpinum* Z4–9 H9–4
- *Epimedium diphyllum* Z5–9 H9–4
- *Epimedium grandiflorum* 'Rose Queen' Z4–8 H8–2
- *Epimedium* x *versicolor* 'Cupreum' Z5–9 H9–4
- *Epimedium* x *youngianum* 'Lilacinum' Z5–9 H9–5

Epimedium grandiflorum
BISHOP'S HAT

☀ ◐ Z5–8 H8–5 ‡↔12in (30cm)

This is one parent of Young's Barrenwort and has similar leaves but without good fall color. Several cultivars have yellow, lilac, violet, or white flowers.

Epimedium x perralchicum
BARRENWORT

☀ ◊ Z5–8 H8–5 ‡18in (45cm) ↔12in (30cm)

Pendent, bright yellow flowers bloom from mid- to late spring. The evergreen foliage of this garden hybrid is bronze when young, later turning deep green.

Epimedium x warleyense
WARLEY BARRENWORT

☀ ◊ Z5–9 H9–5 ‡20in (50cm) ↔36in (90cm)

The leaves on this have 5–9 leaflets and are tinged with red in spring and fall. There are up to 30 flowers on each stem in late spring.

Epimedium x rubrum
RED BARRENWORT

☀ ◊ Z4–8 H8–1 ‡12in (30cm) ↔8in (20cm)

Evergreen leaves are red when young and also turn red with the arrival of cool fall weather. Prefers fertile, organic, well-drained soil.

Epimedium x versicolor var. 'Versicolor'
BICOLORED BARRENWORT

☀ ◊ Z5–9 H9–3 ‡↔12in (30cm)

5–15 leaflets that are tinged coppery-red when young, becoming green later. The flower on this are smaller than those of named forms such as 'Sulphureum'.

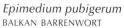

Epimedium pubigerum
BALKAN BARRENWORT

☀ ◊ Z4–8 H8–1 ‡↔18in (45cm)

A spreading plant with 9 shiny leaflets, heart-shaped at the base and hairy beneath. The branched flower spikes, with 12–30 flowers on each, grow in late spring.

Epimedium x cantabrigiense
BARRENWORT

☀ ◊ Z5–8 H8–5 ‡↔24in (60cm)

The flowers appear from midspring to late spring, and can also be yellow. This is a clump-forming plant with evergreen foliage. This hybrid barrenwort prefers organic, fertile soil.

Epimedium x versicolor 'Sulphureum'
YELLOW BARRENWORT

☀ ◊◊ Z5–8 H8–5 ‡12in (30cm) ↔3ft (1m)

Other cultivars of this hybrid cross have pink to copper-red flowers. Prefers fertile, organic, well-drained soil. Susceptible to vine weevil and mosaic virus.

Epimedium grandiflorum 'Lilafee'
LILAC FAIRY BISHOP'S HAT

☀ ◊ Z5–8 H8–5 ‡10in (25cm) ↔12in (30cm)

This is a darker version of the Bishop's hat on the opposite page. The leaves are tinged purple when young, becoming green in summer.

Lilies: The genus *Lilium*

At least one member of this large family of bulbs can find a home in every garden. There are lilies species for sun and shade, wet and dry locations, heavy and light soils, but the most common groups are the Asiatic, trumpet, and Oriental hybrids that each have many named varieties, some of which are shown here.

Lilium 'Black Beauty'
BLACK BEAUTY LILY
☼ ◊ Z3–8 H8–1 ↕6ft (18.m)
Plant this trumpet lily in spring or fall, spacing the bulbs at least 18in (45cm) apart to give them room to multiply for several years without becoming crowded.

Lilium 'Enchantment'
ENCHANTMENT LILY
☼ ◊ Z2–8 H8–1 ↕3ft (1m)
An old Asiatic lily much grown as a potted plant or for cut flowers. One of the easiest lilies to grow, it multiplies readily and survives under poor-soil conditions.

Lilium auratum var. *platyphyllum*
LARGE-FLOWERED GOLDEN-RAY LILY
☼ ◊ Z3–8 H8–1 ↕5ft (1.5m)
Grows best in poor but open soil, without much supplemental food or moisture. Declines if pampered. Outstanding pot plant with a strong fragrance.

Lilium martagon var. album
WHITE MARTAGON LILY

☼ ◊ Z3–7 H7–1 ↕6ft (18.m)

Like the species, this can be slow to establish. It may not appear above ground at all the first summer. Once growing, it can be left undisturbed for many years.

Lilium martagon
MARTAGON LILY

☼ ◊ Z3–8 H8–1 ↕6ft (18.m)

A vigorous clump-forming lily in cultivation for centuries, it is the parent of many modern hybrids. It is shade-tolerant and should be planted in large groups.

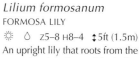

Lilium formosanum
FORMOSA LILY

☼ ◊ Z5–8 H8–4 ↕5ft (1.5m)

An upright lily that roots from the stem below ground and the base of the bulb. Plant in a sheltered spot to give protection from early frosts in fall.

Lilium superbum
TURKSCAP LILY

Ⓝ ☼ ◊ Z4–8 H8–1 ↕5–10ft (1.5–3m)

Flowers in mid- to late summer. Purple mottled stems bear lance-shaped leaves tha spiral around the step. Prefers organic soil.

MORE CHOICES

- *Lilium auratum* Z3–8 H8–1
- *Lilium* x *aurelianense* Z3–8 H8–x1
- *Lilium martagon* v. *cattaniae* Z3–8 H8–x1
- *Lilium michiganense* Z2–7 H7–1
- *Lilium philadelphicum* Z2–6 H6–1
- *Lilium rubellum* Z3–7 H7–1
- *Lilium speciosum* Z3–8 H8–1
- *Lilium speciosum* v. *rubrum* Z3–8 H8–1
- *Lilium* 'Avignon' Z3–8 H8–1

Lilium 'African Queen'
AFRICAN QUEEN LILY

☼ ◊ Z3–8 H8–1 ↕6ft (18.m)

An erect, fragrant trumpet lily that can be forced into early bloom. In the garden, plant 8–10in (20–25cm) deep or the wind may blow them over when in flower.

Lilium lancifolium
TIGER LILY

☼ ◊ Z2–7 H7–1 ↕5ft (1.5m)

A very popular lily that is easy to grow. It is easy to increase from the small black bulbils that form on the stem, May be sold as *L. tigrinum*.

HERBACEOUS PLANTS

HERBACEOUS PLANTS

Lilium henryi
HENRY LILY

☼ ◊ z3–8 H8–1 ↕3–10ft (1–3m)

Much used by hybridizers to produce the modern trumpet lilies. In the garden, it produces up to 12 flowers on a stem. It is tolerant of alkaline soils.

Lilium regale
REGAL LILY

☼ ◊ z3–8 H8–1 ↕6ft (18.m)

One of the easiest of the trumpet lilies although early spring growth is liable to damage from late frosts. Plant with only 1in (2.5cm) of soil over the tip of the bulb.

Lilium 'Star Gazer'
STARGAZER LILY

☼ ◊ z3–8 H8–1 ↕5ft (1.5m)

Asiatic lily hybrids are classified according to the way their flower face; upward, outfacing, or downward. The upfacing group is the largest.

Lilium 'Mont Blanc'
MONT BLANC LILY

☼ ◊ z3–8 H8–1 ↕28in (70cm)

A sturdy lily with scattered brown spots in the center of the petals. Introduced in 1978, this has proven to be a reliable plant that multiplies readily in good soil.

Lilium 'Pink Panther'
PINK PANTHER LILY

☼ ◊ zx–x Hx–x ↕4ft (1.2m)

An outfacing Asiatic hybrid that flowers in early summer. There are many named Asiatic lilies so if you can't find one illustrated, you will find one fairly close.

Lilium 'Casa Blanca'
CASA BLANCA LILY

☼ ◊ z3–8 H8–1 ↕4ft (1.2m)

Although classified as a trumpet lily, this has flattened flowers that open with very little trumpet. It flowers later than many lilies, in late summer..

Lilium canadense
CANADIAN LILY

Ⓝ ☼ ◊ Z2–6 H6–1 ↕5ft (1.5m)

This probably grows better in the north of this region, where it gets frozen in winter. Wet winter soil is detrimental, as is summer drought.

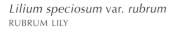

Lilium speciosum var. *rubrum*
RUBRUM LILY

☼ ◊ Z3–8 H8–1 ↕6ft (18.m)

Once widely grown for cutting, it has been surpassed by modern hybrid trumpet lilies, but is still beautiful with raised whiskers toward the center of the petals.

Lilium 'Magic Pink'
MAGIC PINK LILY

☼ ◊ Z3–8 H8–1 ↕4ft (1.2m)

An Oriental hybrid with slightly fragrant flowers in late summer. Like all Oriental lilies, do not plant shallowly or they may blow over in a high wind.

Lilium 'Connecticut King'
CONNECTICUT KING LILY

☼ ◊ Z3–8 H8–1 ↕3ft (1m)

After 'Enchantment', this is probably the most widely grown Asiatic lily. The up-facing flowers are carried on stout stems and defy bad weather. Excellent cut flower.

Lilium pyrenaicum
PYRENEAN LILY

☼ ◊ Z4–7 H7–1 ↕3ft (1m)

One of the earliest lilies to bloom in summer, this thrives in neutral to alkaline soil. It multiplies readily but the scent is unpleasant and attracts flies.

Iris: the genus *Iris*

The most popular group of iris are the bearded or German irises. Varieties of these range from a few inches (10cm) to three feet (1m) in height and bloom in succession from early spring; many are sweetly scented. Siberian and Japanese iris grow best in wet conditions, even in shallow water, while the many bulbous iris (*see* pp.332–337) are a delight in early spring.

Iris 'Beverly Sills'
BEVERLY SILLS BEARDED IRIS
☼ ☼ ◊ Z3–9 H9–1 ↕3ft (1m)
A tall bearded iris that is a strong grower, and should be divided every 3–4 years. This variety won the American Iris Society top award in 1985.

Iris 'Leda's Lover'
LEDA'S LOVER BEARDED IRIS
☼ ◊ Z3–9 H9–1 ↕34in (85cm) ↔12in (30cm)
Irises need a rich soil and must be planted with their fleshy stems just exposed above the soil. They are less likely to be attacked by pests and diseases then.

Iris 'Bride's Halo'
BRIDE'S HALO BEARDED IRIS
☼ ◊ Z3–8 H8–1 ↕3ft (1m) ↔12in (30cm)
Bearded iris get their name from the often prominent "beard" lining the middle of the lower petals. This may be of several colors and often contrasts with the petals.

Iris 'Blazing Saddles'
BLAZING SADDLES BEARDED IRIS
☼ ◊ Z3–9 H9–1 ↕33in (82cm) ↔12in (30cm)
Bearded iris come in a variety of sizes, from 4in (10cm.) tall to over 3ft (1m). The smallest varieties are the earliest to bloom, starting in mid-spring.

Iris 'Mystique'
MYSTIQUE BEARDED IRIS
☼ ◊ Z3–9 H9–1 ↕30in (75cm) ↔12in (30cm)
Lift and divide in late summer to allow them to make new roots before winter comes. Plant on a saddle of soil with their roots down either side, and firm well.

MORE CHOICES

- *Iris chrysographes* Z4–9 H9–1
- *Iris cristata* Z4–10 H10–1
- *Iris foetidissima* Z4–9 H9–2
- *Iris graminea* Z6–9 H9–5
- *Iris japonica* Z7–9 H9–7
- *Iris pseudacorus* Z5–8 H8–3
- *Iris setosa* Z3–8 H8–1
- *Iris spuria* cv. Z6–9 H9–5
- *Iris tectorum* Z5–9 H9–3
- *Iris versicolor* Z3–9 H9–1
- *Iris unguicularis* Z7–9 H9–7

Iris ensata 'Variegata'
VARIEGATED JAPANESE WATER IRIS

☀ ☀ ◊ Z5–8 H8–4 ‡3ft (1m) ↔indefinite
Blooms in early summer. Leaves and stems white-striped. Prefers well-drained, fertile soil and dislikes high nitrogen levels. Plant in midsummer to early fall.

Iris 'Summer Olympics'
SUMMER OLYMPICS BEARDED IRIS

☀ ◊ Z3–9 H9–1 ‡30in (75cm) ↔12in (30cm)
This variety is a reblooming type. These will often bloom again in early fall but need to be given extra fertilizer at the end of their summer flowering to do so.

Iris 'Babbling Brook'
BABBLING BROOK BEARDED IRIS

☀ ◊ Z3–9 H9–1 ‡38in (95cm) ↔12in (30cm)
This won the top iris award in 1972 and is still available. Varieties with standards (upright petals), and falls (outside ones), the same color, are known as selfs.

Iris sibirica 'Caesar's Brother'
CAESAR'S BROTHER SIBERIAN IRIS

☀ ◊◖ Z4–9 H9–1 ‡3ft (1m) ↔12in (30cm)
This is one of the early Siberian iris hybrids, introduced in 1939. Modern hybrids have flowers of pink, lavender, yellow, and even two toned,

Iris sibirica 'Illini Charm'
ILLINI CHARM SIBERIAN IRIS

☀ ◊◖ Z3–9 H9–1 ‡24in (60cm) ↔12in (30cm)
These flower later than the tall bearded irises and don't have the prominent rhizome or beard. They are adaptable and can also grow well in dry soil.

HERBACEOUS PLANTS

Peony: the genus *Paeonia*

Peonies are incredibly tough and long-lived plants; many an old homestead can still be identified by the peony that blooms each spring. The old-wives tale states that peonies don't bloom for seven years if you move them. Planted with the crown buds 1–3in (2.5–8cm) below soil level, they should bloom the following year.

Paeonia 'Bo Peep'
BO PEEP PEONY
☼ ◐ ◑ ◗ Z3–8 H8–1 ↕↔36in (90cm)
Another Japanese-type peony with a stiff-stemmed, vigorous habit. Peony buds often exude a sweet sap that attracts ants, which do not harm the plant.

Paeonia 'Arcturus'
ARCTURUS PEONY
☼ ◑ ◗ Z3–8 H8–1 ↕34in (85cm) ↔36in (90cm)
Peonies are classified by their flower type, depending on the number of petals and the way the stamens are formed. This is a single-flowered type.

Paeonia 'Candy Fluff'
CANDY FLUFF PEONY
☼ ◑ ◗ Z3–8 H8–1 ↕32in (80cm) ↔3ft (1m)
This Japanese-type peony has flattened stamens in the center with some narrow petals growing there as well, and a single row of outer petals.

MORE CHOICES

- *Paeonia* 'America' Z3–8 H8–1
- *Paeonia anomala* Z3–8 H8–1
- *Paeonia* 'Bowl of Beauty' Z3–8 H8–1
- *Paeonia emodi* Z6–8 H8–6
- *Paeonia* 'Festiva Maxima' Z3–8 H8–1
- *Paeonia* 'Felix Crousse' Z3–8 H8–1
- *Paeonia lactiflora* 'Kansas' Z3–8 H8–1
- *Paeonia lactiflora* 'Mons. Jules Elie' Z3–8 H8–1

Paeonia lactiflora 'Edulis Superba'
EDULIS SUPERBA PEONY
☼ ◑ ◗ Z3–8 H8–1 ↕32in (80cm) ↔36in (90cm)
Peony varieties never seem to age and old varieties like this, introduced in 1824, are still widely available. This is an early flowered, very fragrant variety.

Paeonia lactiflora 'Coral Charm'
CORAL CHARM PEONY
☼ ◑ ◗ Z3–8 H8–1 ↕↔36in (90cm)
A very popular, relatively modern, semi-double variety. The flowers fade slightly as they age, giving an interesting two-tone effect to the plant.

Paeonia lactiflora 'Fancy Nancy'
FANCY NANCY PEONY

☀ ☀ ◌ ♦ Z3–8 H8–1 ‡↔30in (75cm)

This has eye-catching Japanese-type flowers. When necessary, move them in late summer because they produce new roots at that time of year.

Paeonia 'June Rose'
JUNE ROSE PEONY

☀ ☀ ◌ ♦ Z3–8 H8–1 ‡32in (80cm) ↔36in (90cm)

This type of double peony, with so many petals the outer ring is not visible, is called a "bomb" type by some experts. It flowers early in the peony season.

Paeonia suffruticosa 'Kinshu'
KINSHU TREE PEONY

☀ ☀ ◌ ♦ Z5–8 H8–5 ‡↔30in (75cm)

Tree peonies have a woody stem that can grow into a small shrub in mild climates. The flowers come in colors not seen in herbaceous peonies.

Paeonia lactiflora 'Moonstone'
MOONSTONE PEONY

☀ ☀ ◌ ♦ Z3–8 H8–1 ‡↔3ft (1m)

This peony looks especially good when back-lit; the petals seem to glow. Plant peonies with their buds 3in (7cm) below soil level to flower the following spring.

MORE CHOICES

- *Paeonia lactiflora* 'Nippon Beauty' Z3–8 H8–1
- *Paeonia lactiflora* 'Paula Fay' Z3–8 H8–1
- *Paeonia lactiflora* 'Raspberry Sundae' Z3–8 H8–1
- *Paeonia lactiflora* 'Red Charm' Z3–8 H8–1
- *Paeonia lactiflora* 'Sarah Bernhardt' Z3–8 H8–1
- *Paeonia lactiflora* 'Shirley Temple' Z3–8 H8–1
- *Paeonia lutea* var. *ludlowii* Z3–8 H8–1
- *Paeonia mlokosewitschii* Z3–8 H8–1
- *Paeonia tenuifolia* Z3–8 H8–1

Paeonia lactiflora 'Red Charm'
RED CHARM PEONY

☀ ☀ ◌ ♦ Z3–8 H8–1 ‡↔30in (75cm)

An early flowering, double variety with stiff stems. This is a very popular variety that was introduced in 1944, comparatively recent in the world of peonies.

Paeonia 'Illini Belle'
ILLINI BELLE PEONY

☀ ☀ ◌ ♦ Z3–8 H8–1 ‡30in (75cm) ↔36in (90cm)

This semi-double variety is early-flowering and particularly striking. Like many peonies, the foliage turns a dark, coppery color in fall.

Ornamental grasses tolerant of shade

Although most ornamental grasses and their relatives are sun-lovers, the ones shown here will grow well in shade, and their narrow foliage makes a good contrast to the broader foliage of most woodland plants. Some of the *Carex* – which are sedges, not true grasses – and the *Phalaris* may tend to be invasive, but they are easy to control in a woodland situation.

HERBACEOUS PLANTS

Calamagrostis brachytricha
KOREAN FEATHER REED GRASS

☼ ☀ ⬤ Z5–9 H9–5 ↕4ft (1.2m) ↔2ft (60cm)
Tolerates full sun if given sufficient moisture. The late summer flowers remain feathery and dry well. Cut back in late winter before growth commences.

MORE CHOICES

- *Carex conica* 'Snowline' Z5–8 H9–1
- *Carex dolichostachya* 'Kaga Nishiki' Z5–9 H9–5
- *Carex elata* 'Bowle's Golden' Z5–9 H9–3
- *Carex flacca* Z5–9 H9–5
- *Carex flaccosperma* z7–9 H9–7
- *Carex nigra* z4–8 H8–1
- *Carex nigra* 'Variegata' z4–8 H8–1
- *Carex pennsylvanica* z4–8 H8–1
- *Carex plantagine* z5–7 H7–4
- *Carex platyphylla* z5–9 H9–5
- *Hystrix patula* z5–9 H9–5
- *Phalaris arundinacea.* 'Feesey' z4–9 H9–3

Imperata cylindrica 'Rubra'
JAPANESE BLOOD GRASS

☼ ⬤ Z5–9 H9–3 ↕20in (50cm) ↔indefinite
Leaves start green but quickly transform to deep blood red. This perennial grass is a slow spreader. Also known as *I. cylindrica* 'Red Baron'.

Hakonechloa macra 'Aureola'
GOLDEN JAPANESE FOREST GRASS

☼ ☀ ⬤ Z5–9 H9–4 ↕14in (35cm) ↔16in (40cm)
Forms mounds of arching leaves that are bright yellow with narrow green stripes until they turn red in fall. Pale green spikelets open late summer to midautumn.

Chasmanthium latifolium
RIVER OATS

Ⓝ ☼ ☀ ⬤ Z5–9 H9–5 ↕3ft (1m) ↔24in (60cm)
A clump-forming, upright grass that grows in most soils and locations. Arching flower stems, which turn red-brown and then buff, can be dried for winter use.

Calamagrostis x acutiflora 'Overdam'
OVERDAM FEATHER REED GRASS

☼ ☀ ⬤ Z5–9 H9–1 ↕4ft (1.2m) ↔4ft (1.2m)
A very effective plant for the border, starting into growth early in spring and continuing to be decorative into winter. The plumes stand up to wind and rain.

Milium effusum 'Aureum'
GOLDEN WOOD MILLET, BOWLES' GOLDEN GRASS
☼ ◑ ◊ Z6–9 H9–6 ‡3ft (1m) ↔1ft (30cm)
A cool-season grass that grows in early spring and
complements spring bulbs. Turns yellow-green in
summer, especially in warm climates.

Juncus effusus 'Spiralis'
CORKSCREW RUSH
☼ ◑ ◖ ᴾᴴ Z6–9 H9–6 ‡18in (45cm) ↔24in (60cm)
The stems form a thick mat of twisted, narrow, leafless
branches in time. Prized by flower arrangers for
Oriental-style arrangements.

Carex siderosticha 'Variegata'
VARIEGATED CREEPING BROADLEAF SEDGE
☼ ◑ ◊◖ Z6–9 H9–6 ‡12in (30cm) ↔16cm (40cm)
Slowly spreading, this tough and adaptable perennial
has pale brown flower spikes in late spring. Prone to
rust, smuts, leaf spots, and aphids.

Carex comans 'Frosted Curls'
NEW ZEALAND HAIR SEDGE
☼ ◑ ◊◖ Z7–9 H9–7 ‡24in (60cm) ↔18in (45cm)
Tolerant of both moist and dry soils, this is best planted on a slope,
where its foliage can trail, or in planters in sun or shade. The flowers
are insignificant. May self-seed slightly in southern parts of the Northeast.

Carex hachijoensis
'Evergold'
VARIEGATED JAPANESE SEDGE
☼ ◊ Z6–9 H9–6 ‡8in (20cm)
↔6–8in (15–20cm)
Bears small brown flower spikes
in mid- to late spring. Best when
grow in reasonably fertile soil.
Can be used as an accent plant
in borders or *en masse* as a an
eye-catching groundcover.

HERBACEOUS PLANTS

Ornamental grasses for moist or waterside sites

Grasses look natural beside a pool or small stream, where their upright spikes can reflect in the water; in fact, many of the sedges and rushes will grow well only in this location. Some of the smaller grasses can be used in decorative pots with a small fountain or waterfall to give the relaxing sound of water on a patio.

Typha minima
DWARF CATTAIL
☼ ◑ Z3–11 H12–1 ‡18–24in (45–60cm) ↔12in (30cm)
Flowers are distinctive, cylindrical spikes that appear from mid- to late summer and can be used in dried arrangements. Can become invasive in unlined ponds.

Typha angustifolia
NARROW-LEAVED CATTAIL
☼ ◑ Z2–11 H12–1 ‡5ft (1.5m) ↔indefinite
Brown flower spikes are borne in midsummer. Can spread quickly by rhizomes and becomes invasive if not contained.

Typha latifolia
CATTAIL
☼ ◑ Z2–11 H12–1 ‡8ft (2.5m) ↔2ft (60cm)
An invasive species useful for the margins of large ponds, but overpowering in small ones. Young shoots are edible; seedheads can be dried for indoor use.

MORE CHOICES

- *Juncus effusus* Z4–9 H9–1
- *Molinia caerulea* subsp. *arundinacea* Z4–8 H8–1
- *Molinia caerulea* subsp. *arundinacea* 'Windspiel' Z4–8 H8–1
- *Molinia caerulea* subsp. *arundinacea* 'Skyracer' Z4–8 H8–1
- *Zizania aquatica* Z3–9 H9–1

Molina caerulea
PURPLE MOOR GRASS

☼ ◊ Z5–9 H9–1 ‡8ft (2.2m) ↔2ft (60cm)

Slow-growing grass bears dense, tufted purple flower clusters that age to tan. Grows well in most soils. Works well in a mixed border or woodland garden.

Carex siderosticha 'Variegata'
VARIEGATED CREEPING BROADLEAF SEDGE

☼ ☀ ◊● Z6–9 H9–3 ‡12in (30cm) ↔16cm (40cm)

Slowly spreading, this tough and adaptable perennial has pale brown flower spikes in late spring. Prone to rust, smuts, leaf spots, and aphids.

Carex elata 'Aurea'
BOWLES' TUFTED SEDGE

☼ ☀ ◊● Z5–9 H9–5 ‡3ft (1m) ↔6in (15cm)

Short rhizomes form a dense clump of gently arching leaves with a fine green edge. Flower spikes appear in late spring and early summer. Prefers fertile soil.

Carex muskingumensis
PALM BRANCH SEDGE

Ⓝ ☼ ☀ ◊● Z3–8 H8–1 ‡28in (75cm) ↔18in (45cm)

Creeping, rhizomatous plant that can form a large mat. Nonshowy flower spikes appear in early summer. Named varieties have white- or yellow- variegated foliage.

Andropogon glomeratus
BUSHY BEARD GRASS, BROOMSEDGE

Ⓝ ☼ ☀ ◊● Z2–7 H7–1 ‡6ft (2m) ↔3ft (1m)

While preferring wet soil, this will grow in drier locations but will not survive drought. Summer foliage is bright green Flowers appear in late summer and are good for drying.

Schoenoplectus tabernaemontani 'Zebrinus'
STRIPED CLUB RUSH

Ⓝ ☼ ● Z5–11 H12–1 ‡5ft (1.2m) ↔indefinite

A clump-forming perennial that spreads by rhizomes; may need to be grown in a container. Often sold as Scirpus in garden centers. The species is native to salt- and freshwater marshes on the East coast.

Juncus effusus 'Spiralis'
CORKSCREW RUSH

Ⓝ ☼ ☀ ● ᵖᴴ Z6–9 H9–6 ‡18in (45cm) ↔24in (60cm)

Spreads slowly from a creeping rootstock. Best suited to a pool margin, but survives in soil that never dries out.

HERBACEOUS PLANTS

Tender ornamental grasses

Some grasses are just so striking that they are grown even though they will not over-winter in our region. Many of the grasses shown here are from tropical or near-tropical climates, such as South Africa. They are either propagated by commercial growers, or can be grown from seed, started indoors about six weeks before last frost date.

Nassella tenuissima
MEXICAN FEATHER GRASS

☼ ◐ ◊ Z7–9 H9–6 ↕↔24in (60cm)

A most attractive grass that blooms in late summer and turns a light yellow-brown in fall. The stems persist into winter. It may go dormant in hot summers.

Pennisetum villosum
FEATHERTOP

☼ ◊ Z9–15 H12–1 ↕↔24in (60cm)

Used by florists as a cut flower, this grass is native to tropical Africa and is normally treated as an annual. It will occasionally overwinter in the south of this region.

Elegia capensis
CAPE ELEGIA, BROOM REED

Ⓝ ☼ ◐ ◊ Z8–15 H12–8 ↕9ft (2.5m) ↔5ft (1.5m)

This looks like a giant horsetail from a distance, but has attractive, brown and white, papery leaves (bracts) enclosing the stem. It makes a good container plant.

MORE CHOICES

- *Chondropetalum tectorum* Z8–10 H10–8
- *Pennisetum alopecuroides* 'Burgundy Giant' Z6–9 H9–6
- *Pennisetum* 'Purple Majesty' Z8–11 H12–1
- *Pennisetum setaceum* 'Rubrum' Z8–11 H12–1
- *Rynchelytrum repens* Z10–11 H12–10
- *Setaria palmifolia* 'Variegata' Z9–10 H10–9

Setaria palmifolia 'Rubra'
RED PALM GRASS

☼ ◐ ◊ Z9–10 H10–9 ↕↔3–6ft (1–2m)

This will not survive temperatures below 40°F (4°C) and should be moved inside before any chance of frost. Excellent container plant, grown for its foliage.

Cymbopogon citratus
LEMON GRASS

☼ ◊ Z10–11 H12–1 ↕5ft (1.5m) ↔3ft (1m)

Favored by Indian and Thai cuisine, it can be planted out for the summer, in the garden or a container, and survive the winter on a sunny window ledge inside.

Large ornamental grasses

The giants of the grass family, these make a bold statement in the garden. Their flower and seed spikes add color to the garden in late fall and early winter and stand up well to winter winds and snow, giving texture even when their color had faded. Site them with care and remember they also take up a lot of ground space and need room to develop.

MORE CHOICES

- *Arundo donax* Z6–11 H12–1
- *Miscanthus giganteus* Z4–9 H9–1
- *Saccharum giganteum* Z9–11 H12–1
- *Spartina pectinata 'Aureomarginata'* Z4–9 H9–1

Saccharum ravennae
RAVENNA GRASS

☼ ◊ Z6–9 H9–6 ↕12ft (4m) ↔6ft (2m)

A good substitute for pampas grass where this is not hardy, but only flowers where summers are long and warm. It is clump-forming and blooms in late summer.

Stipa gigantea
GIANT FEATHER GRASS

☼ ◊ Z8–15 H12–1 ↕8ft (2.5m) ↔4ft (1.2m)

This grass needs a dry soil in winter, it will not survive wet conditions. The flowers, which come out in summer, dry well for winter arrangements.

Panicum virgatum 'Prairie Skies'
PRAIRIE SKIES SWITCH GRASS

Ⓝ ☼ ◊ Z5–9 H9–1 ↕4–5ft (1.2–1.5m) ↔3ft (1m)

Coming into growth late in spring, this species grows strongly once temperatures become high. This variety may be bowed down for a while by heavy rain.

Panicum virgatum 'Cloud Nine'
CLOUD NINE SWITCH GRASS

Ⓝ ☼ ◊ Z3–9 H9–1 ↕5–7ft (1.5–2.1m) ↔3ft (1m)

The new foliage, in late spring, is a good blue-green, turning as fall approaches. The flower spikes weather well and will last all winter, surviving snow and rain.

HERBACEOUS PLANTS

Ornamental grasses with blue foliage

These grasses serve several purposes in the garden, from dwarf edging to temporary seasonal "hedges" to specimen plants. Their silvery blue foliage shows up well against plants with dark green leaves or dark-colored flowers. Taller species help separate other brightly flowered perennials and show them off to perfection.

Panicum virgatum 'Prairie Skies'
PRAIRIE SKIES SWITCH GRASS
Ⓝ ☼ ◊ Z5–9 H9–1 ↕5ft (1.5m) ↔2ft (60cm)
A very blue selection of a native prairie grass. This is a softer, less upright variety that sometimes gets knocked down in a heavy rainstorm.

MORE CHOICES

- *Festuca amethystina* Z4–8 H8–1
- *Festuca amethystina* 'Superba' Z4–8 H8–1
- *Festuca glauca* Z4–8 H8–1
- *Festuca glauca* 'Sea Blue' Z4–8 H8–1
- *Helictotrichon sempervirens* 'Saphirprundel' Z4–8 H9–1
- *Panicum virgatum* 'Dallas Blues' Z5–9 H9–5
- *Sesleria heufleriana* Z5–8 H8–5
- *Sorghastrum nutans* 'Sioux Blue' Z4–9 H9–1

Panicum virgatum 'Heavy Metal'
HEAVY METAL SWITCH GRASS
Ⓝ ☼ ◊ Z5–9 H9–4 ↕3ft (1m) ↔30in (75cm)
A good blue switch grass with an upright habit and stems that are weatherproof and hold up well into winter. The flower spikes have a pink tinge at first.

Panicum virgatum 'Cloud Nine'
CLOUD NINE SWITCH GRASS
Ⓝ ☼ ◊ Z3–9 H9–1 ↕6ft (1.8m) ↔3ft (1m)
A taller selection that is also weatherproof. The stems turn a golden yellow in fall and last through the winter. Cut back in early spring.

Leymus arenarius
BLUE LYME GRASS
☼ ◊ Z4–10 H10–1 ↕5ft (1.5m) ↔indefinite
A fast spreader that should be planted only where it cannot grow into other plants. Underground stems can pierce landscape fabric. May be listed as *Elymus*.

Helictotrichon sempervirens
BLUE OAT GRASS
☼ ◊ Z4–9 H9–1 ↕3ft (1m) ↔2ft (60cm)
Straw-colored spikelets bloom on stiff, upright stems from early to midsummer. Grow in marginally to moderately fertile soil. Clean up plants in spring.

Festuca glauca 'Elijah Blue'
ELIJAH BLUE FESCUE

☼ ◊ Z4–7 H7–1 ↕8in (20cm) ↔10in (25cm)
Produces spikelets of violet-flushed, blue-green
flowers in early to midsummer. Prefers marginally to
moderately fertile soil. Divide every 3 to 4 years.

Festuca glauca 'Blaufuchs'
BLUE FOX BLUE FESCUE

☼ ◊ Z4–8 H8–1 ↕12in (30cm) ↔10in (25cm)
This and the many named forms of blue fescue differ
in their degree of blueness. Good as massed plantings
and container plants. All prefer cool conditions.

Festuca glauca 'Skinner Blue'
SKINNER BLUE BLUE FESCUE

☼ ◊ Z4–8 H8–1 ↕12in (30cm) ↔10in (25cm)
Lift and divide open-centered clumps every third
spring when cutting back the foliage. Blue fescues do
not do well in soil that is waterlogged in winter.

Schizachyrium scoparium 'The Blues'
THE BLUES LITTLE BLUESTEM

☼ ◊ Z2–7 H7–1 ↕3ft (1m) ↔12in (30cm)
Selected for its glaucous foliage and propagated by
division. The species was a main constituent of the
tallgrass prairie and is still grown as a forage grass.

Sesleria caerulea
BLUE MOOR GRASS

☼ ☼ ◊ Z5–8 H8–5 ↕12in (30cm) ↔10in (25cm)
The leaves are blue on top and green beneath, giving a
two-toned effect. Flowers appear in late spring. Grows
best in an alkaline soil and tolerates drought.

HERBACEOUS PLANTS

Ornamental grasses with variegated foliage

Variegation in the narrow foliage of grasses can appear different from that in other plants. While some species have the common linear striping, others have leaves transversely variegated with bands of green and white or green and yellow, giving an entirely different effect. Some of the grasses with highly variegated leaves can be as eye-catching as white flowers.

HERBACEOUS PLANTS

Calamagrostis x *acutiflora* 'Overdam'
OVERDAM FEATHER REED GRASS
☼ ☀ ◐ z5–9 H9–1 ↕↔4ft (1.2m)
An easy-to-grow, clump-forming grass, with foliage that has longitudinal pale yellow striping. Late summer flower spikes are effective in winter and weatherproof.

Carex siderosticha 'Variegata'
VARIEGATED CREEPING BROADLEAF SEDGE
☼ ☀ ◐◐ z6–9 H9–3 ↕12in (30cm) ↔16cm (40cm)
Slowly spreading, this tough and adaptable perennial has pale brown flower spikes in late spring. Prone to rust, smuts, leaf spots, and aphids.

MORE CHOICES

- *Carex conica* 'Snowline' z5–8 H9–1
- *Carex mushingumensis* 'Oehme' z3–8 H8–1
- *Carex nigra* 'Variegata' z4–8 H8–1
- *Glyceria maxima* 'Variegata' z4–9 H10–3
- *Luzula sylvatica* 'Marginata' z4–9 H9–4
- *Miscanthus sinensis* v. *condensatus* 'Cabaret' z5–9 H9–1
- *Miscanthus sinensis* v. *condensatus* 'Cosmopolitan' z4–9 H9–1
- *Molinia caerulea* 'Strahlenquelle' z4–8 H8–1
- *Phalaris arundinacea* 'Feesey' z4–9 H9–3
- *Spartina pectinata* 'Aureomarginata' z4–9 H9–1

Carex morrowii 'Ice Dance'
ICE DANCE JAPANESE SEDGE
☼ ☀ ◐ z5–9 H12–1 ↕20in (30cm) ↔12in (30cm)
Bears panicles of green and brown flower spikes in late spring. Clump-forming perennial with short rhizomes. Best grown in fertile soil.

Arundo donax 'Versicolor'
GIANT REED
☼ ◐ z7–15 H12–1 ↕8–10ft (2.5–3m) ↔2ft (60cm)
Terminal clusters of light green to purple spikelets are produced from mid- to late fall. The habit is suggestive of corn plants. Also called *A. donax* 'Variegata'.

Arrhenatherum elatius subsp. *bulbosum* 'Variegatum'
BULBOUS OAT GRASS, STRIPED TUBER OAT GRASS
☼ ☼ ◊ Z5–8 H8–5 ↕20in (50cm) ↔8in (20cm)
A slowly spreading grass with bulbous swellings at the base of the stems. Grows best in cool climates and may go dormant in summer where they are hot.

Molinia caerulea 'Variegata'
VARIEGATED PURPLE MOOR GRASS
☼ ◊ Z4–8 H8–1 ↕↔2ft (60cm)
A clump-forming grass that makes low mounds of foliage. Bright yellow flower spikes are not freely produced in regions with hot summers.

Miscanthus sinensis 'Kirk Alexander'
KIRK ALEXANDER MAIDENGRASS
☼ ◊ Z4–9 H9–1 ↕6ft (2m) ↔3ft (1m)
This cultivar has tan flowers in fall and yellow banding on the leaves. It is also more compact than the species, making it a good candidate for smaller borders.

Miscanthus sinensis 'Variegatus'
VARIEGATED MAIDENGRASS
☼ ◊ Z5–9 H9–1 ↕6ft (2m) ↔4ft (1.2m)
Autumn-flowering panicles persist throughout winter. Cut back in early spring before new growth starts. Prefers moderately fertile soil. Great accent plant.

Miscanthus sinensis 'Zebrinus'
ZEBRA GRASS
☼ ◊ Z4–9 H9–1 ↕4ft (1.2m) ↔3ft (1m)
Fall-blooming flowers are initially copper then fade to creamy white. Makes a nice living screen. Flowers can be cut for fresh or dry arrangements.

Miscanthus sinensis 'Morning Light'
MORNING LIGHT MAIDENGRASS
☼ ◊ Z5–9 H9–1 ↕↔4ft (1.2m)
Resembles *M. sinensis* 'Gracillimus' except for its narrow white leaf edges. Like other slender-leaved grasses, it looks beautiful when backlit by the sun. Excellent plant for providing a fountainlike illusion in the ground or in a pot.

HERBACEOUS PLANTS

Ornamental grasses with colorful foliage

In addition to the grasses with variegated leaves (*see* pp. 318–319), some grasses and sedges have brightly colored foliage. The bright yellow forms shown here stand out particularly well when associated with shrubs with red or purple foliage, such *Cotinus* 'Royal Purple'. Plant Japanese blood grass (right) where it will be backlit to enhance the color.

HERBACEOUS PLANTS

Carex morrowii 'Expallida'
OHWI JAPANESE SEDGE GRASS

☼ ◐ ◊ Z7–8 H8–1 ↕18in (45cm) ↔12in (30cm)
Evergreen species with arched, narrow foliage with white and green stripes. The foliage looks good through winter, and plants flower in early spring.

Carex elata 'Aurea'
BOWLES' GOLDEN SEDGE

☼ ◑ ◊◊◑ Z5–9 H9–3 ↕28in (70cm) ↔18in (45cm)
Discovered by A.E. Bowles in England, this is a graceful plant with narrow leaves, each with a longitudinal green stripe. In dry soils this needs shade.

Deschampsia cespitosa 'Goldgehänge'
GOLDEN PENDANT TUFTED HAIR GRASS

☼ ◑ ◊◊◑ Z4–8 H8–1 ↕6ft (2m) ↔5ft (1.5m)
Bears cloudlike heads of fine-textured, slightly pendent, golden flowers. A cool-season grass that grows best in damp locations.

Carex hachijoensis 'Evergold'
EVERGOLD ODHIMA KAN SUGE

☼ ◊ Z6–9 H9–6 ↕8in (20cm)
↔6–8in (15–20cm)
A very ornamental grass forming densely tufted tussocks of fine foliage. The leaves are green-white when young, changing to green-yellow with age.

MORE CHOICES

- *Hakonechloa macra* 'Aureola' Z5–9 H9–5
- *Miscanthus* 'Purpurascens' Z4–9 H9–1
- *Panicum virgatum* 'Hanse Herms' Z5–9 H9–1
- *Panicum virgatum* 'Shenandoah' Z5–9 H9–5
- *Pennisetum alopecurioides* 'Cassian' Z5–9 H9–1
- *Spodiopogon sibiricus* Z4–9 H9–1
- *Sporobolus heterolepis* Z3–8 H10–2
- *Themeda triandra* v. *japonica* Z10–11 H12–9

Milium effusum 'Aureum'
GOLDEN WOOD MILLET, BOWLES' GOLDEN GRASS

☼ ◊ Z6–9 H9–6 ↕24in (60cm) ↔12in (30cm)
A cultivar with very yellow spring foliage that keeps its color all summer if grown in moist shade. It may go green in hot climates and then become semi-dormant.

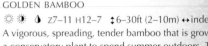

Phyllostachys aurea
GOLDEN BAMBOO

☼ ☼ ◑ ◊ Z7–11 H12–7 ↕6–30ft (2–10m) ↔indefinite
A vigorous, spreading, tender bamboo that is grown as a conservatory plant to spend summer outdoors. The decorative golden stems can be used as walkingsticks.

Melinia repens
PURPLE NATAL RUBY GRASS

☼ ◊ ◑ Z9–10 H10–1 ↕↔2ft (60cm)
Tender grass grown as an annual. Showy flower spikes in summer and fall are brightest when newly opened. Move container-grown plants indoors for winter bloom.

Pleioblastus auricomus
GOLDEN-STRIPED BAMBOO
☼ ◑ Z7–15 H12–1 ↕↔5ft (1.5m)
Fast-growing, rhizomatous bamboo. It makes a good container plant, where its aggressive growth can be controlled. Drought-tolerant when established.

Imperata cylindrica 'Rubra'
JAPANESE BLOOD GRASS
☼ ◑ Z5–9 H9–3 ↕20in (50cm) ↔indefinite
Leaves start green but quickly transform to deep blood red. This perennial grass is a slow spreader. Also known as *I. cylindrica* var *koenigii* 'Red Baron'.

Bromus inermis 'Skinner's Gold'
SKINNER'S GOLD BROME
☼ ◐ ◑ Z6–8 H12–1 ↕↔2ft (60cm)
The species is an important pasture grass, but this is grown for its green-edges leaves and yellow flower stalks. Entire plant appears light yellow from a distance.

Panicum virgatum 'Rehbraun'
RED-BROWN SWITCH GRASS
Ⓝ ☼ ◑ Z4–9 H9–4 ↕3ft (1m) ↔30in (75cm)
A variety of switch grass selected for the red color of the fall foliage and seedheads. Stiff, upright cultivar that withstands fall rainstorms and winter snowfalls well.

HERBACEOUS PLANTS

Ornamental grasses with showy flowers

While all grasses flower, some are grown mainly for their seedheads rather than for their foliage. Most of the tall ones shown here are good for adding fall color but also persist into winter, withstanding storms and quite heavy snowfalls. The shorter species retain their ornamental value until late, and seedheads may persist until spring.

HERBACEOUS PLANTS

Andropogon glomeratus
BUSHY BEARD GRASS, BROOMSEDGE
Ⓝ ☼ ☼ ◊ ◑ Z2–7 H7–1 ‡6ft (2m) ↔3ft (1m)
Blue-green foliage precedes the highly ornamental late summer flowers that are good for cutting and drying. A grass suited to most soils, but not drought-tolerant.

Calamagrostis x *acutiflora* 'Karl Foerster'
KARL FOERSTER REED GRASS
☼ ☼ ◑ Z5–9 H9–5 ‡6ft (1.8m) ↔24in (60cm)
The deep green, shining foliage is attractive from spring until fall, when it turns buff-brown. Stiff flower spikes appear in summer and remain into winter.

MORE CHOICES

- *Eragrostis spectabilis* Z9–10 H10–9
- *Panicum virgatum* 'Dallas Blues' Z5–9 H9–5
- *Saccharum brevibarbe* var. *contortum* Z6–9 H9–1
- *Sorghastrum nutans* Z4–9 H9–1
- *Sporobolus heterolepis* Z3–8 H10–2

Pennisetum alopecuroides 'Moudry'
BLACK FLOWERING MOUNTAIN GRASS
☼ ◊ Z6–9 H9–3 ‡↔3ft (1m)
Bears flower spikes from summer to fall. Seeds of this cultivar are black, giving the spikes a dark cast. Prefers moderately fertile soil.

Chasmanthium latifolium
RIVER OATS
Ⓝ ☼ ☼ ◑ Z5–9 H9–5 ‡3ft (1m) ↔24in (60cm)
Valued for the dangling seedheads that turn rich brown in fall and persist through winter. An inland species native from New Jersey to Texas. Tolerates dry shade.

Miscanthus sinensis 'Graziella'
GRAZIELLA MAIDENGRASS
☼ ◑ Z5–9 H9–1 ‡7ft (2.1m) ↔3ft (1m)
A clump-forming grass, this cultivar has narrow leaves that turn copper to orange in fall. Flowers appear in late summer and open silver, turning color as they age.

Miscanthus sinensis 'Silberfeder'
SILVER FEATHER EULALIA
☼ ◑ Z4–9 H9–1 ‡8ft (2.5m)
A most attractive but fairly invasive form that spreads by underground runners. The pink-tinged new flowers appear slightly earlier than on 'Graziella'.

Muhlenbergia capillaris
PINK HAIR GRASS

Ⓝ ☀ ☀ ◐ ◑ Z7–9 H9–6 ↕↔30 in (75cm)

Flowers appear in fall and, after turning pale brown, remain attractive into winter. Most effective in large plantings. Native from Massachusetts to Florida.

Molinia caerulea subsp. arundinacea
TALL PURPLE MOOR GRASS

☀ ☀ ◐ Z4–8 H8–1 ↕8ft (2.5m) ↔2ft (60cm)

A graceful, clump-forming grass that needs fertile soil. Foliage and flowers turn golden brown in fall and then break off at ground level. There are several named forms.

Pennisetum orientale 'Karley Rose'
KARLEY ROSE ORIENTAL FOUNTAIN GRASS

☀ ◐ Z7–9 H9–7 ↕ ↔3ft (1m)

A long-flowering grass that blooms from midsummer to late fall. It does well in containers. The species has white blooms with a hint of pink, especially in cooler regions.

Saccharum ravennae
RAVENNA GRASS

☀ ◐ Z6–9 H9–6 ↕12ft (4m) ↔6ft (2m)

A drought-tolerant species whose flower spikes tend to droop if grown too moist. Foliage turns orange-brown in late fall, when the flower stems become red-tinted.

Briza media
COMMON QUAKING GRASS, TREMBLING GRASS

☀ ☀ ◐ Z4–11 H12–1 ↕3ft (1m) ↔12in (30cm)

This grows on both acidic and alkaline soils. Flowers appear in late spring and turn from purple-tinted green to straw brown as they age. They dry well.

Ornamental grasses for prairies and meadows

The majority of grasses grown in meadows and prairies are native species, and, while they have a rustic charm and often good fall color, they are not particularly ornamental. The grasses shown here will all adapt to these wild conditions, spread slowly, and compete with the native species, and they are attractive in the bargain.

Pennisetum orientale 'Tall Tails'
TALL TAILS FOUNTAIN GRASS
☼ ◊ z7–9 H9–7 ‡24in (60cm) ↔30in (75cm)
A compact, floriferous grass that blooms from summer into fall. This grows best in the southern parts of this region and needs warm weather to flower well.

Pennisetum villosum
FEATHER TOP GRASS
☼ ◊ z9–15 H12–1 ‡↔24in (60cm)
This marginally hardy grass is easy to grow from seed. It is a very showy species that also does well in containers and is used by florists as a cut flower.

Panicum virgatum
SWITCH GRASS
Ⓝ ☼ ◊ z5–9 H9–1 ‡3ft (1m) ↔30in (75cm)
Native over much of eastern North America, this is one of the tallgrass prairie species. It forms clumps but also spreads by underground shoots.

Molinia caerulea 'Altissima'
ALTISSIMA PURPLE MOOR GRASS
☼ ◊ ᵖᴴ z4–8 H8–1 ‡x to 5ft (1.5m) ↔1ft (30cm)
A clump-forming grass native to wet areas of Europe and Asia. This upright cultivar blooms in midsummer and grows best where summers are cool.

Molinia caerulea 'Variegata'
VARIEGATED PURPLE MOOR GRASS
☼ ◊ ᵖᴴ z4–8 H8–1 ‡24in (60cm) ↔6in (40cm)
Like the cultivar 'Altissima', this flowers best in cool climates. Flower stalks are bright yellow. Worth growing for the foliage alone where summers are hot.

Schizachyrum scoparium
LITTLE BLUESTEM, PRAIRIE BEARD GRASS
Ⓝ ☼ ◊ Z2–7 H7–1 ‡3ft (1m) ↔12in (30cm)
One of the characteristic grasses of tallgrass prairie.
Very tolerant of moisture and soil. Foliage color is
variable, ranging from bluish to bright green.

Chasmanthium latifolium
RIVER OATS
Ⓝ ☼ ☼ ◊ Z5–9 H9–5 ‡3ft (1m) ↔24in (60cm)
An inland native plant that grows well in most soil
conditions. Seedheads are green at first, turning buff
as they mature, and remaining through winter.

Bouteloua gracilis
BLUE GRAMA
Ⓝ ☼ ◊ Z5–9 H9–5 ‡24in (60cm) ↔12in (30cm)
The distinctive mid- to late summer flowers are red-
tinged at first, becoming pale brown. Makes a good
container plant, where the flowers can be seen better.

MORE CHOICES

- *Andropogon gerardii* Z2–7 H7–1
- *Andropogon ternaries* Z2–7 H7–1
- *Andropogon virginicus* Z2–7 H7–1
- *Buchloe dachyloides* Z3–11 H12–2
- *Eragrostis spectabilis* Z9–10 H10–9
- *Koeleria macrantha* H5–1
- *Sorghastrum nutans* Z4–9 H9–1

Elymus canadensis
CANADIAN WILD RYE
Ⓝ ☼ ◊ Z3–8 H8–1 ‡6ft (2m) ↔24in (60cm)
A clump-forming, fast growing grass that may be short-
lived. Flower spikes resemble cultivated rye. Tolerant
of most soils. Native to dry, sandy sites.

Deschampsia cespitosa
TUFTED HAIR GRASS
☼ ☼ ◊ ◊ ◊ Z4–8 H8–1 ‡6ft (2m) ↔5ft (1.5m)
An excellent evergreen grass that prefers cool locations
with adequate moisture but does well in most of this
region. Airy heads of tiny flowers appear in summer.

Briza media
COMMON QUAKING GRASS, TREMBLING GRASS
☼ ☼ ◊ Z4–11 H12–1 ‡3ft (1m) ↔12in (30cm)
A cool-season grass with evergreen foliage. Tolerant of
most soils and situations. Inflated seedpods dance in
the slightest breeze and can be dried for winter use.

HERBACEOUS PLANTS

Aquatic perennials for floral interest

Garden pools are becoming very popular and even small garden centers now carry a choice of suitable plants. By selecting carefully, one can have aquatic plants in flower from early spring until frost. Even in a pond too small for a waterlily, this long season of bloom is possible.

Mentha aquatica
WATER MINT
☼ ◐◖ Z6–11 H12–6 ‡6–36in (15–90cm) ↔3ft (1m)
The essential oils in the intensely aromatic leaves are used in perfumery. It flowers in summer. Grows much like citrus mint. From Eurasia.

Iris ensata 'Variegata'
VARIEGATED JAPANESE WATER IRIS
☼ ☀ ◖ Z5–9 H9–4 ‡3ft (1m)
↔indefinite
Blooms in early summer. Leaves and stems are attractively white-striped. Prefers well-drained, fertile soil and dislikes high levels of nitrogen. Plant from midsummer to early fall.

MORE CHOICES

- *Butomus umbellatus* Z3–11 H8–5
- *Caltha palustris* Z3–7 H7–1
- *Caltha palustris* 'Alba' Z5–7 H7–3
- *Caltha palustris* 'Multiplex' Z5–9 H9–1
- *Heuchera rubescens* Z3–8 H8–1
- *Iris laevigata* 'Snowdrift' Z5–9 H9–1
- *Mimulus ringens* Z4–9 H9–4
- *Myosotis palustris* Z3–9 H8–5
- *Nymphaea* 'Director Moore' Z4–11 H12–1

Iris pseudacorus
YELLOW FLAG
☼ ◖ Z5–8 H8–3 ‡6ft (2m) ↔indefinite
A vigorous iris that blooms from mid- to late spring. Ripe seeds fall from the capsule and then float away and spread to new locations.

Iris versicolor
BLUE FLAG, WILD IRIS
Ⓝ ☼ ◐◖ Z3–9 H9–1 ‡2ft (60cm) ↔indefinite
Blooms in early to midsummer. Prefers fertile, well-drained, loamy soil. Susceptible to aphids and mealybugs, especially when in bloom.

Iris laevigata
JAPANESE WATER IRIS
☼☀ ◐◖ Z4–9 H9–1 ‡2–3ft (60–90cm) or more ↔indefinite
Blooms late spring to early summer in shades of blue, red, purple, and white. Forms sizeable clumps. From wet areas of Japan, N. China, Korea, C. Russia.

Lysichiton americanus
YELLOW SKUNK CABBAGE
Ⓝ ☼ ◖ Z7–9 H9–7 ‡3ft (1m) ↔30in (75cm)
Yellow flowers in early spring precede large, strongly veined, bold leaves. Prefers to be in rich, organic soil. From bogs and wet woodlands of W. North America.

Lysimachia vulgaris
YELLOW LOOSESTRIFE

☼ ◐ ◐ Z4–8 H8–1 ↕4ft (1.2m) ↔3ft (1m)

A upright plant with soft stems that spreads by underground runners and can become somewhat invasive; contain it in a pond planting basket.

Menyanthes trifoliata
BOG BEAN

Ⓝ ☼ ◐ Z4–8 H9–3 ↕9in (23cm) ↔12in (30cm)

Grows well in wet soil beside a pool, or in up to 12in (30cm) of water. It spreads slowly and flowers in early summer. It is named for the beanlike leaves.

Nelumbo 'Mrs. Perry D. Slocum'
MRS. SLOCUM AMERICAN LOTUS

☼ ◐ Z4–11 H12–3 ↕18in (45cm) ↔6ft (1.8m)

A rapidly spreading plant, it can fill a large pond in a single season if planted unconfined. The species was an important food source of the indigenous people.

Sagittaria sagittifolia
JAPANESE ARROWHEAD

☼ ◐ Z5–11 H12–5 ↕18in (45cm) ↔12in (30cm)

Racemes of 1in white flowers with a basal spot appear during summer. Prefers gravelly soil and will spread and self-sow. From shallow to deep waters in Eurasia.

Nymphaea 'Attraction'
ATTRACTION WATERLILY

☼ ◐ Z4–11 H12–1 ↔6ft (2m)

Day-blooming flowers 5in (13cm) wide This hardy waterlily has bronze-green leaves that are purple-brown with dark purple markings when young.

MORE CHOICES

- *Nymphaea 'Green Smoke'* Z4–11 H12–1
- *Nymphaea 'Paula Louise'* Z4–11 H12–1
- *Nymphaea 'Sioux'* Z4–11 H12–1
- *Nymphaea 'Texas Dawn'* Z4–11 H12–1
- *Pyrola elliptica* Z7–9 H9–7
- *Tolmiea menziesii* Z6–9 H9–6

Pontederia cordata
PICKEREL WEED

Ⓝ ☼ ◐ Z3–11 H12–1 ↕30in (75cm) ↔18in (45cm)

Flowers are borne from late spring to fall. When grown in an aquatic container, soil should be a loamy and fertile. Can also grow in water-filled barrels.

Aquatic perennials for foliage or texture

Narrow spikes reaching into the sky, broad arrowheads rising from the water, or large, flat leaves held just above the surface: these are just a few of the foliage choices available from aquatic plants. Naturally, most of these flower as well, but it is the foliage display that remains in your garden for a much longer time and so is worth considering as much as (if not more than) flowers.

Acorus gramineus 'Ogon'
JAPANESE SWEET FLAG
☼ ● Z10–11 H12–2 ‡to 10in (25cm) ↔6in (15cm)
Gives the impression of tall, semi-evergreen iris leaves. Flowers are inconspicuous. Susceptible to wet and dry root rots, rust, and various fungal leaf spots.

Orontium aquaticum
GOLDEN CLUB
Ⓝ ☼ ● Z6–10 H10–4 ↔24in (60cm)
A strange plant, related to calla lilies and jack-in-the-pulpit, that puts on an unusual but colorful display in spring. Leaves are waterproof and appear dry if pushed below the surface.

Acorus calamus 'Variegatus'
VARIEGATED SWEET FLAG
Ⓝ ☼ ● Z10–11 H12–2 ‡30in (75cm) ↔24in
Insignificant flowers appear from late spring to early summer. Does not produce fertile seeds, but it can spread widely by rhizomes.

Eriophorum angustifolium
TALL COTTON GRASS
Ⓝ ☼ ● ◕ Z5–9 H9–5 ‡to 30in(75cm) ↔indefinite
The grasslike foliage (*Eriophorum* is not a true grass) arises from long, creeping rhizomes. The downy flowers appear above the foliage in summer.

Iris pseudacorus
YELLOW FLAG
☼ ● Z5–8 H8–3 ‡6ft (2m) ↔indefinite
A vigorous iris that blooms from mid- to late summer. Ripe seeds fall from the capsules and then float away and spread to new locations.

Typha minima
DWARF CATTAIL

☼ ◑ Z3–11 H12–1 ↕18–24in (45–60cm) ↔12in (30cm)

Flowers are distinctive, cylindrical spikes that appear from mid- to late summer and can be used in dried arrangements. Can become invasive in unlined ponds.

Lysichiton camtschatcensis
JAPANESE SKUNK CABBAGE

☼ ◑ Z5–9 H9–1 ↕30in (75cm) ↔24in (60cm)

Early spring flowers have a more pleasant aroma than *L. americanus*, and the plant is smaller. Prefers rich, organic soil. From bogs and wet woodlands of NE Asia.

Nuphar lutea
YELLOW POND LILY

Ⓝ ☼ ◑ Z3–9 H9–1 ↔5ft (1.5m)

Produces peculiar-smelling flowers in summer Can eventually produce very large colonies along the edge of a body of water. Divide plants regularly to promote flowering.

Sagittaria latifolia
WAPATO, DUCK POTATO

Ⓝ ☼ ◑ Z5–11 H12–5 ↕5ft (1.2m) ↔2ft (60cm)

Similar in appearance and growth habit to the Japanese Arrowhead (*S. sagittifolia*). Susceptible to leaf spots, leaf smut, spider mites, and aphids.

MORE CHOICES

- *Acorus gramineus* 'Oborozuki' Z10–11 H12–2
- *Equisetum hyemale* Z3–11 H12–1
- *Equisetum scirpoides* Z5–11 H12–4
- *Houttuynia cordata* 'Chameleon' Z5–11 H12–1
- *Juncus articulatus* Z6–9 H9–6
- *Juncus balticus* Z6–9 H9–6
- *Juncus effusus* 'Compactus' Z6–9 H9–6
- *Juncus effusus* 'Quartz Creek' Z6–9 H9–6
- *Nuphar pumila* 'Variegata' Z3–9 H9–1
- *Schoenoplectus lacustris* Z4–8 H8–1
- *Typha angusifolia* Z2–11 H12–1
- *Typha latifolia* Z2–11 H12–1

Ranunculus flammula
LESSER SPEARWORT

☼ ◑ Z3–9 H9–1 ↕28in (70cm) ↔30in (75cm)

An aggressive species that needs constant care to keep it from spreading too widely. The foliage is held just clear of the water, showing the red-tinted stems.

Juncus effusus 'Spiralis'
CORKSCREW RUSH

Ⓝ ☼ ◑ ◑ pH Z6–9 H9–6 ↕18in (45cm) ↔24in (60cm)

The leafless stems turn and twist to form a dense, prostrate mat. Small brown flower spikes appear in summer. Stems are prized by flower arrangers.

Nelumbo nucifera
SACRED LOTUS

☼ ◑ Z4–11 H12–3 ↕28–60in (0.7–1.5m) ↔indefinite

Large, platelike leaves are held above the water. Needs a container at least 3ft (1m) across. Some named varieties are smaller and better suited to home gardens.

HERBACEOUS PLANTS

Nelumbo nucifera 'Rosea Plena'
DOUBLE PINK SACRED LOTUS

☼ ● Z4–11 H12–3 ↕4–5ft (1.2–1.5m) ↔indefinite
A fast-spreading, tropical aquatic that needs a long, hot summer to bloom well. Grows well in shallow water or up to 16in (40cm.) deep.

Equisetum hyemale
COMMON HORSETAIL

Ⓝ ☼ ● Z3–11 H12–1 ↕to 4ft (1.2m) ↔indefinite
Invasive species that should be planted in a container to restrict its growth. Extremely adaptable. Ancient species, little changed since the time of the dinosaurs.

Houttuynia cordata 'Chameleon'
CHAMELEON PLANT

☼ ● Z5–11 H12–1 ↕4in (10cm) ↔indefinite
The multicolored foliage is the reason to grow this; flowers are insignificant. Spreading plant that will also grow in dry soil. The green-leaved species is invasive.

Andromeda polifolia
COMMON BOG ROSEMARY, MARSH ANDROMEDA

☼ ◐ ● Z2–6 H6–1 ↕16in (40cm) ↔24in (60cm)
White or pale pink flowers bloom in spring and early summer among leathery, dark green leaves. Native to northern Europe.

Caltha palustris 'Alba'
WHITE MARSH MARIGOLD

Ⓝ ☼ ● Z3–7 H7–1 ↕9in (22cm) ↔12in (30cm)
More compact than the yellow-flowered species. Prefers rich soil and open sites. Does best if water level is less than 2in (5cm). Widespread in the N Hemisphere.

Acorus gramineus 'Variegatus'
VARIEGATED SWEET FLAG

☼ ◊ Z10–11 H12–2 ↕10in (25cm) ↔6in (15cm)
The grasslike foliage is a rich green, striped with white in summer, and fragrant when crushed. Seen here in fall. Grows in water up to 9in (23cm) deep.

Nymphaea 'Attraction'
ATTRACTION WATERLILY

☼ ◊ Z3–11 H12–1 ↔6ft (2m)
Day-blooming flowers 5in (13cm) wide This hardy waterlily has bronze-green leaves that are purple-brown with dark purple markings when young.

Calla palustris
BOG ARUM

Ⓝ ☼ ◊ Z4–8 H8–1 ↕10in (25cm) ↔12in (30cm)
Flowers appear in midsummer. Upright leaves emerge from creeping rhizomes. Use to soften the edges of a bog garden. From N and C Europe, Asia, and N America.

Pontederia cordata
PICKEREL WEED

Ⓝ ☼ ◊ Z3–11 H12–1 ↕30in (75cm) ↔18in (45cm)
Flowers are borne from late spring to fall. When grown in an aquatic container, the soil should be a loamy and fertile. Can also be grown in water-filled barrels.

Nymphaea 'Virginalis'
VIRGINALIS WATERLILY

☼ ◊ Z3–11 H12–1 ↔4ft (1.2m)
A hardy waterlily with rounded leaves that are purple to bronze when they open. The fragrant flowers are up to 5in (14cm) across. Grow in water to 20in (50cm) deep.

Iris ensata 'Variegata'
VARIEGATED JAPANESE WATER IRIS

☼ ☼ ◊ Z5–8 H8–4 ↕3ft (1m) ↔indefinite
Blooms in early summer. Leaves and stems are attractively white-striped. Prefers fertile soil and dislikes high levels of nitrogen. Plant in early fall.

Medium to large bulbs for spring

Often neglected in favor of the better-known tulip and daffodil hybrids, these bulbs will amaze you by the speed with which they emerge and grow in the spring. They are good choices for a woodland garden, since most have die down before the trees are fully in leaf. The fritillaries have a slight skunky smell and are shunned by squirrels for this reason.

Narcissus poeticus
POET'S NARCISSUS

☼ ◐ ◊ Z3–9 H9–1 ↕8–20in (20–50cm)
A late-blooming species that is the parent of several excellent cultivars. Most have the characteristic flat, fragrant flowers with a red-rimmed cup.

Fritillaria meleagris
SNAKE'S-HEAD FRITILLARY

☼ ◊ Z4–9 H8–2 ↕12in (30cm) ↔3in (8cm)
Blooms in spring. Flowers available in purple to pinkish purple and white. Will naturalize in grass or a rock garden. Prefers moderately fertile to fertile, organic soil.

Fritillaria imperialis
CROWN IMPERIAL

☼ ◊ Z4–9 H8–2 ↕3ft (1m) ↔12in (30cm)
A heavy feeder, it needs a mulch of a rich compost or an application of phosphorus and potassium in ealy spring to bloom well the following year.

Fritillaria persica 'Adiyaman'
ADIYAMAN PERSIAN FRITILLARY

☼ ◊ Z6–8 H8–6 ↕3ft (1m) ↔6in (10cm)
Twisted, gray-green leaves cover the lower stem. Plant in fall for spring flowering, if grown in light shade, flowering will be prolonged. May be short-lived.

Hyacinthus orientalis 'Lady Derby'
LADY DERBY HYACINTH

☼ ◐ ◊ Z5–9 H9–5 ↕12in (30cm)
Plant outdoors in fall for late spring flowers, or pot and force indoors for blooms during winter. There are many other cultivars in a wide color range.

Hyacinthoides hispanica 'La Grandesse'
LA GRANDESSE SPANISH BLUEBELL
☼ ◊ Z4–9 H9–1 ↕16in (40cm) ↔4in (10cm)
Flower spikes bloom in late spring above strap-shaped
leaves. Hardier than the English bluebell. Other
named forms in blue and pink are also easy to find.

MORE CHOICES

- *Leucojum aestivum* Z3–9 H9–1
- *Muscari neglectum* Z2–9 H9–1
- *Narcissus tazzeta* Z3–9 H9–1
- *Narcissus* x *poetaz* Z3–9 H9–1
- *Trillium cernuum* Z3–7 H8–1
- *Tulipa* (cultivars) Z3–8 H8–1
- *Tulipa fosteriana* Z3–8 H8–1

Trillium grandiflorum
WAKE ROBIN
Ⓝ ☼ ☀ ◊◊ Z4–7 H7–3 ↕18in (45cm) ↔12in (30cm)
Flowers bloom in midspring and often turn pink as
they age. Prefers acidic to neutral soil rich in organic
matter. Mulch in fall with leaf mold.

Trillium chloropetalum
GIANT WAKE ROBIN
Ⓝ ☼ ☀ ◊ Z6–9 H9–6 ↕16in (40cm) ↔8in (20cm)
The fragrant flowers appear in spring. Prefers acidic to
neutral, organic soil. Mulch in fall with leaf mold.
Susceptible to rust, smut, fungal spot, slugs, and snails.

Trillium cuneatum
WHIPPOORWILL FLOWER
Ⓝ ☼ ☀ ◊ Z6–9 H9–6 ↕18in (45cm) ↔12in (30cm)
An ideal plant for a rich woodland soil, this multiplies
slowly and seeds itself if happy. Native from New York
to Georgia, it may be listed as *Trillium sessile*.

Tulipa greigii
GREIG'S TULIP
☼ ◊ Z3–8 H8–1 ↕20in (50cm)
One of the first tulips to flower in spring, the mottled
foliage keep this attractive even when the petals have
fallen. There are many named cultivars.

Leucojum aestivum 'Gravetye Giant'
GRAVETYE GIANT SNOWFLAKE
☼ ◊ Z4–9 H9–1 ↕3ft (1m) ↔3in (8cm)
This cultivar is much more robust than the species.
Faintly chocolate-scented flowers appear in spring.
Prefers organic soil. Susceptible to narcissus bulb fly.

HERBACEOUS PLANTS

Small bulbs for spring

Many of these are the first flowers to bloom after winter; plant some in a sun-trap to enjoy an early spring. Readily available and economical, plant them in drifts across a perennial or shrub border, not just along the front. They make a superb display and after flowering will be hidden by emerging leaves. These multiply rapidly and are good for naturalizing in lawns.

Crocus tommasinianus 'Ruby Giant'
RUBY GIANT CROCUS
☼ ◊ Z3–8 H8–1 ‡4in (10cm) ↔1in (2.5cm)
An early-flowering crocus that will bloom in late winter in mild climates. Multiplies rapidly and can be lifted and divided every few years as the leaves start to yellow. Plant about 4in (10cm) deep.

Crocus biflorus
SCOTCH CROCUS
☼ ◊ Z3–8 H8–1 ‡2½in (6cm) ↔2in (5cm)
Like all crocuses, this needs extremely good drainage, so coarse sand or fine gravel should be added to heavy soils before planting. Good in a rock garden.

Crocus chrysanthus
SNOW CROCUS
☼ ◊ Z3–8 H10–1 ‡2in (5cm) ↔1½in (4cm)
This is a very early-flowering species. Crosses of this species with C. biflorus have produced a number of hybrids in white, purple, and yellow.

Puschkinia scilloides
STRIPED SQUILL
☼ ◐ ◊ Z3–9 H9–1 ‡8in (20cm) ↔2in (5cm)
Plant bulbs in fall for their striking late winter to early spring flowers. The variety libanotica is pure white. Adaptable to most soil types and will naturalize.

Narcissus jonquilla 'Baby Moon'
BABY MOON NARCISSUS

☼ ◊ Z3–9 H9–1 ‡8in (20cm)

Flowering in late spring, this has several sweetly scented blooms on each stem. Easy to grow and increases readily in good soil. Plant in early autumn.

Muscari armeniacum
ARMENIAN GRAPE HYACINTH

☼ ◊ Z4–8 H8–1 ‡8in (20cm) ↔2in (5cm)

A vigorous species, this increases rapidly. Plant in fall, or in summer following division. There are many other readily available *Muscari* species and cultivars.

Bulbocodium vernum
SPRING MEADOW SAFFRON

☼ ◊ Z7–9 H9–7 ‡3in (8cm)

One of the first bulbs to flower in spring, with blooms appearing before the leaves. Survives best in soil that bakes in summer and will rot if soil is too wet.

Erythronium dens-canis
DOG'S-TOOTH VIOLET

☼ ◐ ◊ Z3–9 H9–1 ‡6in (15cm) ↔4in (10cm)

This is the European counterpart of *E. americanum*. Plant in an organic soil in early fall. There are several named forms with flowers of different shades, including white.

Erythronium americanum
YELLOW TROUT LILY

Ⓝ ◐ ◊ Z3–9 H9–2 ‡2–10in (5–25cm) ↔2–3in (5–8cm)

Prefers organic soil that is not too rich. Sometime large colonies fail to bloom in a given year. Prone to rust, smuts, fungal spots, and slugs. Native to the eastern US.

Chionodoxa luciliae
GLORY OF THE SNOW

☼ ◊ Z3–9 H9–1 ‡10in (25cm) ↔2in (5cm)

Blooms in early spring. This species also has cultivars with white and pink flowers. Adapts to most well-drained soils, where it self-sows. Also called *C. forbesii*.

Leucojum vernum
SPRING SNOWFLAKE

☼ ◊ Z4–8 H9–3 ‡12in (30cm)

A choice species for the front of a woodland bed, but it must not be allowed to become dry in summer, even when the foliage has died down, or flowering will be greatly reduced.

HERBACEOUS PLANTS

Ornithogalum umbellatum
STAR OF BETHLEHEM

☼ ◊ z7–11 H12–7 ↕12in (30cm)
↔4in (10cm)

Midspring flowering, this can become a real weed on light soils, but does not seem as invasive on heavier ones. Multiplies rapidly by seed and division; every small bulblet left in soil will grow.

Eranthis cilicica
TURKISH WINTER ACONITE

☼ ☀ ◊ z4–9 H9–1 ↕3in (8cm) ↔2in (5cm)

This has larger flowers, more divided leaves, and blooms later than the better-known *E. hyemalis*. In its native habitat, it grows on hillsides and in conifer woods.

Eranthis hyemalis
WINTER ACONITE

☼ ☀ ◊ z4–9 H9–1 ↕3in (8cm) ↔2in (5cm)

One of the first flowers to bloom in spring, this can self-seed freely in a woodland situation but is seldom a pest. The foliage dies down soon after flowering.

Anemone blanda 'Violet Star'
GRECIAN WINDFLOWER

☼ ◊ z4–8 H8–1 ↕↔6in (5cm)

This grows best in a woodland location. The flowers close at night or on cloudy days. Soak new bulbs overnight before planting to improve survival.

MORE CHOICES

• *Anemone blanda* z4–8 H8–1
• *Crocus vernus* z3–8 H8–1
• *Eranthis x tubergenii* 'Guinea Gold' z4–9 H9–1

Iris bucharica
HORNED IRIS

☼ ◊ z5–9 H9–5 ↕16in (40cm)

An unusual bulbous iris that is very easy to grow and blooms just before the miniature bearded types. It prefers a slightly alkaline soil that is dry in summer.

Galanthus nivalis
COMMON SNOWDROP

☼ ◊ Z3–8 H8–1 ‡4–6in (10–15cm) ↔2–3in (5–8cm)

A bulbous perennial native from the Pyrenees to Ukraine. Suitable for naturalizing in grass or in a woodland but also at home in borders and rock gardens.

Galanthus elwesii
GIANT SNOWDROP

☼ ◊ Z3–9 H9–1 ‡12in (30cm) ↔3in (8cm)

Honey-scented flowers appear in late winter on surprisingly robust plants. Foliage is sometimes twisted. Best when grown in soil with high organic content.

Scilla siberica
SIBERIAN SQUILL

☼ ☼ ◊ Z5–8 H8–5
‡4–8in (10–20cm)
↔2in (5cm)

Flowers appear in spring. Plant bulbs in fall in moderately fertile, organic soil. Naturalizes well under trees and shrubs.

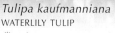

Tulipa tarda
TURKESTAN TULIP

☼ ◊ Z3–8 H8–1 ‡6in (15cm)

This thrives in poor soil and hot, dry places and will multiply rapidly without becoming a nuisance. One of the easiest and most enjoyable of the small tulips.

Tulipa kaufmanniana
WATERLILY TULIP

☼ ◊ Z3–8 H8–1 ‡4–14in (10–35cm)

Flowers can also be cream or flushed with pink, orange, or red. Blooms early to midseason. Prefers well-drained soil kept moist during the growing season.

Allium karataviense
TURKESTAN ONION

☼ ◊ Z3–9 H9–5 ‡10in (25cm)

An unusual species with 2 wide, grayish leaves that lie almost flat on the soil. The large head of flowers is on a short stem and remains attractive when in seed.

Scilla mischtschenkoana
TUBERGEN'S SQUILL

☼ ☼ ◊ Z4–7 H9–6 ‡6in (15cm) ↔2in (5cm)

An easy-to-grow bulb producing 3 or 4 flower spikes with up to 5 blooms per spike. It blends well with the showier Siberian squill and likes the same conditions.

Bulbs for summer

Often stately, frequently eye-catching, and always interesting, summer-flowering bulbs deserve a place in every garden. The species shown here are hardy throughout this region, although the *Crocosmia* may require a winter mulch in the north. Be sure to dead-head the flowering onions *(Allium)* to prevent them from seeding, or they may take over the garden.

HERBACEOUS PLANTS

Calochortus venustus
WHITE MARIPOSA LILY

Ⓝ ☼ ◊ Z6–10 H10–6 ↕to 24in (60cm) ↔3in (8cm)

Mariposa lilies need moisture in spring and early summer and dryer conditions from then on. Named forms, with larger flowers, are sometimes available.

Allium moly
GOLDEN GARLIC

☼ ◊ Z3–9 H9–1 ↕10in (25cm) ↔2in (5cm)

An easy-to-grow onion that is not invasive. The stems curl over, making this a good choice for edging a path. The foliage has a slight garlic scent when crushed.

Allium cernuum
NODDING ONION

Ⓝ ☼ ◊ Z3–9 H9–5 ↕28in (70cm) ↔5in (12cm)

A vigorous, bulbous plant with strap-shaped, dark green basal leaves. Flowers are borne in summer. Plant the bulbs in fertile soil in fall.

Allium giganteum
GIANT ORNAMENTAL ONION

☼ ◊ Z3–9 H9–5 ↕6ft (2m) ↔12–14in (30–35cm)

Amazingly dense flowerheads bloom in summer. Strap-shaped leaves wither before flowers appear. Prefers fertile soil. Excellent cut flower.

Galtonia candicans
SUMMER HYACINTH

☼ ◊ Z7–10 H10–7 ↕3–4ft (1–1.2m) ↔4in (10cm)

Fragrant flowers appear in late summer. Grow in fertile soil from fall-planted bulbs. Provide heavy winter mulch in colder areas, and protection from slugs.

Camassia cusickii
BLUE CAMASS

Ⓝ ☼ ☼ ◊ Z3–11 H12–1 ↕32in (80cm) ↔4in (10cm)

Grows best in a good soil with added organic matter. They multiply slowly and should be dug and divided in late summer as the foliage starts to die down.

Camassia leichtlinii
WHITE CAMASS

Ⓝ ☼ ◐ ◊ Z4–11 H12–1 ‡4½ft
(130cm) ↔4in (10cm)
Native from British Columbia to
California, this is the most showy of
the camass. It likes similar conditions
to *C. cuicksii.* There is also a form
with violet blue flowers.

Crocosmia x 'Lucifer'
LUCIFER MONTBRETIA

☼ ◊ Z6–9 H9–6 ‡to 3ft (1m)
↔10in (25cm)
This is a robust hybrid that blooms in
midsummer and prefers moderately
fertile, organic soil. Can be dug
up and stored like gladiolus where
not hardy.

Gladiolus communis subsp. *byzantinus*
HARDY GLADIOLUS

☼ ◊ Z8–10 H9–1 ‡3ft (1m) ↔6in (15cm)
Modern gladiolus hybrids must be lifted in fall and
over-wintered in a frost-free place, but this species will
survive outdoors year-round in most of the northeast.

Arisaema triphyllum
JACK-IN-THE-PULPIT

Ⓝ ☼ ◊ Z4–9 H9–1 ‡24in (60cm) ↔6in (15cm)
Found in damp woods and swamps throughout most
of eastern North America. Easy to grow in any organic-
rich soil that doesn't get too dry in summer.

Arisaema sikokianum
JAPANESE JACK-IN-THE-PULPIT

☼ ◊ Z4–9 H9–3 ‡20in (50cm) ↔6in (15cm)
This is ideal for a woodland garden and thrives in a
soil with a high organic content. It has become very
popular in the last 20 years. Blooms in early summer.

Arisaema ringens
LARGE-LEAVED JACK-IN-THE-PULPIT

☼ ◊ Z6–9 H9–6 ‡12in (30cm) ↔8in (20cm)
A less common plant that likes similar conditions to
the other *Arisaema* shown. The early summer flower is
green, with purple stripes and lip and a curled hood.

HERBACEOUS PLANTS

Bulbs for fall

It is almost like magic; one day the soil is bare, the next, flowers have appeared. Most of these fall-flowering bulbs produce leaves in spring that disappear for the summer. Flowers shoot up in fall, almost overnight, and last for weeks. The often delicate-looking blooms are incredibly tough, surviving heavy rain and rebounding after even hard frosts.

Sternbergia lutea
AUTUMN DAFFODIL

☼ ◊ ◔ Z7–9 H9–6 ‡6in (15cm) ↔3in (8cm)
Flowers appear in fall. Plant bulbs in late summer. Best when grown in moderately fertile soil. Prefers dry soil while it is dormant. Excellent rock garden plant.

Crocus speciosus
MAUVE FALL CROCUS

☼ ◊ Z3–8 H8–1 ‡6in (15cm) ↔2in (5cm)
A very easy species with tough flowers that withstand late fall rains and even early snowfalls, lying flat in bad weather and becoming upright again in good.

Cyclamen hederifolium
HARDY CYCLAMEN

◑ ◊ Z8–7 H9–7 ‡4in (10cm)
↔4–6in (10–15cm)
Scented flowers bloom in shades of pink or white. Leaf shape ranges from triangular to heart-shaped. Prefers moderately fertile, organic soil.

Schizostylis coccinea
CRIMSON FLAG

☼ ◔ Z7–9 H9–7 ‡24in (60cm) ↔12in (30cm)
Grow this in organic soil in the edge of a small pond. Drought is fatal to these bulbs. Leave undisturbed for several years, since flowering is reduced after division.

Crocus longiflorus
AUTUMN CROCUS

☼ ◊ Z5–8 H8–5 ‡4in (10cm) ↔1¼in (3cm)
The fragrant flowers appear with the leaves in early to midfall. These are best ordered from a specialized bulb nursery, which ships at the correct planting time.

Crinum x *powellii*
POWELL'S SPIDER LILY

☼ ◔ Z7–11 H12–8 ‡5ft (1.5m) ↔12in (30cm)
Grow in fertile, fairly moist soil in the garden or use in containers. In most of this region, bring indoors before danger of hard frost and store over winter like a dahlia.

Gladiolus papilio
HARDY GLADIOLUS

☼ ◑ ◊ Z8–10 H9–1 ‡3ft (1m)
Grow in organic soil with summer moisture. In poor soils, plants will grow well and multiply, but flowering will be poor. Native to South Africa in damp meadows.

Leucojum autumnale
AUTUMN SNOWFLAKE

☼ ◊ Z5–9 H9–1 ‡6in (15cm)

Grows best in soil that is allowed to become dry during summer but needs moisture during the growing season from mid- to late fall. Native to Spain and N. Africa.

Colchicum autumnale
MEADOW SAFFRON, NAKED BOYS

☼ ◊ Z4–9 H9–1 ‡6in (15cm) ↔3in (8cm)

Large, flat leaves appear in spring and die down by midsummer. Flowers emerge in late summer or early fall. There are normally several flowers per bulb.

Colchicum speciosum
SHOWY MEADOW SAFFRON

☼ ◊ Z4–9 H9–1 ‡7in (18cm) ↔4 in (10cm)

This has the largest flowers of the meadow saffrons. Flowers appear in midfall. Do not delay planting, bulbs will start to bloom even on the shelf.

MORE CHOICES

- *Crocus sativus* Z5–8 H8–1
- *Cyclamen pupurascens* Z5–9 H9–4
- *Lycoris squamigera* Z6–11 H12–6
- *Sternbergia clusiana* Z7–10 H10–7

Colchicum x agrippinum
CHECKERED MEADOW SAFFRON

☼ ◊ Z4–9 H9–1 ‡4in (10cm) ↔3in (8cm)

This unusual plant is thought to be a hybrid with the common meadow saffron as one parent. It flowers in midfall, and the narrow leaves grow the following spring.

Colchicum cilicicum
TURKISH MEADOW SAFFRON

☼ ◊ Z4–9 H9–1 ‡4in (10cm) ↔3in (8cm)

Fragrant flowers in mid to late fall are followed by large, dark green leaves that persist over winter and die down the following summer.

Medium to large annuals for shade

Almost every garden has some area of shade that cries out for annuals, because no other group of plants puts on as good or prolonged display. These are the background plants that can be used to hide a concrete wall or the base of a fence, or plant them through fading bulbs to disguise their dying foliage.

Solenostemon scutellarioides 'The Line'
THE LINE COLEUS
☼ ☼ ◗ z11–12 H12–1 ↕↔3ft (1m)
This is the new botanical name for the plant gardeners have long known as Coleus blumei. Easy to grow. Many forms with leaves colored in a multitude of ways.

Impatiens wallerana
IMPATIENS
☼ ☼ ◗ z10–15 H12–1 ↕↔2ft (60cm)
A tender perennial that flowers freely the first year. Plants start blooming in late spring and continue to frost. Many cultivars are available.

Impatiens balsamina
ROSE BALSAM
☼ ◗◗ H12–1 ↕30in (75cm) ↔18in (45cm)
Flowers range from white, pink, and red to lilac as well as bicolors and doubled forms, which have only a light scent. Prefers organic soil.

Cynoglossum amabile 'Firmament'
FIRMAMENT CHINESE FORGET-ME-NOT

☼ ☼ ◊　Z5–8 H8–1　↕16in (40cm) ↔12in (30cm)

A compact, slow-growing annual that can be sown outside or started indoors 6 weeks before last frost. The flowers are fragrant. Removing old flowers promotes rebloom.

Lobelia erinus
BEDDING LOBELIA

☼ ◊　Z2–8 H8–1　↕8in (20cm) ↔6in (15cm)

Flowering continuously from summer through autumn, these trailing perennials (usually grown as annuals) occur in shades of blue, purple, red, and white. Nice in containers, especially hanging baskets.

Mimulus guttatus
LARGE MONKEY FLOWER

Ⓝ ☼ ☼ ●　Z6–9 H9–6　↕12in (30cm) ↔20–48in (50–120cm)

An upright perennial often grown as an annual. Spreads easily by rooting at the leaf joints. Flowers often spotted or marked with red inside the throat.

Torenia fournieri
WISHBONE FLOWER

☼ ◊　Z12–13 H6–1　↕12in (30cm) ↔9in (23cm)

A slow-growing annual. Very fine seed that needs to be sown about 10 weeks before planting time. Should not be allowed to dry out once planted.

Mimulus lewisii
PINK MONKEY FLOWER

Ⓝ ☼ ◊　Z5–8 H8–5　↕24in (60cm) ↔18in (45cm)

Vigorous, spreading plant blooms spring into summer. Will self sow. Prefers fertile, organic soil. Can tolerate standing water levels up to 3in (8cm).

MORE CHOICES

- *Blechnum brasiliense* Z11–11 H12–10
- *Cynoglossum amabile* Z5–8 H8–1
- *Helichrysum petiolare* 'Limelight' Z10–11 H12–1
- *Lobelia erinus* Z2–8 H8–1
- *Mirabilis jalapa* Z11–15 H12–9
- *Strobilanthes dyerianus* Z11–12 H12–1

Asplenium bulbiferum
HEN-AND-CHICKEN FERN

☼ ◊　Z9–11 H12–8　↕↔4ft (1.2m)

An unusual, tender, perennial fern that grows little plantlets on the top of the fronds. These drop off and grow on their own. Winter indoors in good light.

Fuchsia cultivars
LADY'S EARDROPS

☼ ◊　Z9–11 H12–9　↕10ft (3m) ↔6ft (2m)

Bears flowers throughout summer in cooler areas in a wide range of colors and flower shapes, from delicate singles to voluptuous doubles.

HERBACEOUS PLANTS

Tropical perennials grown as annuals

Plant these beside a shady path to hide the bare spots where early spring bulbs like snowdrops have died down. In deep shade, use varieties with white or pale colored flowers, which will stand out better. Try to change the species you choose each year to avoid a buildup of pests and diseases.

Canna x *generalis* 'Pretoria'
PRETORIA CANNA

☼ ◊ z7–11 H12–7 ↕6ft (1.8m) ↔20in (50cm)
This is one of the modern hybrid cannas with colorful foliage and bright flowers. Other varieties have blooms of yellow, red, and pink, or purple-red foliage.

Cyathea cooperi
COOPER'S TREE FERN

☼ ◑ ◊◔ z11–12 H12–10 ↕15ft (5m) ↔12ft (4m)
A fast-growing tree fern that adds a tropical look to the garden. Best grown in a large container so it can be brought inside easily, long before any danger of frost.

Abutilon pictum 'Thompsonii'
THOMPSON'S FLOWERING MAPLE

☼ ◊ z8–10 H12–8 ↕↔15ft (5m)
This can be grown as a shrub or be trained to a single stem like a small tree. Bring indoors before frost and cut back hard. Keep almost dry over winter.

Caladium bicolor 'Pink Beauty'
PINK BEAUTY ANGEL WINGS
☼ ☼ ◗ ⊡ Z15–15 H12–4 ↕↔24in (60cm)
This is one of several hybrids with leaves mottled with maroon, red, pink, or white. Grow in a woodland soil and store at 55°F (13°C) overwinter.

Colocasia esculenta 'Fontanesii'
VIOLET-STEM TARO
☼ ● Z9–11 H12–8 ↕3ft (1m) ↔2ft (60cm)
Where these plants get enough heat, they produce large flowers resembling callas. Overwinter tubers in a dry, frost-free location. Native to tropical E. Asia.

Colocasia esculenta 'Illustris'
IMPERIAL TARO
☼ ◗● ⊡ Z8–11 H12–8 ↕5ft (1.5m) ↔24in (60cm)
Grown as a staple food in tropical countries, the two varieties shown here are more decorative with colored stems and veins. Grow in slightly acidic soil.

MORE CHOICES

- *Alocasia macrorrhiza* Z13–15 H12–10
- *Begonia rex* Z13–15 H12–1
- *Canna* 'Stuttgart' Z7–11 H12–7
- *Cyathea cooperi* Z11–12 H12–10
- *Setaria palmifolia* 'Variegata' Z9–11 H12–9

Begonia 'Non-Stop Red'
NON-STOP RED TUBEROUS BEGONIA
☼ ◗ H7–1 ↕↔12in (30cm)
Can be grown from seed, but takes a long time to make a tuber large enough to save. Allow plants to become frosted in fall to seal the stems, then store frost-free.

Xanthosoma sagittifolium
ARROWHEAD TARO
Ⓝ ☼ ◗ ⊡ Z14–15 H12–10 ↕↔3ft (1m)
Native to tropical U.S., Central and South America, the leaves are a source of food. In the garden, grow in an acidic, organic soil and over-winter indoors.

Impatiens balsamina
ROSE BALSAM, TOUCH-ME-NOT
☼ ◗● H12–1 ↕30in (75cm) ↔18in (45cm)
Not as well known as the common patience-plants, these have a more upright habit and are fairly easy to grow from seed. There are also double-flowered forms.

HERBACEOUS PLANTS

Large annuals or tropicals with bold foliage

Add a touch of the exotic with these striking plants. Use them to fill bare spots at the back of a border, in large planters on the patio, or even as individual specimen plants, as you would use trees and shrubs. Some are strictly annual, but others can be dug in fall and stored in a frost-free place (such as a basement) to grow again the following year.

Canna 'Australia'
AUSTRALIA CANNA
☼ ◊ z7–11 H12–7 ‡5ft (1.5m) ↔20in (50cm)
Frost-tender, these need to be started indoors in the North but can be planted directly into the garden where the growing season is longer. Lift in fall before hard frost.

Canna x generalis 'Pretoria'
PRETORIA CANNA
☼ ◊ z7–11 H12–7 ‡6ft (1.8m) ↔20in (50cm)
One of the most striking of modern canna hybrids, which need to be lifted in fall. Do not wash soil off the rhizomes, store in just-moist peat, then overwinter in a cool, frost-free place at about 45°F (7°C).

MORE CHOICES

- *Alpinia zerumbet* 'Variegata' z14–15 H12–10
- *Colocasia esculenta* 'Fontanesii' z9–11 H12–10
- *Hibiscus acetosella* 'Red Shield' z10–11 H12–1
- *Musa zebrina* z11–11 H12–6
- *Ricinus communis* 'Zanzibar' z11–14 H12–1
- *Tibouchina grandifolia* z13–15 H12–10
- *Xanthosoma sagittifolium* z14–15 H12–10

Canna indica 'Phaison'
PHAISON CANNA
☼ ◊ z7–11 H12–7 ‡7ft (2.1m) ↔4ft (1.2m)
Modern canna hybrids come in a wide range of colors; pink, red, yellow, orange, and bitone. Foliage may be bright green, shades of red, or variously striped.

Ricinus communis
CASTOR BEAN

☼ ◊ Z11–14 H12–1 ‡6ft (1.8m) ↔3ft (1m)

Easy to grow from seed, these make an imposing statement and can grow into a large shrub in a single season if given enough heat and moisture. Seeds are poisonous and should be removed where young children are present.

Ensete ventricosum 'Maurelii'
ABYSSINIAN BANANA

☼ ◑ ◊ Z10–12 H12–10 ‡20ft (6m) ↔15ft (5m)

Plant this in an organic soil in the open ground or in a large container. In good summers, 3ft (1m) long spikes of white flowers may be produced. Bring indoors before frost in fall and overwinter in a frost-free place..

Phormium tenax 'Bronze Baby'
NEW ZEALAND FLAX

☼ ◑ Z9–11 H12–6 ‡↔32in (80cm)

Related to *Agave*, this forms a stiff, upright clump, with leaves that curl downwardsat their tips. There are other cultivars with leaves striped pink or orange.

Gunnera manicata
GIANT RHUBARB

☼ ◑ ● Z7–11 H12–7 ‡8ft (2.5m) ↔10ft (3m)

Plant in organic soil in a location that will be protected from strong winds. This may survive a mild winter, especially if the crown is protected with mulch.

Musa basjoo
JAPANESE BANANA

☼ ◊ Z9–11 H12–1 ‡15ft (5m) ↔12ft (4m)

The large leaves are easily damaged, so plant in a sheltered site in an organic soil. Creamy white flowers give rise to inedible bananas. Good container plant.

Ricinus communis 'Carmencita'
RED CASTOR BEAN

☼ ◊ Z9–11 H12–1 ‡6ft (1.8m) ↔3ft (1m)

This is an imposing, tender shrub that can be grown from seed each spring. The female flowers are bright red, the male ones an off-white. May self-seed.

Dahlia 'Bishop of Llandaff'
BISHOP OF LLANDAFF DAHLIA

☼ ◊ Z9–11 H12–5 ‡3ft (1m) ↔18in (45cm)

A very old variety that is still grown for its dark foliage. Lift in fall, turn upside down to drain the stems, allow to air-dry, and overwinter at about 40°F (4°C).

HERBACEOUS PLANTS

Tender annuals

While not as eye-catching as the plants on the previous page, these are still sufficiently uncommon to cause comment. They are no more difficult to grow than geraniums or petunias but are ideally suited for planters and raised beds. Some can be brought inside in fall and grown as houseplants over winter, and a few can be stored dry.

Nelumbo nucifera 'Rosea Plena'
DOUBLE PINK SACRED LOTUS
☼ ● Z4–11 H12–3 ‡4–5ft (1.2–1.5m) ↔indefinite
An attractive addition to the water garden, this is one of several color forms of this species. It is a vigorous plant and will spread if not contained. Plant out when water is at 65°F (18°C).

Nelumbo nucifera
SACRED LOTUS
☼ ● Z4–11 H12–3 ‡3–5ft (1–1.5m) ↔4 (1.2m)
A very rampant grower, this needs to be planted in a container to prevent it from spreading. It needs at least 12in (30cm) of water above soil level to grow well.

Salvia discolor
TWO-COLOR SAGE
☼ ☼ ● Z9–11 H12–3 ‡18in (45cm) ↔12in (30cm)
An upright plant with fragrant foliage covered with white hairs on the underside. The stems are also woolly. Flowers are in long spikes in late summer.

Plectranthus argentatus
SILVER PLECTRANTHUS

☀ ◊ H12–1 ↕↔3ft (1m)

A spreading, trailing plant that adds contrast to a planter or hanging basket. Roots easily and grows quickly. Leaves have a distinctive odor when touched.

MORE CHOICES

- *Alocascia macrorrhiza.* z13–15 H12–10
- *Begonia rex* z13–15 H12–1
- *Ipomoea batatas* 'Margeurite' z9–15 H12–1
- *Manihot esculenta* 'Variegata' z13–15 H12–1
- *Melianthus major* z8–11 H12–8
- *Neoregelia carolinae* f. tricolor. z13–15 H12–1
- *Strobilanthes dyeranus* z11–12 H12–1

Solanum quitoense
NARANJILLA

☀ ☀ ◊ z9–10 H10–9 ↕4 ft (1.2m) ↔3ft (1m)

A very thorny, dramatic tomato relative native to South America. It must be grown in extremely well-drained soil. The edible fruit are bright orange.

Solenostemon scutellarioides 'The Line'
THE LINE COLEUS

☀ ☀ ◊ z11–12 H12–1 ↕2ft (60cm) ↔3ft (1m)

This is just one of a multitude of coleus cultivars with leaves splashed and marked with different shades. Good houseplants for a sunny windowsill in winter.

Neoregelia carolinae 'Tricolor'
BLUSHING BROMELIAD

☀ ◊ z13–15 H12–1 ↕12in (30cm) ↔24in (60cm)

Although the flowers are insignificant, the color change that suffuses the center of the leaves before flowering is striking. Bring indoors before any danger of frost.

Neoregelia concentrica
CONCENTRIC BROMELIAD

☀ ◊ z13–15 H12–1 ↕12in (30cm) ↔28in (70cm)

Leaves can be up to 12in (30cm) long are edged with black spines. The center of the plant turns purple just before flowering and retains the color for several months.

Ipomoea batatas 'Blackie'
BLACKIE SWEET POTATO

☀ ◊ z11–12 H12–1 ↕20ft (6m)

A tender climber that is often used as a trailing plant for containers and hanging baskets. Purple flowers may be produced in warmer parts of the Northeast.

HERBACEOUS PLANTS

Annual accent plants for the border

New varieties of annuals are introduces every year, but many of the old established ones are still worth growing. Use the ones illustrated here to paint colorful pictures. Taller, upright species can be used in the center of a container or be dotted through a flat planting to give contrast. Those with a spreading habit will trail attractively when grown in planters.

Pentas lanceolata
EGYPTIAN STARCLUSTER
☼ ◊ Z14–15 H12–10 ↕6ft (2m) ↔3ft (1m)
A tender, woody tropical often grown as a houseplant. Needs fertile soil and should be brought indoors before any danger of frost. Available in a range of colors.

Senecio confusus
CLIMBING RAGWORT
☼ ◊ Z13–15 H12–10 ↕20ft (6m)
A bushy, twining, tender climber that can clothe a support and give height to a border. Fragrant flowers turn red with age. Native from Mexico to Honduras.

Leonotis leonurus
LION'S EARS
☼ ◊ Z12–15 H12–6 ↕6ft (2m) ↔3ft (1m)
An upright, South African shrub grown as an annual. Cut back to make it denser. The whorls of two-lipped flowers open in late summer and last until frost.

MORE CHOICES

- *Amaranthus tricolor* Cultivars H12–5
- *Fuchsia* 'Gartenmeister Bonstedt' Z9–11 H12–9
- *Helichrysum sp.* Z7–11 H9–3
- *Lantana camara* Z11–11 H12–1
- *Mirabilis jalapa* Z11–15 H12–9
- *Nicotiana sylvestris* Z10–11 H12–1

Salvia guaranitica 'Black and Blue'
BLACK AND BLUE SAGE
☼ ☼ ◊ Z8–11 H12–8 ↕8ft (2.5m) ↔24in (60cm)
A tender, slightly shrubby perennial native to Brazil, sometimes available with annual plants at nurseries. Flowers from late summer until frost.

Melampodium paludosum
AFRICAN ZINNIA
☼ ☼ ◊ Z11–12 H12–1 ↕6in (15cm) ↔8in (20cm)
A mound-shaped plant that tolerates heat, humidity, and drought. Easy to grow from seed sown 6 weeks before the last frost date. Makes a good container plant.

Calibrachoa 'Brilliant Cherry'
BRILLIANT CHERRY MILLION BELLS
☼ ◊◊ Z8–15 H12–1 ↕4in (10cm) ↔12in (30cm)
Resembles a small-flowered petunia. Mounded plants cover themselves in flowers all summer. Ideal for containers and hanging baskets, as well as the border.

Phygelius aequalis cultivars
CAPE FUCHSIA
☼ ◊ Z7–9 H9–7 ↕↔3ft (1m)
Bushy, upright plants that attract hummingbirds. They can be grown anew each spring, or overwintered on a sunny windowsill. Native to South Africa.

Hebe x franciscana 'Variegata'
VARIEGATED FRANCISCAN HEBE
☼ ☼ ◊ Z9–10 H10–9 ↕↔2–4ft (60–120cm)
A rounded shrub that is grown from cuttings and must be overwintered indoors. It makes a good seasonal border plant, flowering freely from midsummer onward.

MORE CHOICES
- *Nierembergia sp.* Z7–11 H12–7
- *Pelargonium sp.* Z11–12 H12–1
- *Pyrola elliptica* Z7–9 H9–7
- *Tolmiea menziesii* Z6–9 H9–6
- *Salpiglossis sinuata* Z10–11 H12–1
- *Salvia* 'Indigo Spires' Z8–11 H12–7
- *Salvia leucantha* Zx9–11 H12–4
- *Salvia vanhouttei* Z9–11 H12–1

Petunia 'Purple Wave'
PURPLE WAVE PETUNIA
☼ ◊ Z9–11 H12–1 ↕18in (45cm) ↔3ft (1m)
A fairly new type of petunia that makes a ground-hugging carpet and thrives in hot conditions. Be sure the vigorous plants don't smother young perennials.

Heliotropium arborescens
COMMON HELIOTROPE
☼ ◊ Z12–15 H12–9 ↕↔18in (45cm)
A very fragrant flower that can be raised from seed or cuttings. 'Marine' is dwarfer, with darker flowers, but little scent. Special selections are grown from cuttings.

Tithonia rotundifolia
MEXICAN SUNFLOWER
☼ ◊ Z10–11 H12–1 ↕6ft (2m) ↔12in (30cm)
A drought-tolerant annual that can be sown directly where it is to flower or be started indoors 8 weeks before last frost date. A good cut flower.

Annual climbers

These fast-growing plants can provide a temporary screen or can be used to cover a trellis while permanent climbers become established. They can also be planted at the top of a retaining wall to trail downward or be used to cover chain-link fencing and turn it into an attractive feature. With the exception of sweet peas, these climbers need to be planted after danger of frost has passed.

Lablab purpurea
HYACINTH BEAN

☼ ◊ Z10–11 H12–1 ‡6–20ft (2–6m)

A vigorous, twining, perennial climber grown as an annual. Fragrant purple flowers from midsummer onward produce pods (edible after careful cooking).

Bougainvillea 'Mauritius'
MAURITIUS BOUGAINVILLEA

☼ ◊ Z13–15 H12–1 ‡↔3ft (1m) as an annual

A perennial, tropical climber, often with thorny branches, that can be wintered indoors. Many named forms with flowers in a wide color range.

Lathyrus odoratus 'Temptation'
TEMPTATION SWEET PEA

☼ ◊ H8–1 ‡6ft (2m) ↔1ft (30cm)

Grown for their fragrance, sweet peas should be picked regularly. Bloom best during cooler weather.. 'Knee-Hi' and 'Jet Set' are bushy and do not climb.

Lathyrus odoratus 'Lady Penny'
LADY PENNY SWEET PEA

☼ ◊ H8–1 ‡6ft (2m) ↔1ft (30cm)

Sow sweet peas in early spring as soon as the soil is dry enough to work. Pinch out the growing tip when 4 leaves have formed. They flower better on sideshoots.

MORE CHOICES

- *Allamanda cathartica* Z14–15 H12–10
- *Ipomoea quamoclit* Z12–13 H12–6
- *Mandevilla* 'Alice du Pont' Z13–15 H12–1
- *Mina lobata* Z13–15 H12–10
- *Passiflora alato-caerulea* Z11–12 H12–7
- *Thunbergia alata* Z11–15 H12–10
- *Tropaeolum peregrinum* Z11–12 H12–1
- *Vigna caracalla* H12–1

Aristolochia gigantea
DUTCHMAN'S PIPE

☼ ◐ ◊ Z12–15 H12–10 ‡30ft (10m)

Provide support for this woody-stemmed climber. Cut back previous season's growth in spring to 2 or 3 nodes. May be affected by spider mite or whitefly.

Passiflora alata
WINGED-STEM PASSIONFLOWER

☼ ◐ ◊ Z7–9 H9–7 ‡20ft (6m)

A tropical perennial that may be grown as an annual. Leaves are light green with toothed margins. Flowers in spring in a conservatory and in summer outdoors.

Passiflora coccinea
RED GRANADILLA

☼ ◐ ◊ Z14–15 H12–10 ‡12ft (4m)

A vigorous climber with slender red stems and lobed leaves covered in red hairs. Flowers, produced from summer to fall, may produce edible fruit .

Ipomoea purpurea
MORNING GLORY

☼ ◊ H12–1 ‡6–10ft (2–3m)

Twining climber that flowers best in poor soil. Sow this in situ, because seedlings resent disturbance. There are many other color forms.

Solanum jasminoides 'Album'
WHITE POTATO VINE

☼ ◊ Z8–10 H10–8 ‡6ft (2m) ↔6in (15cm)

A nontwining vine that can be grown to scramble through other plants or used in containers and baskets. Flowers appear from summer onward.

Solanum jasminoides 'Album Variegatum'
VARIEGATED WHITE POTATO VINE

☼ ◊ Z8–11 H12–8 ‡6ft (2m) ↔6in (15cm)

Also nontwining, this is slower-growing than the plain-leaved variety. It makes a good houseplant for winter if kept on a sunny window ledge.

Tender succulents for containers or the garden

Many of the succulent plants cultivated indoors during winter will benefit from being outdoors during summer. Because light intensity is much stronger and temperatures fluctuate more, plants should be acclimatized gradually to outside conditions to avoid leaf scorch or drop. In fall, reverse this process well before there is any danger of frost.

Echeveria pilosa
HAIRY ECHEVERIA

☼ ◊ Z12–15 H12–10 ‡4in (10cm) ↔16in (40cm)
A short-stemmed, more or less unbranched plant. Rosettes are covered in short white hairs. Orange and yellow flowers are borne in summer.

Echeveria elegans
MEXICAN GEM

☼ ◊ Z12–15 H12–10 ‡2in (5cm) ↔20 in (50cm)
A fast-growing species that produces many offsets and quickly forms a solid mat. The rosettes become pinkish in the sun and may have a red margin.

Graptopetalum paraguayense
GHOST PLANT, MOTHER OF PEARL

☼ ◐ ◊ Z12–15 H12–10 ‡8in (20cm) ↔indefinite
A prostrate perennial with rosettes up to 6in (15cm) in diameter. Leaves may be tinged pink. Star-shaped white flowers with red spots in late winter.

Sedum nussbaumeranum
GOLDEN STONECROP

☼ ◊ Z4–9 H9–1 ‡9in (23cm) ↔indefinite
Upright at first, the stems become lax later and form a spreading plant. They root readily. In shade the foliage is a greenish yellow. White flowers appear in spring.

Aeonium arboreum 'Zwartkop'
BLACK AEONIUM

☀ ◊ Z9–11 H9–4 ‡↔6ft (2m)

An upright, shrubby succulent that keeps its dark color providing it is in bright light. Long stems of starlike, bright yellow flowers appear in spring.

Opuntia robusta
STOUT PRICKLY PEAR

☀ ◊ Z12–15 H12–10 ‡↔6ft (2m)

A shrubby or treelike cactus with several brown, white, or yellow spines in each of the barbed spine clusters. It will tolerate light freezing for brief periods.

MORE CHOICES

- *Agave americana* 'Mediopicta'
  Z12–15 H12–10
- *Beschorneria yuccoides* Z12–15 H12–10
- *Crassula ovata* Z12–15 H12–10
- *Delosperma cooperi* Z8–10 H10–8
- *Pedilanthus tithymaloides* Z11–11 H12–1
- *Sedum morganianum* Z11–12 H12–1
- *Sanseveria trifasciata* 'Laurentii'
  Z14–15 H12–10
- *Senecio stapeliiformis* Z13–15 H12–10

Opuntia argentina
ARGENTINA PRICKLY PEAR

☀ ◊ Z13–15 H12–10 ‡50ft (15m) ↔10ft (3m)

A treelike cactus, with clusters of barbed brown spines, and a single long spine in the center. The summer flowers produce edible, spineless fruits.

Opuntia microdasys var. albispina
HONEY BUNNY, POLKA-DOT CACTUS

☀ ◊ Z13–15 H12–10 ‡↔16–24in (40–60cm)

Probably the most widely grown cactus indoors, this has barbed spines that detach easily but are almost impossible to remove from the skin.

Aloe aristata
TORCH PLANT, LACE ALOE

☀ ◊ Z13–15 H12–10 ‡5in (13cm) ↔indefinite

The terminal spines are soft and do not cause injury. In winter, the leaves curl toward the center, forming a ball. Red flowers in summer on 3ft (1m) stems.

Agave americana 'Marginata'
YELLOW-EDGED CENTURY PLANT

Ⓝ ☀ ◊ Z12–15 H12–10 ‡6ft (2m) ↔10ft (3m)

The leaves have sharply-pointed tips and backward-pointing spines on the edges. New foliage is edged with yellow that fades to white.

HERBACEOUS PLANTS

Ornamental herbs & vegetables

While these can be combined to give a colorful potager garden in the French style, they are frequently used to mix through existing perennial or annual plantings, as in the old English cottage gardens. With care, leaves or stems can be cut from most of the plants shown here without spoiling their decorative effect.

Allium schubertii
SCHUBERT'S FLOWERING ONION
☼ ◊ Z4–10 H10–1 ‡24in (60cm) ↔8in (20cm)
The individual flower stalks are of different lengths, rather than uniform. The strap-shaped basal leaves die down before the flowers open in early summer.

Foeniculum vulgare 'Purpureum'
PURPLE FENNEL
☼ ◊ Z6–9 H9–6 ‡6ft (1.8m) ↔18in (45cm)
Young foliage is a dull purple, becoming a blue-green as it matures This perennial can be used in cooking, like the regular green fennel. It may seed freely.

Cynara cardunculus
CARDOON
☼ ◊ Z7–9 H9–7 ‡6ft (2m) ↔3ft (1m)
Purple flowerheads bloom from early summer to early fall. A clump-forming perennial that is also an old vegetable related to the artichoke .

Melissa officinalis
LEMON BALM
☼ ◊ Z4–9 H12–1 ‡3ft (1m) ↔18in (45cm)
A bushy perennial with a pronounced lemon taste and smell. Used in cooking or for beverages. It may be dried for winter use. The oil extracted from the leaves is used in perfumes and soaps.

Origanum laevigatum 'Herrenhausen'
HERRENHAUSEN OREGANO
☼ ◊ Z7–11 H12–1 ‡30in (75cm) ↔18in (45cm)
A decorative oregano, not the species used in cooking. Slightly woody perennial that makes a bushy plant with flowers all summer. Cut back by half in spring.

Thymus vulgaris
COMMON THYME
☼ ◊ Z4–9 H9–1 ‡12in (30cm) ↔16in (40cm)
This bushy, cushion-forming subshrub produces purple or white flowers in spring and early summer. The most widely grown thyme for culinary use.

Zea mays
CORN
Ⓝ ☼ ◊ H12–1 ‡to 12ft (4m) ↔24in (60cm)
In addition to the varieties grown for eating, there are several ornamental varieties with colorful foliage. Other selections have multicolored kernels.

Capsicum annuum cultivars
SWEET PEPPER

☼ ◊ ◐ z9–11 H12–1 ‡↔2ft (60cm)

Sweet peppers come in a variety of sizes and shapes. White flowers are followed by green fruit that turn shades of red, yelow, orange, purple, and ivory. Annual.

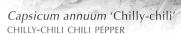

Capsicum annuum 'Chilly-chili'
CHILLY-CHILI CHILI PEPPER

☼ ◊ ◐ z9–15 H12–1 ‡↔ 1ft (30cm)

Tolerant of high heat, peppers should not be planted out until the soil is warm, or flower buds may abort. The hot flavor comes from the white pith and seeds.

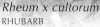

Rheum x cultorum
RHUBARB

☼ ☼ ◊ z3–9 H9–1 ‡5ft (1.5m) ↔3ft (1m)

In addition to its use in pies and preserves, rhubarb makes a very ornamental border plant with large leaves and towering spikes of creamy white flowers.

Teucrium fruticans
TREE GERMANDER

☼ ◊ z5–9 H9–5 ‡3ft (1m) ↔12ft (4m)

A bushy subshrub with arching branches and aromatic leaves. The closely related Wall Germander (*T. chamaedrys*) makes a good low, tightly clipped hedge.

MORE CHOICES

- *Angelica gigas* z4–9 H8–2
- *Artemisia dracunculus* z3–7 H7–1
- *Asparagus officinalis* 'Jersey Knight' z4–8 H8–1
- *Brassica oleracea* 'Osaka' z7–11 H6–1
- *Levisticum officinale* z4–8 H8–1
- *Origanum dictamnus* z8–11 H12–8
- *Rosmarinus officinalis* z8–11 H12–8
- *Saccharum* 'Pele's Smoke' z9–11 H12–9
- *Salvia officinalis* 'Tricolor' z4–10 H12–1
- *Tulbaghia violacea* 'Silver Lace' z7–10 H10–7
- *Thymus x citriodorus* 'Aureus' z6–9 H9–5

Origanum 'Kent Beauty'
KENT BEAUTY OREGANO

☼ ◊ z5–8 H8–5 ‡4in (10cm) ↔8in (20cm)

A trailing perennial that is well suited to growing over a low wall or on a rock garden. It will not survive in wet soil. An ornamental variety, not culinary.

Ipomoea batatas 'Blackie'
BLACKIE SWEET POTATO

☼ ◊ z11–12 H12–1 ‡20ft (6m)

A tender tropical plant, useful for large hanging baskets and containers, where it can trail. Store the tubers over winter like dahlias.

PART III

GARDENING TECHNIQUES

including Selecting Plants, Planting, Pruning, and Propagation

Once you've planned your SMARTGARDEN™ and have determined what you'd like to grow, it's time to put on the gardening gloves. Here are pointers on selecting healthy plants and detecting potentially unhealthy ones; planting them correctly; pruning trees, shrubs, and other woody plants; and propagating new plants by various methods.

SELECTING PLANTS

Choosing plants at the nursery or garden center does not need to be a long, complicated process: basically, look for plants that appear healthy and avoid extremes, such as too much top-growth compared to the root ball, or too little foliage on stems that barely support the leaves. Spend more time on choosing longer-lived and more expensive trees and shrubs than on herbaceous plants.

CHOOSING A TREE

Container-grown tree

Before buying one of these, remove it from its container to examine the roots. Do not buy a potbound tree (with a mass of congested roots) or one with thick roots protruding from the holes.

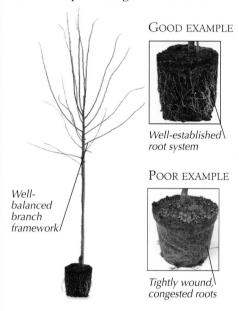

GOOD EXAMPLE

Well-established root system

POOR EXAMPLE

Well-balanced branch framework

Tightly wound, congested roots

Bare-root tree

These have virtually no soil around the roots. Examine the roots to check that they are not damaged or diseased and that there is no sign of dryness that may have been caused by exposure to air or sunlight.

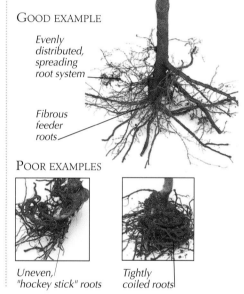

GOOD EXAMPLE

Evenly distributed, spreading root system

Fibrous feeder roots

POOR EXAMPLES

Uneven, "hockey stick" roots

Tightly coiled roots

Balled-and-burlapped tree

Buy and plant a balled-and-burlapped tree when it is dormant in fall or early spring, following the same basic examination criteria as for both container-grown and bare-root trees.

GOOD EXAMPLE

X CUPRESSOCYPARIS LEYLANDII

Firm root ball with the covering intact

SELECTING A CONTAINER-GROWN SHRUB

Look through the drainage holes (or carefully slide the shrub out of its container) to check for a well-developed root system. If present, the shrub is probably container-grown and is not containerized (meaning it was recently removed from the open ground and put into a container). The roots should have healthy, white tips. Reject plants with poorly developed root systems, with coiled roots or root balls, or with roots protruding from the container, since these rarely establish or grow well.

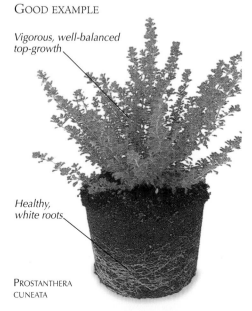

GOOD EXAMPLE

Vigorous, well-balanced top-growth

Healthy, white roots

PROSTANTHERA CUNEATA

POOR EXAMPLE

Twiggy, sparse stems showing little new growth

Potbound roots

Pruning congested roots

Tease out potbound roots, and cut back any that are very long and damaged.

SELECTING CLIMBERS

Climbing plants are usually sold container-grown, although a few may be sold bare-root. Choose a healthy-looking plant with a well-balanced framework of strong shoots, and reject any that show signs of pest infestation or disease. For potgrown plants, turn the pot over and check that the tips of the young roots are just showing. If so, the plant is well rooted. Reject potbound plants – those that have tightly coiled roots or a mass of roots protruding through the drainage holes. Bare-root plants should have plenty of healthy, well-developed fibrous roots that are in proportion to the amount of top-growth.

GOOD EXAMPLE

Vigorous, sturdy stems

Healthy buds

LONICERA

POOR EXAMPLES

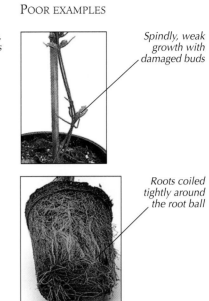

Spindly, weak growth with damaged buds

Roots coiled tightly around the root ball

SELECTING HEALTHY ROSES

Bare-root bush rose

Examine the plant carefully: if the stems appear dried out (the bark will be shriveled), or buds have started growing prematurely (producing blanched, thin shoots), do not buy it.

GOOD EXAMPLE

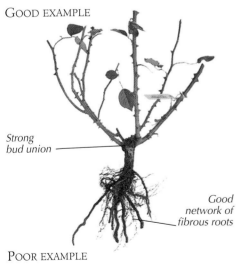

Strong bud union

Good network of fibrous roots

POOR EXAMPLE

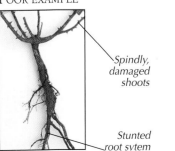

Spindly, damaged shoots

Stunted root sytem

Container-grown rose

Check that the plant has not been recently potted up: hold the plant by its main shoot and gently shake it. If it does not move around in the soil mix, it is well established and a good buy.

GOOD EXAMPLE

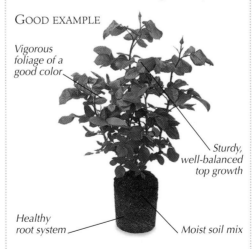

Vigorous foliage of a good color

Sturdy, well-balanced top growth

Healthy root system

Moist soil mix

POOR EXAMPLE

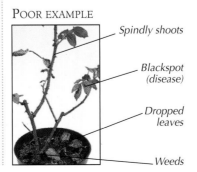

Spindly shoots

Blackspot (disease)

Dropped leaves

Weeds

Standard rose

Choose a standard rose with a balanced head of shoots, since it is likely to be viewed from all sides. A straight main stem is best, although a slightly crooked stem is acceptable.

GOOD EXAMPLE

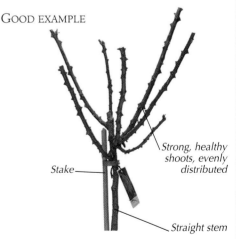

Strong, healthy shoots, evenly distributed

Stake

Straight stem

POOR EXAMPLE

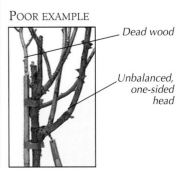

Dead wood

Unbalanced, one-sided head

CHOOSING HERBACEOUS PLANTS

Most herbaceous plants are sold container-grown, but bare-root plants are also sometimes available from fall to early spring, when they are dormant. If buying herbaceous plants at the beginning of the growing season, check that there are strong, emerging shoots. Plants that have a few fat, healthy-looking buds are better than those that have a large number of weaker ones.

GOOD EXAMPLE

IMPATIENS CULTIVAR

Bushy, sturdy growth

Healthy buds developing

Moist soil mix

GOOD EXAMPLE

Strong, healthy top growth

Moist soil mix

Established, vigorous roots

LUPINE

POOR EXAMPLES

Weak and woody top-growth

Dry soil mix

Underdeveloped root system

Leggy, bare stems

Dead leaves

Moss and weeds growing on soil mix

Potbound roots

Yellowing, discolored leaves

SELECTING BULBS, CORMS, TUBERS, AND SIMILAR PLANTS

Most bulbs are sold in a dry state during their dormant period. Buy these as early as possible before they start into growth; most daffodils, for example, normally start producing roots in late summer, and most other spring-flowering bulbs will begin to grow by early fall. Fall-flowering crocuses and *Colchicum* species and hybrids especially benefit from early planting: specialized nurseries sell them in midsummer. All fall-flowering bulbs are best bought and planted by late summer. Summer-flowering bulbs (such as *Gladiolus*, *Dahlia*, and *Canna*) are available for purchase in spring.

Bulbs tend to deteriorate if kept dry too long; they will have a shorter growing period and take some time to recover and flower satisfactorily, so buy and plant them as soon as they are available. Do not buy or plant any bulbs that are mushy or slimy, or any that feel much lighter than a bulb of similar size of the same kind (they are probably dried up and dead).

GOOD EXAMPLES

DAFFODIL (SINGLE-NOSED)   DAFFODIL (TWIN-NOSED)

Fresh, plump tubers

Moist peat or similar packing

ERYTHRONIUM OREGONUM

POOR EXAMPLES

Diseased tissue

Damaged outer scales

No tunic (covering)

Deterioration of bulb tissue

Small nose

Offset too small to flower

CORYDALIS SOLIDA

Distinct growing point on corm

SELECTING PLANTS FOR THE WATER GARDEN

When selecting aquatic plants at the nursery or garden center, look for clean, fresh-looking, and vigorous specimens, growing in tanks that are free from algae and duckweed (*Wolffia*). Check that the undersides of the leaves are free from jellylike deposits of snail eggs and that there are no strands of blanketweed in the foliage. Mail-order plants should appear plump and green; if they look weak and limp, they are unlikely to grow well. If buying plants by mail order, use a specialized supplier.

Marginal plant

GOOD EXAMPLE

Strong flowering stem

Healthy leaves

CALTHA PALUSTRIS

POOR EXAMPLE

Weak growth

Weed-infested soil mix

Surface floater

GOOD EXAMPLE

Young, fresh growth

STRATIOTES ALOIDES

POOR EXAMPLE

Damaged growth

Old, rotting foliage

SELECTING CACTI AND OTHER SUCCULENTS

When buying cacti and other succulents, choose healthy, pest- and disease-free, unblemished plants that show strong new growth (unless you are buying the plants when they are dormant) or have flower buds forming. Do not buy damaged or even slightly shriveled specimens, or any with dull, dry, or limp segments. Also reject plants that have outgrown their pots.

GOOD EXAMPLE

Healthy-looking body

New buds forming

REBUTIA SPECIES

POOR EXAMPLE

Damaged growth

GOOD EXAMPLE

Plump, fleshy leaves

Sturdy stem

CRASSULA OVATA

POOR EXAMPLE

Shriveled and cut leaves

PLANTING

When selecting and planting trees, shrubs, and woody climbers, it is vital to take account of the general weather pattern of your area as well as your garden's individual microclimate, because these factors will determine whether a given plant is hardy and has a reasonable chance of surviving in your garden. Proper planting and aftercare will increase the likelihood of survival.

PLANTING A CONTAINER-GROWN TREE

First, thoroughly moisten the soil mix in the container – if it is very dry, stand the container in water for half an hour or until the soil mix is moist throughout (the bubbles will stop rising). Then remove the container, cutting it away if necessary, taking care not to damage the roots excessively. Gently tease out the roots with your fingers or a hand fork (or with pruners, if the roots are thickly congested) to encourage them to grow into the surrounding soil; this is essential with a potbound plant. If there are any broken or damaged roots, trim them back with pruners. It is important to check that the planting depth is correct. If a tree is planted too deeply, its roots may not receive enough oxygen and the tree may grow more slowly or even die; if planted too shallowly, the roots may dry out.

Mark out the area of the hole to be dug – about 3 or 4 times the diameter of the tree's root ball. Remove any grass or weeds, then dig out the hole to about 1½ times the depth of the root ball.

2 Scarify the sides and bottom of the hole with a fork. There is no need to improve the soil unless the quality is very poor, such as dense, heavy clay or very infertile sand.

3 Drive a stake into the hole, just off center and on the windward side. Lay the tree on its side and slide it out of the pot. Gently tease out the roots without breaking up the root ball.

4 Hold the tree next to the stake and spread out roots. Lay a stake across the hole to check the planting depth. Adjust by adding or removing soil. Plant tree at same depth it was in its container.

5 Backfill around the tree with more topsoil, working it down the root ball, and then gently firm the soil. Build up soil around the hole to form a watering ring.

6 Cut back damaged stems, long sideshoots, and weaker, lower branches (see inset). Apply a mulch 2–3in (5–7cm) deep around the area.

PLANTING A CONTAINER-GROWN SHRUB

Fall and spring are the optimum times for planting container-grown and containerized shrubs. Planting in fall allows the roots to establish while the ground is still warm, so the shrub should be growing vigorously before hot, dry weather the next summer. In some areas, planting can be carried out during mild weather in winter, but not when the ground is very cold or frozen. Roots will not begin growth in very cold soil, and there is a risk that they may freeze. A possible disadvantage to spring planting is that top-growth is likely to develop before the roots establish adequately and, if there is a long spell of hot, dry weather, watering may be required to help the plants survive.

Using a watering ring

To help retain water, create a shallow depression and a low wall of soil around the shrub. Cover the area with mulch, then allow the ring to settle on its own.

Placing one hand on top of the soil mix and around the shrub to support it, carefully ease the plant out of its container. Place the shrub in the prepared hole.

Lay a stake alongside to check that the soil level is the same as before. If necessary, adjust the planting depth by adding or removing topsoil beneath the shrub.

Backfill around the shrub with the removed soil, firming in stages to prevent air pockets from forming. Once the hole has been filled with soil, carefully firm around the shrub with your heel or hands.

Prune any diseased, damaged, or weak wood, and cut back any inward-growing or crossing stems to an outward-growing shoot or bud.

TRANSPLANTING A SHRUB

Careful selection and siting of a shrub should make transplanting unnecessary, although sometimes it may be desirable or unavoidable. In general, the younger the shrub, the more likely it is to reestablish after being moved. Most young shrubs may be lifted bare-root when dormant. Established shrubs that have large root systems should be lifted with a ball of soil around the roots before being moved. Spring (before bud break) and mid- to late fall are the best times to do this.

Using a spade, mark out a circle around the extent of the shrub's branches (here *Ilex aquifolium* 'Golden Milkboy'). Tie in (or prune off) any trailing stems, or wrap the shrub in burlap, to prevent the stems from being damaged. Dig a circular trench around the plant.

Use a fork to loosen the soil around the root ball. Continue to carefully fork away soil from around the shrub's root ball to reduce its size and weight.

Undercut the root ball with a spade, cutting through woody roots if necessary to separate them from the surrounding soil.

Pull some burlap up around the root ball and tie it securely. Remove the shrub from its hole, then transport it to its new position.

Remove or untie the burlap when replanting. Plant with the soil mark at the same level as before. Firm, water well, and mulch.

PLANTING A CLIMBER AGAINST A WALL

Before removing the plant from its pot, make sure that the soil mix is moist. Water the plant well, so that the root ball is thoroughly wet, and then allow it to drain for at least an hour. Remove the surface layer of soil mix to eliminate weeds, and then invert the pot, taking care to support the plant as it slides out. If the roots have begun to curl around inside the pot, gently tease them out. Any dead, damaged, or protruding roots should be cut back to the perimeter of the root ball. Position the plant so that the top of the root ball is just level with the surrounding soil. It is advisable to plant clematis more deeply, however. Climbers that have been grafted (as is the case with most wisterias) should be planted with the graft union 2½in (6cm) below soil level to encourage rooting of the cultivar.

1 Attach a support 12in (30cm) above the soil and 2in (5cm) from the wall. Dig a hole 18in (45cm) from the wall. Loosen the soil at the base and add compost.

2 Soak the climbers root ball well. Position it in the hole at a 45° angle, placing a stake across to check the planting level. Spread the roots away from the wall.

3 Fill in around the plant and firm and level the soil, ensuring that no air pockets remain between the roots and that the plant is fully supported.

4 Untie the stems from the central stake and select 4 or 5 strong shoots. Insert a stake for each shoot and attach it to the lowest wire. Tie in the shoots.

5 Using pruners, trim back any weak, damaged, or wayward shoots to the central stem. This establishes the initial framework for the climber.

6 Water the plant thoroughly (here *Jasminum mesnyi*). Cover the surrounding soil with a deep mulch to retain moisture and discourage weeds.

PLANTING A BARE-ROOT ROSE

Bare-root roses are best planted just before or at the beginning of their dormant period (in fall or early winter) to lessen the shock of transplanting. Early spring is better in areas that have bad winters. Plant roses as soon as possible after purchase. If there is any delay, perhaps because of unsuitable weather, it is best to heel them into a spare piece of ground, with the roots buried in a shallow trench. Alternatively, store the roses in a cool and frost-free place, and keep the roots moist. If the roots of a bare-root rose look dry before planting, soak the roots in a bucket of water for an hour or two until they are thoroughly moist.

Remove diseased, damaged , or crossing shoots and straggly stems; trim thick roots by one-third. Dig a hole and fork in compost mixed with bone meal or fertilizer.

Center the rose in the hole and spread out the roots evenly. Lay a stake across the hole to check that the bud union will be at the correct depth for the type of rose and your climate zone.

In 2 or 3 stages, water the hole and backfill with soil after the water has drained out. Do not walk on the backfilled soil to avoid compacting the soil and breaking the roots.

PLANTING A CLIMBING ROSE

Train climbers grown against a wall or fence along horizontal wires that are about 18in (45cm) apart and held in place by vine eyes or strong nails. If the brickwork or masonry is very hard, drill holes for the vine eyes with a ³⁄₁₆in (4.7mm) bit. Keep the wires 3in (7cm) away from the wall to allow air circulation and discourage diseases. The ground next to a wall is likely to be dry, since it is in a rain shadow and the masonry absorbs moisture from the soil. Plant about 18in (45cm) from the wall where the soil is less dry and water from eaves will not drip on the rose. Prepare the soil and planting hole, and trim the rose, as for bush roses. Fan out its roots. Train the shoots along stakes, but keep each stake far enough from the roots to avoid damaging them.

Place the rose in the planting hole, leaning it toward the wall at an angle of about 45° so that the shoots reach the lowest support wire. Place a stake across the hole to check the planting depth.

Use stakes to guide the shorter shoots toward the wires. Tie all the shoots to the stakes or wires with plastic straps (see insert).

PLANTING A STANDARD ROSE

A standard rose needs a stake, placed on the side of the prevailing wind, to support it. Paint the entire stake with a preservative that is not toxic to plants, then allow it to dry. Insert the stake very firmly near the center of the planting hole before positioning the rose to avoid damaging the roots and, as a result, encouraging suckers from below the graft union. Position the rose next to the stake, and check that it just reaches the base of the lowest branches; if necessary, adjust the height of the stake. Use a stake or rake handle to make sure that the bud union is at the correct level (above ground in warmer areas, below in colder).

Position the stake in the hole so that the rose stem will be in the center. Drive the stake into the ground and check that the top is just below the head of the rose.

Place a stake across the hole to check the planting depth. Use the old soil mark on the stem as a guide and plant at the correct depth. Fill in the hole, then water.

Use a tie just below the head of the rose, and another halfway up the stem, to attach the rose to the stake. Cut out weak or crossing shoots.

PLANTING A CONTAINER-GROWN PERENNIAL

Perennials grown in containers may be planted out at any time of year when the soil is workable, but the best seasons are spring and fall. Planting in fall helps the plants establish quickly before the onset of winter, because the soil is still warm enough to promote root growth, yet it is unlikely to dry out. In cold areas, however, spring planting is better for perennials that are not entirely hardy or that dislike wet conditions.

In a prepared bed, dig a hole 1½ times wider and deeper than the plant's root ball.

Gently scrape off the top 1¼in (3cm) of soil to remove weeds and weed seeds. Carefully tease out the roots around the sides and base of the root ball.

Check that the plant crown is at the correct depth when planted and fill in around the root ball. Firm gently around the plant, then water it in thoroughly.

PLANTING ANNUALS INTO OPEN GROUND

Before you plant out annuals, first prepare the bed, water the young plants thoroughly, and then allow them to drain for an hour or so. To remove a plant from its pot, invert it, supporting the stem with a finger on either side. Then tap the rim against a hard surface. If plants are in trays without divisions, hold the tray firmly with both hands, then tap one side sharply on the ground to loosen the medium.

Break the pack apart and carefully remove each seedling (here *Tagetes*) with its root ball intact.

Place each plant in a hole large enough to take its root ball, making sure the plant is slightly lower in the soil than it was in its container.

Gently firm the soil in the well around the plant so that there are no air pockets. Water the area.

PLANTING DEPTHS

While most perennials are best planted out at the same soil level as they were in their pots, a number grow better if planted higher or deeper, depending on their individual requirements. Some prefer a raised, well-drained site, while others thrive in deeper, moist conditions.

ASTER

GROUND-LEVEL PLANTING
The majority of perennials should be planted so that the crown of the plant is level with the surrounding soil.

SISYRINCHIUM STRIATUM 'AUNT MAY'

RAISED PLANTING
Set plants that are prone to rot at the base, and variegated plants that tend to revert, with their crowns slightly above the ground.

HOSTA

SHALLOW PLANTING
Plant perennials that require a moist environment with their crowns about 1in (2.5cm) below ground level.

POLYGONATUM

DEEP PLANTING
Plant perennials with tuberous root systems so that their crowns are about 4in (10cm) below the soil surface.

PLANTING LARGE BULBS IN GRASS

When planting bulbs that are to be naturalized in grass, first cut the grass as short as possible. Random rather than regimented planting achieves a more natural effect; scatter the bulbs gently by hand over the area and plant them where they have fallen, making sure that they are at least one bulb's width apart. Dig holes with a trowel or use a bulb planter, which cuts out plugs of sod and soil to a depth of about 4–6in (10–15cm); dig deeper if necessary for larger bulbs. Check that all the holes are at the correct depth and that the bulbs are the right way up before inserting them and replacing the sod, then give them a good watering.

Clean the bulbs (here daffodils), removing any loose outer coatings and old roots. Scatter the bulbs randomly over the planting area, then make sure that they are at least their own width apart.

Make an individual hole for each bulb, using a bulb planter to remove a circle of sod and a core of soil to a depth of about 4–6in (10–15cm).

Place a pinch of bone meal, mixed with a little of the soil from the core, into each hole and put in a bulb with the growing point uppermost.

Break up the underside of the core over the bulb so that it is completely covered with loose soil. Then replace the remains of the core on top of it.

Replace the lid of sod and firm it in gently, taking care not to damage the growing point of the bulb. Fill in any gaps in the grass with more soil.

PLANTING BULBS IN THE OPEN

Dry, loose bulbs should be planted as soon as possible after purchase, usually in late summer or early fall (plant summer-flowering bulbs in early to midspring); otherwise, keep them cool and dry until you can plant them. Bulbs are usually best planted several to a large hole dug out with a spade, but they may also be planted singly. Do not make the outline of the planting area or the spacing of the bulbs symmetrical: this looks unnatural, and if one or two bulbs fail, they will leave unsightly gaps.

Dig out a large hole in well-prepared ground. Plant the bulbs (here tulips), at least 3 times their own depth, and 2–3 widths apart.

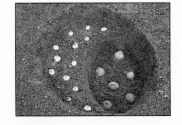

For a natural effect, space the bulbs randomly. Once they are in position, gently draw the soil over them with your hand to avoid displacing or damaging them.

Tamp down the soil over the planted area with the back of a rake. Avoid walking heavily on the soil surface, because this might damage the growing points.

Planting bulbs

SINGLY
Plant each bulb in a separate hole at the appropriate depth. Draw back the prepared soil with a trowel, and firm it down gently afterward.

IN LAYERS
Two or more kinds of bulb may be planted in the same space. Plant each kind at its correct depth, carefully covering each layer before planting the next type of bulb.

PLANTING DEEP-WATER AND MARGINAL PLANTS

Whether planting in beds or free-standing containers, settle the plants firmly in the soil, because they are very buoyant and may become dislodged. Always plant in moist soil, and soak containers well before immersing them in the pond. A top-dressing of grit, coarse sand, or pea gravel to a depth of 1in (2.5cm) prevents soil from floating out and clouding the water and discourages hungry or curious fish from disturbing the plants. When submerging the containers in deep water, thread string through the sides to form handles; this makes it much easier to position the basket, which can then be gradually lowered onto the bottom.

Choose a planting basket to accommodate the plant roots, and line it with burlap or closely woven polypropylene.

Fill the basket with heavy, moist soil to a depth of at least 2in (5cm). Center the plant (here *Aponogeton distachyos*).

Fill with more soil to within ½in (1cm) of the rim of the basket, firming the plant in well to give it good anchorage.

Top-dress the container with washed grit or pea gravel to a depth of 1in (2.5cm).

Trim away any surplus liner with scissors. Tie string handles to the rim of the basket on opposite sides.

Hold the basket by the string handles, then gently lower it onto blocks or the marginal shelf. Release the handles.

Surface floaters

With a new planting, include some surface-floating plants to discourage the growth of algae. When the ornamental plants become more established, some of the floaters should be removed. In a large pond, a line may be drawn across the pond from both ends to bring plants within reach. Duckweed in particular is very persistent, so choose less vigorous species.

Surface-floating plants have no anchorage because their roots obtain nutrients directly from the water. Their initial positioning is unimportant, since the groups are moved around on the surface by wind.

Surface-floating plants (here *Stratiotes aloides*) may be placed on the water's surface; in warm weather they multiply rapidly, giving valuable surface shade.

PLANTING IN A HANGING BASKET

Awide range of plants can be grown in a hanging basket, including annuals, tender perennials, succulents (as shown here) and even weak-stemmed shrubs, such as fuchsias. Make sure that the basket is completely clean. Wire baskets should be lined with a commercial liner or a layer of sphagnum moss. Do not line the basket with plastic, since this restricts drainage. If using a plastic basket that has an attached drainage tray, be sure to place a piece of screening over the drainage hole(s) to prevent the soil mix from washing out.

Line a wire hanging basket with a layer of moist sphagnum moss. The layer should be 1¼in (3cm) thick when compressed.

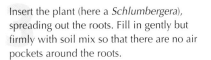

Fill the basket almost to the brim with a mix of 1 part sharp sand to 3 parts soil-based potting mix. Prepare a hole for the plant in the center of the basket.

Insert the plant (here a *Schlumbergera*), spreading out the roots. Fill in gently but firmly with soil mix so that there are no air pockets around the roots.

If planting succulents, as here, wait for 2–3 days after planting before watering the finished basket. Otherwise, water immediately and then allow the basket to drain before hanging it.

REPOTTING AN INDOOR PLANT

Indoor plants need repotting to accommodate their growth and to replenish the soil mix. A potbound plant has retarded growth, and water runs straight through the soil mix. Repot before this happens, so that the plant develops well. A few plants, such as amaryllis (*Hippeastrum*), enjoy confined roots, so repot them less often, and top-dress occasionally. The best time to repot is at the start of the growing season, although fast-growing plants may need repotting a few times in one season. The process may delay flowering, because the plant initially concentrates its energy on new root growth. Avoid repotting a dormant plant; it will not respond to the moisture and fertility, and it may rot.

Before potting on a plant (here *Dracaena deremensis* 'Souvenir de Schriever'), make sure that its root ball is moist by watering it thoroughly about an hour beforehand. Select a pot that is one or two sizes larger than the old one. Make sure the pot is clean (whether washed, disinfected, or new) to avoid spreading diseases. The fresh potting mix should be of the same type as that in the old pot.

Remove the plant by inverting the pot and sharply tapping the rim on a hard surface to loosen the root ball. Support the plant as it slides out of the pot.

Gently tease out the root ball with a small fork or your fingers. Put some moist potting mix in the base of the new pot.

Insert the plant so that its soil mark is level with the rim base. Fill in with soil mix to within ½in (1.5cm) of the rim, firm, water, and place in position (right).

PRUNING

Pruning and training both aim to make sure that plants are as vigorous and healthy as possible, are at the least risk of infection from disease, and are free of structural weakness at maturity. They can also create striking features by enhancing ornamental qualities, such as bark, flowers, foliage, and fruit. However, pruning always causes some stress, so learn when and how to prune.

PRUNING AND TRAINING YOUNG TREES

Young trees benefit from formative pruning to make sure that they develop a strong, well-balanced framework of evenly spaced branches. This involves the removal of dead, damaged, and diseased wood, as well as any weak or crossing branches. Formative pruning may also be used to determine the tree's shape as it grows: for example, a young feathered tree may be pruned over several years to form a standard, or perhaps trained against a wall as an espalier.

Feathered tree
Remove congested and crossing shoots, then cut out any laterals that are small, spindly, or badly positioned, to achieve a well-balanced framework of branches.

Feathered tree

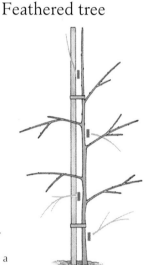

Central-leader standard

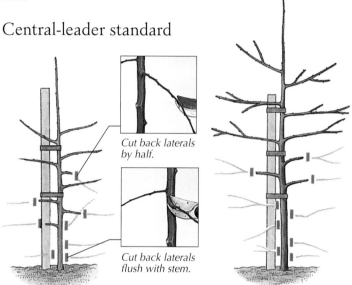

Cut back laterals by half.

Cut back laterals flush with stem.

Year 1
On the lowest third of the tree, cut back laterals to the main stem; on the middle third, cut back laterals by half. Remove any weak or competing leaders.

Years 2 and 3
Continue the process, removing the lowest laterals completely and cutting back by about half those laterals that are on the middle third of the tree.

Branched-head standard

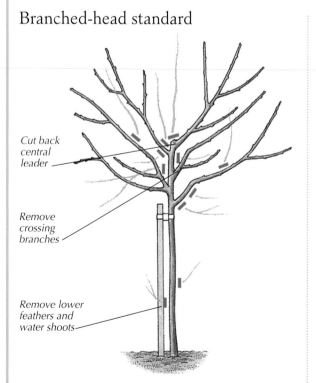

Cut back central leader

Remove crossing branches

Remove lower feathers and water shoots

Remove crossing laterals and any growths on the lower third of the tree. Cut back the leader to a healthy bud or shoot.

Weeping tree

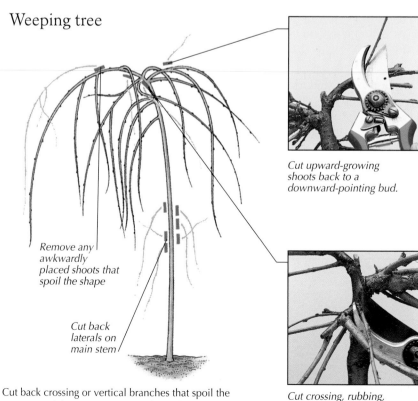

Remove any awkwardly placed shoots that spoil the shape

Cut back laterals on main stem

Cut upward-growing shoots back to a downward-pointing bud.

Cut crossing, rubbing, or congested growth.

Cut back crossing or vertical branches that spoil the symmetry of the tree. Remove any growths on the main stem.

FORMATIVE PRUNING AND TRAINING

The aim of formative pruning is to make sure that a shrub has a framework of well-spaced branches. The amount of formative pruning required depends very much on the type of shrub and on the quality of the plants available. (It is usually best to start with a quality plant from a good source.) Evergreen shrubs generally need little formative pruning. Excessive growth resulting in an unbalanced shape should be lightly pruned in midspring, after the shrub has been planted. Deciduous shrubs are much more likely to require formative pruning than evergreen shrubs. This should be carried out in the dormant season, between midfall and midspring, at or after planting.

Coppicing a shrub for winter stem color

Coppicing stimulates the growth of colorful, vigorous stems. Cut back all stems to about 2–3in (5–8cm) from the base before growth begins in spring, and then fertilize and mulch well.

Prune back crossing or congested shoots to an outward-facing bud or cut right back to the base.

Prune out any very weak and spindly, or long and straggly, stems, cutting them right back to the base.

Also remove any very awkward stems that spoil the shape of the shrub, to leave an evenly balanced framework.

WHY, HOW, AND WHERE TO CUT

Pruning normally stimulates growth. The actively growing terminal shoot or dormant growth bud of a stem is often dominant, inhibiting by chemical means the growth of buds or shoots below it. Pruning to remove the ends of stems affects the control mechanism, resulting in more vigorous development of lower shoots or growth buds. Hard pruning promotes more vigorous growth than light pruning. This needs to be borne in mind when correcting the shape of an unbalanced shrub. Prune weak growth hard, but strong growth only lightly.

Opposite shoots
Prune stems with opposite buds to just above a strong pair of buds or shoots, using a clean, straight cut.

Alternate shoots
For plants with alternate buds, prune to just above a bud or shoot, using a clean, angled cut.

Making an angled cut
Angle the cut so that its lowest point is opposite the base of the bud and the top just clears the bud.

PRUNING ROSES

The purpose of pruning roses is to promote new, vigorous, disease-free shoots developing to replace the old, weakened ones, and so produce a reasonably attractive shape and the optimum display of blooms. Training a plant stimulates the production of flowering sideshoots and directs new growth. A pair of sharp, high-quality pruners is essential, and always wear thornproof gloves.

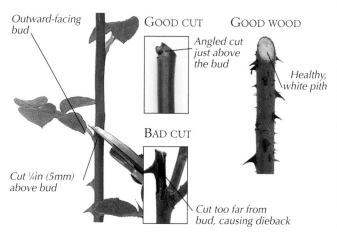

Outward-facing bud

GOOD CUT

Angled cut just above the bud

GOOD WOOD

Healthy, white pith

Cut ¼in (5mm) above bud

BAD CUT

Cut too far from bud, causing dieback

Pruning a newly planted bush rose

Prune a newly planted bush rose to about 3in (8cm) above ground level. Cut back to outward-facing buds, and remove any cold-damaged growth.

PRUNING HYBRID TEA AND GRANDIFLORA ROSES

Depending on the extent of winter kill and on the differences among cultivars, in colder areas the main shoots should be pruned back to between 8–10in (20–25cm). In milder areas, the shoots may be cut down less severely, to about 18–24in (45–60cm). For exhibition-quality blooms, cut the main shoots back hard to leave only two or three buds.

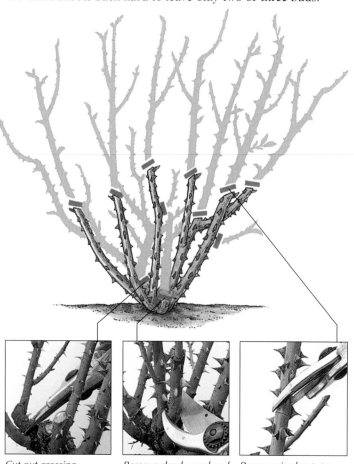

Cut out crossing, congested, and twiggy or spindly growth.

Remove dead wood and any that shows signs of damage or disease.

Prune main shoots to within about 8–10in (20–25cm) of ground level.

PRUNING FLORIBUNDA ROSES

When pruning Floribundas, cut out any unproductive wood as for Hybrid Teas. Reduce sideshoots by about one-third on smaller cultivars, and by two-thirds on taller-growing ones. Cut back the main shoots to 12–15in (30–38cm), but reduce the shoots of taller cultivars by about one-third. Do not prune them any harder, (unless growing for exhibition) because this will significantly reduce the number of blooms.

Remove crossing or congested wood and twiggy, spindly growth.

Prune out all dead, damaged or diseased wood to a healthy bud.

Prune main shoots to 12–15in (30–38cm) from ground level.

Reduce sideshoots by one- to two-thirds, cutting to a bud.

PRUNING STANDARD AND MINIATURE ROSES

Most standards are formed from Hybrid Teas or Floribundas budded onto a straight, unbranched stem. Prune as for their bush relatives, but cut back the main shoots so that they are all roughly equal in length. If the head is unbalanced, prune the shoots on the denser side less hard so that they do not produce as much new growth as those on the thinner side.

There are two methods: either give them the minimum of attention (remove dead growth, thin out tangles, and shorten overly long shoots) or treat them like small Hybrid Teas or Floribundas (remove all growth except the strongest shoots, and then cut them back by one-third or more).

Standard rose

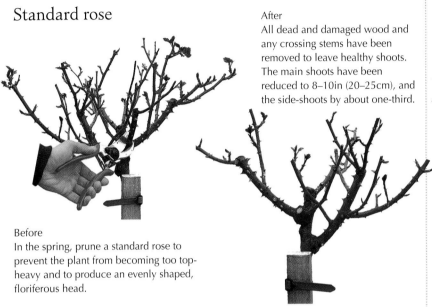

After
All dead and damaged wood and any crossing stems have been removed to leave healthy shoots. The main shoots have been reduced to 8–10in (20–25cm), and the side-shoots by about one-third.

Before
In the spring, prune a standard rose to prevent the plant from becoming too top-heavy and to produce an evenly shaped, floriferous head.

Miniature rose

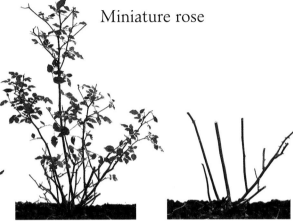

Before (Method Two)
Miniature roses often produce a mass of twiggy growth. The shape of this plant is unbalanced by overly vigorous shoots growing from the base.

After (Method Two)
Excessively twiggy and spindly growth, crossing shoots, and damaged wood have been removed, and vigorous shoots have been cut back by half.

DEALING WITH SUCKERS

Suckers usually look quite different from the rest of the plant, often with leaves of a different shape or color, and they often grow more strongly. Remove any suckers as soon as they appear. This prevents the rootstock from wasting energy on the sucker's growth. Damage to the roots, caused by severe cold or any accidental nicks from hoes, other implements, or a stake, may stimulate the production of suckers. Shoots on the stem of a standard rose are also suckers, since the stem is actually part of the understock. As with other grafted roses, any suckers will look different from the cultivar you want to grow.

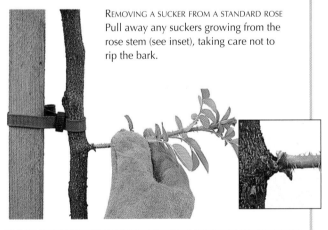

REMOVING A SUCKER FROM A STANDARD ROSE
Pull away any suckers growing from the rose stem (see inset), taking care not to rip the bark.

With a trowel, carefully scrape away the soil to expose the top of the rootstock. Check that the suspect shoot arises from below the bud union.

Using gloves to protect your hands, pull the sucker down and away from the rootstock. Trim the wound, refill the hole, and gently firm the soil.

How a sucker grows

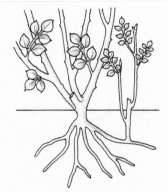

The sucker (right) grows directly from the rootstock. If cut back only at ground level it will regrow and divert further energy from the main part of the plant.

PEGGING DOWN ROSES

This technique is an effective (although time-consuming) way of increasing flower production on roses that tend to send up long, ungainly shoots with flowers only at the tips. In late summer or fall, bend the shoots over gently, taking great care not to snap them, then peg the shoots firmly into the ground. This has much the same result as horizontally training the shoots of climbing and rambler roses.

Select long, noflowering shoots, and prune the soft tips. Gently bend each shoot over, then peg it to the soil with sturdy wire pins (see insert)

PRUNING GALLICA ROSES

Many of these old-fashioned roses produce a twiggy tangle of shoots that should be regularly thinned out to improve air circulation and bloom quality and to make the plant more attractive. After flowering, shorten the sideshoots only, and remove any dead or diseased wood. Gently clip Gallica roses used for hedging to maintain a neat shape. Follow their natural outline: do not attempt to shape them into a formal hedge, since this would remove many of the sideshoots on which flowers are produced in the following year.

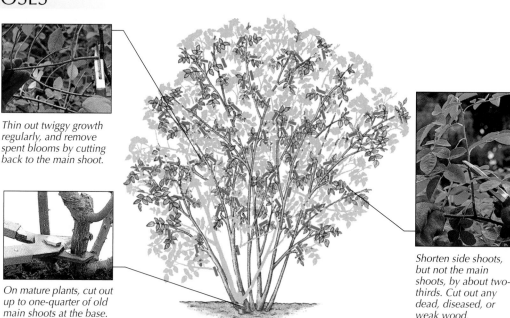

Thin out twiggy growth regularly, and remove spent blooms by cutting back to the main shoot.

On mature plants, cut out up to one-quarter of old main shoots at the base.

Shorten side shoots, but not the main shoots, by about two-thirds. Cut out any dead, diseased, or weak wood.

PRUNING ALBA, CENTIFOLIA, DAMASK, AND MOSS ROSES

After flowering, reduce both main shoots and sideshoots. At the end of summer, cut back any overly long shoots that might whip about in the wind and cause wind-rock damage to the roots.

A general note on pruning the old-fashioned roses: some of these roses have a very individual growth habit and do not conform neatly to a specific pruning program. For these, it is best to observe the way the plant grows for the first few years, and then adapt a specific program (such as one of those given here) to how the rose reacts to the program. Some old-fashioned roses resent pruning and will respond by turning into very unattractive plants.

Cut back any overly long, whippy shoots by about one-third.

Prune sideshoots to about two-thirds of their length.

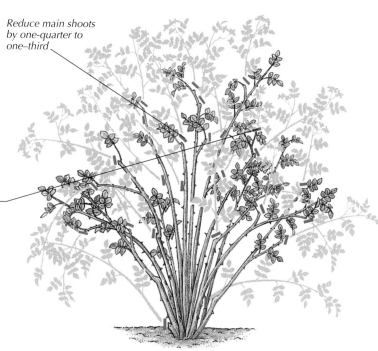

Reduce main shoots by one-quarter to one–third

PRUNING AND TRAINING CLIMBING ROSES

These roses require minor pruning but regular annual training. In their first year (and in their second unless they have made exceptional growth), do not prune climbers, except to remove any dead, diseased, or weak growth. Never hard prune climbing sports of bush roses (roses with the word "climbing" in their name; for example 'Climbing Peace') in the first two years, since they may revert to the bush form. Begin training as soon as the new shoots are long enough to reach the supports; train them sideways along horizontal supports to encourage flowering. Where this is not possible, choose a cultivar that is halfway between a tall shrub and a climbing rose. Many of these flower well from the plant base without special training.

Reduce the sideshoots by about two-thirds or about 6in (15cm), cutting above an outward-facing bud.

Tie all new shoots into horizontal wires 6–8in (15–20cm) apart. The shoots should not cross each other.

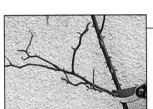

Remove any diseased, dead, or twiggy growth, cutting back to healthy wood or the main shoot.

PRUNING AND TRAINING MATURE RAMBLER ROSES

Ramblers produce much more growth from the base than most climbers and, if not carefully managed, grow into a vicious tangle of unmanageable shoots. Prune ramblers in summer, after they flower. In the first two years, restrict pruning to cutting back all the sideshoots by about 3in (7.5cm) to a vigorous shoot; also, remove dead or diseased wood. In later years, prune and train more heavily to maintain the framework: remove the oldest shoots to the ground, and train in new shoots that spring up from the base.

Cut sideshoots back to leave between 2 to 4 healthy buds or shoots.

Cut back any old, spent shoots to ground level, using loppers.

Tie all shoots to the wires as close to the horizontal as possible.

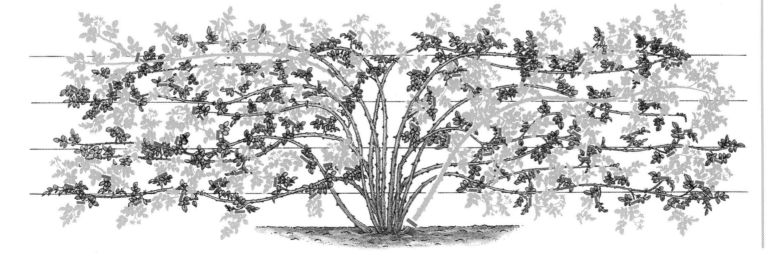

PROPAGATION

Producing new plants from existing ones is one of the most satisfying of all horticultural pursuits. From a simpler technique (sowing seeds) to the more elaborate (such as layering), growing your own allows you to raise a number of plants at minimum expense, such as for a hedge, and greatly increases your selections, especially if you grow annuals and vegetables from seed.

HARDWOOD CUTTINGS

Many deciduous trees and shrubs (as well as some evergreens) may be rooted from hardwood cuttings outdoors in fall and winter. If your winters are long and harsh or excessively wet, the cuttings usually die if left outside, but they can be rooted in deep boxes in a frost-free basement or root cellar instead. Select cuttings just after a hard frost. Choose strong, vigorous shoots of the current season's growth. For species that do not root easily, tie cuttings into small bundles, then plunge them into a sand bed.

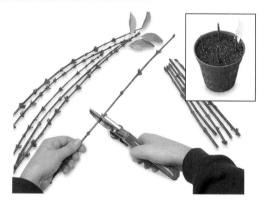

Strip leaves and sideshoots from bottom half of cutting

For deciduous plants: trim off tips and cut stems into 8in (20cm) lengths. Make a horizontal cut just below a node, and a sloping cut to mark the top. Dip the base in hormone rooting compound. Insert them 2in (5cm) apart, 6in (5cm) deep, in soil-based rooting medium in pots, either in a cold place or outdoors.

For evergreens: cut shoots into sections 8–10in (20–25cm) long. Trim just above a leaf at the tip and below another at the base. Strip leaves from bottom half of cutting. Insert 5–8 cuttings in a 6in (15cm) pot. Place in a closed case with slight bottom heat, or in a clear plastic bag. Rooting occurs in 6–10 weeks.

SEMIRIPE CUTTINGS

Many conifers, as well as certain broadleaved evergreens such as hollies (*Ilex*) and *Magnolia grandiflora*, may be propagated readily from semiripe cuttings. After insertion, check the cuttings periodically, watering them only to keep them from drying out. Remove any fallen leaves as soon as they appear, since these may rot and spread disease to the cuttings. During cold spells, cold frames should be insulated with burlap or a similar covering.

The ideal semiripe cutting is taken from current season's growth that has begun to firm up; the base is quite firm, while the tip is soft and still actively growing. Such stems will offer some resistance when bent.

Stem wood is firm but flexible

Wood is stiff and fully ripe

Stem is soft and sappy

Cutting is trimmed below a stem joint

Too soft Semiripe Too hard

DISTINGUSHING SEMIRIPE WOOD

In mid- to late summer, select a healthy, semiripe shoot of the current season's growth (here, *Aucuba*), then sever the cutting jut above a stem joint with clean, sharp pruners.

Remove sideshoots from the stem with a sharp knife. Trim the stem to 4–6in (10–15cm), cutting just below a stem joint. Remove the soft tip and the lowest pair of leaves.

To stimulate rooting, cut a shallow sliver of bark, ½–1in (1–2.5cm) long, from the base of the stem; do not expose the pith. This process is known as wounding.

Dip the base of the cutting in hormone rooting compound. Make sure that the entire wound receives the thinnest possible (but uniform) coating, then shake off the excess.

Place cuttings 2–3in (5–8cm) apart in standard rooting medium in a nursery bed outdoors (or in pots in a closed case). Label with name and date. Water and cover.

SOFTWOOD AND GREENWOOD CUTTINGS

This method of propagation is suitable for some tree species, although it is more commonly used for shrubs. Softwood cuttings are taken from the fast-growing tips of new shoots and usually root very easily. They wilt rapidly, however, so it is vital to prepare and insert them as quickly as possible after removing them from the parent plant.

SOFTWOOD CUTTINGS
Take softwood cuttings in spring and early summer from the new season's growth before it has begun to firm up. Choose vigorous nonflowering shoots with 2 or 3 pairs of leaves, cutting just below a stem joint.

GREENWOOD CUTTINGS
Take greenwood cuttings in late spring to midsummer, just as new stems begin to firm up. They are less prone to wilt and easier to handle than softwood and root as readily. Treat them exactly as for softwood cuttings

Remove the soft tip, because it is vulnerable to rot and scorch

Remove the soft tip just above a leaf joint, as well as the lowest pair of leaves. Cut large leaves in half to reduce moisture loss. Trim the base just below a leaf joint; the stem should be 1½–2in (4–5cm) long.

Fill a 5in (13cm) pot with rooting medium. Make 2 or 3 holes around the edge, then insert the cuttings so that the lowest leaves lie just above the surface and are not touching each other.

Vent of closed case will be opened gradually to harden off rooted cuttings

After watering thoroughly with a commercial fungicidal solution, label and place pots in a closed case heated, if possible, at the base to 59°F (15°C). Keep in a shaded place, out of direct sun.

Once cuttings have rooted, admit more air to harden them off. Knock out of the pot, tease apart, and pot up singly into 3½in (9cm) pots of soil mix. Pinch out growing tips to encourage bushy growth.

SIMPLE LAYERING

The long, trailing shoots of climbers may often be propagated by simple layering if they do not root naturally. A shoot is wounded and pegged down into the surrounding soil. This induces it to root at a node to provide a young plant that is later separated from the parent. Layers of many climbers that have been pegged down in spring will develop strong root systems by fall, at which time they can be separated from the parent plant. Layering also works for many shrubs and a few trees.

Dig a hole, about 3in (8cm) deep in prepared soil, with a shallowly sloping side next to the parent plant and a nearly vertical slope on the far side. Mix a little sand and organic matter into the bottom of the hole if soil is heavy.

Trim off sideshoots and leaves. At the point where the underside of the stem touches the soil, make a slanting cut through to the middle of the stem to make a "tongue" of bark, or remove a 1in (2.5cm) sliver of bark.

Dust the wound with some hormone rooting compound. Peg the stem down securely into the bottom of the hole using several U-shaped, galvanized wire pins, placing them on either side of the wound.

Bend the stem tip up against the vertical side of the hole and secure with a stake. Backfill, firm, and water in. Keep weed-free and moist. A layer should be well rooted within a year, and can be cut from the parent.

Plant the layer in a 5in (13cm) pot of standard soil mix, then water and label it. You could plant it into its permanent position in the garden if it has produced enough roots. Watch its watering needs carefully.

PROPAGATING PERENNIALS BY DIVISION

This method is suitable for propagating many perennials that have a spreading rootstock and produce plenty of shoots from the base. As well as being a way of increasing stocks, in many cases division rejuvenates the plants and keeps them vigorous, since old or unproductive parts are discarded. Most plants should be divided when they are dormant (or are about to go dormant, or are just emerging from dormancy) from late fall to early spring, but not in extremely cold, wet, or dry weather, because these conditions may make it difficult for the divided plants to reestablish successfully. Try to do this on an overcast, calm day.

Lift the plant to be divided, taking care to insert the fork far enough away from the plant so that the roots are not damaged. Shake off surplus soil.

Separate plants with a woody center by chopping through the crown with a spade. Use a trowel for smaller, less dense clumps.

Alternative method

Divide densely rooted herbaceous plants (here *Hemerocallis*) using 2 forks inserted back to back in the center. Larger, tougher clumps will require the help of an assistant.

Divide the plant into smaller pieces by hand, retaining only healthy, vigorous sections, each with several new shoots.

Cut back the old top-growth, then replant the divided sections to the same depth as before. Firm in and water thoroughly.

DIVIDING HOSTAS

Large hostas with tough rootstocks should be divided using a spade or back-to-back forks. Hostas that have looser, fleshy rootstocks may be separated by hand; this technique may be necessary to avoid damaging smaller-growing cultivars. For quick reestablishment of a clump, include several buds on an individual division, but if making many plants is your goal and you can wait longer for mature clumps, separate the clump into single or double buds, as long as each division has enough roots to sustain it. Trim any damaged parts with a knife, then replant as soon as possible. If there is a delay, store the plants under cover and keep moist.

Tough, fibrous roots
Divide the crown with a spade. Each section should include several developing buds.

Loose, fleshy roots
Divide small plants and those with a loose rootstock by pulling the clump apart by hand.

DIVIDING RHIZOMATOUS PLANTS

Divide plants with thick rhizomes, such as *Bergenia* and rhizomatous irises, by splitting the clump into pieces by hand, then cutting the rhizomes into sections, each with one or more growth points. Bamboos have tough rootstocks that either form dense clumps with short rhizomes or have long, spreading rhizomes. Divide dense clumps with a spade or two back-to-back forks; cut spreading rhizomes into sections (each of which should have three nodes or joints) with pruners. In all cases, trim excessively long roots before replanting.

Lift the plant to be divided (here an iris), inserting the fork well away from the rhizomes to avoid damaging them.

Shake the clump to remove any loose soil. Using your hands or a hand fork, split the clump into manageable pieces.

Discard any old rhizomes, then detach the new, young rhizomes from the clump and neatly trim off their ends.

Dust the cut areas with fungicide. Trim long roots by one-third. For irises, cut the leaves into a "fan" about 6in (15cm) tall to prevent wind-rock.

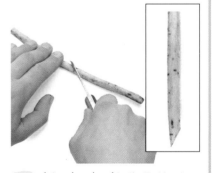

Plant the rhizomes at least 6in (15cm) apart. The rhizomes should be half buried, with their leaves and buds upright. Firm in well, then water.

PROPAGATING PERENNIALS BY ROOT CUTTINGS

This is a useful method of propagating perennials that have fairly thick, fleshy roots, such as *Papaver orientale*; it also works very well for horseradish (*Armoracia*). Take care to minimize damage to the parent plant when cutting its roots, and replant it immediately. Root cuttings are most successful when they are taken during the plant's dormant period, usually just before winter. Note: plants with thinner roots, such as *Anemone*, are done slightly differently. Lay the cuttings flat on the medium, then cover and treat as for thicker root cuttings.

Lift the plant (here *Acanthus*) when dormant and wash the roots. Cut roots of pencil thickness close to the crown.

Cut each into lengths of 2–4in (5–10cm). Make a straight cut at the upper end and an angled cut at the lower (inset).

Insert the cuttings into holes made in pots of moist rooting medium, then firm. The top end of each cutting should be flush with the surface.

Top-dress the pots of cuttings with coarse grit, label them, and place them in a cold frame until the cuttings root.

When the cuttings have developed young shoots, pot them up into individual pots filled with soil-based potting mix. Water and label the pots (see inset).

SOWING IN DRILLS

Seeds sown in drills produce seedlings growing in straight rows at regular intervals, so they are readily distinguished from weed seedlings, which are randomly distributed. Using either a trowel tip or the corner of a hoe, mark out shallow drills at a width depending on the ultimate size of the plants. Sow seeds thinly and evenly by sprinkling or placing them in each drill at the appropriate depth for the plants being sown, then carefully draw back the displaced soil. Label each row, then water gently but thoroughly with a fine spray. This technique is traditionally used for sowing vegetables, but it works equally well for annuals and biennials, especially in cutting gardens.

Using a line of string as a guide, make a furrow about 1in (2.5cm) deep with a hoe.

Alternative Step

If the seeds are pelleted, place them individually in the base of the drill.

Dribble the seeds from your hand to make sure they are scattered evenly.

Carefully rake the soil back over the drill without dislodging the seeds.

BROADCAST SOWING

Before sowing, mark the outline of the area for different plants with sand to keep track the balance of colors, heights, and habits of each of the plants to be used, especially annuals. After sowing, label the area, then water the area gently but thoroughly with a fine spray. This method is particularly suitable for taprooted annuals, such as *Clarkia*, *Gypsophila*, and poppies (*Papaver*), which are best sown where they are to flower, since they do not transplant readily.

Prepare the soil by raking to produce a fine tilth. Scatter the seeds thinly over the prepared area from your hand or from the packet.

Rake over the area lightly at right angles to cover the seeds so that they are disturbed as little as possible. Water gently but thoroughly.

THINNING SEEDLINGS

To prevent overcrowding, seedlings usually need to be thinned. Do this when the soil is moist and the weather mild, taking care to retain the sturdier seedlings where possible and to achieve even spacing. To minimize disturbance to a seedling being retained, press the soil around it with your fingers as the surplus seedlings are extracted. Thinnings may be used to fill sparse areas caused by uneven sowing or irregular germination, or they may be planted elsewhere in the garden.

To thin small seedlings, nip them out at ground level so that the roots of the remaining seedlings are not disturbed.

Lift seedlings gently, keeping as much soil around them as possible. If moving them, place them in a clear plastic bag to retain moisture.

SOWING IN A TRAY

Many annuals, biennials, perennials, herbs, and vegetables are usually sown in containers so that they can germinate and develop under cover and then be planted out as young plants when conditions are favorable. Pots, seed pans (shallow pots), seed trays, and packs are all suitable containers, depending on the number of seeds to be sown and the space they require. Most seedlings will need to be pricked out before they are large enough to be planted out (see below). Peat pots are useful for seedlings that do not transplant well, since the whole pot may be planted out without disturbing the roots.

Fill the seed tray with a standard sowing medium, then level with a presser board to ½in (1cm) below the rim.

Sprinkle the seeds thinly over the surface of the medium to achieve an even distribution.

Cover the seeds with a layer of sieved, moist soil mix to about the same thickness as the seeds themselves. Water the seeds in lightly.

Place a piece of glass or clear plastic sheeting over the tray to maintain even humidity.

Shade the tray with netting if the tray is in direct sunlight. Remove both glass and netting as soon as germination starts.

PRICKING OUT OF A PACK

Seedlings raised in trays or pans need to be transplanted into larger containers before they become overcrowded, because they may quickly become weak and spindly if deprived of sufficient space or light, and damping off (a disease) may develop. This process is known as pricking out. It enables the seedlings to continue to develop properly until they are ready for planting out in the open garden. Fill the new containers with a soil-based mix, then firm gently to eliminate any air pockets. Small pots, no more than 3in (6cm) in diameter, or compartmentalized plastic packs are ideal for individual seedlings; larger pots, pans, or trays can be used for several plants.

Carefully separate the seedlings, handling them by their seed leaves, not their more delicate stems. Try to keep plenty of medium around the roots.

Transplant each seedling into a separate section of a pack. Firm the soil mix around each one with your fingers or a dibber, then water.

APPENDICES

Connecticut
University of Connecticut
Ratcliffe Hicks School of Agriculture
Storrs-Mansfield, CT 06269
(860) 486-6271
http://www.canr.uconn.edu/ces

Illinois
University of Illinois, Department of
Horticulture
125 Mumford Hall
1301 W Gregory Drive
Urbana-Champaign, IL 61801
(217) 333-5900
http://www.extension.uiuc.edu

Indiana
Purdue University
Department of Horticulture & Landscape
Architecture
625 Agriculture Mall Drive
West Layfayette, IN 47907-2010
(888) EXT INFO
http://www.hort.purdue.edu

Iowa
Iowa State University
Ames, IA 50010
(515) 294-2751
http://www.extension.iastate.edu

Maine
University of Maine
Department of Plant, Soil &
Environmental Sciences
5722 Deering Hall
Orono, ME 04469-5722
(207) 581-3188
http://www.umext.maine.edu

Massachusetts
University of Massachusetts
Landscape, Nursery & Urban Forestry
Amherst, MA 01003
(413) 545-4800
http://www.umassgreeninfo.org

Michigan
Michigan State University
Department of Horticulture
A146 Plant & Soil Sciences Building.
East Lansing, MI 48824-1325
(517) 355-2308

Minnesota
University of Minnesota
St. Paul, MN 55108
(612) 625-1915
http://www.extension.umn.edu

Missouri
University of Missouri
Department of Horticulture
1-40 Agriculture Building
Columbia, MO 65211 (573) 882-7511
http://muextension.missouri.edu

New Hampshire
University of New Hampshire
Thompson School of Applied Sciences
Durham, NH 03824
(603) 629-9494
http://ceinfo.unh.edu

New Jersey
Rutgers, the State University of New Jersey
New Brunswick, NJ 08903
(732) 932-9306
http://www.rce.rutgers.edu

New York
Cornell University
Department of Horticulture
134A Plant Science Building
Ithaca, NY 14853
(607) 255-2237
http://www.hort.cornell.edu

Ohio
Ohio State University
Department of Horticulture & Crop Science
Columbus, OH 43210
(614) 247-7313
http://ohioline.osu.edu

Pennsylvania
Penn State University
Department of Horticulture
102 Tyson Building.
University Park, PA 16802
(814) 355-4897
http://hortweb.cas.psu.edu

Rhode Island
University of Rhode Island
Department of Plant Sciences
Kingston, RI 02881
(800) 448-1011
http://www.uri.edu/ce

Vermont
University of Vermont
Department of Plant & Soil Science
Hills Agricultural Building.
105 Carrigan Dr.
Burlington, VT 05405
(802) 656-2990
http://www.uvm.edu/extension

Wisconsin
University of Wisconsin
Department of Horticulture
1575 Linden Dr.
Madison, WI 53706
(608) 262-3980
http://www.hort.wisc.edu

GARDENING WEB SITES

The Internet provides a rich source of information on every facet of the horticultural world. In addition to the web sites maintained by many botanical gardens and research facilities, many gardening centers offer their plants and horticultural products on the internet. The following sites may be particularly helpful or enlightening.

Betrock's Hortworld
http://www.hortworld.com

Directory of Horticulture Web Sites
http://depts.washington.edu/hortlib/resources/dir_hort_websites.shtml

GardenNet
http://gardennet.com

GardenWeb
http://www.gardenweb.com

Hortiplex database
http://hortiplex.gardenweb.com/plants

HortNet Plant Image Gallery
http://www.hort.net/gallery

Internet Directory for Botany
http://www.botany.net/IDB

Lady Bird Johnson Wildflower Center
http://www.wildflower.org

NeoFlora
http://www.neoflora.com/Internet

Plant Facts
http://plantfacts.ohio-state.edu

RHS Horticultural Database
http://www.rhs.org.uk/databases/summary.asp

Tropicos Image Index
http://mobot.mobot.org/W3T/Search/vast.html

USDA Plant Database
http://plants.usda.gov

OTHER USEFUL HORTICULTURAL ORGANIZATIONS

A good source of information about specific plants and many have local chapters where you can meet fellow enthusiasts. Most do not have a settled office. Use their web-sites to find the closest chapter.

American Horticultural Society
http://www.ahs.org

All-America Selections
A non-profit organization devoted to promoting the best annuals. They have display gardens across the country.
http://www.all-americaselections.org

All-America Rose Selections
A similar organization devoted to the rose.
http://www.rose.org

American Hemerocallis Society
http://www.daylilies.org

American Hosta Society
http://www.hosta.org

American Iris Society
Local shows and meetings
http://www.irises.org

American Peony Society
Local shows and meetings
http://www.americanpeonysociety.org

American Rhododendron Society
http://www.rhododendron.org

American Rose Society
http://www.ars.org/

The International Lilac Society
http://lilacs.freeservers.com

New England Wildflower Society
A good source of information
http://www.newfs.org

North American Lily Society
Local shows and meetings
http://www.lilies.org

North American Rock Garden Society
A good source of rare plants
http://www.nargs.org

BOTANIC GARDENS AND ARBORETA

Most have good, labeled collections of trees, shrubs, perennials, and often annual display beds. Many run classes and demonstrations. They are good places to see mature plants you may be considering for your own garden.

Connecticut
Bartlett Arboretum
University of Connecticut
151 Brookdale Road
Stamford, CT 06903-4199
(203) 322-6971
http://bartlett.arboretum.uconn.edu

Marsh Botanical Garden
Yale University
227 Mansfield Street
New Haven, CT 06511
(203) 436-8665

Illinois
Chicago Botanic Garden
P.O. Box 400
Glencoe, IL 60022
(708) 835-5440
http://www.chicago-botanic.org/

Luthy Memorial Botanical Garden
Peoria Park District
2218 N. Prospect
Peoria, IL 61603
(309) 686-3352
http://www.peoriaparks.org/luthy/

Morton Arboretum
4100 Route 53
Lisle, IL 60532-1293
(630) 968-0074
http://www.mortonarb.org/

Indiana
Holcomb Botanical Garden
Butler University
4600 Sunset Avenue
Indianapolis, IN 46208
(317) 283-9413

Perdue University Horticultural Gardens
West Lafayette, IN 47907
(317) 494-1296
http://www.hort.purdue.edu/hort/

Iowa

Bickelhaupt Arboretum
340 South 14th Street
Clinton, IA 52732
(319) 242-4771
http://www.bickarb.org/

Des Moines Botanical Center
909 East River Drive
Des Moines, IA 50316
(515) 283-4148
http://www.botanicalcenter.com/

Iowa Arboretum
Box 44A, Route 1
Madrid. IA 50156
(515) 795-3216
http://www.iowaarboretum.com/

Iowa State University Horticultural Garden
Ames, IA 50001
(515) 294-2751
http://www.hort.iastate.edu

Maine

Fay Hyland Botanical Plantation, U. Maine
Orono, ME 04469
(207) 581-7461
http://www.botanique.com

Massachusetts

Alexandra Botanic Garden at Wellesley
108 Central Street
Wellesley, MA 02181
(617) 235-0320
http://www.wellesley.edu

Arnold Arboretum of Harvard University
125 Arborway
Jamaica Plain, MA 02130
(617) 524-1718
http://www.arboretum.harvard.edu

Berkshire Garden Center
P.O. Box 826
Stockbridge, MA. 01262
(413) 298-3926

Botanic Garden of Smith College
Lyman Plant House
Northampton, MA 01063
(413) 585-2748
http://www.smith.edu/

Michigan

Cooley Gardens
P.O. Box 14164
Lansing, MI 48901
(517) 351-5707
http://www.cooleysgardens.com

Fernwood Gardens
13988 Range Line Road
Niles, MI 49120
(616) 695-6491
http://www.fernwoodgarden.com

Matthaei Botanical Gardens
University of Michigan
1800 N. Dixboro Road
Ann Arbor, MI 48105
(313) 998-7061
http://www.lsa.umich.edu/mbg

Michigan State University
Horticulture Gardens
East Lansing, MI 48823
(517) 355-0348
http://www.hrt.msu.edu/

Missouri

Missouri Botanical Garden
P.O. Box 299
St. Louis. MO 63166
(314) 577-5100
http://www.mobot.org/

New Hampshire

Prescott Park Gardens
University of New Hampshire, Nesmith Hall
Durham, NH 03824
(603) 862-1520
http://www.ilovegardens.com/New_
Hampshire_Gardens

New Jersey

George Frelinghuysen Arboretum
53 East Hanover Avenue, Box 1295
Morristown NJ 07962-1295
(201) 326-7600
http://nynjctbotany.org/njnbtofc/frelingh.html

Reeves-Reed Arboretum
165 Hobart Avenue
Summit, NJ 07901
(201)273-8787
http://www.reeves-reedarboretum.org/

Rutgers Display Gardens
New Brunswick, NJ 08903
(201) 932-9639
http://aesop.rutgers.edu/~rugardens/

New York

Bailey Arboretum
Lattingtown, Long Island, NY 11560
(516) 676-4497
http://www.fieldtrip.com/ny/65718020.htm

Bayard Cutting Arboretum
P.O. Box 466
Oakdale, NY 11769
(516) 581-1002
http://www.fieldtrip.com/ny/65811002.htm

Brooklyn Botanic Garden
1000 Washington Avenue
Brooklyn, NY 11225-1099
(718) 622-4433
http://www.bbg.org/

Cornell Plantations
One Plantations Road
Ithaca, NY 14850
(607) 255-3020
http://www.plantations.cornell.edu/

Highland Botanical Park
180 Reservoir Avenue
Rochester, NY 14620
(716) 244-8079

New York Botanical Gardens
200th Street & Southern Boulevard
Bronx, NY 10458-5126
(718) 817-8700
http://www.nybg.org/

Planting Fields Arboretum
Planting Fields Road
Oyster Bay, NY 11771
(516) 922-9206
http://www.plantingfields.com/

Ohio

Chadwick Arboretum
Ohio State University
2120 Fyffe Road
Columbus, OH 43210
(614) 292-0473
http://chadwickarboretum.osu.edu/

Dawes Arboretum
7770 Jacksontown Road Southeast
Newark OH 43055
(614) 323-2355
http://www.dawesarb.org/

Gardenview Horticultural Park
16711 Pearl Road
Strongville, OH 44136
(216) 238-6653
http://www.gardenclub.net/gardenview.htm

Holden Arboretum
9500 Sperry Road
Mentor, OH 44060
(216) 256-1110
http://www.holdenarb.org/

Inniswood Botanical Garden
940 Hempstead Road
Westerville, OH 43081
(614) 895-6216

Kingwood Center
900 Park Avenue West
Mansfield, OH 44906
(419) 522-0211

Secrest Arboretum
1680 Madison Avenue
Wooster, OH 44691-4096
(216) 264-3761
http://www.oardc.ohio-
state.edu/centernet/secrest.htm

Toledo Botanical Garden
5403 Elmer Drive
Toledo, OH 43615
(419) 536-8365
http://www.toledogarden.org/

Pennsylvania
Arboretum of the Barnes Foundation
P.O. Box 128
Merion Station, PA. 19066
(215) 664-8880
http://www.barnesfoundation.org/

Longwood Gardens
Route 1, P.O. Box 501
Kennett Square, PA 19348-0501
(215) 388-6741
http://www.longwoodgardens.org/

Morris Arboretum
9414 Meadowbrook Avenue
Philadelphia, PA 19118
(215) 247-5777
http://www.upenn.edu/morris/

Scott Arboretum
500 College Avenue
Swarthmore College
Swarthmore, PA. 19081
(215) 328-8025
http://www.scottarboretum.org/

Rhode Island
Green Animals Topiary Garden
380 Cory's Lane
Portsmouth RI 02871
(401)683-1267
http://www.ohwy.com/ri/g/grantopg.htm

Vermont
University of Vermont Display Gardens
Hills Building
University of Vermont
Burlington, VT 05405
(802) 656-2630
http://pss.uvm.edu/ppp/vpdgli.html

Wisconsin
Boerner Botanical Gardens
5879 South 92nd Street
Halws Corner, WI 53130
(414) 425-1130
http://www.boernerbotanicalgardens.org/

Botanical Gardens of the University of
Wisconsin
144 Birge Hall
430 Lincoln Drive
Madison, WI 53706
(608) 262-2235
http://www.wisc.edu/arboretum/

Olbrich Botanical Gardens
3330 Atwood Ave.
Madison, WI 53704
(608) 246-4551

ALL-AMERICA SELECTIONS
A non-profit organization devoted to the improvement and promotion of annuals grown from seed. New introductions, submitted by commercial seed companies, are evaluated each year by judges all across North America, and compared to similar, existing varieties when possible. The results are compiled in All-America headquarters and worthy varieties are awarded the AAS Winner logo. Selected gardens have displays of recent winners where you can see how they perform in your climate and get ideas for your own garden. Display gardens in this region are as follows.

Connecticut
Elizabeth Park
Asylum & Prospect Avenue
Hartford, CT 06119

Bartlett Arboretum and Gardens
151 Brookdale Road
Stamford, CT 06903

Illinois
Alwerdt's Gardens
1 mile south of I-70, Exit 82
Altamont, IL 62411

Illinois Central College
One College Drive
East Peoria, IL 61635

Chicago Botanic Garden
100 Lake Cook Road
Glencoe, IL 60022

Bird Haven Greenhouse
225 N. Gougar Road
Joliet, IL 60432

Mabery Gelvin Botanical Gardens
Route 47
Mahomet, IL 61853

Triton College Botanical Garden
2000 5th Avenue
River Grove, IL 60171

Washington Park Botanical Garden
Fayette & Chatham Road
Springfield, IL 62704

Cantigny Gardens
One South 151 Winfield Road
Wheaton, IL 60187

Indiana
Foster Gardens
3900 Old Mill Road
Fort Wayne, IN 46807

Hamilton County Master Gardeners
2003 East Pleasant Street
Noblesville IN 46060

Iowa
Iowa State University Reiman Gardens
1407 Elwood Drive
Ames, IA 50011

Noelridge Park
4900 Council Street Northeast
Cedar Rapids, IA 52404

Vander Veer Botanical Park
215 West Central Park Avenue
Davenport, IA 52803

Des Moines Botanical Center
909 East River Drive
Des Moines, IA 50316

Dubuque Arboretum Botanical Gardens
3800 Arboretum Drive
Dubuque, IA 52001

ISU Home Demonstration Garden
53020 Hitchcock Avenue
Lewis, IA 51544

Amana Colonies Community Gardens
Village Perimeter
South Amana, IA 52334

Maine
University of Maine Rogers Farm
Bennoch Road
Stillwater, ME 04489

Massachusetts
University of Massachusetts
Durfee Conservatory
Amherst, MA 01003

Newton Center Green
Langley Road
Newton, MA 02459

Berkshire Botanical Garden
5 West Stockbridge Road
Stockbridge, MA 01262

Massachusetts Horticultural Society
New England Trial Garden
900 Washington Street
Wellesley, MA 02482

Michigan
Michigan State University
Horticulture Demonstration Garden
East Lansing, MI 48824

Frankenmuth Mutual Insurance Company
One Mutual Avenue
Frankenmuth, MI 48787

Dow Gardens
1018 West Main Street
Midland, MI 48640

Fernwood Botanic Gardens
13988 Rangeline Road
Niles, MI 49120

Michigan State U. Hidden Lake Gardens
Route M-50
Tipton, MI 49287

Minnesota
Minnesota Landscape Arboretum
3675 Arboretum Drive
Chanhassen, MN 55317

University of Minnesota North Central Reserve
1861 Highway 169 East
Grand Rapids, MN 55744

Lyndale Park Gardens
4125 East Lake Harriet Parkway
Minneapolis, MN 55409

University of Minnesota West Central Reserve
State Highway 329
Morris, MN 56267

University of Minnesota, St. Paul
Gortner & Folwell Avenue
St. Paul, MN 55108

Missouri
Horticulture Display Gardens
Southeast Missouri State University
New Madrid Drive
Cape Girardeau, MO 63701

St. Louis County Government Center
41 South Central Avenue
Clayton, MO 63105

U. of Missouri Dept. of Horticulture
I-87 Agriculture Building
Columbia, MO 65211

Loose Park Gardens
5200 Pennsylvania Avenue
Kansas City, MO 64114

Powell Gardens
1609 Northwest US Highway. 50
Kingsville, MO 64061

Missouri Botanical Garden
4344 Shaw Boulevard
St. Louis, MO 63110

New Hampshire
Balsams Grand Resort Hotel
Route 26
Dixville Notch, NH 03862

Fuller Gardens
10 Willow Avenue
North Hampton, NH 03862

University of New Hampshire Trial Garden
Prescott Park, Marcy Street
Portsmouth, NH 03801

New Jersey
Hunterdon County Arboretum
1020 Highway 31
Lebanon, NJ 08833

Ramapo College of New Jersey
505 Ramapo Valley Road
Mahwah, NJ 07430

Deep Cut Gardens
352 Red Hill Road
Middletown, NJ 07748

Frelinghuysen Arbortetum
53 East Hanover Avenue
Morristown, NJ 07962

Rutgers University Lacey Display Gardens
Route 1 & Ryders Lane
New Brunswick, NJ 08901

Skylands Botanical Garden, Ringwood Park
1304 Sloatsburg Road
Ringwood, NJ 07456

New York
Boldt Castle Formal Gardens
1000 Island Bridge Authority
Alexandria Bay, NY 13607

Dickman Farm Gardens
13 Archie Street
Auburn, NY 13021

Cutler Botanic Gardens
840 Upper Front Street
Binghampton, NY 13905

Brooklyn Botanic Gardens
1000 Washington Avenue
Brooklyn, NY 11225

Buffalo and Erie County Botanical Gardens
2655 South Park Avenue
Buffalo, NY 14218

Erie Basin Marina Park
Joan Fuzak Memorial Gardens
1 Erie Street
Buffalo, NY 14202

Sonnenburg Gardens
151 Charlotte Street
Canandaigua, NY 14424

Queens Botanical Garden Society, Inc.
45-50 Main Street
Flushing, NY 11355

Mohonk Mountain House
Mountain Rest Road
New Paltz, NY 12561

Old Westbury Gardens
71 Old Westbury Road
Old Westbury, NY 11568

Cornell Cooperative Extension of Nassau Co.
1425 Old County Road
Plainview, NY 11803

Cornell Cooperative Extension of Dutchess Co.
Dutchess County Fairground, Route 9
Rhinebeck, NY 12572

The Potager
116 Sullivan Street
Wurtsboro, NY 12790

Ohio
Krohn Conservatory
1501 Eden Park Drive
Cincinnati, OH 45202

Spring Grove Cemetery & Arboretum
4521 Spring Grove Avenue
Cincinnati, OH 45232

Rockefeller Park Greenhouse Gardens
750 E. 88th Street
Cleveland, OH 44108

Kingwood Center
900 Park Avenue West
Mansfield, OH 44906

Dawes Arboretum
7770 Jacksontown Road Southeast
Newark, OH 43056-9380

Wilson's Hillview Display Garden
10923 Lambs Lane Northeast
Newark, OH 43055

Miami University Formal Gardens
Boyd Hall, Fisher Drive
Oxford, OH 45056

Gardenview Horticultural Park
16711 Pearl Road
Strongsville, OH 44136

Toledo Botanical Garden
5403 Elmer Drive
Toledo, OH 43615

Ohio State U. Agricultural Technical Inst.
Route 250 & US 83
Wooster, OH 44691

Mill Creek Metro Parks
Fellows Riverside Gardens
123 McKinley Avenue
Youngstown, OH 44509

Pennsylvania
Temple University Ambler Research Gardens
580 Meetinghouse Road
Ambler, PA 19002-3994

Longwood Gardens
US Route 1 South
Kennett Square, PA 19348

Rodale Research Center
611 Siegfriedale Road
Kutztown, PA 19530

Pennsylvania State University
Department of Horticulture
101 Tyson Building
University Park, PA 16802

Vermont
Waterfront Park
College Street at Lakefront
Burlington, VT 05405

Vermont Community Botanical Garden
1100 Dorset Street
South Burlington, VT 05403

Wisconsin
Boerner Botanical Gardens
5879 South 92nd Street
Hales Corners, WI 53130

A.R. Albert Horticultural Garden
Hancock Agricultural Research Station
N3909 County Highway
Hancock, WI 54943

W. Madison Research Station, U. Wisconsin
Mineral Point Road
Madison, WI 53706

Vincent HS Agribusiness/Natural Resources
7501 North Granville Road
Milwaukee, WI 53224

Jung Seed Company
335 South High Street
Randolph, WI 53957

INDEX

Page numbers given in italics refer to catalog pages on which the plants are illustrated. In plant entries, topics that relate to the main entries appear first; subentries for species and cultivars always follow the general subentries.

ACKNOWLEDGMENTS

DK Publishing Inc. and the American Horticultural Society would like to express special thanks to Dr. H. Marc Cathey for his vision of a SMARTGARDEN™ and for promoting these important principles to the American gardener; to Katy Moss Warner for her keen eye and superb leadership; to Arabella Dane for the use of her Showtime database and her countless hours of support; to Mary Ann Patterson for believing in and coordinating this project from its conception; to Mark Miller for hours of research; to David Ellis for his editor's savvy.

Rita Pelczar, author of the core text for the SMARTGARDEN™ Regional Guides, has written for several American gardening magazines and has contributed to several books. As an associate editor for *The American Gardener,* she wrote a four-year series of articles highlighting principles of the SMARTGARDEN™ plan.

The Northeast regional author, Trevor Cole, trained at Hampton Court Palace gardens and the Royal Botanic Gardens, Kew. He emigrated to Canada in 1967 and started working at the Central Experimental Farm, Ottawa. Initially he was working on the adaptation of native flora to cultivation. He was appointed curator of the Dominion Arboretum in 1972, and retired in 1995. Author of three gardening books and many articles, he has received awards for his writing from the Garden Writers Association of America, the International Lilac Society, and the North American Rock Garden Society. He is horticultural consultant for DK Publishing in the US and Canada, Reader's Digest, and Mitchel Beazley.

PHOTO CREDITS

American Gardener Magazine: Mary Yee 18L, 19CR

Ball Horticultural Company: 77 R, 350 BR, 357 TR

Paul Bromfield Aquatics: 223 BR, 328 BR, 330 BR

Courtesy of W. Atlee Burpee: 221 TL

Chicago Botanical Garden: Bill Biderbost 76 BL

Corbis: W.Cody, 54TR: Larry Lee Photography 54 BL; Arthur Morris 42 TL; Richard Hamilton Smith 54 TL

Emerald Coast Growers: 140 BR, 310 TL, 314 TR, 322 BC, 323 TC, 324 TC

FLPA: S. Maslowski 61

GardenPhotos.com: Graham Rice 350 BL; Judy White 94 TC, 96 L, 103 TC, 110 BR, 207 TR, 209 BR, 220 TR, 226 BL, 241 BR, 282 BC, 304 BC, 327 R, 333 BL, 355 TR, 357 TL

Garden and Wildlife Matters Photo Library: Sheila Apps 46 T; M. Collins 60 BR; John Feltwell 202 TL, 234 TL, 265 CL, 336 TC, 337 CL, 341 BC; Garden & Wildlife Matters Photo Library 7 CL, 7 C, 7 BL, 14 TL, 26 TR, 26 BL, 32 BL, 36 BL, 37 BL, 38 BR, 39 TR, 42 BR, 45 TR, 50 BR, 60 BL, 62 BL, 65 TR, 67 R, 69 TL, 69 BR, 72 TL, 72 TR, 73 B, 90 BR, C, 101 TC, 102 TL, 104 TL, 124TC, 124 TR, 126 TR, 128 TL, 137 TL, 141 BR, 157 TR, 162 BC, 168 TL, 175 TL, 175 TR, 202 TC, 212 BR, 213 CL, 214 TR, 221 CR, 221 BL, 231 TL, 236 CR, 243 BC, 246 TL, 254 BL, 255 CL, 268 TC, 284 TL, 286 TL, 293 BL, 293 TC, 311 TR, 319 TL, 320 TR, 323 BL, 323 BR, 324 TR, 324 BL, 324 BR, 325 BL, 325 BC, 331 TL, 338 BR, 347 TC, 349 TL, 349 BL, 353 TC, 356 TC; Martin P. Land 304 TL, 304 BR, 332 BR; Colin Milkins 51 BL; John & Irene Palmer 352 BL; Steffie Sheilds 230 TR, 246 BR, 256 BR, 286 R, 353 BL; Debi Wager 47 BL

Garden Picture Library: Mark Bolton 112 TC; Philippe Bonduel 180 TL, 314 TC; Lynne Botchie 250 TL; Brian Carter 100 TR, 122 TL, 137 BR, 155 TL, 196 BR; Jack Elliot 229 BL; Ron Evans 207 TL; Christopher Fairweather 133 CR; Suzie

Gibbons 59 BR Garden Design by Karen Maskeu; John Glover 25 TL Garden Design by Alan Titchmarsh, 79, 87 BL, 154 LC, 170 TC, 352 R; Sunniva Harte 24 B Garden Design Beth Chatto, 175 CL, 291 BL, 293 TL; Neil Holmes 222 BR, 257 BR, 273 BR, 284 BC; Michael Howes 155 BL; Jacqui Hurst 327 TL; Lamontagne 305 BR; Jane Legate 29 TR; Mayer/LeScanff 315 TR; Marie O'Hara 70 BL, 80-81; Howard Rice 19 BR, 30 BL, 174 TL, 174 TR, 255 TR, 263 TR, 268 BL, 325 TL, 333 BR, 340 BL, 341 BL, 351 BR; Ellen Rooney: 23 TR; JS Sira 153 BR, 155 BC, 181 BR, 233 C, 267 BC, 286 BL, 313 BL, 353 TL; Ron Sutherland 75 Garden Design Anthony Paul; Ros Wickham 238 TR; Didier Willery 87 TR, 112 TL, 154 BR, 172 TL, 176 BC, 222 TC, 301 BL; Kit Young 174 B; Green Bay Botanical Garden: Brenda Hansen 76 BR

Andrew Lawson: Andrew Lawson 3-4

Monrovia: 82 TR, 82 BL, 83 BR, 88 TL, 90 TR, 94 BR, 99 BC, 101 CL, 107 TR, 115 BR, 120 BR, 121 BR, 123 TR, 124 BC, 125 BR, 126 TC, 129 BL, 145 TR, 146 TL, 147 TL, 149 TC, 150 TC, 151 TR, 151 BR, 153 TC, 162 TR, 162 BC, 172 BC, 173 CL, 177 TL, 177 BL, 178 CR, 179 TR, 181 TC, 187 TL, 188 CR, 195 TR, 198 BR, 200 BR, 202 BL, 203 BR, 204 TL, 205 BR, 209 TL, 209 TR, 210 TC, 210 TR, 213 C, 218 TC, 219 TL, 230 BR, 233 TC, 234 BL, 237 TL, 240 TL, 241 TC, 241 TR, 242 BL, 243 TR, 243 BR, 247 BR, 248 BR, 252 BR, 255 BL, 260 BR, 261 CL, 261 BR, 265 R, 267 BR, 277 TR, 277 CR, 285 CR, 292 TL, 292 BL, 294 BR, 295 BR, 296 BR, 307 TR, 307 CR, 307 BR, 311 BC, 319 TR, 319 CR, 319 BL, 319 BR, 322 TL, 326 TC, 331 BR, 340 TR, 353 BC, 357 CL

Netherlands Flower Bulb Information Center: 335 TC

Plant Delights Nursery: Tony Avent BR, 130 TL, 132 TR, 195 BR, 207 BL, 218 CR, 229 BC, 235 TC, 235 TR, 246 BL, 249 CL, 249 BC, 250 BL, 252 BL, 263 BL, 264 TL, 267 TR, 273 TL, 291 TL, 292 TR, 292 BC, 295 C, 313 C, 315 BL, 315 BR, 316 TL, 316 TR, 318 BC, 322 TC, 323 TR, 324 TL, 325 TC, 339 BR, 346 L, 346 BR Steven Nikkila: 88 TC, 118 CR, 121 TR, 137 BC, 162 TR, 175 BL, 207 CR, 279 TL, 329 BR, 330 TL, 348 L, 348 TR

Trevor Cole: 87 TL, 87 C, 105 TR, 105 CR, 133 TR, 133 CL, 133 BR, 163 TC, 163 TR, 163 BR, 163 TL, 163 TR, 163 CR, 163 CL, 163 BC, 163 BR, 211 C, 234 TC, 236 TL, 247 BL, 251 TL, 264 CR, 306 TL, 306 TR, 306 CL, 306 BL, 306 BR, 307 L, 307 C, 308 TL, 308 TC, 308 TR, 308 BR, 308 BL, 309 TL, 309 TR, 309 CL, 309 C, 309 BL, 309 BR, 316 BL, 317 BL, 317 TR, 317 BR, 320 TL, 320 BL, 320 CR, 320 BR, 321 TL, 321 TC, 321 TR, 321 B

Courtesy of the Online Virginia Tech Weed ID Guide, http://www.ppws.vt.edu/weedindex.htm: 73 TC

The Publisher would also like to thank the following DK photographers who have contributed to this book:

Peter Anderson, Sue Atkinson, Blooms of Bressingham, Michael Booher, Booker Seeds, Clive Boursnell, Deni Bown, Jonathan Buckley, Andrew Butler, Cambridge Botanic Garden, Beth Chatto, Eric Crichton, Geoff Dann, Andrew de Lory, Christine M. Douglas, Alistair Duncan, Andreas Einsiedel, John Fielding, Neil Fletcher, Roger Foley, John Glover, Derek Hall, David W. Hardon, Jerry Harpur, Stephan Hayward, Dr. Alan Hemsley, C. Andrew Henley, Ian Howes, Jacqui Hurst, Anne Hyde, International Coffee Organization, Dave King, Jane Miller, RHS Garden Wisley, Howard Rice, Tim Ridley, Barbara Rothenberger, Royal Botanical Garden, Edinburgh, Bob Rundle, Les Saucier, Savill Garden, Windsor, Mike Severns, Steven Still, Joseph Strauch, Richard Surman, R. Tidman, Juliette Wade, Colin Walton, Matthew Ward, Alex Watson, Steven Wooster, Francesca York